Environmental Management

Environmental Management introduces the principles, practice and key policy issues of this important topic, providing a comprehensive introduction and resource for students and practitioners alike.

It draws together the common themes which run through the various areas of application, which include: the precautionary principle; the 'polluter-pays' principle; a multidisciplinary and anticipatory approach; the goal of sustainable development; assessment of risks, hazards and impacts; and environmental stewardship. C. J. Barrow explores how environmental management may be pursued by individuals, companies, governments, NGOs and international bodies.

Environmental management is a broad and rapidly evolving discipline, and this book highlights the subject's core themes and principles.

C. J. Barrow is Senior Lecturer in the School of Social Sciences and International Development of the University of Wales Swansea.

Routledge Environmental Management Series

This important series presents a comprehensive introduction to the principles and practices of environmental management across a wide range of fields. Introducing the theories and practices fundamental to modern environmental management, the series features a number of focused volumes to examine applications in specific environments and topics, all offering a wealth of real-life examples and practical guidance.

MANAGING ENVIRONMENTAL POLLUTION
Andrew Farmer

COASTAL AND ESTUARINE MANAGEMENT
Peter W. French

ENVIRONMENTAL ASSESSMENT IN PRACTICE
D. Owen Harrop and J. Ashley Nixon

ENVIRONMENTAL MANAGEMENT
Principles and practice
C. J. Barrow

Forthcoming titles:

WETLAND MANAGEMENT
L. Heathwaite

COUNTRYSIDE MANAGEMENT
R. Clarke

Environmental Management

Principles and practice

C. J. Barrow

London and New York

First published 1999
by Routledge
11 New Fetter Lane, London EC4P 4EE

Simultaneously published in the USA and Canada
by Routledge
29 West 35th Street, New York, NY 10001

Routledge is an imprint of the Taylor & Francis Group

Typeset in Ehrhardt by Keystroke, Jacaranda Lodge, Wolverhampton
Printed and bound in Great Britain by TJ International Ltd, Padstow, Cornwall

British Library Cataloguing in Publication Data
A catalogue record for this book is available from the British Library

Library of Congress Cataloging in Publication Data
Barrow, Christopher J.
    Environmental management : principles and practice / C.J. Barrow.
        p.   cm. – (Routledge environmental management series)
    1. Environmental management. I. Title. II. Series.
    GE300.B375 1999   99-17744
    363.7′05–dc21

ISBN 0–415–18560–2 (hbk)
ISBN 0–415–18561–0 (pbk)

Contents

Figures and boxes

Figures

Boxes

Preface

This book explores the nature, scope and role of environmental management. It offers a foundation for a series of texts which deal with the application of environmental management, including:

- *Environmental Risk Management*
- *Managing Environmental Pollution*
- *Coastal and Estuarine Management*
- *Countryside Management*
- *Environmental Assessment in Practice*

Environmental management is a broad and rapidly evolving discipline. This book explores the subject's core themes and principles, which include:

- a multidisciplinary, interdisciplinary or holistic approach;
- support for the 'polluter-pays' principle;
- a goal of sustainable development;
- concern for limits, hazards and potential;
- an attempt to act beyond the local or project level;
- support for long-term not just short-term planning;
- adherence to the 'precautionary principle';
- translation of theory to effective practice;
- the integration of environmental science, planning and management, policy making and public involvement;
- an awareness of the need to change the ethics of peoples, businesses and governments.

The practical issues and challenges faced during the environmental management process are introduced.

CJB 4 October 1998

Introduction

The evolution of environmental management

From prehistory humankind have accumulated environmental know-how and developed strategies for exploiting nature. To help regulate resource use people evolved taboos, superstitions and common rights, formulated laws to improve stewardship, and even undertook national resource inventories (such as the twelfth-century AD Domesday survey). While some managed to sustain reasonable lifestyles for long periods, the idea that pre-modern people 'close to nature' caused little environmental damage is largely an arcadian myth. Indeed, with populations a fraction of today's, prehistoric people, using fire and weapons of flint, bone, wood and leather, managed to alter the vegetation of most continents and probably to wipe out many species of large mammals (Tudge, 1995).

Developments apparent in the late twentieth century make it critical that environmental management be got right; these include: global pollution; loss of biodiversity; soil degradation; and urban growth. The challenges are great, but there have been advances in understanding the structure and function of the environment, in monitoring impacts, data handling and analysis, modelling, assessment, and planning. It is the role of environmental management to co-ordinate and focus such developments, to improve human well-being, and mitigate or prevent further damage to the Earth and its organisms.

Technological optimism apparent in the west, particularly from the 1830s onward, and expressed in natural resources management, faltered a little after 1945 as awareness of environmental problems grew (Mitchell, 1997). Limited efforts were made to ensure natural resources exploitation was integrated with social and economic development before the 1970s – e.g. integrated or comprehensive regional planning and management had been undertaken as early as the 1930s with the establishment of river basin bodies (Barrow, 1997). Urban and regional planning also have some roots in holistic, ecosystem approaches (things which have more recently attracted those interested in environmental management) (Slocombe, 1993: 290). However, natural resources management (in contrast with environmental management) is more concerned with specific components of the Earth – resources – which have utility and can be exploited, mainly for short-term gain and the benefit of special-interest groups, companies or governments. Also, natural resources management responses to problems tend to be reactive, and often rely on quick-fix technological means and a project-by-project approach. Natural resources managers have often been drawn from a limited range of disciplines, typically with little sociological and limited environmental expertise. Their management can be authoritarian and may fail to involve the public; they also tend to miss off-site and delayed impacts. Because of these failings natural resources management has lost ground to environmental management in the last 40 years or so.

Some feel environmental management has, or is developing, a more flexible and sensitive style than natural resources management: assessment of a situation leading to an appropriate approach, emphasising stewardship rather than exploitation. Stewardship implies the management of something with the goal of long-term careful use and sustainable benefit. The focus of such an approach to environmental management is multidisciplinary, interdisciplinary, or holistic (see chapter 7), and the style precautionary and participatory. Increasingly, the aim is to promote sustainable development (Royston, 1978a; Dorney, 1989). It should be noted that a multidisciplinary approach draws upon various disciplines for information, analytical skills and insight, but does not seek an integrated understanding. An interdisciplinary approach draws upon common themes and goes beyond close collaboration between different specialists to attempt integration, and is very difficult because it involves blending differently derived concepts (O'Riordan, 1995: 2–4). These approaches demand awareness that issues may be part of complex transnational, even global environmental, economic and social interaction, which is likely to be affected by politics, perception and ethics.

Others dismiss much of present-day environmental management as 'environmental managerialism' which pays insufficient attention to human–environment interaction, has become institutionalized, and is essentially a state-centred process concerned with formulating and implementing laws, policies and regulations which relate to the environment (Bryant and Wilson, 1998). The difference in viewpoint may partly reflect theory and practice. Whatever one might wish for environmental management as a subject, it is used for real-world problems and consequently managerialism and other shortcomings may creep in. It should be stressed that environmental management is currently evolving and is far from being fixed in form.

Environmental management, whatever its approach, is related to, overlaps, and has to work with environmental planning. The focus of environmental management is on implementation, monitoring and auditing; on practice and coping with real-world issues (like modifying human habits that damage nature), rather than theoretical planning (Hillary, 1995). While a close integration with environmental planning is desirable, environmental management is a field of study dedicated to understanding human–environment interactions and the application of science and common sense to solving problems.

General acceptance that economic development and environmental issues should not be approached separately came somewhere between 1972 (the UN Conference on the Human Environment, Stockholm) and 1992 (the UN Conference on Environment and Development, Rio de Janeiro – the 'Earth Summit'). By the early 1990s natural resources management had given way, as Wisner (1990) observed, perhaps unfairly, to 'a murky philosophical plunge' towards environmental management.

The definition and scope of environmental management

There is no concise universal definition of environmental management. This is understandable, given the very broad scope and the diversity of specialisms involved.

A glance at the first four dictionaries on environmental science I came across proved fruitless, as did an examination of a number of M.Sc. environmental management course brochures, and a recently published environmental studies book! I offer a selection of definitions of environmental management culled from the literature in Box 1.1, which indicates that environmental management displays the following characteristics:

◆ it is often used as a generic term;
◆ it supports sustainable development;
◆ it deals with a world affected by humans (there are few, if any, wholly natural environments today);
◆ it demands a multidisciplinary or interdisciplinary approach;
◆ it has to integrate different development viewpoints;
◆ it seeks to integrate science, social science, policy making and planning;
◆ it recognizes the desirability of meeting, and if possible exceeding basic human needs;
◆ the timescale involved extends beyond the short term, and concern ranges from local to global;
◆ it should show opportunities as well as address threats and problems;
◆ it stresses stewardship, rather than exploitation.

Most sources quoted in Box 1.1 assume there is an optimum balance of natural resource uses, and that the environmental manager must decide where that lies, using planning and administrative skills to reach it. This conceptualization usually adopted by mainstream environmental management is clearly biased towards the anthropocentric, i.e., the view that environmental issues are considered after development objectives have been set (Redclift, 1985). There are many who would object to this and advocate other approaches, for in environmental management there is a wide diversity of beliefs ranging from anthropocentric to ecocentric. There are growing calls for a reshaping of environmental management towards greater emphasis on social aspects, perhaps to move the field closer to human geography to ensure that it is not divorced from key issues of human–environment interaction (Bryant and Wilson, 1998).

At its simplest, environmental management must do three things: (1) identify goals; (2) establish whether these can be met; (3) develop and implement the means to do what it deems possible. (1) is seldom easy: a society may have no clear idea of what it needs. Indeed, some people may want things damaging to themselves, others, and the environment. Environmental managers may have to identify goals, and then win over the public and special-interest groups. (2) and (3) require the environmental manager to interface with ecology, economics, law, politics, people, etc., to co-ordinate development. To co-ordinate a diversity of things is difficult because development proceeds on a piecemeal, short-term basis – the manner and scale at which most humans operate. The fact that much of what is done at a given point in time and space has wider and longer-term impacts, makes it desirable for development to be managed and co-ordinated at all levels: regional, national and international – the environmental

BOX 1.1 Some definitions of environmental management

◆ An approach which goes beyond natural resources management to encompass the political and social as well as the natural environment . . . it is concerned with questions of value and distribution, with the nature of regulatory mechanisms and with interpersonal, geographic and intergenerational equity (R. Clarke, Birkbeck College, University of London: pers. comm.).

◆ Formulation of environmentally sound development strategies.

◆ An interface between scientific endeavour and policy development and implementation (S. Macgill, Leeds University, UK: pers. comm.).

◆ The process of allocating natural and artificial resources so as to make optimum use of the environment in satisfying basic human needs at the minimum, and more if possible, on a sustainable basis (Jolly, 1978).

◆ Seeking the best possible environmental option to promote sustainable development (paraphrased from several 1990s sustainable development sources).

◆ Seeking the best practicable environmental option (BPEO), generally using the best available techniques not entailing excessive cost (BATNEEC) (based on two widely used environmental management acronyms).

◆ The control of all human activities which have a significant impact on the environment.

◆ Management of the environmental performance of organizations, bodies and companies (Sharratt, 1995).

◆ A decision-making process which regulates the impact of human activities on the environment in such a manner that the capacity of the environment to sustain human development will not be impaired (paraphrase from various 1990s 'green development' sources).

◆ Environmental management cannot hope to master all of the issues and environmental components it has to deal with. Rather, the environmental manager's job is to study and try to control processes to try and reach particular objectives (Royston, 1978b).

◆ Environmental management – a generic description of a process undertaken by systems-oriented professionals with a natural science, social science, or less commonly, an engineering, law, or design background, tackling problems of the human-altered environment on an interdisciplinary basis from a quantitative and/or futuristic viewpoint (Dorney, 1989: 15).

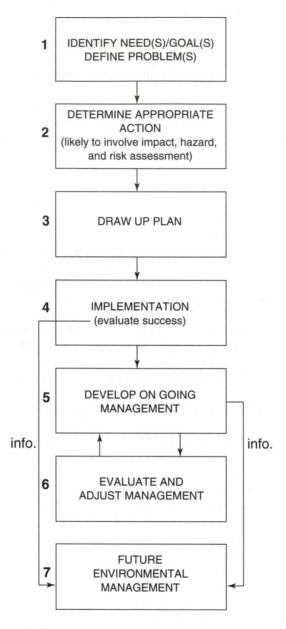

FIGURE 1.1 A typical scheme of practice adopted for environmental management
Note: Increasingly, stages 1, 2 and 3 are influenced by broad strategic policies, and are accountable to public scrutiny (as is stage 5). Ideally, lessons learnt at every stage should be passed on to improve future environmental management – the evaluation of stages 4 and 5 is especially valuable for future management. At stage 1 the public or a developer may not have a clear idea of needs or goals, so the environmental manager may need to establish these.

manager must somehow, as Henderson (1981a) advised, 'think globally, act locally' – and adopt a long-term outlook. Figure 1.1 suggests how environmental management is typically conducted.

Problems and opportunities

Often considerable effort and much money is expended treating *symptoms* of a problem but not the *causes*, which may be difficult to identify and lie well away (in space or time), along a chain of causation. The risk of making this sort of mistake should be reduced by the adoption of a careful approach. Even if such an approach can be used, there is a risk that management will be based on 'snapshot' views, so it is important to use broad-view, long-term and, if possible, gap-free monitoring and auditing to try to reduce this risk (Born and Sonzogni, 1995).

Environmental management will need to modify the ethics of individuals, groups and societies to achieve its goals. There are three main approaches:

1 *Advisory*
   ◆ through education;
   ◆ through demonstration (e.g. model farms or factories);
   ◆ through the media (overt or covert approaches – the latter includes 'messages' incorporated in entertainment);
   ◆ through advice (leaflets, drop-in shops, helplines, etc.).

2 *Economic or fiscal*
   ◆ through taxation ('green' taxes);
   ◆ through grants, loans, aid;
   ◆ through subsidies;
   ◆ through quotas or trade agreements.

3 *Regulatory*
   ◆ through standards;
   ◆ through restrictions and monitoring;
   ◆ through licensing;
   ◆ through zoning (restricting activities to a given area).

One problem faced by environmental managers is that the goal of sustainable development is not fully formed and its fundamental concepts are still debated. Sustainable development, like environmental management, is not easily defined (see Box 1.2). The concept, although it had appeared in the 1970s, was widely disseminated in the early 1980s by the *World Conservation Strategy* (IUCN, UNEP and WWF, 1980), which called for the maintenance of essential ecological processes; the preservation of biodiversity; and sustainable use of species and ecosystems. The Brundtland Report, *Our Common Future* (World Commission on Environment and Development, 1987), placed it on the world's political agenda and helped rekindle public interest in the environment. It also spread the messages that global environmental management

BOX 1.2 Some definitions of sustainable development

◆   Environmental care 'married' to development.
◆   Improving the quality of human life while living within the carrying capacity of supporting ecosystems.
◆   Development based on the principle of inter-generational (i.e. bequeathing the same or improved resource endowment to the future that has been inherited), inter-species and inter-group equity.
◆   Development that meets the needs of the present without compromising the ability of future generations to meet their own needs.
◆   An environmental 'handrail' to guide development.
◆   A change in consumption patterns towards more benign products, and a shift in investment patterns towards augmenting environmental capital.
◆   A process that seeks to make manifest a higher standard of living (however interpreted) for human beings . . . that recognizes this cannot be achieved at the expense of environmental integrity.

Source: Barrow, 1995b: 372

was needed; and that without a reduction of poverty ecosystem damage would be difficult to counter. Environmental management is thus clearly interrelated with socioeconomic development. Twenty years after the *World Conservation Strategy* the same three bodies published *Caring for the Earth* (IUCN, UNEP and WWF, 1991), which proposed principles intended to help move from theory to practice.

Sustainable development was in part generated by fears that the materially comfortable way of life enjoyed in some countries probably cannot be maintained on anything like a global scale with likely population growth (Pirages, 1994). As a concept, sustainable development draws upon two, often opposed, intellectual traditions: one concerned with the limits nature presents to humans, the other with the potential for human material development (Redclift, 1987: 199; Barrow, 1995b). Interpretation varies a lot:

◆   Some see it as a quest for harmony between humans and their environment;
◆   Some fail to accept that in a finite world there cannot be unlimited growth;
◆   Some feel there can be a shift to less environmentally damaging improvements in the quality of human life;
◆   Some hope technology will allow limits to be stretched.

There are too many situations where naive, ill-thought-out appeals for sustainable development are made. This harms the concept, risking its dismissal by the public and decision makers as shallow, unworkable, and so on. Worse, there are cases where sustainable development is being used as rhetoric or cunning deceit to mislead people. Some fear calls for sustainable development may be a way of side-stepping more radical socioeconomic reform. Environmental management must police the use of the concept to prevent its misuse for propaganda or it will become devalued (genetic engineering is subject to similar misleading propaganda which could make its responsible use difficult if the public loses trust).

'Mainstream' sustainable development typically urges:

◆ the maintenance of ecological integrity;
◆ the integration of environmental care and development;
◆ the adoption of an internationalist (North–South interdependence) stance;
◆ the satisfaction of at least basic, human needs for all;
◆ 'utilitarian conservation';
◆ concern for inter-generational, inter-group and inter-species equity;
◆ the application of science, technology and environmental knowledge to world development;
◆ the acceptance of some economic growth (within limits);
◆ the adoption of a long-term view.

The question is whether sustainable development is going to act just as a guiding principle (which in itself is valuable) or whether it generates practical strategies that improve human well-being and prevent environmental degradation. It is not only misuse of sustainable development language by the media, politicians, activists and commerce that poses a problem: some academics and environmental managers are careless. Care is needed to ensure that sustainable development is a realistic objective based on workable strategy.

Environmental problems often do not have a single simple solution. Their solution presents alternatives and challenges; environmental management therefore faces dilemmas (Bennett, 1992: 5–9): (1) Ethical dilemmas – e.g. what to conserve – Inuit hunters or whales? (2) Efficiency dilemmas – e.g. how much environmental damage is acceptable? (3) Equity dilemmas – e.g. who benefits from environmental management decisions, and who pays? (4) Liberty dilemmas – e.g. to what degree must people be restricted to protect the environment? (5) Uncertainty dilemmas – e.g. how to choose a course of action without adequate knowledge or data? (6) Evaluation dilemmas – e.g. how to compare different effects of various options or actions?

Human beings often respond to perceived crisis, rather than carefully assessing the situation and acting to prevent problems. With sustainable development as a central goal, crisis management is a dangerous practice, for, once manifest, problems may not be easily solved and could jeopardize sustainability. The solution is to adopt the precautionary principle (see chapter 3 for further discussion) (Bodansky, 1991; Costanza and Cornwell, 1992; O'Riordan and Cameron, 1995; Francis, 1996). The precautionary principle shifts the burden of proof that a proposal is safe from the 'victim' to the 'developer' (O'Riordan, 1995: 8–10). It also makes sense because environmental management often deals with inadequate data, may have to rely on modelling that is deficient, and has to cope with issues that are complex and not fully understood.

Decision making is often affected by 'polarized perceptions' (ideas based more on stakeholders' prejudice, misconception or greed than objectivity) (Baarschers, 1996). Even if the environmental manager is objective, powerful special-interest groups (e.g. the rich; government ministers; lobby groups; non-governmental organizations (NGOs), industry, the military) may not be. Problems are often caused by sovereignty or strategic arguments which threaten common-sense decisions and make transboundary issues difficult to resolve. The environmental manager must manipulate these forces, trading off stakeholders' desires against protecting the environment. Little remains fixed: demands from various stakeholders alter, the environment changes, public attitudes shift, human capabilities vary – so environmental management must be flexible, adaptive and perceptive (Holling, 1978).

Co-ordination of environment and development requires awareness of environmental and human *limits*, *potential* and *risks* or *hazards*. For most of human history worries have mainly been caused by the acquisition of inputs (food, water, fuel, etc.); over the last century have appeared added problems over outputs (pollution and waste). Environmental problems are commonly caused by human behaviour, notably consumerism; another challenge is the growing human population; another is poverty. Somehow, environmental management has to separate what is real from vague abstractions and fashionable attitudes (Wisner, 1990). It is widely argued that environmental management must address poverty and encourage the use of aid to prevent people degrading their surroundings. These issues were debated, but by no means resolved, at the 1992 Earth Summit, and most environmental managers accept that a component of any strategy for sustainable development is the satisfaction of basic human needs.

Environmental managers are increasingly likely to face:

◆ an unproven threat;
◆ transboundary or global challenges;
◆ problems demanding rapid decisions;
◆ an increasing exchange of information with NGOs via the Internet and various other networks. This means that environmental managers must keep abreast of the activities of many bodies (it also offers possibilities for alliances, and data gathering from different sources).

Modern science has traditionally adopted a reductionist approach, with disciplinary specialists studying components of a problem and avoiding any judgement or advice to managers or planners *before there is adequate proof*. Environmental managers have to deal with uncertainty and complex problems which often cannot afford to wait long enough for proof to be obtained. Reductionist approaches may be too slow when there is pressure to give advice (Funtowicz and Ravetz, 1991). Something may have the potential to cause serious, possibly irreversible problems unless prompt action is taken but it has not actually been proved to be a threat (the classic case being global warming). Environmental management may have to rely on modelling, simulation and forecasts rather than factual predictions – it may be necessary to resort to advocacy without proof, and identify the agency and the mechanism whereby advocacy can be pursued (Redclift, 1984: 44).

The last few decades have seen the recognition of more and more transboundary or global threats. However, there have been helpful developments: environmental management can now draw on improved knowledge of the structure and function of the environment, and of human institution-building, group interaction and perceptions, and new tools are available which improve monitoring, data gathering, impact assessment, information processing, decision making and communication. Though environmental managers face growing problems, they have more powerful aids to draw upon. These developments mean it is possible for environmental management to move away from corrective to anticipatory approaches (adopting the precautionary principle).

Who are environmental managers? A wide range of bodies professionals are involved in environmental management: government agencies (e.g. the European Environmental Agency), international bodies and aid organizations (like the UNEP, FAO, World Bank, USAID, etc.), research institutes (e.g. the Worldwatch Institute, IIED, etc.), NGOs (e.g. WWF, IUCN, Friends of the Earth, etc.); the public (see Box 1.2). Identifying a single environmental manager in a given situation may be like trying to identify who built a Boeing 747 aircraft.

What motivates environmental management? One or more of the following may lead to its adoption:

- Pragmatic reasons – fear or common sense makes people or administrators seek to avoid a problem.
- Desire to save costs – it may be cheaper to avoid problems or counter them than suffer the consequences (pollution, litigation, etc.). There may also be advantages in waste recovery, energy conservation, and maintaining environmental quality.
- Compliance – individuals, local government, companies, states, etc., may be required by laws, national or international agreement to care for the environment.
- Shift in ethics – research, the media, individuals or groups of activists may trigger new attitudes, agreements or laws.
- Macro-economics – promotion of environmental management may lead to economic expansion: a market for pollution control equipment, use of recovered waste, more secure and efficient energy and raw materials supply; or there may be advantages in 'internalizing externalities' (see pareto optimum discussion in chapter 5).

Criticism of environmental management

With something as broad and ambitious as environmental management, criticism is inevitable. The problem of its definition has been discussed, another frequently voiced worry is that it is prescriptive and insufficiently analytical. It also attracts criticism because it involves subjective judgement as well as scientific enquiry, and is as much an art as a science.

Sometimes it is the approach to environmental management that causes offence – some over-zealous efforts have been tantamount to 'eco-fascism' (Pepper, 1984: 204). Redclift (1985) warned of 'environmental managerialism', symptoms of which include: the consideration of the environment after development objectives have been set; the tendency to plunge into techniques regardless of whether they are needed; and failing to see the wood for the trees. Too often environmental management is pursued as a reactive, piecemeal approach, working on projects that have environmental objectives or components designed to mitigate, rather than avoid, environmental impacts (Schramm and Warford, 1989: 8). Environmental management must go beyond monitoring and reacting and adopt a longer term view than has been the case with most planners and politicians. A longer term view improves the chances of avoiding problems and, when it does not, allows time to develop contingency plans, acquire technology, etc.

Environmental management has developed in western democracies where there is relative freedom of access to information (e.g. in the USA through the Freedom of Information Act; in Europe through the European Directive 82/501/EEC – Article 8 of which requires that local communities have information about any hazardous installation) (Haefele, 1973). Now environmental management needs to be adapted to suit different social and political conditions.

The establishment of environmental management

A number of developments have helped establish environmental management:

1   The public in an increasing number of countries have become environmentally aware and unwilling to trust government and corporations to protect the environment. This has largely grown out of their witnessing accidents, misuse of resources, and from concern about ecological threats.
2   NGOs, international agencies, business and governments have started to pursue environmental management.
3   The media monitor and report on environmental issues.
4   International conferences, agreements and declarations have publicized issues and supported environmental management.
5   The establishment in 1973 of the UN Environment Programme (UNEP).
6   The 1969 US National Environmental Protection Act (passed 1970) and the creation of the US Environmental Protection Agency (EPA) in 1970.
7   Publications in North America and Europe which raised environmental concern after the mid-1960s.
8   The development of green politics since the 1970s.
9   Aid and funding agencies in the late 1970s began to require environmental assessments and environmental management before supporting development.
10 The Brundtland Report (World Commission on Environment and Development, 1987) increased awareness of the need for environmental care.

At the time of the UN Conference on the Human Environment, Stockholm (1972) few countries had environmental ministries, few newspapers had environmental editors, or broadcasting companies environmental producers. By the 1992 UN Conference on Environment and Development, Rio (the Earth Summit) most countries had environmental ministries and media interest had vastly increased. The release of *Agenda 21* (UN, 1992; Keating, 1993; Local Government Management Board, 1994) encouraged governments and other bodies to develop environmental management. For example, *Agenda 21* has been adapted to local needs in a number of countries (Patterson and Theobald, 1995; Evans, 1995). Since the early 1990s the European Union (EU) and the UK have published policy documents on sustainable development (Commission of the European Community, 1992; Department of Environment, 1994), Europe has established an Environmental Management and Audit System (EMAS), international environmental standards have been developed, and most countries now require impact assessments before developments proceed.

Environmental management shows considerable variation in style and it is still evolving. It is applied to very different environments, some more 'natural' than others: marine, urban, rural, arid, mountainous, wetlands, etc. A step towards further improvement is to assess what problems it has encountered and why (Trudgill, 1990).

After this brief outline of the evolution, characteristics and problems of environmental management, it is useful to present a picture of its principles (i.e. its main truths and laws), or at least its main themes. Broadly, the main principles of environmental management are prudence and stewardship. These are pursued via:

- forward-looking, broad-view policy making and planning (mainly left to various planners to undertake);
- establishing standards and rules, monitoring and auditing;
- co-ordination (the environmental manager adopting a multidisciplinary, interdisciplinary or holistic approach);
- operationalization/implementation.

Sustainable development is linked to prudence and stewardship as a goal; another is usually human welfare, though there might be situations where long-term human well-being or conservation aims overrule this.

Since the mid-1980s new branches have appeared on the evolutionary tree of environmental management (and are discussed in the following chapters):

- environmental law;
- green business;
- impact, risk and hazard assessment;
- total quality management (TQM), which has led to total environmental quality management;
- environmental standards;
- eco-auditing;
- environmental management systems.

Recommended reading and resources

Introductory books and handbooks

Brown, L.R. (ed.) (annual) *State of the World: a WorldWatch Institute report on progress toward a sustainable society*. Norton, New York (readable annual review of environmental issues and release of data collected by WWI).

O'Riordan, T. (ed.) (1995) *Environmental Science for Environmental Management*. Addison Wesley Longman, Harlow.

O'Riordan, T. and Turner, R.K. (eds) (1983) *An Annotated Reader in Environmental Planning and Management*. Pergamon, Oxford.

Owen, L. and Unwin, T. (1997) *Environmental Management: readings and case studies*. Blackwell, Oxford.

Theodore, L., Dupont, R.R. and Baxter, T.E. (1998) *Environmental Management: problems and solutions*. CRC Press, Boulder (Springer, New York) (see part 1).

UNDP (1992) *Handbook and Guidelines for Environmental Management and Sustainable Development*. United Nations Development Programme, New York.

UNEP/INFOTERRA/IDS (1997) *Guide to Environment and Development Sources of Information on CD-ROM and the Internet*. Intermediate Technology Publications, London.

Wilson, G.A. and Bryant, R.L. (1997) *Environmental Management: new directions for the twenty-first century*. University College London Press, London.

Abstracts

Cambridge Scientific Abstracts
Environmental Abstracts – Bethesda MD 20814–3389
GeoAbstracts – Elsevier, Norwich, UK NR3 3AP

Internet

This is a small selection, and it should be noted that these sources change, may disappear, and are often of unknown provenance (compared with established journals, etc.).

Katz, M. and Thornton, D. (1997) *Environmental Management Tools on the Internet*. Soil and Water Conservation Society, Ankeny, ISBN 1–57444059–4.

Schumann, R.W. III (ed.) (1994) *Eco-data: using your PC to obtain free environmental information*. Government Institutes Inc., Rockville (MD 20850).

http://www.eea.dk/frames/main.html – European Environmental Agency.

http://www.epa.gov/global warming – Global warming.

http://www.gn.apc.org – Green Net home page.

http://www.iied.org – International Institute for Environment and Development (in UK telephone 0171 388 2117).

http://www.iucn.org – IUCN home page.
http://www.Panda.org/home.htm – WWF International.
http://www.unep.ch – UNEP site, conference information.
http://www.www.wyw.ac.uk – University of London, Wye College postgraduate environ-
    mental management courses by distance learning.

Professional bodies

The Chartered Institution of Water and Environmental Management (UK)
EIA Centre, Manchester University (UK)
Environmental Auditors Registration Association (UK)
Institute of Environmental Assessment (UK)
Institution of Environmental Sciences (UK)
International Association of Impact Assessment (USA)

Journals which publish environmental management and related articles

Ambio
Costing the Earth
Ecological Economics
Ecological Modelling
Ecologist
ENDS – Environmental Data Service UK
Environment
Environment and Behavior
Environment & Ecology
Environment and Planning-A
Environment and Urbanization
Environmental Assessment
Environmental Conservation
Environmental Impact Assessment Review
Environmental Law
Environmental Management
Environmental Monitoring & Assessment
Environmental & Resource Economics
Environmental Science & Technology
Environmental Values
Environmentalist
Environmetrics
European Environment
GeoJournal
Global Environment Change
Human Ecology

Impact Assessment (now *Impact Assessment and Project Appraisal*)
International Environmental Affairs
International Journal of Ecology & Environmental Sciences
International Journal of Environmental Studies (section A)
Journal of Arid Environments
Journal of Environment & Development
Journal of Environmental Economics
Journal of Environmental Economics and Management
Journal of Environmental Management
Journal of Environmental Law
Journal of Environmental Planning & Management
Journal of Risk Analysis
Journal of Sustainable Agriculture
Journal of Sustainable Development
Land Degradation & Development
Natural Resources Forum
Natural Resources Journal
Nature & Resources
Resources Policy
Risk, Decision and Policy
Rocky Mountain Institute Newsletter
Science of the Total Environment
Society & Environment
Society & Natural Resources
Sustainable Development (UK)
Sustainable Development (New Delhi, India)

Chapter 2

Environmental management fundamentals and goals

In 1975 Sewell (1975: ix) felt the environmental manager should 'be able to manipulate both social institutions and appropriate technologies but must do this with the sensitivity of an artist, the insights of a poet, and, perhaps, the moral purity and determination of a religious zealot'.

The nature of environmental management

Environmental management is an approach to environmental stewardship which integrates ecology, policy making, planning and social development. Its goals include:

- the prevention and resolution of environmental problems;
- establishing limits;
- establishing and nurturing institutions that effectively support environmental research, monitoring and management;
- warning of threats and identifying opportunities;
- sustaining and, if possible improving, existing resources;
- where possible improving 'quality of life';
- identifying new technology or policies that are useful.

It is clear that these goals conceal a wealth of issues. Clearly, short-term goals must be embedded within an overall vision (Dorney, 1989: 5). Without overall vision it is difficult to avoid fragmented decision making, or to adopt a long-term view, or to prioritize and identify urgent tasks. Environmental management thus demands 'scoping' (deciding goals and setting limits on efforts) before acting. However, this is often neglected.

Since the early 1970s popular texts have often published variants of 'Laws of Ecology' (based on four 'laws' published by Commoner (1971) (environmental management implications are in parenthesis):

1   Any intrusion into nature has numerous effects, many of which are un-predictable (*environmental management must cope with the unexpected*).
2   Because 'everything is connected', humans and nature are inextricably bound together; what one person does affects others (*environmental management must consider chains of causation, looking beyond the local and short term*).
3   Care needs to be taken that substances produced by humans do not interfere with any of the Earth's biogeochemical processes (*environmental management must monitor natural processes and human activities to ensure no crucial process is upset*).

In recent years some environmental managers have begun to express their overall vision and goals by publishing an environmental policy statement – to show intent, identify priorities and principles, and give a sense of purpose. While this informs the public, it does not guarantee sound environmental management. Environmental managers must assume there is an optimum balance between environmental protection and allowing human activities. Establishing where that balance lies depends largely on ethics. Clark (1989) argued that at its core environmental management asks two questions: (1) What kind of planet do we want? (2) What kind of planet can we get? Even if agreement on an optimum balance can be reached, the approach to environmental management goals can take different paths.

Environmental management has not evolved in isolation: regional planners often adopt a human ecology approach, other planners a systems analysis or an ecosystem approach. For example, McHarg (1969) used river basins, and Doxiadis (1977) tried to develop a science of planning settlement in balance with nature – ekistics. Rapoport (1993: 175) recognized two main groupings: those who adopt a horticultural metaphor – Garden Earth – and those who prefer one that is more technological – Spaceship Earth. The variety of challenges, and the fact that many different actors are involved (e.g. the public, commercial interests, professions, local and national government, special-interest groups, the voluntary sector), means that in practice environmental managers often focus on a region, ecosystem, sector of activity, or resource (Box 2.1).

Environmental managers may not achieve their objectives, might be criticized (or sued), fall into disrepute with those who employ them, and lose public trust. So, like most administrators, environmental managers are likely to follow risk-aversion strategies, including:

- working to safe minimum standards;
- adopting sustainability constraints;
- following a 'win–win' or 'least regrets' approach (i.e. actions which seek benefits *whatever the outcome*; actions which seek to reduce unwanted impacts, respectively).

Effectively, these all conserve or protect the environment unless social costs are very high. Following the precautionary principle is not costless. In many situations it has high costs as some things have to be forgone to keep open escape options (Earll, 1992; Pearce, 1994: 1337).

The implications of human population growth

In the late eighteenth century Thomas Malthus examined the factors limiting human population growth. His thesis was that human population growth puts pressure on the means of subsistence, throwing it out of balance with the environment so that there is population collapse. Interest in the limits to human population was rekindled in the 1970s by a group of ecologists, systems analysts, demographers and 'environmentalists'

BOX 2.1 Approaches to environmental management

(There may be overlap between groupings, and within categories. Environmental managers may be more or less anthropocentric or ecocentric, more or less 'green', more or less supportive of technology. There is also a wide spectrum of political and philosophical stances, all of which colour the approach adopted)

Ad hoc approach: approach developed in reaction to a specific situation

Problem-solving approach: follows a series of logical steps to identify problems and needs and implement solutions (see Figure 1.1)

Systems approach: for example

♦ ecosystem (mountain; high latitude; savanna; desert; island; lake, etc.) (Dasmann *et al.*, 1973; Ruddle and Manshard, 1981)[†]
♦ agro–ecosystem (Conway, 1985a and b)

Regional approach: mainly ecological zones or biogeophysical units, which can sometimes be international – i.e. involve different states, e.g. an internationally-shared river basin. For example:

♦ watershed (Easter *et al.*, 1986)[†]
♦ river basin (Friedman and Weaver, 1979; Barrow, 1998)[†]
♦ coastal zone[†]
♦ island
♦ command area development authority (irrigation-related)
♦ administrative region
♦ sea (e.g. Mediterranean; North Sea; Baltic; Aral Sea, etc.)[†]

Specialist discipline approach: often adopted by professionals. For example:

♦ air quality management
♦ water quality management
♦ land management
♦ environmental health
♦ urban management
♦ ocean management
♦ human ecology approach
♦ tourism management/ecotourism
♦ conservation area management

Strategic environmental management approach: (see chapter 6)

Voluntary sector approach: environmental management by, or encouraged and supported by NGOs. For example

- debt-for-nature swaps
- private reserves
- 'ginger groups' which try to prompt environmental management
- private funding for research or environmental management

Commercial approach: environmental management for business/public bodies

Political economy or political ecology approach: (see chapter 13) (Blaikie, 1985)

Human ecology approach: (see chapter 13)

† = biogeophysical systems

who came to be known as neo–Malthusians (e.g. Ehrlich *et al.*, 1970). For a given species and situation, population tends to grow until it encounters a critical resource limit or controlling factor, whereupon there is a gradual or sudden, limited or catastrophic decline in numbers, or a shift to a cyclic boom-and-bust pattern. Neo–Malthusians saw population growth as the primary cause for concern, although a few also focused on the growing threat from 'careless technology' (Farvar and Milton, 1972). One of the neo–Malthusians, Hardin (1968), focused on collective damage as a consequence of inadequately controlled individual actions, something of concern to modern environmental management. Hardin's 'tragedy of the commons' essay (and related works) argued that commonly owned natural resources under conditions of population growth would be damaged because each user would seek to maximize their short-term interests (see chapter 5). This thesis is now largely dismissed as simplistic, together with much of the neo–Malthusian theory, for failing to examine the social and historical context of population growth. The link between population growth and environment is more complex than neo–Malthusians acknowledged.

While 1970s neo–Malthusian and environmentalist publications were largely dogmatic warnings or pleas for change (Hardin, 1974a; 1974b), weak on proof and workable strategies, they did trigger an awareness that in a finite world there were *limits*. In practice, there are complex environment–population linkages and feedbacks, for example, the speed of population growth related to the ability to upgrade technology may be crucial. Damage to the environment can be a function of:

1 human population numbers;
2 high levels of consumption of that population (i.e. lifestyle);
3 technology used to satisfy consumption and dispose of waste (Harrison, 1990).

Contradicting neo–Malthusian theories, Boserüp (1965; 1981; 1990) explored how population increase, provided it does not overwhelm the adaptive ability of people, may prompt social and technological changes leading to improved quality of life (see also: Turner and Ali, 1996). Tiffen(1993; 1995; *et al.*, 1994) documents situations where not only has population growth led to innovation that improved quality of life, it has also reduced environmental degradation. This prompts the questions: How often can that pattern be achieved? What must be done to encourage such a pattern?

While there are Boserüpian grounds for tempering Malthusian and neo-Malthusian pessimism, world-wide there has been breakdown of established livelihood strategies and environmental degradation. There are also situations where a very low human population, or transboundary pollution of virtually undisturbed areas, are causing environmental damage. On a global scale there do seem to be too many humans, so environmental managers will have to establish what optimum sustainable population is, and how it can best be reached. Some demographers argue that only within the next decade or so will it be possible to achieve such a population with humane approaches (Hartshorn, 1991: 401).

Limits to growth, sustainable development and environmental ethics

When neo-Malthusians were drawing attention to limits, the Club of Rome (an informal international group concerned about the predicament of humanity) reported on a systems dynamics computer world-model (Meadows *et al.*, 1972: *The Limits to Growth*). This publication reported on studies to determine future scenarios, using global forecasts of accelerating industrialization; population growth; rates of malnutrition; depletion of non-renewable resources; and a deteriorating environment. The report was designed to promote public interest, and concluded that 'If present growth trends . . . continue unchanged, the limits to growth on this planet will be reached within the next hundred years' (by 2072). Meadows and his colleagues concluded that by effective environmental management – a condition of adequate 'ecological and economic stability' could be sustained.

With *The Limits to Growth* in mind, some began calling for reduced or even 'zero growth'. However, any state embracing such ethics would face considerable disruption of its economy. From the early 1970s there was a much more palatable alternative – sustainable development. This seemed to offer a way for continued growth to avoid conflict with environmental limits (Barrow, 1995b). The goals of sustainable development and the Club of Rome are the same – adequate sustained quality of life for all without exceeding environmental limits. It is possible to stretch some limits, using technology, so sustainable development may be pursued not just by altering demands or finding resource substitutes.

In a sequel to *The Limits to Growth* the same principal authors refined their original systems dynamics model and fed in much-improved data. *Beyond the Limits* (Meadows *et al.*, 1992) argued that the 1972 warnings were broadly correct, that some of the limits have already been exceeded, and that, if present trends continue, there is virtually certain to be global collapse within the lifetime of children alive today

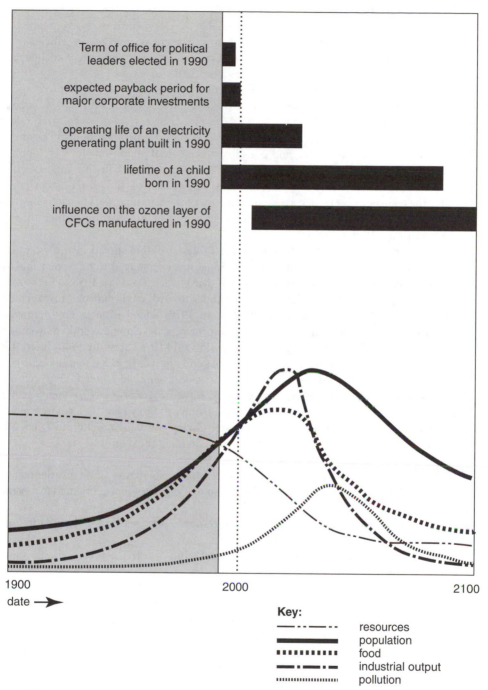

FIGURE 2.1 Time horizon of the *World3* model
Source: Meadows *et al.* (1992: 235, Fig. 8.1)

(see Figure 2.1). However, they argue that it is still possible to have 'overshoot but not collapse', and to achieve the goal of sustainable development if excessive population growth and material consumption are cut and there is increase in efficiency of materials and energy use soon. *Beyond the Limits* throws down an urgent challenge to environmental management and indicates a timescale for action.

For effective environmental management there must be means of resolving controversies regarding proper conduct (Cairns and Crawford, 1991: 23): to a large degree ethics enable this. Ethics can be defined as a system of cultural values motivating people's behaviour (Rapoport, 1993). They draw upon human reasoning, morals, knowledge of nature, and goals to act as a sort of plumb-line for development and shape a worldview. Ethics operate at the level of individuals, institutions, societies, and internationally. Some environmentalists have blamed Judaeo–Christian ethics for the tendency over the last two thousand years for western peoples to see themselves in dominion over nature, and to pursue strategies of exploitation, rather than of stewardship (White, 1967).

From the late sixteenth century the Protestant ethic spread in the west, and ideas of utopia were discussed – the individual was encouraged to be responsible for self-improvement through good acts and hard work (Weber, 1958; Hill, 1964). However, few tried to shift *laissez-faire* attitudes towards environmental management before the 1960s. Activists in the 1960s and 1970s added little to environmental science; however, they did stimulate a quest for new development and environment ethics (Cheny, 1989; Dower, 1989; Barrow, 1995a: 14–16). From the 1980s interest in the environment has grown, stimulating books and journals (e.g. *Environmental Ethics; Ethics & Behaviour; Ethics, Place and Environment; Environmental Values; Science, Technology & Human Values*). Interestingly, some progressive environmental ethics literature has come from business. Unfortunately, there is plenty of environmental ethics theory, but little ethical pragmatism! Carley and Christie (1992: 78) tried to summarize the range of environmental ethics, dividing them into:

(a) *Technocratic* environmental ethics = resource-exploitative, growth-oriented;
(b) *Managerial* environmental ethics = resource-conservationist, oriented to sustainable growth;
(c) *Communalist* environmental ethics = resource-preservationist, oriented to limited or zero growth;
(d) *Bioethicist* or *deep ecology* environmental ethics = extreme preservationist, anti-growth.

Grouping (a) is anthropocentric and places faith in the capacity of technology to overcome problems. Grouping (d) is unlikely to attract support from enough people to be a viable approach, and offers little guidance to environmental managers. Carley and Christie felt the ethics of groups (b) and (c) were more likely to support sustainable development and provide guidance for environmental management.

Environmental management: problems and needs

Westerners have tended to see themselves as being at war with nature, rather than seeking to understand it and then trying to exist within its constraints. The environment was to be 'tamed', and unspoilt lands were 'wastelands'. Since the 1930s the last land frontiers have been closing, and unsettled areas capable of giving a good livelihood are increasingly difficult to find. By the mid-1960s the limitless world was seen to have shrunk to Spaceship Earth, a finite and delicate system which must be taken care of if it is to support humanity. The Gaian viewpoint goes further, regarding the Earth as a system which, if upset by careless development, might adjust in such a way as to make current lifestyles impossible or even eliminate humans.

Environmental management therefore faces complex environmental challenges which may reach crisis level within fifty years. It will have to cope with these in the face of growing human population, increasing poverty, likely social unrest, and perhaps natural disasters. Anticipatory action seems to hold most promise, and people will have to be involved more than has been the case with planning and management in the past. How will environmental management achieve its policy goals? Through a mix of moral pressure, the spread of appropriate ethics, and by ensuring economics, business and law are sufficiently sensitive to the needs of the environment. Environmental management will need to make use of education and the media to alter social attitudes so that there is an acceptance of a new ethics. It will also have to draw upon other fields to achieve its goals, and must have effective institutions. Manuals, guides, checklists, conventions and agreements can help guide the identification of goals and preparation of action plans and their implementation.

The reductionist approach of splitting problems into component parts for study and solution lies at the core of western rational, scientific study. Some feel a holistic 'overall view' approach should replace 'compartmentalized and inflexible science'; I feel that is a mistake – there is a need for both (Risser, 1985; Savory, 1988; Atkinson, 1991a: 154; Rapoport, 1993: 176).

Environmental management involves a series of decisions (Figure 2.2). How these are made depends on whether a technocratic or a consultative model is adopted. The latter has become the usual pattern in the USA and Canada, and is increasingly being chosen in Japan and Europe, reflecting the trend towards freedom of information. Whatever the overall approach, environmental management is, as Matthews *et al.* (1976: 5) noted, a 'myriad of individual and collective decisions by persons, groups, and organizations' and 'together these decisions and interactions constitute a process – a process that in effect results in management (or mismanagement) of the environmental resources of a society'.

Of the many problems that beset environmental management, inadequate data is a common hindrance: there are still huge gaps in knowledge of the structure and function of the environment, the workings of global, regional and local economics, and of how societies and individual humans behave. The ideal is adequate data that can be presented in real time, so that the scenario can be observed as it changes. With improved computers, software and the development of tools like geographical information systems (GIS) this may one day be possible, but often all that is available today is an occasional, incomplete snapshot view.

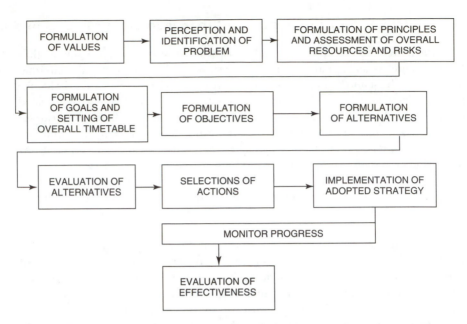

FIGURE 2.2 Major decision-making steps in a typical environmental management process
Source: Part-based on Matthews *et al.* (1976: 10, Fig. 1)

Decision making is often made difficult by politics; lobbying; media, public and NGOs' attention; lack of funding and expertise. Environmental managers are faced with two temporal challenges: (1) problems may suddenly demand attention and allow little time for solution; (2) the desirability that planning horizons stretch further into the future than has been usual practice. Decisions are easier to make and policies more easily adjusted if there is time available – for example, a 3°C climate change over 150 years may not be too much of a challenge, but if it happens over 20 years it certainly would be (Chiapponi, 1992). Predictions are difficult enough with stable environments; once stability has been upset there may be unexpected and sudden feedbacks or shifts to different states, all of which are difficult to forecast. The behaviour of economic systems are even more difficult to predict, and human behaviour is especially fickle as tastes and attitudes alter. The unpredictability and rapidity of challenges prompted Holling (1978) to argue for adaptive assessment and management.

Sustainable development calls for trade-offs. For example, it may be necessary to forgo immediate benefits to secure long-term yields – which may far outweigh the former. Such trade-offs can be a cruel choice for individuals, groups or countries, and a minefield for the environmental manager (and it is a situation where foreign aid could be focused to cushion trade-offs).

Institutional problems probably present more difficulties for environmental management than technical or scientific challenges (Cairns and Crawford, 1991). Human institutions change and can be difficult to understand and control and building new ones may be hard. It is vital that the institutions involved in environmental management are effective. Even if there is technology and funding and a will to solve a problem, success will be unlikely without the right type of sustainable institution. A growing number of social scientists have been focusing on institution building: this gives us grounds for optimism. The major international body charged with environmental management, the United Nations Environment Program (UNEP), was designed in the 1960s (and founded in 1973), and needs remodelling to be more effective (Von Moltke, 1992). The UNEP was located away from Paris, Geneva or New York, in Nairobi, which has had mixed results – some argue it is off the beaten track and this partly explains its poor funding and lack of power. To be fair to institutions like the UNEP, they must rely on the quality of their arguments to convince countries and multinational companies (MNCs) or transnational companies (TNCs) to accept a strategy, and have been given little in the way of sanctions to enforce policies.

Recommended reading

Journals which publish articles on the fundamentals of environmental management

Environmental Management
Ethics, Place and Environment
Journal of Environmental Management

Environmental management – business and law

'Our products reflect our philosophy . . . respect for other cultures, the past, the natural world, and our customers. It's a partnership of profits with principles'.
(Anita Roddick – The Body Shop promotional literature 1990)

Business and legal aspects of environmental management have developed greatly and generated huge interest in recent decades. This chapter presents an overview.

In many respects business and legal aspects are the cutting-edge of environmental management. Business drives a lot of human activity, and can degrade people and the environment, or offer routes to new development ethics and sustainable development. Law provides guidelines and rules for arbitration, without which chaos and destruction ensue. Both these aspects of environmental management must evolve rapidly to face challenges like globalization and transboundary problems adequately.

ENVIRONMENTAL MANAGEMENT AND BUSINESS

By the late seventeenth century in the Caribbean, Mauritius, and many other places, trade in sugar, timber and other commodities by bodies like the Dutch East Indies Company and the (British) East India Company and clearances by numerous smaller plantation owners were causing deforestation and soil erosion (Grove, 1995). By the 1830s, English Romantic socialist-environmentalists like William Morris, and in Russia the proto-anarchist Pyotr Kropotkin began to criticize industrialization for its pollution, human degradation and shoddy products (MacCarthy, 1994). But there was little popular protest until the 1960s, by which time people in developed countries had improved standards of living and enjoyed sufficient free time and access to a more or less democratic media, to become aware of and lobby for environmental issues. Accidents like the *Torrey Canyon* oil-tanker spillage and pollution disasters like Three Mile Island, Love Canal and Seveso had raised public awareness in USA and Europe by the mid-1970s. Also environmental NGOs, consumer protection groups and popular writers (like Carson, 1962) fanned public interest.

Accidents prompted environmental controls. Also by the 1970s American NGOs and groups of lawyers interested in environmental issues (notably the Environmental Defense Fund and the Natural Resources Defense Fund) began to fight group court actions against those damaging nature and lobbied for environmental legislation. In Europe and New Zealand green politics began to emerge. Research and contact between scientists increased after the 1957–8 International Geophysical Year, leading to improving awareness of environmental issues, better understanding of Earth's structure and function, the development of international standards, and sharing of data.

The USA passed the 1969 National Environmental Policy Act (NEPA) in 1970, and established an Environmental Protection Agency (Seldner and Cottrel, 1994: 61–96). The UN held the 1972 Conference on the Human Environment in Stockholm, and in 1973 established the UN Environmental Program (UNEP). A deluge of publications fanned concern for the environment and realization there was a need to review practices and ethics, e.g. Schumacher's (1973) *Small Is Beautiful* voiced concern about material consumption, pollution and uncaring business. Overall, the mid-sixties to mid-seventies was a decade of increasing environmental concern.

NEPA required developers to meet environmental standards, and effectively promoted the precautionary principle. Business was also being prompted by legislation, public opinion and self-interest to pay attention to the environment. It was not enough to obey the law and reduce liability, there was a need to look concerned – what Brenton called 'defensive greenness' (1994: 148). Some companies saw opportunities for commercial gain through environmental management – building a green image and marketing environmentally friendly products or providing services for environmental management (Greeno and Robinson, 1992). There was a realization that 'end-of-pipe' solutions (i.e. cleaning up rather than prevention) were more costly, gave a bad public image, and that environmental management could be a way of cutting costs to get a 'competitive edge' (Beaumont, 1992: 201; Taylor, 1992; Winter, 1994).

Other factors have prompted business interest in environmental management:

♦   globalization (i.e. media, finance, etc., becoming global);
♦   'glasnost' (i.e. increasing public demand for access to information);
♦   activity of green business groups, especially since the 1992 UN Conference on Environment and Development;
♦   trade union and NGO concern for environmental issues;
♦   a wish by companies to reduce inspection by regulatory bodies;
♦   insistence by funding, insurance and licensing bodies that impact assessment and eco-audit be conducted;
♦   ethical (green) investment policies adopted by some companies (in the USA a group of powerful investors now apply a set of environmental policy principles – the 'Valdez Principles') (North, 1992);
♦   genuine sense of responsibility (some companies have been founded by people with a strong sense of moral duty);
♦   avoidance of litigation;
♦   the establishment since the 1970s of increasingly powerful environmental ministries in most countries;
♦   formation of bodies like the Institute of Environmental Management (UK);
♦   promotion of the Integrated Systems for Environmental Management and the Business Charter for Sustainable Development (International Chamber of Commerce, 1991);
♦   provision of courses on environmental management at university business schools;
♦   the UN Center on Transnational Corporations has promoted sustainable development.

Corporate environmental management in the 1990s

Business interacts with a wide range of parties (Figure 3.1). Satisfying the investors and shareholders is at present the driving force; the adoption of environmental management implies concern for a wider range of stakeholders: the public, bystanders, employees, consumers, the regional and global environment. Environmental management must address its objectives within the context of company practices (e.g. if at all possible it should not slow completion schedules) (Seldner and Cottrel, 1994). As its value is proven, those practices may be modified to help environmental management. 'Company', 'firm' or 'business' is used in this chapter, but environmental management, eco-audit and environmental management systems are also practised by government departments, city administrations, etc.

The tasks of a business environmental manager include:

◆ education of employees to be aware of environmental issues;
◆ updating management on relevant environmental regulation, laws and issues;
◆ selecting specialists and checking that environmental management tasks contracted out to consultants have been satisfactorily conducted and are properly acted upon;
◆ ensuring waste management is satisfactory;
◆ avoiding legal costs, reducing insurance premiums, risk and hazard assessment;
◆ if need be correcting mistakes of the past.

FIGURE 3.1 Corporate environmental management: the parties involved
Sources: Partly based on Royston (1978a: 7, Fig. 3); Hunt and Johnson (1995: 69, Fig. 4.1)

A typical definition of business environmental management would be: 'efforts to minimize the negative environmental impact of the firm's products throughout their life cycle' (Klassen and McLaughlin, 1996: 119). The range of tasks is so wide, and involves working with so many people or bodies outside the company, that 'environmental co-ordinator' might be a better term.

If business fails to adopt environmental management in a serious fashion there will be little progress, for, as Hawken (1993) noted, corporations are Earth's dominant institutions – many corporations have earnings in excess of those of most developing countries, and some command more riches than some developed nations. Governments are often lobbied and prevailed upon to do what national business, MNCs or TNCs want. Big business often has better access to information, resources and skills than poor nations, and may have greater stability for year-to-year planning than some governments.

For the last ten years there has been an increasing flow of books on environmental management and sustainable development for business (e.g. Elkington and Burke, 1989; Davis, 1991; Sadgrove, 1992; Schmidheiny, 1992; Smith, 1992; Allenby and Richards, 1994; Hutchinson and Hutchinson, 1997). This literature may be subdivided into:

- greening of business (often by sector, e.g. tourism management and environment);
- environmental management for sustainable development of business;
- green corporate environmental management;
- total quality management/environmental management systems;
- eco-audit;
- impact assessment, hazard and risk assessment;
- green business ethics;
- green marketing, labelling, life-cycle assessment;
- recycling and waste disposal;
- health and safety;
- environmentally sound investment and funding;
- environmental law and business.

By 1992 the chemical industry in developed countries was spending an estimated 3 to 4 per cent of its sales income per annum on environment, health and safety in the USA alone: that constituted about US$10 billion a year (Greeno and Robinson, 1992: 231). Spending is rapidly increasing. With accidents like the *Exxon Valdez* costing over US$2 billion it is easy to see why.

Corporate visions of stewardship – a paradigm shift to environmental management ethics?

'Fordism' of the 1920s to 1960s emphasized mass production, mass consumption, corporate control and resource exploitation (Amin, 1994: 2). Since the 1960s various thinkers, 'barefoot economists' and environmentalists have questioned growing consumerism, i.e. excessive consumption, stimulated through marketing (Elkington and Hailes, 1988; Adams *et al.*, 1991). The problem is, how will people (consumers) and business (supplying the consumers) shift to something more supportive of environmental goals? Hawken (1993) in *The Ecology of Commerce* argued that free market capitalism, the economic and social credo of most of the world, must rapidly shift to a 'restorative economy' based on 'industrial ecology' (see later this chapter). Only business, he argued, and no other human institution, has the power to make adequate changes. Allenby and Richards (1994) also saw industrial ecology as a means of integrating environmental concern with economic activity.

Whether it is termed post-Fordian, postmodern or post-industrial, what Hawken and others argue is that the world's future economy should be organized with guiding principles coming from industrial ecology. These post-Fordians seem convinced that the profit motive will be replaced by a more environmentally sensitive approach. Some even suggest that environmental management values are supplanting shareholder interests and a paradigm shift is beginning. However, there is a risk that 'greening' of business is appearance rather than substance, simply the adoption of environmental management tools to improve profits and public relations (Garrod and Chadwick, 1996).

While there might seem to be few incentives at present to encourage a shift to better environmental management, there have been efforts to promote it (Greeno and Robertson, 1992: 224; Welford, 1996; 1997). One of the more significant moves has been the publication in 1991 of a *Business Charter for Sustainable Development* by the International Chamber of Commerce at the 1991 World Industry Conference on Environmental Management (see Box 3.1). One of the first questions asked by business of such proposals is 'can they improve financial performance as well as lead to sustainable development?'. Klassen and McLaughlin (1996) put this to the test, and concluded from studies of firms' performances that the adoption of environmental management *did* increase profits.

Approaches adopted to promote environmental management in business

Klassen and McLaughlin (1996) noted: 'the long-term goal of environmental management is to move toward . . . considering environmental aspects in an integrated fashion in product design, the entire manufacturing process, marketing, product delivery and use, consumer service, and post-consumer product disposition.' Already, several fields are well developed, including: industrial ecology, green marketing, consumer protection bodies, ecolabelling, total quality management, covenants, life-cycle analysis.

BOX 3.1 Business Charter for Sustainable Development: principles for environmental management

1 *Corporate priority* To recognize environmental management as among the highest corporate priorities and as a key determinant to sustainable development; to establish policies, programmes and practices for conducting operations in an environmentally sound manner.

2 *Integrated management* To integrate these policies, programmes and practices fully into each business as an essential element of management in all its functions.

3 *Process of improvement* To continue to improve corporate policies, programmes and environmental performance, taking into account technical developments, scientific understanding, consumer needs and community expectations, with legal regulations as a starting-point; and to apply the same environmental criteria internationally.

4 *Employee education* To educate, train and motivate employees to conduct their activities in an environmentally responsible manner.

5 *Prior assessment* To assess environmental impacts before starting a new activity or project, and before decommissioning a facility or leaving a site.

6 *Products and services* To develop and provide products or services that have no undue environmental impact and are safe in their intended use, that are efficient in their consumption of energy and natural resources, and that can be recycled, reused, or disposed of safely.

7 *Customer advice* To advise, and where relevant educate, customers, distributors and the public, in the safe use, transportation, storage and disposal of products provided; and to apply similar considerations to the provision of services.

8 *Facilities and operations* To develop, design and operate facilities and conduct activities, taking into consideration the efficient use of energy and materials, the sustainable use of renewable resources, the minimization of adverse environmental impact and waste generation, and the safe and responsible disposal of residual waste.

9 *Research* To conduct or support research on the environmental impacts of raw materials, products, processes, emissions and wastes, associated with the enterprise, and on the means of minimizing any adverse impacts.

10 *Precautionary approach* To modify the manufacture, marketing or use of products or services or the conduct of activities, consistent with scientific and technical understanding, to prevent serious or irreversible environmental

continued . . .

degradation. The 1991 Second World Industry Conference on Environmental Management (Rotterdam) promoted the 'precautionary principle'. One problem for those proposing a development is how much proof of a risk they need before taking possibly expensive precautions – what seems to be be widely followed is to establish whether there is a 'reasonably foreseeable risk' or a 'significant risk' (Birnie and Boyle, 1992: 95–6).

11 *Contractors and suppliers* To promote the adoption of these principles by contractors acting on behalf of the enterprise, encouraging and, where appropriate, requiring improvements in their practices to make them consistent with those of the enterprise; and to encourage the widest adoption of these principles by suppliers.

12 *Emergency preparedness* To develop and maintain, where significant hazards exist, emergency preparedness plans in conjunction with the emergency services, relevant authorities and the local community, recognizing potential trans-boundary impacts.

13 *Transfer of technology* To contribute to the transfer of environmentally sound technology and management methods throughout the industrial and public sectors.

14 *Contributing to the common effort* To contribute to the development of public policy and to business, governmental and intergovernmental programmes and educational initiatives that will enhance environmental awareness and protection.

15 *Openness of concerns* To foster openness and dialogue with employees and the public, anticipating and responding to their concerns about the potential hazards and impacts of operations, products, wastes or services, including those of transboundary or global significance.

16 *Compliance and reporting* To measure environmental performance; to conduct regular environmental audits and assessments of compliance with company requirements, legal requirements, and these principles; and periodically to provide appropriate information to the Board of Directors, shareholders, employees, the authorities and the public.

Note: The International Chamber of Commerce established a task-force of business representatives to create this Business Charter for Sustainable Development – it was launched in April 1991.

Source: International Chamber of Commerce, 1993

Industrial ecology

This is an approach which examines industrial, economic and resource activities from a biological and environmental, rather than a monetary point of view (Frosch and Gallopoulos, 1989). Allenby and Richards (1994) saw it as integrating environmental concern into economic activity. Industrial ecology regards waste and pollution as uneconomic and harmful, and seeks to 'dovetail' them with raw materials. This means that wherever possible industry should use by-products, and go beyond the reduction of wastes to make use of what remains by the producer or other bodies. The product does not cause damage, and leads to a system of commerce where each and every act is inherently sustainable and restorative (Hawken, 1993: xvi). Effectively, *the environmental price of a product is included in its retail price.*

This application of the ecosystem concept to industry means linking the 'metabolism' of one company or body to that of others. This is not far-fetched: some groupings of companies and settlements do it already. For example, Kalundborg (Denmark) has a coal-fired power station, oil refinery, pharmaceutical companies, concrete producer, sulphuric acid producer, fish farms, horticultural greenhouses and district heating – which are well integrated. Kalundborg's industrial ecology has happened more or less spontaneously, as companies seek to minimize costs of energy and raw materials and cut the output of waste. There are a number of similar examples in Sweden (Hawken, 1993: 62) and Denmark, where sewage, agricultural waste and household refuse disposal are often integrated with district heating and electricity generation.

Pigouvian taxes

Some people advocate going beyond the sort of industrial ecology-based strategy adopted by Kalundborg to a fully cyclic economy, i.e. one which yields virtually no waste because recycling and by-product recovery are complete. Making manufacturers responsible for some or all of the costs of recycling or waste disposal is one way of encouraging waste reduction and industrial ecology. There are various ways of doing this: one is to levy Pigouvian taxes (see chapter 5). Named after the 1920s UK economist Arthur Pigou, these aim to ensure a manufacturer pays *all* costs from raw material and energy provision to final collection and recycling.

Pigouvian taxes may present problems: large companies may make sufficient profits to afford fines, but small companies could be crippled. So, the 'polluter-pays' principle can be a virtual licence to pollute if the fines are not set high enough, and that can damage small businesses (Beaumont, 1992). One way of avoiding such problems is to use licences; for example, in Germany manufacturers pay a fee to the government to display a green dot on packaging which authorizes (compulsory) recycling. As the costs have to be passed on to the customer, this encourages companies to reduce expensive packaging and use cheap, recyclable materials.

Green marketing

Some companies and public bodies had recognized by the early 1980s that a satisfactory green image could improve public relations, and perhaps provide a marketing niche (Charter, 1992; Coddington, 1993; Peattie, 1995). There are manufacturers that have gained from this, and offer genuinely improved products – e.g. refrigerators that use less electricity, do not leak CFCs, and which are easier to recycle, and firms which manufacture equipment for monitoring and managing environmental quality. Less enlightened companies may sell goods because of public fears about the environment – e.g. sunblock creams and sunglasses for those afraid of increased UV. AEG reputedly increased sales by ca. 30 per cent in a static market by running a marketing campaign on its green strengths. In America in the 1980s McDonald's commissioned an environmental audit and acted on it to shift from plastic packaging foamed with CFCs to environmentally friendly cardboard. This proved good for public relations and was much cheaper (Elkington and Hailes, 1988).

Consumer protection bodies

Alongside the growth in green marketing there has been a spread of green consumerism (The Council of Economic Priorities of the United States, 1989; Mintel, 1990; Irvine, 1989). Consumer protection bodies have been active since the 1960s, and have not been restricted to the developed countries, e.g. one Malaysian body has been active in its own country and works for consumers elsewhere – the Consumers Association Penang.

Ecolabelling

The marking of goods to indicate that they are environmentally friendly (ecolabelling) has been adopted in many countries, including Canada, the USA, Germany and Sweden (Figure 3.2). In most cases the product is judged against similar goods by an independent agency to establish whether it has less environmental impact (without formal eco-auditing). Germany was one of the first countries to introduce ecolabelling in 1978, with its Umweltzeichen or Blaue Engel system (Hemmelskamp and Brockmann, 1997). This relies on a jury of experts supervised by the Federal Environment Ministry to award the right to display a mark on packaging or in adverts. This is a way of influencing the behaviour of consumers, helping them identify the environmental impacts of products, and encourages manufacturers to reduce the impacts of their products.

Ecolabelling assesses environmental impact and communicates this to the consumer or middle merchant. The focus is on the product and often nothing is said about the process of production or distribution. So, an 'environmentally friendly' product might come from a factory which causes pollution or present a disposal problem after use. There is also a need for standardization and policing of ecolabelling.

Blue Angel
West Germany (1978)

EcoMark
Japan (1989)

EcoLogo
Canada (1989)

Ecolabelling Scheme
European Union (1992)

Environment Mark
Nordic Council (1989)

FIGURE 3.2 Ecolabelling
Note: Date of introduction in parenthesis

However, under current World Trade Organization (WTO) rules this may not be easy. West (1995) warned that without better legal enforcement, it tended to become a marketing gimmick.

Total quality management and environmental management systems

(Environmental management systems and eco-audit are further discussed in chapter 4.)

Total quality management (TQM) (also called company-wide quality management) aims to provide assurance of adherence to policy and specifications through a structured management system, and to enable demonstration of it to third parties through documentation and record-keeping. TQM was first formulated in the USA, and largely developed in Japan in the early post-war period to try to improve industrial competitiveness. Environmental management systems (EMSs) show adherence to a suitable environmental policy, the meeting of appropriate environmental objectives (equivalent to specifications in quality management) and the ability to demonstrate to a wide range of interested parties ('customers' in TQM) that the system requirements and objectives are met. EMSs, usually require that a company or body publishes and regularly updates an Environmental Policy Statement. An EMS provides an organizational structure, procedures and resources for implementing environmental policy. It also provides a language of performance and quality that can be understood by management (Willig, 1994; British Standards Institution, 1996). So far, adoption of EMS has mainly been voluntary with rapid growth of interest and continuing modification and improvement. Hunt and Johnson (1995: 4) suggested this indicates business has shifted from 'defensive environmental management' to accepting the need for probity.

There are critics of EMSs, who argue it is possible to rig them by setting easy-to-achieve targets; that it is more important (and difficult) to nurture satisfactory environmental ethics; and that EMS is still being developed and tested (for a critique see: Welford, 1996: 52).

Covenants

A government or other regulatory body can provide companies with a more stable regulatory environment and encourage development of better pollution control plans or adoption of an EMS (Beardsley *et al.*, 1997: 33) through a covenant. This is a written, voluntary agreement signed by the company or other body and the government or agency seeking regulation. The Netherlands has made extensive use of covenants as part of an integrated approach to national environmental management policy. A Dutch company undertaking a covenant would be expected to produce a development plan every four years, to be reviewed by local authorizing bodies. The plan coverage includes pollution control and energy conservation and it is seen as a way of getting national policies implemented at local level. Measures were initiated by the National Environmental Policy Plans (adopted by the Dutch Parliament in 1989), and by 1997 over 1,200 companies had signed covenants. The covenanting approach can be quite effective, particularly in cutting pollution. However, some NGOs are not keen on the approach, viewing it as closed or cosy and not sufficiently open to third parties to check. There are also some worries that it may lead to a softening of enforcement controls. Nevertheless, it is an approach which encourages company self-regulation.

Life-cycle analysis

Many development activities are processes which have different stages – for example, manufacturing a car or running a power station involve raw materials and energy provision, plant construction, manufacturing, distribution, use and disposal or decommissioning. Equipment is usually subject to wear and tear, and so varies in performance and presents different risks as it ages and as management acquire experience (or become complacent). Industrial and power generation sites, for example, often accumulate contamination, and so the environmental threat is not constant. It is therefore undesirable to assess impacts or develop environmental management policies by simply taking a snapshot view. Life-cycle analysis (or assessment) has been developed to try to consider the whole of an activity, which may extend beyond the time horizon of a single owner. It is cradle-to-grave study of an activity or company (British Standards Institution, 1994a; Fava, 1994; Pidgeon and Brown, 1994; Franklin, 1995).

Environmental management and business: the current situation

One may summarize the present situation (see Beaumont, 1992: 202) as:

◆ the majority of businesses are aware that environmental issues are important;
◆ some businesses are doing something – it may be from genuine concern, but often it is for public relations or profit motives;
◆ too often businesses adopt a 'react and repair' approach, rather than following precautionary principles;
◆ only a few businesses are acting at a strategic level;
◆ business is in need of strategies like industrial ecology, but will need to be encouraged or forced to adopt them.

ENVIRONMENTAL MANAGEMENT AND LAW

Law should provide a framework for regulating use of the environment (Harte, 1992; McEldowney, 1996; Bell, 1997) (Box 3.2). Law is crucial for environmental management in a number of ways, aiding:

◆   regulation of resource use;
◆   protection of the environment and biodiversity;
◆   mediation, conflict resolution and conciliation;
◆   formulation of stable, unambiguous undertakings and agreements.

Environmental management may involve a number of resource situations, e.g. individually-owned (private) resources; national resources; shared resources; open-access resources; common property resources; global resources. Some of these are better covered by law than others (Berkes, 1989; The Ecologist, 1993). There are different legal systems – for example, based on Roman Law, on customary laws, Islamic Law, the Code Napoléon – to name but a few. Some countries have legal systems that combine more than one of these, say indigenous and colonial era legislation, plus Islamic Law. Areas may be subject to state and federal laws and to secular and religious laws. In most countries statutory law is written by politicians and passed by national legislature; and common law is compiled by judges (with reference to past cases and prior statutory law).

Most legislation evolves in response to problems, so there is often delay between need and the establishment of satisfactory law. Without effective legislation, resource use, pollution control, conservation, and most fields of human activity are likely to fall into chaos and conflict. Law can encourage satisfactory performance, enable authorities to punish those who infringe environmental management legislation, or confiscate equipment that is misused or faulty, or close a company; it may also be possible for employees, bystanders and product or service users to sue for damages if they are harmed.

Some countries have been active in developing environmental management law, notably Sweden, The Netherlands, the USA, Canada, Australia and New Zealand. Some environmental laws are ancient: Indian rulers promulgated controls on hunting and forest felling centuries ago; the UK had local pollution control laws as early as the twelfth century AD, and passed nationally enforced pollution control legislation like the Alkali Act (1863) over a century ago.

Environmental management increasingly involves transboundary problems that reach beyond traditional sovereignty limits, issues of negligence, and the need for nations to co-operate. International law is evolving to address such issues, although it is difficult to develop and enforce (McAuslan, 1991). Often powerful MNCs or TNCs are involved in issues and these may prompt and drive forward innovation, not necessarily to the benefit of the environment or the public. Walker (1989: 30) likened them to seventeenth-century city states that had insufficient public accountability. The problem is to ensure that changes are for the good of the environment and the greater common good, rather than just suiting a large company or more countries.

Most laws, whether civil or criminal, are corrective – punishing wrong-doers and deterring others from infringing rules and agreements or from causing nuisance or injury. In the main, therefore, legislation has not been very pre-emptive. Environmental managers must also be aware that there is little point in passing laws or making international agreements if there cannot be adequate enforcement.

BOX 3.2 Forms of regulation or legislation (principles, standards, guidelines, etc., which are not firm laws, but help lawmakers. Definitions are not rigidly fixed.)

Principle broadly, a step towards establishing a law. Once established, tested and working, it can be incorporated into law.

Standard levels of pollution, energy efficiency, etc., that are desirable or required. They provide a benchmark so that different individuals, bodies, countries, are as far as possible dealing with the same values. A treaty may incorporate standards.

Guideline suggestions as to how to proceed, usually without real force of law.

Directive documents that set out a desired outcome, but to some extent leave the ways of reaching it to companies, states or countries.

Licence a right granted to a body, which agrees to terms or pays, which requires adherence to strict practice and does not give any guarantee of permanent ownership or usufruct.

Law laws and statutes that require certain actions or standards, and may punish failure to achieve them.

Treaty a solemn binding agreement between international entities – especially states. Treaties can lay down rules or treaty constraints. Stricter, more precise treaties are likely to involve fewer states, and the process of drafting, adopting and ratifying means that this can be a slow process, and environmental management often needs rapid action. Vague treaties are quicker and easier to get signed. Few multilateral treaties are adopted in less than five years: the UN Law of the Sea Convention took nine years (1973–1982), and some take much more. Treaties can be difficult to enforce – often enforcement is attempted by an international organization: e.g. the International Whaling Commission. Treaties should bind states that sign and ratify them to accept terms as customary law, but in practice they do not always get transformed into customary law, and some are largely ignored.

Declaration a general statement of intent or drafting of guidelines to follow. 'Softer' than the obligations of a treaty.

Convention multilateral instrument signed by many states or international institutions. Conventions can be vague, which ensures that countries are not afraid of signing but this can undermine effectiveness.

Protocol less formal agreement, often subsidiary or ancillary to a convention.

Contingency agreement a good way of dealing with uncertainty surrounding many global environmental management issues. Agreement of what to do if something happens.

Three things are especially important for environmental legislation:

1   The precautionary principle, which has evolved to deal with risks and uncertainties faced by environmental management (Rogers *et al.*, 1997). The meaning is still not firmly established by law. The principle implies that an ounce of prevention is worth a pound of cure – it does not prevent problems but may reduce their occurrence and helps ensure contingency plans are made (Mitchell, 1997: 80). The application of this principle requires either cautious progress until a development can be judged 'innocent', or avoiding development until research indicates exactly what the risks are, and then proceeding to minimize them. Once a threat is identified, action should be taken to prevent or control damage even if there is uncertainty about whether the threat is real. Some environmental problems become impossible or costly to solve if there is delay, so waiting for research and legal proof is not costless.

Some hold that the principle should be applied in situations where both the probability and cost of impacts are unknown. The principle was stressed in many of the decisions reached at the Rio Earth Summit in 1992. For example, it was endorsed by Article 15 of the 1992 Rio Declaration on Environment and Development (Freestone, 1994: 209–211). Article 130r of the Maastricht Treaty (Treaty on European Union) of February 1992 states that EU policy on the environment shall be based on the precautionary principle.

2   The polluter-pays principle – in addition to the obvious – the polluter pays for damage caused by a development – this principle also implies that a polluter pays for monitoring and policing. A problem with this approach is that fines may bankrupt small businesses, yet be low enough for a large company to write them off as an occasional overhead, which does little for pollution control. There is debate as to whether the principle should be retrospective – e.g. today a purchaser who acquires contaminated land in good faith is often forced to clean up the mess others left (if the polluter pays, how long back does liability stretch?). Developing countries are seeking to have developed countries pay more for carbon dioxide controls, arguing that they polluted the world during the Industrial Revolution, yet enjoy the fruits of invention from that era.

The polluter-pays principle is more a way of allocating costs to the polluter than a legal principle. OECD member countries adopted the principle in 1972, at least in theory (OECD, 1975).

3   Freedom of information – if the public, NGOs ('green watchdogs') or even official bodies are unable to get information, environmental planning and management is hindered. Democracies have begun to release more information – the USA has a Freedom of Information Act, the EU is moving in that direction, and in the UK the (1994) Environmental Protection Act has helped. Few countries have such well-developed disclosure as the USA, which requires public registers of development activities, publication of Environmental Impact Statements, hazard warning on products, etc. Some governments and multinational corporations fear industrial secrets will leak to competitors if there is too much disclosure, and there are situations where authorities declare 'strategic' needs and suspend disclosure.

In many countries, court actions, even if they were fought in the public interest, had to be brought by an individual, who, if they lost, paid costs. This acted as a deterrent for anyone to tackle government or large company wrongdoings, because they lacked equivalent resources. It is desirable that NGOs and individuals be allowed to bring legal actions to protect the environment, if need be as group cases (class actions). In the USA the Environmental Defense Fund, the Sierra Club, and environmental lawyers like Joseph Sax managed to achieve the right to bring class actions (or group actions) in the 1970s. Subsequently Canada, the UK and several other countries saw similar legal changes.

The 1969 US National Environmental Policy Act (NEPA) – 'environmental Magna Carta'?

Discussions leading to NEPA began in the early 1960s, when the need was perceived for the USA to have a basic declaration of national environmental policy and an action-forcing provision. The US Government was largely reacting to public opinion that conventional planning did not adequately take account of the environment; it already had responsibility to steward resources and protect the environment under the Public Trust Doctrine. However, before NEPA the USA had little effective federal control over the environment and lacked land use regulations which some other countries had. NEPA was signed into US Law on 1 January 1970, to reform federal policy-making, and influence the private sector to reorientate values (Barrow, 1997: 168). Originally it was intended that NEPA would change the nature of federal decision-making. However, it has become more of a procedural requirement. Caldwell (1989) – one of the architects of NEPA – felt that, had it not happened in the USA, something similar would have appeared elsewhere.

NEPA required environmental impact assessment (EIA) prior to federally funded projects that might 'significantly' affect the environment – a message to officials to 'look before you leap'. NEPA Section 101 set regulations to protect the environment, Section 102 (2) (c) ensured they were pursued, and Section 103 included provision for EIA statements to be challenged in court. That happened a lot at first because NEPA was untested and used expressions like 'significant' and 'human environment' that were poorly defined. There was also some need to clarify which developments required EIA, and how and by whom it was to be conducted.

Virtually the world's first use of the expression 'EIA' occurs in Section 102 (2) c of NEPA, which requires US federal agencies to prepare an environmental impact statement (EIS) (bearing the costs against taxes, and sending copies to federal and state agencies and to the public) using EIA, prior to taking action.

There were three main elements in NEPA:

1   NEPA announced a US national policy for the environment.
2   It outlined procedures for achieving the objectives of that policy.
3   Provision was made for the establishment of a US Council on Environmental Quality (CEQ) which was to advise the US President on the environment,

review the EIA process, review draft EISs, and see NEPA was followed. Also in 1970 the US Government created the US Environmental Protection Agency (EPA), its brief to co-ordinate the attack on environmental pollution and to be responsible for the EIA process (the EPA is in effect 'overseer' of impact assessment in the USA).

NEPA was the first time US Law had really allowed for development to be delayed or abandoned for the long-term good of the environment, and for efforts to be made to co-ordinate public, state, federal and local activities. Effectively, NEPA put environmental quality on a level with economic growth, a revolution in values in a country where state intrusion was anathema – for this reason many see it as a sort of Magna Carta, although it stopped short of making a healthy environment a Constitutional Right. Public participation is written into NEPA to the extent it might be described as a corner-stone.

NEPA is statutory law: it was written after deliberation, and did not evolve from custom, practice or tradition. Consequently, like a charter, it was imperfect; there were problems, especially delay, as litigation took place over various issues. Many felt NEPA had been abducted by lawyers and could become a bureaucratic delaying tactic. These teething problems have largely been resolved, although some feel NEPA should be strengthened, possibly leading to changes in the US Constitution to better manage the environment (Caldwell, 1989). NEPA has been a seminal concept and catalyst for EIA in other countries, although bodies like the Canadian Environmental Assessment Research Council and the International Association for Impact Analysis also deserve credit for spreading and developing mandatory development review processes.

Effective implementation of EIA demands legislation and law enforcement to ensure that:

◆ there are no loopholes, so that no activity likely to cause impacts escapes EIA;
◆ the assessment is adequate;
◆ the assessment is heeded;
◆ the public are kept sufficiently informed or, ideally, involved in assessment.

European law and environmental management

The European Community (EC) grew from the six original states which signed the Treaty of Rome in 1957 to form a closer European Union of 15 nations in 1995 which is set to expand further in the future. EU members like Sweden and The Netherlands have long-established traditions of environmental concern; others have given the environment far less attention. Growing EU integration should prompt and support better policies more widely. It will also ensure common rules and ways of monitoring, setting standards, etc. In 1992 the EU established a European Environmental Agency as a clearing-house for environmental information. Its role is also to evaluate and disseminate information and develop means for applying the precautionary principle, but not enforcement of environmental policy.

The Council of Europe (established 1949) had 35 EU and other member states in 1995 (many former colonies, trading partners, etc.), and is active in advocacy, cultural relations and raising awareness of issues including conservation and environmental protection. A UN agency that acts as a pan-European forum is the UN Commission for Europe (UNECE), which supports sustainable development, environmental research, and has launched or serviced several agreements dealing with issues like pollution (e.g. the 1992 Convention on Transboundary Effects of Industrial Accidents) (Hewett, 1995). Environmental legislation is an important part of the emerging pan-European legal system (with the European Court of Justice as an overall arbitrator). The European Environmental Agency has not got as much enforcement power as the US Environmental Protection Agency, and serves mainly to gather information on the state of the European environment. The EU has also established a European Environmental Information and Observation Network; a European Economic Community (EEC) Directive on Environmental Impact Assessment (Directive 85/337) – which requires environmental assessment to be undertaken by developers; an EEC Directive on Freedom of Access to Information on the Environment (Directive 90/313/EEC) – which requires authorities to ensure public access to relevant environmental information; and an EC Regulation on Eco-Management and Auditing (EMAS) (Regulation 1836/93).

One could make the broad generalization that EU environmental law has focused on co-ordination, codification and integration (Ball and Bell, 1991; Vaughn, 1991; Lister, 1996). Since about 1973 there has been more interest in integrating wider environmental issues into politics alongside concern for achieving economic growth. In 1985 the European Commission decided environmental protection should be an integral part of economic and social policies at macroeconomic level and by sector. This was incorporated into the Treaty of Rome in 1987 (Article 130r) and was strengthened by the Maastrict Treaty (1993), which included a statement of concern for sustainable growth (Winter, 1996: 7, 271). EU legislation seems to be increasingly aligning itself with global conventions such as those relating to global warming or waste management. Since 1993 EU law has been enacted to support more freedom of environmental information, better standard setting, the precautionary principle, and the polluter-pays principle; Winter (1996: 277) has listed the core objectives:

◆ preserve, protect and improve the quality of the environment.
◆ protect human health.
◆ prudent and rational use of natural resources.
◆ promote measures at international level to deal with regional or world-wide environmental problems.

Hughes (1992: 86) has noted that environmental management law should be 'vertically integrated' between regional, national and international systems. The EEC system allows this to some extent. Efforts to develop an overall EEC environmental policy resulted in the publication in 1973 of the First Programme of Action on the Environment; the Second, Third, Fourth and Fifth Action Programmes appeared in 1977, 1983, 1987, 1992 (reviewed in 1995), and lay down principles that EEC environmental legislation should adhere to (Hughes, 1992: 89). The Fifth Programme of Action on the European Environment seeks to incorporate good environmental policy into all Community policies (CEC, 1992). In the UK the 1995 Environment Act created a powerful, wide-ranging Environmental Agency for England and Wales (also a Scottish Environmental Protection Agency), which brought together the functions previously spread among many agencies (pollution control, fisheries management, flood defence, etc.) (Lane and Peto, 1995).

International law and environmental management

International law governs relations between states, and has no direct effect on domestic law or individuals. It is often difficult to force a sovereign state to sign, and then honour, a treaty or similar agreement. International law must thus depend a great deal on voluntary agreements by governments and international bodies (the Brussels and Lugano Conventions on Environmental Law cover this issue of ensuring compliance) (Székely, 1990a; 1990b). When negotiation fails a possibility is to refer the case to the International Court of Justice (The Hague) (not a very friendly process), or set up an International Joint Commission. International law has tended to be *laissez-faire* and *ad hoc* (Birnie and Boyle, 1992).

From the mid-nineteenth century until the 1950s co-operation, exchange of information, agreement and international guidelines or rules were often initiated by international public unions, e.g. the International Postal Union, or the International Telegraphic Union. Nowadays, the UN and its 15 specialist agencies (the FAO, WHO, UNESCO, UNEP, etc.) often initiate the development of international environmental law. For example, the UNEP has published guidelines on principles of conduct over shared natural resources (1978) and, more recently, on exchange of information on chemicals in international trade. NGOs like Greenpeace, Friends of the Earth and the World-Wide Fund for Nature also lobby for environmental legislation.

Various observers note the UN-supported system of environmental treaty making is valuable, although it needs strengthening – e.g. the UN General Assembly can only recommend, not insist that law be made. Developing countries have complained that international law is too US- or Eurocentric and there is a wish in some countries to see more application of Islamic Law. Since the 1972 UN Conference on the Human Environment (Stockholm), most of the UN-prompted multilateral treaties have been developed by a two-step process: a relatively vague framework convention which acknowledges a problem is presented (most countries are happy to sign such a non-binding agreement); that step prompts action, especially data collection, discussion and propaganda, which reduces opposition and raises interest so that a protocol can be introduced and agreed to (Susskind, 1992: 67).

International law faces a number of challenges. One of the greatest is the management of 'global commons': oceans and their resources; world weather and climate; atmosphere; stratospheric ozone; space; etc. (Cleveland, 1990). Many resources, and also pests, migrate or move, so that effective management of ocean fisheries, migratory fish in rivers, whaling, disease or locust control, etc., needs to be through multilateral agreement.

In the late 1970s a class action by an NGO forced the US Agency for International Development (USAID) to insist on pre-development environmental assessments before granting funds. In effect the precautionary principle embodied in NEPA was extended to the Third World with respect to aid. Within a few years most aid agencies had adopted environmental guidelines and rules (Wirth, 1986). The end of the Cold War may mean more opportunities and resources for international environmental law to develop (Walker, 1989).

Indigenous peoples and environmental law

IUCN (1997: 27) estimates suggest there are over 250 million indigenous peoples who interact with environmental law with respect to:

1   protection of natural environment together with indigenous people;
2   rights of indigenous people over natural resources;
3   rights over traditional knowledge – e.g. to prevent ethnobotany becoming 'bio-piracy' (gathering indigenous knowledge which is patented and sold);
4   damages to indigenous people for past environmental wrongs by 'outsiders';
5   views of indigenous people which could be fed into environmental law making.

Indigenous people often retain knowledge, skills and beliefs that relate closely to the natural environment. The protection of the environment is often vital to their physical and cultural survival, and they have insight which may aid environmental management and law making.

The rights of indigenous peoples are recognized by the UN Commission on Economic Development (UNCED) 1992 Convention on Biological Diversity and by the 1994 Draft UN Declaration of the Rights of Indigenous Peoples. Nevertheless, indigenous people often still have no written land tenure, making them vulnerable to abuse or resettlement if there are natural resources to be exploited.

In recent decades several countries have made changes to improve indigenous peoples' control of their environment and natural resources (see chapter 8). Whether this will lead to better environmental management is debated. In Australia, New Zealand, the USA, Canada and Amazonian Brazil aboriginal people have fought for their sovereign rights to control and manage, or at least share in, resources (Dale, 1992; Shutkin, 1991). In Australia debate about aboriginal territorial rights has become heated recently. The Australian High Court has ruled that Australia's indigenous people enjoy native title and access rights to land leased by Euro-Australian farmers, which means two land-users should legally coexist. An Aboriginal claim to coastal waters and the Great Barrier Reef, if awarded, would have considerable impact on fishing and coastal resorts (*The Times* (UK), 30 December 1997: 11).

A question increasingly asked is: who should bear the cost of rehabilitation after resources exploitation? For example, the Pacific island of Nauru, now independent, provided phosphates for some 90 years. Does it have any claim on past colonial powers to remedy damage? Nauru claimed through the International Court of Justice for damage done before its independence in 1967 (Anderson, 1992). Similar retrospective actions have arisen in Australia and in other Pacific islands, over nuclear weapons test sites, and in Papua New Guinea concerning mining.

The 1992 UN Conference on Environment and Development

Sometimes referred to as the 'Earth Summit' or abbreviated to UNCED, held in 1992 the Rio Conference was a test of the ability of the international political and legal order to reach a consensus for the good of the whole world (Tromans, 1992; Grubb *et al.*, 1993). Originally there were hopes that UNCED would agree an Earth Charter, but this was not achieved, although several new declarations were made and conventions were established (see Box 3.3) (Freestone, 1994; Johnson, 1993). Freestone (1994) reviewed the implications of UNCED, stressing that it did crystallize principles which contribute to the development of international environmental law. However, some feel the Earth Summit tended to weaken international environmental law by focusing on development issues (see Sands, 1993). A follow-up meeting to UNCED, the Rio II Conference was held in New York in 1997 (see chapter 14).

BOX 3.3 Agreements made at the Earth Summit, 1992

◆ *Rio Declaration on Environment and Development* updated version of the Stockholm Declaration (of 1972); published general principles for future international action on environment and development.
◆ *Framework Convention on Climate Change* framework for negotiation of detailed protocols to deal with control of greenhouse gas emissions, deforestation, sea-level change, etc.
◆ *Convention on Biological Diversity* intended to arrest alarming rate of species loss (criticized for having been poorly and hurriedly drafted).
◆ *Declaration on Forests* a principle, not legally binding, this was substituted for original idea of a Forest Convention.
◆ *Agenda 21* an action plan for the rest of the century and framework for dealing with environment and development issues. Consists of 40 chapters (not a legally binding instrument).
◆ *Global Environmental Facility* a fund established for global problem-solving. Under the auspices of the World Bank, UNEP and UNDP. Designed to be 'democratic and transparent' and helpful to poor nations. Amongst other things, intended to support Biodiversity and Climate Change Conventions.

International law and sovereignty issues

Sovereignty affects access to data and monitoring, and can be a major constraint on environmental management. Countries are usually reluctant to sign any agreement which affects their sovereign powers. Yet growing transboundary and global environmental problems make it important to get co-operation. There are transnational and multinational corporations sufficiently powerful to threaten and bribe their way around sovereignty and other controls. Terrorism can have transnational or global impact, so there should be better international controls and co-operation to counter it. Unfortunately for many environmental management issues, getting multi-state agreements is a slow process.

In 1977 the Stockholm Declaration on the Human Environment affirmed the sovereign right of states to exploit their own resources and their responsibility to ensure that activities within their jurisdiction or control do not cause damage to the environment beyond the limits of their national jurisdiction (Stockholm Principle 21). This affirmation has had considerable influence on subsequent international environmental law making (Birnie and Boyle, 1992: 90).

International trade agreements, notably the GATT/WTO provisions (see chapter 5), mean that if a country has environmental protection laws, say controlling the import of pesticide-contaminated produce, timber cut in an environmentally unsound fashion, or fish caught using nets that kill dolphins, these measures may be unenforceable because they impair 'free trade' (Sinner, 1994). The level playing field demanded by trade agreements may make it difficult to control importation of food and commodities produced by means of genetic engineering and growth- or lactation-enhancing hormones. Conversely, there may be situations where globalization helps countries adopt and enforce better standards (care must be taken to ensure that the motive is to improve environmental quality and not an attempt to make production costs uniform or create a global market for standardized products that enjoy economies of scale). Globalization of patent rights has generated concern; MNCs and TNCs seek to recoup research costs and control markets; poor countries fear bio-piracy with corporations patenting and claiming intellectual rights on genetic resources and ideas derived from such resources. The patenting and control of sales of crop seeds (modern varieties) and pharmaceutical products has also caused much friction.

Protection and extension of sovereignty can lead to wars; testing and storage of weapons; and territorial claims. These affect the environment and need to be more firmly addressed by international agreements and law (Shaw, 1993). The pollution associated with the Gulf War underlines the importance of negotiation. Hostile environmental modification is covered by the 1977 Environmental Modification Convention (invoked to hold Iran to reparations for damage to Kuwait), and there are controls on nuclear, chemical and biological weapons.

Box 3.4 presents some of the treaties and agreements relevant to environmental management (it is *not* complete but a selection). A number of trends are apparent here. There has been a move towards the precautionary principle – since about 1972 countries have been guided to try to prevent pollution accidents and misdemeanours. Obtaining damages for, or penalizing, transnational pollution has been patchy, e.g. there were no adjudications over Chernobyl, *Amoco Cadiz* and many similar disasters. There has been little progress in establishing 'environmental rights' (i.e. rights of natural objects or organisms), although in some western countries there is a vociferous animal rights lobby. Various agreements and conventions have reaffirmed and

BOX 3.4 A selection of treaties, agreements, etc., relating to environmental management

Internationally shared resources
In 1972 the USA and Canada signed the Great Lakes Transboundary Agreement for the comprehensive management of the water quality of the Great Lakes.

Protection of endangered species
1946 International Convention for the Regulation of Whaling. 1973 Convention on International Trade in Endangered Species (CITES). 1979 Bern Convention on the Conservation of European Wildlife.

Protection of environmentally important areas
There are many areas agreed by scientists, social scientists and other specialists to be in need of formal protection. Protection may be supported by a state; privately funded by a group or individual; or by an international body or bodies. For example, there is a worldwide scatter of Biosphere Reserves; the UK has state-protected Sites of Special Scientific Interest (SSSIs); many countries have reserves and national parks. Some conservation areas are established and watched over by international treaty – the 1971 Ramsar Convention (Convention on Wetlands of International Importance) provides a framework for protection of wetland habitats, especially those used by migrating birds. The UN Educational, Scientific and Cultural Organization (UNESCO) supports and oversees many sites of special cultural value.

The Antarctic
In Antarctica territorial claims have been put aside (but not eliminated) under the Antarctic Treaty which came into force in 1960 (signed 1959) (Theutenberg, 1984) (see Figure 3.3). Basically this is an international treaty by which signatories have agreed to keep Antarctica and its surrounding seas open for scientific research by all nations deemed to be pursuing scientific exploration south of 60°S. The treaty requires demilitarization, no nuclear weapons and a commitment to conservation (Triggs, 1988; Holdgate, 1990). (For a review of Antarctic law see Auburn, 1982; Beck, 1986.)

While it has been quite a flexible treaty, modified as need arose, it has been put under some pressure as interest in resource development (notably oil, minerals, krill, squid and fish) comes into conflict with its conservation requirements. There are also demands from non-treaty nations (basically those which have not maintained a significant research presence there) and some NGOs for there to be changes to give the whole world (probably through the UN), not just signatory nations, control of Antarctica (a coalition of over 200 NGOs and non-treaty nations – the Atlantic and Southern Ocean Coalition – has been seeking such a goal). There have been some moves which in theory could

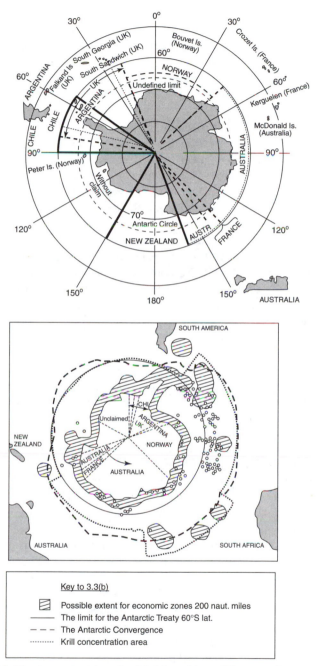

FIGURE 3.3 The Antarctic: (a) territorial claims; (b) possible economic zones to 200 nautical miles, and limit of Antarctic Treaty (60°S lat)

continued . . .

allow mineral resources to be used – the 1988 Convention on the Regulation of Antarctic Mineral Resource Activities allows exploitation only if very stringent environmental assessments are made and accepted by treaty nations. The Falklands conflict is a warning that if potentially attractive mineral resources are identified territorial claims may reappear in Antarctica.

Transboundary pollution
In 1965 Canada and the USA became involved in the Trail Smelter pollution case. The outcome was acceptance that no state has the right to permit use of its territory in such a way as to injure another territory. The 1972 UN Conference on the Human Environment in Stockholm was in part called for by Sweden, because of concern about acid deposition generated by other countries. In 1979 the Geneva Convention on Long-Range Transboundary Air Pollution addressed the problem of transboundary sulphur dioxide atmospheric emissions, but did not lay down firm rules. By the late 1980s the resolution of transboundary impacts had become an increasingly active field of diplomacy (Carroll, 1988). The 1991 UN Economic Commission for Europe Convention on Environmental Impact Assessment in a Transboundary Context obliged signatory states to act to control transboundary environmental impacts from proposed activities.

Controls on global warming
The UN Framework Convention on Climate Change (signed at UNCED 1992) obliged signatories to stabilize CO_2 emissions at 1990 levels by AD 2000. The 1997 Kyoto Conference was intended to settle details of CO_2 reduction and to see that targets were enforced by international law. However, a coalition of USA industries was opposed to any limit on greenhouse gas emissions, and lobbied to hinder agreements. Finally agreements were made by the EU to make an 8 per cent cut in emissions by AD 2010 and arrangements for Tradeable Emissions Quotas (TEQs) were approved (with Russia able to sell its unused quotas to the USA)(see chapter 12 for discussion of TEQs).

Ozone damage controls
Efforts to phase out and if possible ban the use of CFCs were made at the 1985 Vienna Convention for the Protection of the Ozone Layer. The 1987 Montreal Protocol on Substances that Deplete the Ozone Layer – revised 1990 – derives from the Vienna Convention. The protocol aimed for a 50 per cent cut in CFCs over a short period (24, mainly developed nations signed – by 1994 this had increased to 74, including some developing countries) and was signed in the face of considerable uncertainty about ozone damage. The protocol is a landmark, in that *for the first time nations agreed to impose significant costs on their economies in order to protect the global environment*. India and China held out, seeking agreement for funding to assist with ozone controls.

The Law of the Sea

In 1954 the International Convention for the Prevention of Pollution from Ships was undertaken to try to reduce the discharge of waste oil from oil-tankers and other ship-related discharges (with limited success). For ocean pollution control to be effective, agreements that cover rivers, effluent outfalls, air pollution, etc. are required, because pollutants arrive in the sea from such sources (Boyle, 1992). In 1958 the First Conference on Law of the Sea took place (the second was in 1960), and in 1959 the UN established the International Maritime Organization to deal with marine safety, law, pollution control, etc.

From the early 1970s some of the nations with coastlines began to declare extensions of their territorial waters from the accepted 3 to 12, or even 200 nautical miles. The 1950 Continental Shelf Convention was largely behind this trend towards extension of exclusive sovereign rights to continental shelf or seabed resources. To try to formalize these trends the Third Conference on Law of the Sea was held in 1974.

The UNEP's Regional Seas Programme has brought together coastal states of a number of marine regions, resulting in several Regional Seas Treaties, covering: the Mediterranean; the Gulf; West Africa; Southeast Pacific; Red Sea; Caribbean; East Africa; and the South Pacific. These treaties led to the development of Environmental Action Plans and then co-ordination to fight pollution, etc. In 1977 the North Sea ceased to be 'high seas' as far as fish and mineral exploitation were concerned, when the EC established zones laying claim to the continental shelf. A number of the regional seas, e.g. the North Sea, Japan's Inland Sea, the Baltic and the Mediterranean have been the subject of convention or treaty agreements in addition to the efforts of the UNEP to try to control pollution more effectively.

Meeting in Jamaica in 1982, the UN launched the Convention on the Law of the Sea (with agreements effective to 2500 m depth from the shore). Some developing countries are keen to see the oceans, like Antarctica, declared common heritage, rather than becoming *de facto* possessions of those countries with the wealth and technology to exploit the resources.

extended state sovereignty over natural resources (especially apparent in respect to ocean territorial limits). There has been some progress, e.g.: the EU is developing a form of supranational legislation, and the UNEP argues that international law should deal with protecting the world's life support systems.

Alternative dispute resolution

Disputes about resource exploitation and environmental management can be addressed in a number of ways (see Mitchell, 1997: 218–239 for an overview; Napier, 1998 for more detailed coverage of environmental conflict resolution):

1   through legal measures (judicial);
2   through political measures;
3   through administrative measures;
4   through alternative dispute resolution measures (which may not use law).

Legal measures rely upon courts, litigation, protocols and procedures, etc. Political measures rely upon elected or established representatives to decide. Administrative measures can be used to improve resources and environmental management. Alternative dispute resolution can be through a range of measures, including:

◆   negotiation;
◆   mediation;
◆   arbitration;
◆   public consultation.

Environmental management legislation may specify the use of some of these measures, or they may be adopted voluntarily. Negotiation is a process whereby two or more groups agree to meet to explore solutions, in the hope of reaching consensus. Mediation is similar to negotiation, but involves a mutually accepted neutral third party who finds facts and tries to facilitate discussion. The mediator may act with groups that are unwilling to meet face to face, if need be 'filtering' the exchanges to help reach agreement. Arbitration involves a third party like mediation, but at the outset the parties involved agree to give the arbitrator power to make decisions (which may or may not be binding).

Recommended reading and resources

Journals which publish articles on business and environmental management

Business and Environment Abstracts
Business Ethics
Business Strategy and the Environment
Corporate Environmental Policy
Eco-Management and Auditing
Greener Management International
Industry and the Environment
Journal of Environmental Economics and Management
Journal of Industrial Ecology
Management Science
Total Quality Environmental Management

Some organizations and bodies concerned with business and environmental management

- Business for Social Responsibility
- Coalition for Environmentally Responsible Economics (USA)
- Green Ethics Investors, e.g.:
  Commercial Union Environmental Exempt Pension Fund
  Eagle Star Environmental Opportunities Trust
  Merlin International Green Investment Trust
  Social Investment Forum (USA)
  TSB Environmental Investor Fund (UK)
- Institute of Business Ethics
- International Network for Environmental Management (seeks to develop and apply principles of environmental management – over 500 member companies in 1994; non-profit organization established in 1991 by Austrian, Swedish and German businesses)

Journals which publish articles on law and environmental management

Ecology Law Quarterly
Environmental Policy and Law
Journal of Environmental Law
Journal of Planning and Environment Law
Land Management and Environmental Law Report
Ocean & Coastal Management

Chapter 4

Standards, monitoring, modelling, eco-auditing and environmental management systems

In chapter 1 two principles of environmental management were noted: prudence and stewardship. Standards, monitoring, and the other approaches covered in this chapter are crucial for pursuing those principles. They are vital for meaningful evaluation on which to base forward planning and policy decisions, for law making and enforcement, for effective implementation, co-ordination, and for avoiding unwanted impacts. The establishment of widely applicable scientific standards has been one of the most important achievements of western civilization ('standards of behaviour' – ethics – have been discussed earlier, pp. 22–24). Monitoring, modelling, auditing and environmental management systems help ensure ongoing objectives are set and met, check progress and warn of problems and opportunities. Put crudely, standards are benchmarks and the other things discussed in this chapter are concerned with understanding what is happening, checking and stock-taking, using those benchmarks.

Standards

A *standard* may be defined as a widely accepted or approved example of something against which others may be measured. They allow meaningful evaluation, exchange and comparison of data, improve objectivity of judgement (so are important to science), aid recognition of crucial thresholds and limits, support negotiation, law making and comparison (between sites, between countries and between years). Standards have existed from ancient times: the Egyptians, Greeks and Romans had units of measurement and coinage, medieval European craft guilds set standards for the quality of goods, and by the nineteenth century Britain, France and some other countries had institutes and observatories which developed, managed and regulated the standard units used to record data.

Unfortunately, national standards often ran in parallel, so that data collected in, say, a French colony would have to be converted to units used in Britain. Conversion may sometimes be easy, but if the indicators used or the means of gathering data differ, even rough comparison may be difficult. A useful standard in a temperate country may be meaningless in the humid tropics (there are still tropical countries which have building standards inherited from temperate colonial powers which specify roofs to cope with snowfall). Without world-wide standards it is difficult to research the structure and function of the environment and to monitor global conditions. Before the late 1950s various international unions had agreed standards for some fields, such as telegraphy and radio, but not so much for the environmental sciences. One achievement of the International Geophysical Year (1957–58) and subsequent global exchanges of hydrological, meteorological, geophysical and biological data was the development of better international environmental standards.

As research into environmental issues progresses, new standards are needed, for example to assess 'safe' levels of chemical pollution or radioactivity. The process is ongoing, involving various national and international institutes and standards organizations (e.g. the British Standards Institution or the International Standards Organization). Advances in medical knowledge, toxicology, ecology, etc., force the revision of some established standards. Ozone-damaging CFCs were considered inert and safe in the late 1930s, and environmental levels of DDT caused little concern before the 1960s. New standards are being developed which take into account factors like the greater vulnerability of children to some pollutants.

There are a number of ways of developing a standard, each with advantages and disadvantages, e.g. a standard for checking that fruit does not exceed 'safe' levels of a pesticide might be based on a simple maximum residue level (MRL), or a sort of lump sum, or an acceptable daily intake (ADI) – which assumes consumers all eat a given amount per day. It is consequently important that an environmental manager knows the characteristics of a standard as well as the levels measured by it (and the reliability of the measurements). The methods of data collection as well as the agreed units must be standardized. Taking the same meteorological measurements in the lee of a house and in open countryside or at various times of day gives quite different results, making comparison difficult. Collecting data is often expensive; it is therefore important to avoid poorly focused, encyclopaedic data collection, and it is a good idea to 'scope' first (assess what should be measured and how).

Standards often rely upon indicators, things that can be relatively easily measured, and which have specific meaning. Some indicators are precise and reliable, others less so. Sometimes when a broader focus is needed, or the process to be monitored is complex, a composite index may be devised which is the sum of a number of different measurements, e.g. the Human Development Index (OECD, 1991; UNDP, 1991). Environmental standards may be divided into broad groups: those concerned with ensuring human health and safety; those concerned with maintaining environmental quality; those concerned with the quality of consumer items.

Standards play a crucial part in:

◆ monitoring;
◆ modelling to understand the environment and establish trends;
◆ negotiation;
◆ enforcement of rules;
◆ environmental auditing;
◆ maintaining environmental quality.

The fields of activity which make use of standards include:

◆ pollution control;
◆ health and safety;
◆ public hygiene and health (especially domestic water supplies, sewage and waste disposal);
◆ consumer goods (food standards; electrical safety; electromagnetic radiation safety);

- pharmaceutical products;
- transport safety and quality;
- disclosure of information to the public.

Standards are of little use if they are not effectively enforced. Another difficulty is that standards may sometimes be relaxed, usually for profit or strategic reasons. The expression REGNEG (renegotiation of regulations) has been applied to the situation where a developer succeeds in persuading the authorities to relax or modify regulations in its favour, making it easier to meet standards or avoid assessments.

Monitoring

Monitoring aims to establish a system of continued observation, measurement and evaluation for defined purposes. It may provide information at the start of a development, during implementation or after completion. Without monitoring, it can be difficult or impossible to establish how things are performing. Monitoring is the process of keeping the health of the environment (and with social monitoring, of society) in view (Spellerberg, 1991: xi). If sustainable development is a goal, monitoring is vital.

Monitoring should be operated to agreed schedules with comparable methods. The focus may be on biology, chemical pollution, air pollution, or any other aspect of the environment. It is seldom possible to obtain a precise, detailed picture of all environmental parameters (let alone social, economic ones, etc.). Monitoring is therefore often undertaken for a specific reason (or reasons), for the systematic measurement of selected variables (Mitchell, 1997: 261), to:

- improve understanding of environmental, social or economic processes;
- provide early warning;
- help optimize use of the environment and resources;
- assist in regulating environmental and resources usage (e.g. it may provide information for law courts);
- assess conditions;
- establish baseline data, trends, cumulative effects, etc;
- check that required standards are being met, or see whether something of interest has changed;
- document sinks, sources, etc;
- test models, verify hypotheses or research;
- determine the effectiveness of measures or regulations;
- provide information for decision-making;
- advise the public.

The UNEP promoted global environmental monitoring at the 1972 UN Conference on the Human Environment. There has been increasing interest, spurred by transboundary problems, in developing international monitoring systems. These seek to monitor at the global level and ideally offer wide access to their information (those bodies involved include the UNEP, OECD, EEC; and the International Atomic Energy Commission). The UNEP has established the Global Environmental Monitoring System (GEMS), which is a co-ordinated programme for gathering data for use in environmental management and for early warning of disasters. An independent international research unit was founded in 1975 to assist international organizations with monitoring – the Monitoring and Assessment Research Centre (MARC). This concentrates on biological and ecological monitoring, particularly pollution. The World Conservation Monitoring Centre was established in 1980 by upgrading an IUCN-run body, to monitor endangered plant and animal species. The US Food and Drugs Administration monitors pharmaceutics and foods. The spread and use of weapons (especially nuclear, chemical and biological) are increasingly monitored by international bodies. In most countries, doctors, vets and other professionals report observed effects to central monitoring bodies.

Monitoring may show how the environment, a society, or economy changes, aiding understanding of structure and function. Monitoring, surveillance and screening (the checking of a specific thing, e.g. a particular disease in a population – not to be confused with impact assessment screening) are valuable development aids but they can generate problems over who should administer, enforce and pay for them.

Surveillance

Surveillance is repetitive measurement of selected variables over a period of time, but with a less clearly defined purpose than monitoring. It is more exploratory and can be undertaken to determine trends, calibrate or validate models, make short-term forecasts, ensure optimal development, warn of the unexpected, etc. Surveillance, like monitoring, can focus on the environment, people or an economy, and may:

- check whether statutory regulations are complied with (without monitoring and surveillance the setting of standards and rules is of little value);
- provide information for systems control or management;
- assess environmental quality to see whether it remains satisfactory;
- detect unexpected changes.

Where monitoring seeks to establish the ongoing picture, it may be important to examine past conditions and establish trends to understand the present and permit extrapolation of possible future scenarios. For example, studies of climate changes and ecological responses give clues to possible future conditions.

Environmental, social and economic monitoring have each generated their own practitioners and literature, which may focus at local, regional, national or global level or study 'pathways' (e.g. for pollution). Surveillance and monitoring can be done at source (where something is being generated), at selected sample points, at random, along transects, or by sampling some suitable material or organism. For example, pollution might be monitored by checking a smokestack, by a network of instruments, or by surveying lichen species diversity and growth. Regulatory monitoring checks its findings against set, in-house, national or international standards or stated objectives.

For the last few decades, and at a gathering pace, remote monitoring and surveillance have been possible: at its most extreme, data gathering by unmanned space vehicles; also by orbiting or geo-stationary satellites, reconnaissance aircraft and automatic weather or oceanographic data-gathering stations. The best data are of little use if poorly co-ordinated, so bodies have evolved to support surveillance and monitoring on an international scale and disseminate results to where they are useful.

Modelling

A model is a caricature or simplification of reality: often a set of equations, used to predict the behaviour of a variable or variables. The predictions can be imperfect, but good modelling should cope with change and inadequate data. There are many types of model, developed by various disciplines: computer models, analogue models, conceptual models, role-play exercises, etc. Conceptual models are used to see what needs study and to help formulate and check hypotheses and to organize ideas. Simulation or predictive models can provide EIA with an indication of what may happen in the future, and can help environmental managers see how something is proceeding. Hydrologists may set up a scale model of a river estuary and release flows of water to study tides, currents, flooding, scour and deposition. Climatologists are developing general circulation models, using powerful computers to try to establish likely future climate change. Input–output models have been used by regional planners and environmental managers for integrated environmental management and strategic environmental management. Futures models or world models were used to produce *The Limits to Growth* and other futures predictions. Ecosystem simulation modelling is applied to specific ecosystems; social scientists use social modelling to predict socioeconomic impact, and economists use economic models to try to establish micro- or macro-economic trends and to test ideas for manipulating an economy.

Environmental auditing, environmental accounting, eco-audit, assessment, and evaluation

The environmental manager needs to have an idea of the state of the environment, and of any threats, future problems or opportunities. There has been some confusion over the use of the terms 'environmental auditing' and 'assessment'. Environmental auditing has been applied to stock-taking, eco-review, eco-survey, eco-audit, eco-evaluation, environmental assessment (another vague expression), state-of-the-environment assessment, the production of 'green charters' and the checking of impact assessments to determine their effectiveness (Cahill, 1989; Edwards, 1992; Grayson, 1992; Thomson, 1993; Buckley, 1995).

Environmental accounting is reasonably distinct from auditing; state-of-the-environment accounts (see chapter 5) and environmental quality evaluation use knowledge of how the ecosystem is structured and functions to collect data showing the state of an area (not only terrestrial; seas like the Baltic have been assessed). These approaches seek to establish the *current* status of an ecosystem; EIA (see later) focuses on the *future* effects of development. Ecological evaluation seeks to establish what is of value.

At first glance environmental auditing would seem to mean establishing the latest picture provided by monitoring; however, it is more complex. Environmental audit can be conducted at company, institution, state, national or global levels, and may mean: (1) an auditing (i.e. stock-taking or inventory-focus) approach to the environment which seeks to review conditions and evaluate impacts of development (e.g. new systems of national accounts); (2) studies aimed at avoiding or reducing environmental damage; or (3) a means by which a body systematically and holistically monitors the quality of the environment it interacts with or is responsible for (vital in any quest for sustainable development). The latter activity is now usually termed 'eco-audit', an internal review of the activities and plans of a company or other body.

State-of-the-environment accounts set out a region's or nation's environmental, social and economic assets. Norway, France, The Netherlands, Canada and the World Bank have developed national state-of-the-environmental accounts systems – for example, France's Comptes du Patrimoine Naturel ('national heritage accounts'), developed since 1978. National state-of-the-environment accounts make use of environmental assessment and have been promoted as improvements on indicators like gross domestic product to document development status. They may prove important in future trade agreements to ensure that environmental effects are counted, and in the quest for sustainable development (Ahmad *et al.*, 1989). However, there has been criticism of environmental accounting, mainly that it is just stock-taking and stops short of encouraging a change of attitude towards the environment and a precautionary approach.

In the UK environmental assessment has been used by government bodies to mean EIA; elsewhere the term is applied to pre-development stock-taking, for example site-selection for a nuclear waste repository. In the USA an environmental assessment means a concise public document which should provide enough evidence for a decision to be made on whether or not to proceed to a full EIA. Environmental assessment has also been applied to surveillance or screening – like checking drugs or industrial activities, and it is used for study which seeks to establish the state of an environment with less focus on impacts than EIA.

Environmental appraisal is a generic term used in the UK for the evaluation of the environmental implications of proposals. Environmental appraisal is sometimes used as an equivalent of environmental assessment or environmental evaluation. A number of agencies have published environmental appraisal guidelines (see Barrow 1997: 23).

Eco-auditing

Eco-auditing (corporate environmental auditing or environmental management systems auditing) may be defined as a systematic multidisciplinary methodology used periodically and objectively to assess the environmental performance of a company, public authority or, in some instances, a region. Eco-audits can be done in-house, by a government team, or by an independent, accredited specialist or team. So far, it has been mainly a *voluntary* process (in relation to finance and company matters, 'auditing' implies involuntary) that seeks to increase public awareness and aid the quest for sustainable development. Sometimes eco-audits are not voluntary: there have been cases where shareholders have demanded eco-audits at public meetings (*The Times*, 11 April 1997: 25), and aid agencies increasingly demand them before granting funding.

Impact assessment deals with *potential* effects of proposed developments; eco-auditing focuses on *actual* effects of established activities. Both impact assessment and eco-audit can be valuable tools for environmental management provided that management is committed to adequate action on the findings.

Eco-audit evolved as a management tool in the USA in the 1980s as companies were held more responsible for the damage they caused and realized the need for a green image (EPA, 1988; Shillito, 1994; Buckley, 1995; Gilpin, 1995). It has been promoted in Europe by the International Chamber of Commerce and by some multinational corporations as a means of getting effective environmental management (International Chamber of Commerce, 1989; 1991). A significant step forward has been the development of eco-audit standards/environmental management and audit systems, the world's first being offered by the British Standards Institution (BS 7750) in 1992. This moved beyond assessment of environmental effects to ensure that bodies made commitments to continual environmental improvement.

Eco-audit handbooks and guidebooks began to appear in the mid-1980s (Harrison, 1984; Blakeslee and Grabowski, 1985; Grayson, 1992; Local Government Management Board, 1991; 1992; Thompson and Therivel, 1991; Spedding *et al.*, 1993; McKenna & Co., 1993; Richards and Biddick, 1994). In 1986 the US Environmental Protection Agency issued an Environmental Auditing Policy Statement, designed to encourage the use of eco-audits by US companies, and laid down guidelines.

Eco-audit is increasingly practised in the USA, Europe, Australia and other developed countries, further impetus being given by the publication of *Agenda 21*, and by the European Commission's Fifth Environmental Action Programme (1992). The latter seeks to promote 'shared responsibility' (by people, commerce and government) for the environment, popular green awareness, and a move towards sustainable development, and it supports eco-audit (see Figure 4.1). In 1992 18 of the UK's top companies undertook eco-audits; by 1996 roughly half the country's firms had eco-audited – a rapid, voluntary spread. Eco-auditing is part of a growing shift from mere compliance with regulations to developing forward-looking environmental management strategies (Willig, 1994; Sunderland, 1996), so it supports the principle of prudence. There has been less progress in developing countries, although India has

FIGURE 4.1 European Union Eco-Management and Audit Scheme (EMAS) eco-audit award logo
Note: This can be used on a company's brochures, letterhead, reports and advertisements, but must make no reference to specific products or services, and may not be used on product pacakages.

modified its Companies Act to include a requirement for eco-audits, and Indonesia has required companies to conduct eco-audits since 1995.

Eco-audits offer some or all of the following benefits:

- they generate valuable data for regional or national state-of-the-environment reports;
- they are a means for ensuring the continual improvement of environmental management;
- they may be a valuable way of monitoring;
- they can help establish an effective environmental protection scheme, which may reduce insurance premiums (Finsinger and Marx, 1996);
- they can assist efforts for sustainable development;
- they can inform the public about the body's environmental performance, which is good PR;
- they can help involve the public in environmental management;
- they help identify cost recovery through recycling, opportunities for sale of by-products, etc;
- they reduce risks of being accused of negligence and losing court cases;
- they may reduce the need for government inspections;
- they can ensure that often complex regulations are known about and followed and licences are obtained;
- they offer management more peace of mind.

There may also be risks associated with eco-audits:

- they may spot a problem that is costly to cure, which might otherwise have been overlooked without too much harm;

- they can be expensive;
- a body may fear trade secrets will be exposed to competitors;
- smaller companies cannot do eco-auditing in-house and must use specialists from outside (costly, with a risk of loss of trade secrets).

There are two broad categories of eco-audit: (a) industrial – private sector corporate eco-audits, (b) local authority or higher-level government eco-audits (sometimes called 'green charters') – these are more standardized than industrial (private sector) corporate eco-audits, and are commissioned by local authorities to show local environmental quality (Levett, 1993; Barrett, 1995; Leu *et al.*, 1995) (Box 4.1). Some local authorities produce state-of-the-environment reports which are not the same as audits carried out as part of an environmental management system approach (see later in this chapter).

BOX 4.1 Types of eco-audit

- *Site* or *facility audit* a company or body audits to see how it conforms to safety and other regulations and care for the environment.
- *Compliance audit* to assess whether regulations are being heeded and/or policy is being followed.
- *Issues audit* assessment of the impact of a company's or other body's activities on a specific environmental or social issue, e.g. rainforest loss (Grayson, 1992: 40).
- *Minimization audit* to see if it is possible to reduce: waste; inputs; emission of pollutants (including noise); energy consumption, etc.
- *Property transfer audits* (pre-acquisition audit, merger audit, disvestiture audit, transactional audit, liability audit) – a company or body audits prior to disvestiture, takeover, joint venture, alliance, altering a lease, sale of assets, etc., to show if there are any problems such as contaminated land.
- *Waste audits* to see if regulations are met, whether costs can be reduced by sale of by-products, etc. (Ledgerwood *et al.*, 1992; Thompson and Wilson, 1994). The motivation to audit may be to comply with legislation or come from a desire to prevent problems.
- *Life-cycle assessment/analysis* evaluation that can extend beyond the time horizon of a single owner, company or government (it is cradle-to-grave), e.g. impacts of something from manufacture, through use to disposal (Fava, 1994; British Standards Institution, 1994c).

Note: Even within a single company eco-audit must check for variation from unit to unit and allow for change that takes place as plant ages. Eco-audit may extend to checking environmental impacts of suppliers, subsidiaries, use and disposal of products and packaging.

In the UK the first eco-audit by a local authority took place in 1989 (Kirklees District Council, assisted by Friends of the Earth). Roughly 87 per cent of UK local government authorities had used eco-audit or planned to by 1991, encouraged by the UK 1990 Environmental Protection Act (Grayson, 1992: 50). Unfortunately, some of the eco-audits produced little more than publicity documents.

There is considerable overlap between eco-audit and health and safety management – some countries now test the environmental quality of new buildings to ensure that they do not harm employees, that they use eco-friendly construction materials and do not waste energy. Energy efficiency and better employment conditions mean savings on power bills and less absenteeism.

Barton and Bruder (1995: xv) see local eco-audit as a key measure in the delivery of sustainable development as 'a process for establishing what sustainable development means in practice – how to interpret it locally, how to test whether you are achieving it'. They recognized two components in eco-audit: (1) external – collation of available data to produce a state-of-the-environment report, and (2) internal – the state-of-the-environment report as a foundation for efforts to assess policies and practices (Barton and Bruder, 1995: 12). First-time audits are usually more complex than follow-up audits.

Various bodies and companies publish eco-audit guidelines or manuals which can help other auditors, and there is also use of computers, expert systems and information technology (retrieval systems like LEXIS conceptual, or hypertext searching). However, guidelines and computer aids are not enough: effective environmental management demands commitment. Some companies, authorities and educational establishments have tried to do eco-auditing on the cheap, which tends to give inadequate results. Doing this also poses risks from institutional politics – e.g. ministries may compete; companies may be rivals; internal squabbles may distort things.

Once standards like BS 7750 improve and spread, together with better training and accreditation of auditors, these problems should be reduced (Buckley, 1995: 292–293; Gleckman and Krut, 1996). The standards that have so far evolved mainly relate to developed countries, and require modification for use in poorer countries. There is also a need for internationally recognized standards (or even a single world standard) for eco-audit. Worries have been voiced that some standards are determined more by politics, special-interest groups and public opinion than by objective science (Ludwig et al., 1992; Rensvik, 1994; Reisenweber, 1995). Box 4.2 presents some eco-audit–environmental management system standards.

Environmental management systems

Eco-audits alone are snapshot views: they are more effective if they are part of a structured environmental management system. Environmental management systems (EMSs) were developed in response to the realization that there was a need for an integrated and proactive approach to environmental issues. They are a means for helping industry, or other bodies, comply with environmental regulations, obtain

---

BOX 4.2 Eco-audit–environmental management system standards

Note: These standards, which deal with environmental management systems (EMSs), have evolved from total quality management (TQM), and are quality auditing systems. They must be widely applicable, effective at getting regulation, yet flexible. It is also desirable that they help integrate environmental management quality standards with commercial quality management (product/ service quality) standards and occupational health and safety quality management standards (Young, 1994).

BS7750

In early 1992 the world's first eco-audit standard was published – British Standards Institute's BS7750 Specification for Environmental Management Systems (British Standards Institution, 1992; 1994a; 1994b; Hunt and Johnson, 1995: 89) – derived from an earlier Management Quality System BS5750. A number of countries adopted it and it was revised in 1993 and 1994 to make it more compatible with the more recently introduced Eco-Management and Audit Scheme (EMAS – which has drawn upon BS7750) (Bohoris and O'Mahoney, 1994; Sharratt, 1995: 41–53; Willig, 1994: 33–42; Buckley, 1995). BS7750 is a means by which an organization can establish an EMS. To obtain BS7750 a body has to establish and maintain environmental procedures and an environmental protection system which meets BS7750 specifications and demonstrate compliance. It must also be committed to cycles of self-improvement through internal eco-audit. There are three elements to BS7750: (1) possession of an environmental policy; (2) a documented EMS; (3) a register of effects on the environment.

Critics of BS7750 argue that it is possible to get the standard by *promising* to do better and then to release relatively little information to the public (it is not as open as, say, the US Toxic Releases Inventory). At the time of writing BS7750 did not provide for a publicity logo and was being superseded by the ISO14001 series.

EMAS

The Eco-Management and Audit Scheme (EMAS) was launched in 1993 (EU Council Regulation 1836/93) although it was not until April 1995 that it came into force in the UK (Welford, 1992; EEC, 1993; Brown, 1995). EMAS goes beyond eco-audit to require an approved EMS and the production of an independently verified public statement. EMAS seeks to encourage industries in EU states to adopt a site-specific, proactive approach to environmental management and improve their performance. EMAS is in some ways similar to, and is broadly compatible with, the already established BS7750, but is much broader in scope and requires greater public reporting of audits. It is stronger

---

than BS7750 on environmental protection, and is aimed more at industrial activities. EMAS is also stronger on *ensuring* that a body regulates its environmental impacts.

EMAS registration is voluntary (but is established in the EEC by regulation so that consistent rules are supposed to be set for all those participating). Participants write and adopt an environmental policy which includes commitments to: meeting all legislative requirements and ensuring continued improvement of performance; implementation of an environmental programme with objectives and targets derived from a comprehensive review process; establishing a management system (which includes future environmental audits) to deliver these objectives and targets; issue public environmental statements (EMAS does not insist on *full* publication of audits). Originally it had been planned to make full public disclosure compulsory but this was abandoned. An accredited third party verifies all these things (see *Journal of the Institution of Environmental Sciences* 4(3) – May 1995, pp. 4–7). If these terms are broken, the organization may be suspended from EMAS, and so lose their right to a special logo (green credentials), which means loss of publicity advantage and possibly increased insurance premiums or supplier, investment, or sales–outlet boycott (see Figure 4.1).

Criticisms of EMAS include the charge that its auditing criteria are vague (Karl, 1994); that it disrupts the activities of an organization; that it may reveal trade secrets and; perhaps cause public or workforce hostility. There are signs in the UK that small companies find the cost of BS7750 more of a challenge than do larger companies. There are also calls for EMAS to increase the focus on sustainable development (Spencer-Cooke, 1996).

Europe is improving EMAS by introducing strategic environmental assessment to all plans, policies and programmes (Barton and Bruder, 1995: 11) (see chapter 3). There were also plans at the time of writing to expand EMAS to make it more compatible with the ISO14001 series. If the EEC adopts an Environmental Charter, eco-audit will become more widespread, possibly even compulsory.

ISO14000

The International Standards Organization (ISO) has been seeking to develop a standard (or rather, a series of standards, some advisory, some contractual) broadly compatible with EMAS and BS7750. ISO[DIS]14001 was introduced in 1996, and the series also incorporates ISO14004. ISO14001 provides information on the requirements for an EMS, and ISO14004 has the elements needed and guidance on implementation of an EMS.

The ISO1400 series are roughly equivalent to BS7750 and EMAS, but more user-friendly and easier to understand, and seem likely to gain world-wide adoption (for details see Rothery, 1993; Baxter and Bacon, 1996; Jackson, 1997; Sheldon, 1997). These ISO standards are related to the ISO9000 series (roughly

continued . . .

equivalent to BS5750) which are widely used by business world-wide and deal with quality systems (TQM) registration. The ISO14001 standard is taking over from BS7750 and is periodically updated (details are usually published in *ENDS* – see list of journals at the end of chapter 1 (Knight, 1997)).

technical and economic benefits, and are designed to ensure that an environmental policy and environmental objectives are adopted and followed (standards like BS7750 or EMAS require an EMS to be established and maintained). Hunt and Johnson (1995: 89) argued that EMSs:

◆ help to develop a proactive environmental approach;
◆ ensure a balanced view across all functions;
◆ enable effective, directed environmental goal-setting;
◆ make the environmental auditing process effective.

An EMS usually requires a participating body to publish an environmental policy statement and regularly update it. The standards used to eco-audit typically test whether the body:

◆ has identified overall aims;
◆ understands constraints on achieving aims;
◆ identifies who is responsible for what;
◆ sets an overall timetable for achieving aims;
◆ has determined resource needs;
◆ has selected a project management approach;
◆ has a progress monitoring system.

EMSs rely on independent certification of compliance with set eco-audit standards to encourage more careful planning. EMSs can in practice be difficult to pursue effectively as a result of real-world institutional politics, funding problems, data shortages, need for industrial secrecy, health and safety issues. There is a need to improve the sustainable development aspects of eco-audits. Figure 4.2 illustrates a basic EMS approach. The EMAS approach is presented in Figure 4.3; see also Box 4.2.

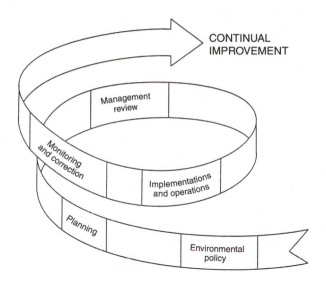

FIGURE 4.2 Basic environmental management system approach
Source: Based, with modifications, on Hunt and Johnson (1995: 6, Fig. 1.2)

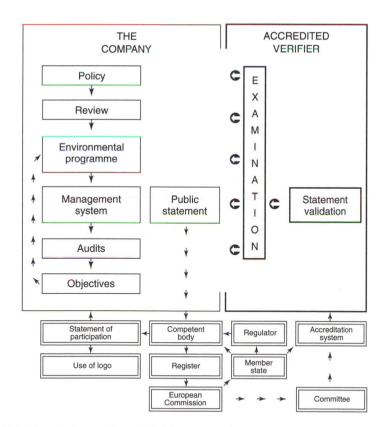

FIGURE 4.3 The basic provisions of the European Union's EMAS
Source: Hunt and Johnson (1995: 74, Fig. 4.2)

Recommended reading

Journals which publish articles on monitoring, eco-auditing and EMSs

Eco-Management and Auditing
Environmental Accounting and Auditing Reporter
Environmental Assessment
Environmental Auditing
Environmental Management
Environmental Monitoring and Assessment
Impact Assessment and Project Appraisal
Journal of Environmental Planning and Management

Chapter 5

Environmental management and economics

Regardless of the stance adopted, whether utopian, utilitarian, libertarian, Malthusian, cornucopian, etc., for almost as long as economics has existed, economists have invoked the 'invisible hand of the market' as a mechanism that supposedly ensures that it becomes uneconomical to exploit a potentially renewable resource before it is badly damaged. Pareto optimum, a basic theorem of welfare economics, states that through market exchange, with each person pursuing their private interests, there are effective controls over resources exploitation and use of the environment; it also states that, except in inefficient market situations, it is not possible to make anyone better off without making at least one person worse off. Unfortunately, the market has not been an effective control: there are plenty of examples of ruined fisheries, lost forests, etc. to prove it. At present:

> '"the free market" does not provide consumers with proper information, because the social and environmental costs of production are not part of current economic models. . . . Private profits are being made at public costs in the deterioration of the environment and the general quality of life, and at the expense of future generations.'
>
> (Capra, 1997: 291)

The market may fail to control exploitation for various reasons, including difficulty in valuing many resources (e.g. what is the worth of a rare plant?); some things are valueless as a use has yet to be found for them. Resources and environment may be used to give outputs (such as crops) or benefits (such as recreational use) or there may be non-use (intrinsic) value (e.g. conservation provides material for future pharmaceutical use or crop-breeding). When a resource or the environment has current utility (i.e. can give 'satisfaction'), this may be gained directly (e.g. use of land for recreation or tourism) or indirectly though manufacturing (Perman *et al.*, 1996). Figure 5.1 lists the elements of total economic value.

The 'greening' of economics

Many of the attempts at a concise definition of economics mention 'resources', 'the Earth', 'the environment', e.g. 'economics is essentially the stewardship of resources' (Hanson, 1977); or 'economics offers a framework within which to analyse the problems which we face in making choices about the environment in which we live' (Hodge, 1995: 3); or 'economics is concerned with the allocation, distribution and use of environmental resources' (Perman *et al.*, 1996: 24). It is thus puzzling why, before the last decade, there was little contact between economics and environmental studies.

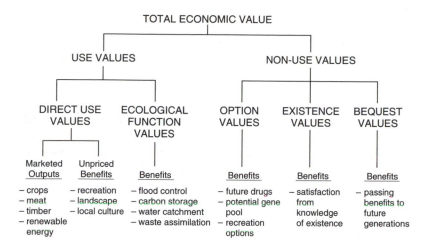

FIGURE 5.1 The elements of total economic value
Source: Hodge (1995: 7, Fig. 1.2)

The failure to weave environmental sensitivity into economics has been flagged as a cause of many of the world's problems. Given the difficulties involved in effectively valuing nature, and in dealing with human use of the environment and resources, such criticisms are perhaps unfair. Nevertheless, before the 1980s few economists recognized the Earth was finite, and most encouraged expansion.

In 1798 Thomas Malthus published his first essay: its warnings about limits were largely ignored until after the 1940s, when it became clear that open frontiers (i.e. further vacant land for development) were closing, and pollution disasters warned of the need for environmental sensitivity. One of the first to publish on resource and conservation economics was Ciracy-Wantrup (1952). Fourteen years later Boulding (1966) inspired many with his writings on the economics of Spaceship Earth which acknowledged that the world was finite and vulnerable. Further impetus to 'greening' was given by the publications of Meadows *et al.* (1972) and Schumacher (1973). By the late 1970s a little greening of economics was apparent (Krutilla and Fisher, 1975; Hanson, 1977; Kneese, 1977; Cooper, 1981). Green economics is essentially concerned with the consequences of the drive to amass wealth (Ekins, 1992a; Buarque, 1993).

Work on theoretical and practical environmental economics expanded after the mid-1980s (Lowe and Lewis, 1980). Since the 1970s considerable effort has gone into seeking alternatives to reliance upon market controls (Redclift, 1992). A particular boost was given by the publication of *Blueprint for a Green Economy* (Pearce *et al.*, 1989) and related texts (Pearce *et al.*, 1990; 1991; Pearce, 1995). From the early 1990s there has been an increasing interest in economics and environmental management (Marcandya and Richardson, 1992; Redclift, 1992; Turner *et al.*, 1994; Barbier, 1993; Funtowicz and Ravetz, 1994; Mikesell, 1995; McGillivray, 1996). Increasingly the focus is on sustainable development (Pearce *et al.*, 1990; Tisdell, 1993), on pollution control economics (e.g. Forsund and Strom, 1988), on economic development and environmental management (Schramm and Warford, 1990), and on environmental taxes. Some economists adopt the concept of sustainable development without acknowledging that the Earth and its resources are finite, then talk of 'sustained growth' and explore ways of achieving it. There is debate about the likelihood of real, sustainable growth.

There is no single unified market, and large sections of the world's population are not directly affected by economics. The reality is that many of those suffering from environmental problems are 'marginal' – economically and socially deprived, perhaps living in remote situations. Also, one must not assume universal co-operation between nations to protect the environment: some countries or power groups may try to gain from global challenges, and exploit situations.

Today, two widely stated goals of environmental economics are: (1) to cut extravagant resource exploitation; (2) to seek sustainable development. Some economists argue that environmental care should stimulate economic growth by improving the health of the workforce, making it more productive and creating employment in the green sector (pollution control and environmental remediation, etc.).

BOX 5.1 An example which may have widespread promise: Curitiba City, Brazil

Much of the success of Curitiba's greening since the mid-1970s has been through the efforts of its Mayor, Jaime Lerner, and have not depended on much outside funding. He established an effective refuse collecting system for Curitiba's slums (*favelas*), where narrow alleyways make it impossible to use lorries. Recycling bins were placed around the *favelas* and the people were paid in city transport system tokens or welfare tokens for sorted, recyclable trash. Organic wastes went to farmers for composting, and people collecting this were rewarded with food stamps. The approach provides a sort of social security system for the poor, who in return scour the city for refuse. The travel tokens offer better access to employment and boost the use of public transport, there are no costs for running garbage trucks and less need for street construction.

Numerous other, largely self-help, innovations have made Curitiba a landmark in green urban development. Curitiba has improved living conditions for the poor and upgraded its infrastructure in spite of having had one of Brazil's most rapid growth rates (Rabinovitch, 1996). The city has been able to become self-funding and no longer seeks aid from state government, is comparatively clean and relatively prosperous. The city has an improved bus transport system and crime rates have been kept low compared with other Brazilian cities.

There is no obvious tested model for improving people's well-being and protecting the environment – the USA has problems, as do Russia and China, Japan and developing countries. A few glimmers of green are apparent, though, for example the city of Curitiba (see Box 5.1). There have also been economists who are keen to avoid the 'commodity fetishism of mainstream economics', and develop workable 'green economics' and 'barefoot economics' (Scitovsky, 1976; Max-Neef, 1986; 1992a; 1992b; Henderson, 1981a; 1981b; McBurney, 1990; Dodds, 1997). One supposition is that steady-state economics might be developed to ensure that growth does not lead to serious environmental degradation. How much inroad on mainstream economics this makes remains to be seen (Booth, 1997). There has also been some greening of mainstream accountancy (Gray, 1990).

Environmental economics

By the 1980s 'new economics' had appeared and environmental economics was expanding (Costanza, 1991; Common, 1996). Bodies like the London Environmental Economics Centre had been established and environmental issues had gained a much higher profile (Tietenberg and Folmer, 1998). Even so, economics is still far from becoming green – being aware of a problem is no guarantee that people change their ways. Things like shadow pricing may be more often used, but macro-economics is still generally reluctant to include environmental costs in calculations of things like gross national product (GNP); economic growth is still a major goal, little change from the 1970s when an environmentalist observed that 'growth for the sake of growth is the ideology of the cancer-cell'. A recent UK press advert called for an 'environmental economist'

> to explore how economic factors should be taken into account when drafting and applying environmental regulations; to establish the value of economic instruments within a mixed regime of regulations; to establish economic measures of trends in the employing nation's environmental capital.

There have been attempts to incorporate economic evaluation into environmental impact assessment (James, 1994). Valuation of the environment must be improved for developing and developed countries (Georgiou *et al.*, 1997). For an introduction to the economic theory involved in policy making for environmental management see Baumol and Oates (1988).

Global environmental problems and economics

Those exploring policies to cope with climate change, transboundary pollution and other global environmental problems need to know the likely costs, approaches which may be useful, and economic controls. The economics of global climate change is attracting considerable attention to try to resolve disagreement between various countries and institutions over the apportionment of blame, estimation of costs, and development of controls (Agarwal and Narain, 1991; Funkhauser, 1995; Tietenberg, 1997; Proost and Braden, 1998). Another area of interest is technology change: in the early 1970s Farvar and Milton (1972) suggested that careless application of technology caused socioeconomic problems. Nowadays economists try to forecast the impacts of proposed innovations (Tylecote and Van der Straaten, 1997).

Environmental accounts

Environmental auditing has been applied to: eco-audits (see chapter 4), stock-taking, eco-review, eco-survey, etc. State-of-the-environment accounts, environmental quality evaluations and environmental accounts systems collect data on the environment and resources to try and show the state of an area (or sea like the Baltic or Aegean). Most of these accounting procedures treat the environment as natural capital and try to measure its depletion or enhancement. Valuing environmental features in monetary terms can be difficult.

The foundation for these procedures has often been the UN model of Standard National Accounts, usually with 'satellite accounts' added for environmental items – some call these 'environmentally adjusted national accounts' (UN, 1993). Such accounts seek to establish the stocks of resources, value of environmental features, and their use over time (Newson, 1992: 92). National environmental accounts systems (new systems of national accounts, green accounts, patrimonial accounts, or state-of-the-environment accounts) have been developed to assist with data gathering and storage and to value environment and natural resources (Pearce *et al.*, 1989: 93–119). Canada, Denmark, Norway, France, Japan, USA, The Netherlands and the World Bank have developed national state-of-the-environment accounts since the early 1970s and the UNEP has been promoting this type of accounting in developing countries (Schramm and Warford, 1989: 30; Alfsen and Bye, 1990; Hartwick, 1990; Common and Norton, 1994; McGillivray, 1994). Most follow the Dutch model, comparing output of each sector of the economy with how much it depletes finite resources such as fossil fuel. Some countries are moving to include water pollution, radioactive waste and other factors in their accounting.

These accounting systems seek to set out a region's environmental, social and economic assets, and can be used to assess whether economic development is consistent with sustainable development, or help ensure optimal use of natural resources and environment (Ahmad *et al.*, 1989; Hamilton *et al.*, 1994). For example, a natural resource accounting system can help a manager establish what percentage of, say, mineral exploitation profits to invest in long-term sustainable development so that a region or country does not suffer boom and decline. In practice, being able to make such investments depends on the type of government, people's attitudes and the persuasiveness of environmental management. Natural resource accounts can show the linkages between the environment and the economy, may be useful for forecasting, and can establish which habitats, etc., are of importance. They should make land use more rational, and are an improvement on the use of indicators like GNP (Thompson and Wilson, 1994: 613) but stop short of encouraging a crucial change in people's and administrators' attitudes towards environmentally sound development.

In the mid-1990s the UK Office of National Statistics produced national environmental accounts to try to measure the country's economic performance, assessing the environmental impact of each industry, using 1993 statistics. These accounts show for various economic sectors the percentage contribution to the national economy against percentage of total: greenhouse gas emission; responsibility for acid deposition; and smoke emission (*New Scientist* 4 September 1996: 11).

Evaluating the environment and natural resources

Ever since Ciracy-Wantrup (1952), resource inputs have been divided by assessors into: renewable (regardless of management, also called 'stock resources'); potentially renewable (dependent on management); and non-renewable (Figure 5.2). Some renewable resources can be converted to non-renewable through poor management or natural disaster. Certain resources cannot be remade if damaged or exhausted (e.g.

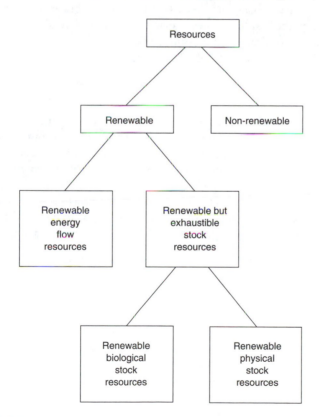

FIGURE 5.2 A classification of environmental resources
Source: Perman *et al.* (1996: 4, Fig. 1.1)

biodiversity). The absorptive capacity of the environment (its ability to absorb and neutralize damaging compounds or activities) is a resource which should be assessed by economists. There may be opportunities to substitute for a given resource, using labour, capital or alternative materials.

Cost–benefit analysis

Cost–benefit analysis (CBA) seeks to identify the impact of development on each person affected at various points in time, and so estimate the aggregate value which each person gains or loses. There is a huge literature on CBA, its shortcomings, modifications and alternatives (Brent, 1997). Widespread dissatisfaction with CBA's effectiveness in valuing environmental issues has led to many suggested improvements or alternatives, some favouring quantitative approaches, and others qualitative (Munda *et al.*, 1994). One focus has been to try to improve its consideration of environmental issues, but this is still far from adequately solved (Hanley and Spash, 1994). A development since the early 1990s is the concept of best available techniques not involving excessive economic costs (BATNEEC). This places the onus on developers to adopt the best techniques available, with only 'excessive cost' as a viable excuse for not doing so (Pearce and Brisson, 1993).

Shadow prices

The difficulty of establishing the value of 'externalities', including environmental factors, in monetary units has been addressed in several ways: one is to use shadow prices. A shadow price is a value that reflects the true opportunity cost of a resource or service. The real value of something reflects the most desirable alternative for it, e.g. (in production) the opportunity cost of producing an extra unit of manufactured goods is the lost output of childcare, food production, etc., forgone as a result of transferring resources to manufacturing activities. In consumption, opportunity cost is the amount of one commodity that must be forgone in order to consume more of another (Todaro, 1994).

Green taxes

The use of taxation is an important tool for seeking environmental management goals. Pearce (1995) urged environmental management to seek a balance between using economic command and control (largely through taxes) and incentives. Capra (1997: 292) suggested that one of the most effective ways of countering environmental damage and supporting sustainable development would be to shift the tax burden from income to 'eco-taxes'. These could be added to products, energy, services and materials, to reflect true costs. This means the *consumer* pays. While there have been national measures for some time, interest in green taxation on an international scale is recent (and still mainly theoretical), triggered by increasing transboundary pollution, competition for internationally shared resources, and the threat of global environmental change.

The function of green taxes is not to raise revenue for government but rather to provide participants in the marketplace with accurate information about true costs. For example, a tax on CFCs reflects their impact on ozone (Farber *et al.*, 1995). Green taxes counter the pursuit of lower prices by externalizing the true costs, ensuring that the purchaser is aware of the costs of environmental impacts. It is important that attempts to integrate external costs of production into prices does not burden the poor or 'punish' the middle classes. The aim is to give people and companies incentives to invent, innovate and respond to environmental challenges (Repetto *et al.*, 1992). Green taxation should encourage manufacturers to seek to reduce waste and other environmental damage to keep down their costs and thus prices to the purchaser – i.e. there is incentive to improve environmental practice. Taxation is also becoming an important tool in the quest for sustainable development (Von Weisäcker and Jesinghaus, 1992).

One problem associated with attempts to agree international green taxation is that it may come into conflict with sovereignty (Nellor, 1987). There are a number of taxation approaches that have potential for controlling global climate change: tradeable emission quotas; carbon (emissions) tax; energy use tax; taxation associated with technology transfers; reduced taxation for providing carbon sinks.

Pigouvian taxes

The idea of 1920s' UK economist Arthur Pigou, these are intended to be levied on (externalities) pollution, or activities it is desirable to discourage to achieve sound environmental management (see chapter 4).

Carbon emissions taxes

A number of countries have already taken steps to adopt these. For an examination of them and their welfare effects see Cornwall (1997). The prospects of a widely practised global carbon tax is some way off. At the time of writing the EU looked close to setting carbon taxes designed to stabilize emissions at the 1990 level by AD 2000.

Tradeable emissions quotas

Tradeable emissions quotas (TEQs) (marketable or auctionable permits or tradeable emissions permits) have been applied in a number of countries. In the USA they have been used for control of air pollution emissions for over a decade, and in France to control water-borne effluent since 1969 (Owen and Unwin, 1997: 402). There has been considerable interest in the use of TEQs for dealing with transboundary atmospheric pollution, especially carbon dioxide emissions (for coverage of TEQ developments in the EU see Koutstaal, 1997).

The 1997 Kyoto Climate Change Agreement has established a TEQ 'club' (Canada, Japan, USA, Russia) which will trade emissions permits among its members – in effect, the USA and Japan have first rights to any permits offered by Russia. This has left the EU to bear the burden of emission controls but saved negotiations from collapse (*New Scientist* 18 December 1997: 10).

Energy use taxes

Tax on vehicle fuel, domestic power supplies and household heating fuel can be used to discourage excessive consumption. The cost of vehicle fuel in the USA is still three to four times less than it is in Europe, so there is scope for taxation. Energy taxes encourage efficient use and change to non-polluting alternatives, but could be unfair to countries with less scope for the latter (such as those lacking hydroelectricity or already committed to coal or oil).

Green funding

Funding and aid agencies are increasingly focusing on environmental management and sustainable development (Rich, 1986; Turnham, 1991; Feitelson, 1992), and they also check for risks, such as contaminated land, before supporting developments (Kopitsky and Betzenberger, 1987).

The Global Environmental Facility (GEF), launched in 1990, is a corporate venture between governments of industrialized and developing countries. The GEF is jointly managed by the World Bank, UNDP and UNEP to assist developing countries to tackle globally relevant environmental problems such as climate change; loss of biodiversity; management of international waters; and stratospheric ozone depletion. The GEF is targeted at poorer countries and involves NGOs in identifying, monitoring and implementing projects. There were efforts in 1992 at the Earth Summit to increase the profile of the GEF. Criticisms include the complaint that donors to the GEF have simply cut back on other aid to finance it; that participation is not open enough or wide enough; and that some developing countries want poverty alleviation included.

Aid and the environment

There is a wide range of forms and in the practice of aid: recipients may be governments, bodies, groups of people or individuals. International agencies, NGOs, individuals and groupings of governments may be donors. Sometimes donors contribute aid directly to recipients, or it can be via an intermediary such as an NGO or a UN body. When aid is government to government it is termed bilateral aid; when several governments or an international organization have contributed it is multilateral aid.

Frequently aid is tied or is conditional, i.e. requirements are attached to the funding – a recipient may have to behave in a particular way or a percentage of the aid must be used to buy goods and services from the donor nation. The latter arrangement is known as 'aid for trade provision', and it is not unknown for obsolete, overpriced or unsuitable goods or services to be traded (Hayter, 1989: 21, 92). Aid may be in the form of funding, foodstuffs or other supplies, sometimes training or secondment of skilled manpower rather than donation of goods or funds. There are situations where conditionality makes sense (environmental care or improvement may be a condition), others where it is perceived as neo-protectionism or neo-colonialism, as an extra cost and as a sign that there is a risk that support could be diverted. Environmental care is increasingly a condition of aid (Keohane and Levy, 1996).

There has been criticism of some agencies' aid policy for its impact on the environment (Dinham, 1991; Hildyard, 1991). At the Earth Summit in 1992, Japan offered more aid for the environment than any other nation, much tied to her export or resources import policy and, according to Forrest (1991), has tended to support large superprojects which have sometimes caused serious environmental impacts. Aid may be well intended, but even providing roads can cause problems. Environmentally benign aid is not easy to achieve. What to to a donor seems like sensible safe-guards to avoid unwanted environmental (and socioeconomic) impacts may appear to a recipient to be excuses for more conditionality, delay and perhaps loss of a portion of funding to pay for appraisals, safeguards and remedial measures, and intrusion into sovereignty.

To combat global environmental problems will require considerable aid to poor countries. At the Earth Summit richer nations were clearly reluctant to commit themselves to the GEF, either for fear it would slow their economies or because they wished to ensure tight control over how the aid was spent. The 'democratization' of the USSR and its allies has meant less spending on arms and propaganda in both the east and west but it may divert aid there which would have gone to developing countries.

Academics and aid agencies have examined environmental (and socioeconomic) aspects of aid, although surprisingly little has been published, given the huge sums and considerable impacts involved (Linear, 1982; 1985; Adams and Solomon, 1985; Hayter, 1989). Hayter (1989: 83) listed a number of reasons why this might be. Agencies have developed environmental guidelines and have staff to assess impacts prior to granting assistance. For example, the World Bank established an Office of Environmental Affairs in 1970 (Warford and Partow, 1989), and the UK Overseas Development Administration (now the DFID) established environmental appraisal procedures (ODA, 1984; 1989a; 1989b).

Debt, structural adjustment and environment

Debt and environment

The 'debt crisis' broke in 1982, and soon claims were made that it resulted in environmental degradation, although there was little clear proof (Adams, 1991; George, 1988; 1992; Reed, 1992a: 143; UN, 1992). During the 1970s many developing countries financed their economies by taking loans. Falling prices for exports of primary produce, rising costs for oil imports, and in some cases disorder and maladministration led to escalating debt. The 1973–1974 OPEC oil price increase caused further recession, driving down export prices and making debt repayment difficult. Various impacts of debt have been recognized: (1) money diverted to servicing debt is unavailable for environmental management; (2) resources are put under pressure to earn foreign exchange for interest or to pay off debt; (3) means to combat debt cause difficulty, notably structural adjustment measures.

By the 1990s Latin American and sub–Saharan countries were spending roughly 25 per cent of their total foreign exchange each year servicing debt (Davidson *et al.*, 1992: 161). In spite of paying US\$6,500 million a month interest between 1982 and 1990, debtor countries were still 61 per cent more indebted in 1991. The struggle to earn foreign exchange to service debts damages biodiversity and the environment. Debt problems, by reducing biodiversity and degrading the global environment, and by causing poverty and conflict, also affect richer nations indirectly (George, 1992: 1–33). In 1991 under the Trinidad Terms the Paris Club of creditors agreed to cancel some debts.

Linkages between economics and environment are often complex and caution should be exercised when debt–damage relationships are recognized. Debt servicing is not the only reason countries exploit resources: it might be to support urban facilities, industrialization or special-interest groups.

Structural adjustment and the environment

Structural adjustment refers to strategies adopted as a response to debt. When recession began to take hold in the developed countries, the World Bank and the International Monetary Fund began to impose structural adjustment programmes to try to stabilize the economies of debtor nations (developing countries), protect creditors and generally shore up the international economy (Bello and Cunningham, 1994). The tool used to try and stimulate growth and ensure debt repayment was the structural adjustment loan – this was intended to counter the spiralling debt situation, fight various inefficiencies, and improve the flow of traded goods. The World Bank began in Turkey in 1980, and by 1990 another 64 countries had adopted measures. These measures varied from country to country, although they usually took the form of loans to reduce balance of payments problems, which were granted on condition the recipient deregulated their economy, reduced state expenditure, and freed exchange rates. The goal was to give priority to export earnings, make the economy more efficient by cutting spending on wages and welfare, and reduce state controls to boost productive sectors. There was limited success, but in some countries there were significant or marked ill-effects: reduced household incomes, increased unemployment, inflation, cut-back in support for welfare and public services, and less spending on environmental management. Limited impacts have been felt in developed countries, but in some poorer nations there has been significant increase in poverty, greater childhood mortality (George, 1988), land abandonment, riots and rural–urban migration. One of the consequences of structural adjustment that may have an impact on the environment is the progressive disempowerment of the poor (Redclift, 1995). At its worst structural adjustment has obliged many people to sacrifice environmental assets for short-term survival.

At first these conditional loans gave little consideration to environmental impacts. Since the mid-1990s there has been interest in the effects of structural adjustment policies on the environment (Reed, 1992a; 1992b; 1996; World Bank, 1994). The World Bank and some other agencies involved in formulating structural adjustment policies increasingly try to support better environmental management and seek sustainable development.

Paying for conservation

The value of conservation in economic terms is considerable, but not adequately realized. An assessment in the late 1970s suggested the contribution of plant and animal species to the USA economy was roughly 4.5 per cent of GDP (in the region of US$ 87,000 million) (McNeely et al., 1990: 18). If the value were better known, conservation might be given better funding. Provided it is compatible with conservation, forest extraction, tourism and sport may generate supporting funds. Eco-tourism has attracted particular attention as a means of funding conservation (see chapter 10). So far, there has been little progress with taxing biotechnology or pharmaceutical industries to support conservation, yet both draw upon biodiversity. However, ways have been found of trading off debt for conservation or other forms of environmental care.

There have been promising developments since the 1980s of debt-for-nature swaps (Thomas Lovejoy has been credited with their invention in 1984). These have been negotiated in a number of countries, and are widely seen to provide a way for the recipient to pay off some or all foreign debt with less loss of face than would be caused by defaulting. The debtor country avoids defaulting and still retains control over conservation or environmental activities, and USA banks should be able to write off some of the expense against taxes (Simons, 1988; Pearce, 1989; 1995: 35, 47–48; Cartwright, 1989: 124; McNeely, 1989; Shiva et al., 1991: 63). Opponents, especially in the recipient countries and on the staff of NGOs, are less supportive (Hayter, 1989: 258; Sarkar and Ebbs, 1992). The earliest debt swaps were negotiated in Ecuador and Bolivia by 1987, and subsequently in Costa Rica, the Philippines, the Dominican Republic, Mexico, Malagasy, Jamaica, Cameroon, and other countries (George, 1988: 168; Patterson, 1990; Yearley, 1991: 182; 258).

Debt–swaps take a variety of forms, but most involve conversion of hard currency debt to local currency debt. When a lender realizes it will probably never recoup, it sells the debt, at a discount, to another (donor) who then releases cash to the debtor country in local currency, so the donation goes further to support environmental management or conservation. Some debt-swaps are bond-based (a central bank pays interest on a bond created, usually for an NGO, over a period typically of five to seven years); others are government policy programmes (under which the recipient government pledges to implement a policy or initiatives aimed at improving the environment or conservation). Debt–debt swaps are the interchange of foreign loans between creditors. Debt-rescue swaps ('buybacks') are the repurchase of a country's debt in secondary markets. Sometimes linked to debt-for-nature swaps are carbon sequestration deals, whereby a developed country or corporation establishes tree plantations to lock up carbon dioxide to compensate for their emissions elsewhere.

Criticisms levelled at debt-for-nature swaps are that:

◆ they offer limited potential to pay off existing debts (i.e. are tiny compared with typical national indebtedness);

◆ they may be used to 'smear' indigenous environmental groups efforts, i.e. opponents of environmental protection spread rumours of foreign interference to divert attention from other issues;

◆ there may be difficulties in adopting them in some countries because of different accounting and regulatory systems;

◆ there is no guarantee of ongoing protection or care;

◆ they may be seen as an erosion of a developing country's sovereignty;

◆ if operated through NGOs, swaps may not assist or train local agencies;

◆ they do little to change commercial forces that damage the environment;

◆ they have so far been applied to a limited range of activities, mainly park and reserve establishment and maintenance;

◆ the main beneficiaries, it has been argued, were the debt-seller banks (Mahony, 1992).

Trade and environmental management

Trade impacts upon environment for example, it affects:

◆ rates of deforestation;

◆ demand for animal and plant products, and may be a major reason why a species is endangered;

◆ global carbon dioxide levels;

◆ extraction of mineral resources, production of food and commodity crops;

◆ levels of pollution in developed countries;

◆ pollution controls in developing countries.

Some forms of trade can be less damaging than others: export of forest products should be less damaging than logging, and may discourage deforestation if it is carefully controlled and local people benefit (Buckley, 1993). To combat logging the Body Shop store chain has tried to encourage environmentally benign forest product trade by minimizing middleman profits. However, such products may have limited markets, which restricts what can be achieved. Falling commodity prices on the world market mean farmers get poor returns on crops, yet, committed to purchasing inputs, they are forced to expand the area farmed, or intensify production, or practise shifting cultivation and the extraction of other resources to supplement their farming activities, leading to environmental degradation. The problem cannot be solved by going back to a pre-cashcrop economy. Through trade, countries can obtain materials and continue to expand production. It can also mean that production impacts (pollution due to manufacture and problems associated with consumption of goods) are felt over a wider area.

Trade and the environment

In the early 1990s probably over 80 per cent of the world trade was in the hands of MNCs and TNCs (Anon, 1993: 220). In 1974 the Group of 77 (G77) – a coalition of 100, mainly developing, countries – demanded a New International Economic Order (NIEO) at the UN General Assembly. The NIEO included plans for new commodity agreements, alteration of what were seen as unfair patents laws and general North–South economic reform, especially expanded free trade as a way of creating employment and wealth. These demands have received considerable support, and TNCs and MNCs can benefit from better access to world markets. Some are less keen, and advocate a new protectionism, i.e. a reduction in the volume of trade, as an alternative to free trade, to cure the market problems that led to demands for NIEO but have not had much success (Lang and Hines, 1993).

The main vehicle for reform has been the General Agreement on Tariffs and Trade (GATT) (Morris, 1990; Shrybman, 1990; Davidson et al., 1992: 174). There are other multilateral trade agreements, e.g. the North American Free Trade Agreement (NAFTA) (between the USA, Canada and Mexico in late 1993) (Ritchie, 1992); the Asia Pacific Economic Cooperation (APEC) (founded in 1989 as a loose grouping of 15 nations); the Common Agricultural Policy (CAP), which seeks to promote production and effective use of agricultural resources to maintain food supplies and give EC farmers a fair standard of living. The CAP uses price supports and has had significant effects on the environment of Europe and other countries which trade with Europe.

The GATT, which became the World Trade Organization (WTO) in 1994, is a multilateral agreement covering roughly 90 per cent of the world's trade, first drafted in 1947 to establish rules for the conduct of international trade, the hope being to lower tariff barriers erected in the 1930s that were held to be a hindrance to world development. There were eight rounds of meetings to discuss GATT prior to

---

BOX 5.2 The positive and negative effects of free trade on environmental management

Free trade might help environmental management through:
- ending tariff barriers that raise produce prices, causing farmers to overstress land for profit;
- reducing the dumping of cheap US and European food surpluses, which, by making it difficult for developing country producers to get a fair price, discourage them from leaving land fallow or investing in land improvement, erosion control, etc.;
- removing restrictions that make it difficult for developing countries to produce and sell finished wood products to developing countries. This should give much better profits and reduce logging;
- harmonizing standards and co-ordinating trade impacts on the environment on a global scale;

Free trade might harm environmental management because:
- much existing or proposed environmental legislation could be interpreted as illegal non-tariff trade barriers. There is thus a reduction in controls which discouraged logging, trade in endangered species, use of cattle growth hormones like BST, etc.;
- trade liberalization may lead to increased specialization of production that may over-stress a resource or environment;
- the struggle to keep down costs to be competitive may mean exports are expanded to compensate and resources or the environment are put under stress;
- reduced import restrictions will remove opportunities to counter trade in hardwoods, endangered species, etc. (see Box 5.3);
- there may be increased opportunities to sell commodities like beef, sugar, etc., and this might encourage increased forest clearance and poor land management in countries that are keen to boost production;
- producers may think twice about spending money on pollution control or other forms of environmental management if another country does not, and they are competing with it to sell similar goods, on otherwise equal terms (Ritchie, 1992);
- it may be less easy, without the threat of trade restrictions, to get countries to reduce carbon dioxide emissions or other pollution;
- poor countries may reduce domestic food prices, import grain, and raise more export crops like soya (e.g. as happened in Brazil);
- any domestic support for the peasantry in developing countries or poorer farmers in developed countries could be interpreted as unfair protection. Small farmers might become marginalized and then damage the land trying to survive;

- larger farmers, encouraged by free trade to practise industrial (agrochemical-using) agriculture to produce export crops, may damage the land;
- there is a risk that foreign inputs and MNC controls will increase, leading to more dependency;
- if free trade leads to reduced home production there is a risk of problems if overseas supplies fail;
- it could be difficult to pass and enforce national environment and resource management or health protection laws.

1985–1986, the last, the Uruguay Round, should have run from 1986 to 1990 but failed to reach agreement until some years later (Raghavan, 1990; Anon., 1992). Things had stalled over cutting subsidies to agriculture: in particular the French farming lobby was opposed to the 1992 Blair House Agreements to reduce farm subsidies. In 1993 in Tokyo the Quad Group of GATT (Japan, USA, Canada and the EC) agreed to abolish or reduce many tariffs, effectively agreeing new world trade rules.

Free trade can lead to environmental damage: when the Roman Empire adopted it grain prices seem to have fallen, prompting large landowners with many slaves to practise more ruthless commercial farming, while smaller agriculturalists were forced out of business. Richard Cobden was aware of the environmental implications for the UK of freeing up trade by the repeal of the Corn Laws (1846) (legislation which had protected farmers from falling wheat prices) – with free trade landowners drained and cleared more land and intensified land use.

While free trade may bring some benefits, then, there are worries that it causes environmental problems (Boxes 5.2 and 5.3). Difficulties outlined in Box 5.3 continue, e.g. in April 1998 the WTO were still in disagreement with the USA over restricting imports of shrimps caught with nets that endanger wildlife (*The Times* 28 April 1998). The main problem is that signatory countries have less control over imports because most quotas and controls are outlawed (Bown, 1990; Westlund, 1994). There are also worries that free trade could favour developed countries' biotechnology (Raghavan, 1990; Acharya, 1991).

GATT established a Disputes Panel to resolve problems but so far it has not been effective enough at dealing with environmental issues. Interest in further greening free trade has resulted in a growing literature (Sorsa, 1992; Esty, 1994; Marsh, 1994; Rugman and Kirton, 1998). GATT set up a group on Environmental Means and International Trade, and bodies like the OECD are keen to harmonize free trade and environment (De Miraman and Stevens, 1992; Zarsky, 1994). It would also be wise to seek greater co-ordination between the various free trade organizations and the UN Commission on Trade and Development (UNCTAD).

In 1985 the 85 signatories of GATT undertook to try to restrict the export of hazardous materials. However, pollution control activities are not easy because of difficulties in disseminating information on pesticides and other compounds and their effects, and because monitoring and enforcing controls in the real world are often problematic. Measures were taken to improve controls; for example, in 1986 the FAO

BOX 5.3 Clash between free trade and environmental management: the yellow-fin tuna case

From 1972 the USA had restrictions on its own tuna fishing. Between 1988 and 1991 conflict arose because America felt the Mexicans were using purse-sein netting techniques that killed marine mammals and other wildlife. In 1992 the USA enacted the International Dolphin Conservation Act, which prohibited the import of fish or fish products from countries which were deemed to have inadequate measures for protecting marine mammals.

The 1992 Act led the USA to place an embargo on imports of Mexican canned yellow-fin tuna. Mexico complained (before the Act was passed) in 1991 that it would violate free trade rules. GATT found in favour of Mexico (the ban being a violation of its Article XI) (Anderson and Blackhurst, 1992; Charnovitz, 1993; Musgrave, 1993).

Similar problems have been caused by the USA's (1987) Driftnet Enforcement Act and (1992) Wild Bird Conservation Act. Problems with the former are continuing at the time of writing. The difficulty is deciding whether this sort of restriction is justified under free trade rules.

issued an International Code of Conduct on the Distribution and Use of Pesticides, and by 1990 about 100 countries were signatories. The FAO and WHO set up the Codex Alimentarius Commission to establish food standards, including acceptable pesticide levels, and this annually publishes standards. Under GATT the Codex seems likely to have increased powers. However, it has been argued that Codex decisions are determined too much by developed countries and MNCs or TNCs (Avery *et al.*, 1993). Any nation that already has, or is setting standards higher than the Codex may well be deemed to be putting up trade barriers and could suffer sanctions (for a recent study of WTO agreements and the environment, focusing on how to solve the difficulties, see Cameron and Fijalkowski, 1998).

Recommended reading

Journals which publish articles on environmental management and economics

Ecological Economics
Environmental Economics
Environmental & Resource Economics
Local Environment
Natural Resource and Environmental Economics
New Economics

Chapter 6

Environmental risk management, impact, hazard and risk assessment

'Ecology is the science which warns people who won't listen, about ways they won't follow, to save an environment they don't appreciate' (Anon).

This chapter examines approaches used to forecast future scenarios, assess the impacts caused by development, and the risks and hazards posed by nature and human activity. These approaches are often linked with the assessment of economic impacts, notably by CBA (see chapter 5), and often feed into eco-auditing (see chapter 4). For those seeking greater depth of coverage, the following books in the Routledge Environmental Management Series are recommended:

A. Nixon and O. Harrop (1998) *Environmental Impact Assessment*
S. McGill (1999) *Environmental Risk Management*

Environmental risk management

Environmental risk management incorporates a range of approaches (including risk assessment, discussed later in this chapter) to:

◆   estimate risk;
◆   evaluate risk;
◆   respond to risk.

It deals with multidimensional risks (often involving interrelated physical and social impacts) and demands political judgement to improve the chances of optimum decision making (O'Riordan, 1979; Pollard *et al.*, 1995). There have been calls for these approaches to become more holistic (Harvey *et al.*, 1995), and some already overlap with or are combined together in eco-auditing. There is growing interest in risks associated with global environmental change, including: biospheric catastrophe (unstoppable shift to conditions that threaten human and other life); climatic perturbation (natural or human-induced which threatens the well-being of people and wildlife); reduced provision of basic needs (threats to sustained production of food, access to adequate water, energy, etc.); and pollution (O'Riordan and Rayner, 1991).

Environmental risk management and most of the approaches discussed in this chapter are imprecise, partly because the world is complex; a common cliché is that 'everything in the environment is connected to everything else'. The media often refer to the 'butterfly effect' (a concept from chaos theory, implying that a trivial event can lead to a vast cascade of changes that are impossible to predict accurately). Since the 1960s there has been a shift towards more appropriate development, and the right to damage the environment and people in the name of 'progress' is questioned. There is increased awareness that technology and biotechnology can pose threats and there is growing interest in sustainable development. This chapter looks at the approaches developed to identify and avoid problems or missed opportunities. In addition to warning of impacts, risks and hazards, some of these approaches can help make planning and management more accountable to the public, and may encourage more careful decision making. They are often not the quantitative scientific approaches they seem; rather, they are ordered but *subjective* methods for improving judgement (Fairweather, 1993: 10).

Environmental impact assessment

There is no universal definition of what exactly environmental impact assessment (EIA) is, so it is best treated as a generic term for a process which seeks to blend administration, planning, analysis and public involvement in pre-decision assessment. A shorter explanation might be 'an approach which seeks to improve development by *a priori* assessment' (Boxes 6.1 and 6.2). Figure 6.1 illustrates how EIA fits into planning, Figures 6.2 and 6.3 show how it relates to other approaches.

Identifying consequences of a proposed activity is common sense, rather than a revolutionary idea. However, for much of history it has not been the planning and management approach adopted. Impact assessment has been evolving for over a quarter-century, but it is still imperfect and is often misapplied or misused. The field has been dominated by EIA; however, there are a number of approaches running parallel (and sometimes overlapping), with broadly similar goals, frequently exchanging information, techniques and methods, which are of value for environmental management. These include social impact assessment (SIA) (see later this chapter), hazard assessment, risk assessment, technology impact assessment, eco-auditing, CBA, and a range of forecasting or futures scenario-prediction methods (Ryecroft *et al.*, 1988). These approaches have a lot in common: for example, there is usually an effects focus; they are systematic, focused, interdisciplinary and comprehensive, and generally iterative.

EIA can offer much more than simply a common-sense approach to development: it can be a policy instrument, a planning tool, a means of public involvement and part of a framework crucial to environmental management and the drive for sustainable development. Some view impact assessment as a philosophy rather than just a technique; Graham Smith (1993: 12) argued that it should be treated as 'a bridge that integrates the science of environmental analysis with the policies of resource management'.

Attitudes towards EIA vary from the view that it is just a required rubber-stamping activity, or that it determines optimal development, to the idea that it has a vital role to play in improving environmental management and planning to achieve sustainable development (Lawrence, 1997).

Until recently planners and managers mainly asked:

- Is it technically feasible?
- Is it financially viable?
- Is it legally permissible?

BOX 6.1 An overview of EIA

The following observations describe EIA:

◆ It is proactive assessment, and should be initiated pre-project/programme/ policy, before development decisions are made. In-project/programme/policy and post-project/programme/policy assessment are common. While these may not allow much problem avoidance, they can advise on problem miti- gation, gather data, feed into future impact assessment, improve damage control and the exploitation of unexpected benefits.

◆ It is systematic evaluation of all significant environmental (including social and economic) consequences an action is likely to have upon the environment.

◆ It is a process leading to a statement to guide decision makers.

◆ It is a structured, systematic, comprehensive approach.

◆ It is a learning process and means to find the optimum development path.

◆ It is a process by which information is collected and assessed to determine whether it is wise to proceed with a proposed development.

◆ It is an activity designed to identify and predict the impacts of an action on the biogeophysical environment and on human health and well-being, and to interpret and communicate information about such impacts.

◆ It is a process which forces (or should force) developers to reconsider proposals.

◆ It is a process which has the potential to increase developers' accountability to the public.

◆ It usually involves initial screening and scoping (to determine what is to be subjected to EIA, and decide what form the assessment should take).

◆ It should be subject to independent, objective review of results.

◆ It should publish a clear statement of identified impacts with an indication of their significance (especially if any are irreversible).

◆ It should include a declaration of possible alternative development options, including nil-development, and their likely impacts.

◆ Ideally there should be public participation in EIA (often it is partial or avoided).

◆ There should be effective integration of EIA into the planning/legal process.

Source: Part-based on Barrow, 1997: Box 1.1, p. 3

BOX 6.2 The figure below illustrates the typical stepwise EIA process.
Note the idealized steps or phases 0 to 6.

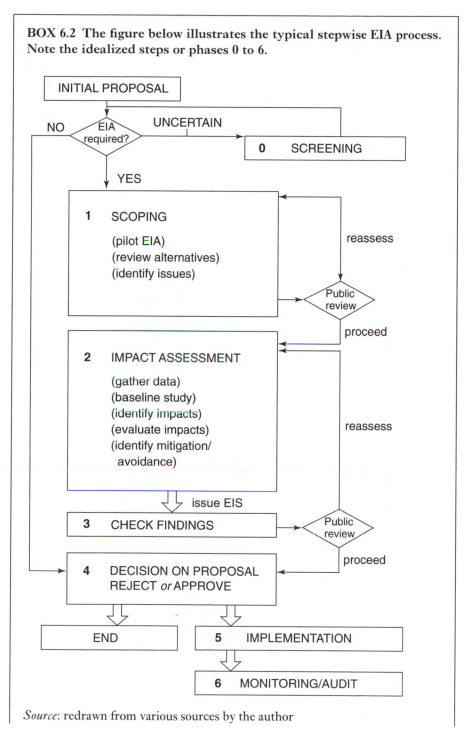

Source: redrawn from various sources by the author

continued . . .

Screening (phase 0) is concerned with deciding which developments require an EIA. This *should* prevent unnecessary assessment, yet ensure that there is no escape when assessment is needed (in practice that is difficult). Screening may not be mandatory in some countries. Note that the term 'environmental assessment' is used for screening in the USA, but in the UK has been applied to EIA. In the USA if environmental assessment/screening (also called *initial environmental evaluation*) indicates no need to proceed to a full EIA a statement of Finding of No Significant Impact (FONSI) is issued publicly, allowing time for objection/appeal before a final decision is arrived at.

Scoping (phase 1) overlaps phase 0 and should help determine the terms of reference for an EIA, the approach, timetable, limits of study, tactics, staffing, etc. By this stage the EIA should consider alternative developments. In practice, a decision as to how to proceed may already have been made by a developer.

Identification, measurement and evaluation of impacts (phase 2) may proceed with or without public review(s). A variety of techniques may be used to determine possible impacts: as human judgement is involved, this is an art rather than a wholly objective scientific process, regardless of the statistics used. The difficulty of identifying indirect and cumulative impacts makes this a tricky and often only partially satisfactory process. This phase is much assisted if an adequate set of baseline data is available – often it is not and extensive desk and field research is needed.

Check findings (phase 3) may follow a public review and/or may involve an independent third party to ensure objectivity. A statement, report, chart or presentation is usually released – effectively the product of an EIA, this is termed the Environmental Impact Statement (EIS) and is what the decision makers, environmental managers (and perhaps public) have to interpret.

Decision on proposal (phase 4): in practice, where a development has already been decided on or is even under way, corrective measures can be perfected. It is a way of passing on hindsight knowledge to planners in the future. The EIS may not be clear or easy to use: some countries require irreversible, dangerous and costly impacts to be clearly shown. It also useful if alternatives and potential benefits are indicated. The environmental manager must be able to read the EIS and identify gaps, weaknesses, limitations. An EIA must not be allowed to give a false sense of security.

Implementation (phase 5): this is where an environmental manager is especially active. Unexpected problems may arise.

Monitoring and audit (phase 6): in practice it is often omitted or is poorly done. If planning and management are to improve, efforts should be made to assess whether the EIA worked well. It is also important to keep on monitoring to catch unexpected developments. Efforts to assess EIA are generally termed Post-EIA Audits. An EIA can easily be a snapshot view and ongoing monitoring or a repeat EIA can help counter that.

By considering goals, realities and available alternatives, it should be possible to identify the *best options* rather than simply acceptable proposals. EIA has tended to flag negative impacts but can also ensure that opportunities are not missed. It is important to stress that EIA should consider all options, including no development/ no change.

By improving understanding of relationships between development and environment and prompting studies, EIA can actively lead to better environmental management. If EIA is to become an integral part of planning, it must be applied before development decisions are made. However, in practice, much is retrospective, initialled after decisions have been made or even after development is under way or completed. This is still of value because it can help clarify problems and add to hindsight knowledge. Nevertheless, if EIA is done after key decisions have been made, it is unlikely to be able to force a change of plan to less damaging options. At worst it may simply be cosmetic – done to try to reduce opposition. Also, while not a blatant cosmetic exercise, EIA is frequently an inflexible and devalued part of a development legitimization process.

The world is facing the possibility of damaging impacts that may be costly or impossible to cure. There should be efforts to avoid them, and an *ad hoc* narrow approach is not enough. EIA can be a powerful tool in the quest for sustainable development, particularly through strategic environmental assessment (see later this

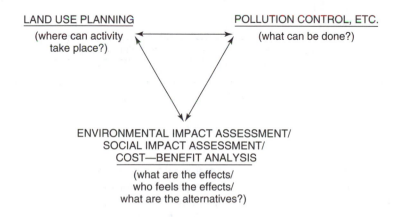

FIGURE 6.1 How impact assessment fits into planning

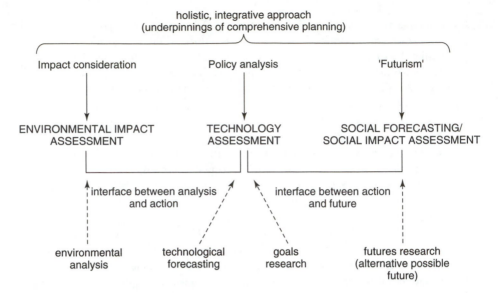

FIGURE 6.2 Relationship of environmental impact assessment (EIA), technology assessment, social forecasting and social impact assessment (SIA)
Source: Adapted from Vlachos (1985: 54, unnumbered figure)

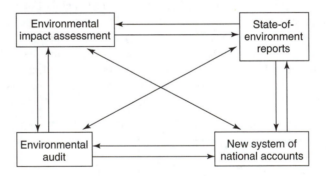

FIGURE 6.3 Relationships, possible exchanges of information and methodologies for environmental impact assessments, environmental audits, new systems of national accounts and state-of-the-environment reports.
Source: Thompson and Wilson (1994: 612, Fig. 5)

chapter). What is needed is integration of environmental and development planning – and EIA may help bring about this integration (Jacobs and Saddler, 1989; Dalal-Clayton, 1992; D. Pritchard, 1993). Environmental managers must cope with uncertainty, and err on the side of caution, following the precautionary principle, which means where there are threats of serious or irreversible environmental changes, lack of full scientific certainty should not be used as a reason for postponing measures to prevent environmental degradation (Dovers and Handmer, 1995: 92). The 1992 Earth Summit stressed the value of impact assessment – 17 of its 27 principal declarations deal with some aspect of EIA.

EIA should be more widely used early in planning and needs to be improved to consider more effectively indirect and cumulative impacts (Gardiner 1989; Jacobs and Sadler, 1989; Anon, 1990; Jenkins, 1991; Wallington *et al.*, 1994). A cumulative impact is the consequence of more than one direct or indirect impact acting together. Such impacts can be very difficult to predict. An indirect impact is the result of a second, third or subsequent impact in a chain of causation in space and/or time. A number of direct or indirect impacts could combine to pose a cumulative impact. Chemical and biological timebombs are insidious forms of cumulative impact: a chemical accumulates, or a biological process continues, without causing a problem, perhaps without being apparent, until a threshold is suddenly exceeded, either through continued accumulation or activity, or because some environmental or socioeconomic change(s) triggers it (Stigliani *et al.*, 1991). For example, pesticide gradually accumulating in the soil may suddenly be flushed out when acid deposition brings soil chemistry to a threshold; another example might be the insidious accumulation of a chemical in the environment which suddenly reaches a threshold where it triggers infertility in a species. One vital role of environmental management is to recognize threats and warn if thresholds are approached.

The development of EIA

Nothing quite like EIA appeared before 1967, although the *Report of the Volta Preparatory Commission* (HMSO, 1956a; 1956b) was a proactive development assessment. Countries like the UK and France have made use of commissions of inquiry to assess impacts and, to some extent, to keep the public informed since the sixteenth century or earlier. However, these generally took a good deal of time to deliver results, and were applied in an *ad hoc* manner only to some developments, in response to ministerial or popular concern. Their involvement of the public is in a very limited or controlled way, and they are not as systematic as EIA (an example of a UK commission of inquiry which had public meetings is the early 1970s Roskill Commission on the Third London Airport (HMSO, 1971). McHarg's (1969) *Design with Nature* stressed the value of anticipatory and systematic consideration of environmental limits, development impacts and alternatives, and is seen as a forerunner of EIA. White also came close to proposing EIA in the 1960s (White, 1968). The first true EIA was probably in 1967, investigating copper mining in Puerto Rico (Mayda, 1993; Gilpin, 1995: 115). EIA evolved from land use planning, CBA, multiple objective analysis, modelling and simulation, and was established by the 1969 USA National Environmental Policy Act (NEPA) (Flamm, 1973; Ditton and Goodale, 1974: 145–151) (Box 6.3). NEPA has not been the only EIA initiative in the USA (16 states, plus the District of Columbia, had passed similar laws by 1991) but it was the most crucial (Canter, 1996: 20).

BOX 6.3 The 1969 US National Environmental Policy Act

President Theodore Roosevelt called for foresight in respect to pollution control during his 1908 Conference on Conservation, but it was not until 1969 that effective legislation was enacted. Preparations leading to the National Environmental Policy Act (NEPA) began in the early 1960s, when the need was perceived for the USA to have a declaration of national environmental policy and an action-forcing provision (Ditton and Goodale, 1974; Canter, 1996: 1–35). Before NEPA the USA had little effective federal control over the environment and lacked land use regulations which countries like the UK or France had (Wood, 1995: 16). NEPA became Law on 1 January 1970.

It was designed to reform federal policy making with the intent to influence the private sector – the hope being to transform and reorientate values (Heer and Hagerty, 1977; Caldwell, 1989). Originally it was intended that NEPA would change the nature of federal decision making. However, over the years it has become more of a procedural requirement (Wood, 1995: 75).

NEPA required an EIA prior to approval of federally funded projects that 'significantly' affected the environment – a message to federal officials to 'look before they leap' (Cheremisinoff and Morresi, 1977). NEPA Section 101 set regulations to protect the environment, Section 102(2) (c) ensured that they were pursued, and Section 103 included provision for inadequate EIA statements to be challenged in court (see chapter 3) (Wathern, 1988: 24; Hildebrand and Cannon, 1993). US federal agencies are required to prepare an environmental impact statement (EIS) (bearing the costs against taxes and sending copies to federal and state agencies and to the public) using EIA, *prior* to taking action (for a list of the federal agencies involved see Corwin *et al.*, 1975: 41). There was also some need to clarify what developments required assessment and how it was to be conducted.

There were three main elements in NEPA:

1   NEPA announced a US national policy for the environment.
2   It outlined procedures for achieving the objectives of that policy.
3   Provision was made for initiating the establishment of a US Council on Environmental Quality (CEQ) which was to advise the US President on the environment, review the EIA process, review draft EISs and see that NEPA was followed (i.e. recommendations and co-ordination). The CEQ effectively administers EIA legislation in the USA and issues the regulations that ensure effective EISs are produced.

Also in 1970 the US Government created the US Environmental Protection Agency (EPA), its role to co-ordinate the attack on environmental pollution and to be responsible for the EIA process (the EPA is in effect 'overseer'of impact assessment in the USA).

NEPA created a more systematic, product-driven process of environ-mentally-informed decision making. This was the first time US Law had really allowed for development to be delayed or abandoned for the long-term good of the environment. Efforts were also made to co-ordinate public, state, federal and local activities. Overall, it was a revolution in values in a country where state intrusion was anathema – for this reason many see it as a sort of Magna Carta, although it stopped short of making a healthy environment a constitutional right, and some have been seeking to change that (Yost, 1990).

NEPA is statutory law, i.e., it was written after deliberation and did not evolve from custom, practice or tradition. Consequently, like a charter, it was not perfect.

By the late 1980s some of the initial weaknesses had been overcome and at least 30 other countries had adopted similar procedures (Manheim, 1994). Bodies like the Canadian Environmental Assessment Research Council and the International Association for Impact Analysis deserve credit for spreading and developing impact assessment. The results have been mixed: in some countries satisfactory, in others the NEPA approach is socioeconomically and culturally inappropriate and needs further adaptation.

What was new about EIA when it spread after 1970 was its systematic assessment and presentation of predicted impacts, available alternatives and mitigation possibilities. EIA evolved in an era dominated by a technocratic perspective on problem solving and with an emphasis on biophysical impacts. This may help explain why SIA has received less support, although activities similar to SIA pre-date EIA. NEPA was improved in 1971, 1973, 1976, 1977, and in 1978 the Council on Environmental Quality (CEQ) was established to give NEPA regulations more force. Although it had issued EIA guidelines in 1974, the US Agency for International Development (USAID) failed to apply them strongly enough. In 1975 a US public-interest group sued to force it to prepare EISs on its grants and loans. Consequently, by 1976 USAID and other bodies, notably lending banks and the USA State Department, were applying EIA to overseas investments and aid. In 1979 the Foreign Assistance Act effectively extended NEPA to the USA's foreign activities. By the 1980s there were calls for further reform, including better incorporation of social impacts into EIA procedures, and for NEPA to be more strongly written into the US Constitution (something yet to happen) (Renwick, 1988). Attempts to amend NEPA in 1990 to increase its overseas application to global change, biodiversity loss and transboundary pollution has had limited effect.

By 1995, about half the world's governments required EIA in some form (Robinson, 1992). Adoption has usually involved modification of techniques and pro-cedures, because US experience may not be sufficiently relevant, and approaches and techniques are constantly evolving. The quality of impact assessment varies greatly (Coenen, 1993; McCormick, 1993). So far, the greatest progress has probably been made in Australia, Canada, The Netherlands, Sweden, Norway and the USA (Prasad, 1993).

There are a number of ways EIA can be adopted:

◆ Adapt existing planning procedures to incorporate it (as in Germany, Sweden, Denmark, UK).
◆ Create impact assessment legislation, like the USA, Australia and Canada.
◆ Develop global impact assessment regulations and supportive institutions.

Global and transboundary impact assessment

Even though there were few binding agreements reached at Rio in 1992, nor much funding made available, the Earth Summit made clear that global and transboundary impact assessment were important. So far, attention has mainly focused on predicting impacts of global warming, ozone damage, world trade developments and structural adjustment policies. Less attention has been given to the impacts of soil degradation, ocean and atmospheric pollution, and loss of biodiversity, though these are very real threats (Barrow, 1997: 172–225).

In 1991 the UN Economic Commission for Europe (UNECE) launched the Convention on Environmental Impact Assessment in a Transboundary Context at Espoo, Finland (signed by 28 countries, including the USA and the European Community). This Espoo Convention was the first multilateral treaty on trans-boundary rights relating to *proposed activities* (at the time of writing it had yet to be fully adopted by the signatories). The Convention provides for the notification of all affected parties likely to suffer an adverse transboundary impact from a proposed development. Signatories also undertake to give equal rights concerning impact assessment to all affected by a development. Even if they are citizens of different countries, they can therefore be represented in the developer nation's public inquiries, etc. The EC Environmental Assessment Directive (85/337EEC of 1985) makes similar but less wide-ranging provisions, which permit affected parties to participate in the developer's impact assessment if they so wish (Jorissen and Coenen, 1992). This directive goes beyond making provisions for project-level impact assessment to encourage programme- and policy-level assessments. This is effectively strategic environmental assessment (SEA) (see later this chapter) and offers a promising route to EIA able to deal with transboundary impacts (Therivel *et al.*, 1992: 131).

Social impact assessment

Social impact assessment (SIA) seeks to assess whether a proposed development alters quality of life and sense of well-being, and how well individuals, groups and communities adapt to change caused by development (for an introduction and bibliographies see Vanclay and Bronstein, 1995; Barrow, 1997: 226–259). EIA and SIA deal with opposite ends of the same spectrum and overlap (some also recognize cultural impact assessment, concerned with effects on archaeological remains, holy places, traditions, etc.). Freudenburg (1986: 452) saw mainstream SIA as part social science, part policy making, part environmental sociology. SIA often uses qualitative data and may deal with more intangibles than EIA, and consequently it has attracted the criticism that it is 'soft' and imprecise. Yet qualitative data, provided they are objectively gathered, can be as valuable as quantitative data for many purposes. Some of the issues SIA deals with are difficult to quantify: for example, sense of belonging, community cohesion (maintenance of functional and effective ties between a group), lifestyle, feelings of security, local pride, perception of threats and opportunities. However, these are things an environmental manager needs to know about.

According to Burdge and Vanclay (1996: 59), social impacts are alterations in the ways in which people live, work, play, relate to one another, organize to meet their needs, and generally cope as members of a society (and involve lifestyle, community cohesion, mental health, etc.); while cultural impacts involve changes to the norms, values and beliefs of individuals that guide and rationalize their cognition of themselves and their society. SIA and cultural impact assessment consider how a proposed or actual activity affects way of life and attitudes. One may argue that socioeconomic and biophysical aspects of the environment are so interconnected that impact assessment should not treat them separately. This is not a universally held view, and such a holistic total impact assessment is more of a goal than reality. Yet often there is no distinct division between the EIA and SIA.

Social scientists and social historians were studying social impacts long before EIA and SIA appeared, but the emphasis was almost always on retrospective analysis. It is the focus on prediction, planning and decision making which separates SIA from other fields of social research, which tend to concentrate on causal analysis.

The first use of the term 'SIA' was probably in 1973 in connection with the impact of the Trans-Alaska Pipeline on the Inuit People (Burdge, 1994). In general SIA has remained underfunded and neglected compared with EIA, although attention in the USA increased following the CEQ's 1978 requirement that NEPA direct more attention to assessing socioeconomic as well as physical impacts. Various disasters around the world prompted the demand for SIA. The Three Mile Island incident (a US nuclear facility which suffered a near-meltdown that necessitated evacuation of householders in 1983) is seen by many as a landmark event because it was forced to use SIA to assess threats and public fears before re-starting the reactor (Moss and Stills, 1981; Freudenburg, 1986: 454; Llewellyn and Freudenburg, 1989). The US Federal Highways Administration and the US Army Corps of Engineers have been active in developing SIA (mainly in relation to road developments); there has also been considerable activity in New Zealand from the early 1970s – prompted by the Environmental Protection and Enhancement Procedures (1973), the Town and Country Planning Act (1977) and the Resource Management Bill (1989). New Zealand had a Social Impact Assessment Working Group, established to develop and promote SIA by 1984 (and in 1990 an SIA Association was formed). It is probably fair to say that up to the late 1980s there had been less interest in SIA in Europe than the USA or Canada (for example, the physical effects of the Chernobyl disaster received attention but, apart from health impacts, the socioeconomic effects had much less).

Methods and techniques used by SIA originate from a wide range of disciplines: social welfare, sociology, behavioural geography, social psychology, social anthropology, etc. This diversity, the complexity of SIA, and the relative lack of funding, have resulted in its becoming less standardized than EIA and it has spread more slowly.

In addition to claiming that it is imprecise, critics of SIA argue it is too theoretical; too descriptive (rather than analytical and explanatory); weak at prediction; *ad hoc*; mainly applied at the local scale; likely to delay development (causing 'paralysis by analysis'). Another criticism is that few of the theories it uses are tightly defined so it is difficult to make comparisons between successive studies. Nevertheless, Burdge and Vanclay (1996) were of the opinion that its definition and process had been clarified, and that much progress had been made, although it needed to be better integrated with the development process.

SIA can help ensure that projects, programmes and policies generate few or no socioeconomic problems. SIA can guide the management of social change in advance of the implementation of proposed developments, and has the potential to bring together various disciplines and types of decision-maker (Soderstrom, 1981: v).

The socioeconomic component of the environment differs from the biophysical in that it can react in anticipation of change; it can also be adapted if an adequate planning process is in place. It is also different in that reactions can be more fickle, because individuals or groups in a population are more often than not inconstant in response. There may also be difference in timing as well as degree of impact on various sections of society, some of which may be especially vulnerable. For example: property owners will probably react differently from non-property owners. As with EIA, different socioeconomic or sociocultural impacts may be generated at various stages in a policy, programme or project cycle, for example: during construction, when the facility is functioning, and after it is closed down – too narrow a temporal focus and SIA may miss impacts (Gramling and Freudenburg, 1992). Spatially it is also important to adopt a wide enough view, as social impacts may be felt at the individual, family, community, regional, national, or international level (or more than one level), not necessarily at the same time. Like EIA, SIA has been applied more at project rather than programme, plan or policy level. The crucial thing is that SIA, like EIA, should identify undesirable and irreversible impacts.

Methods used by SIA include: social surveys; questionnaires; interviews; use of available statistics such as census data, nutritional status data, findings from public hearings; operations research; systems analysis; social cost–benefit analysis; the Delphi technique (see later); marketing and consumer information; field research by social scientists, etc. Behavioural psychologists are often involved in SIA to ascertain things like: likely reactions, whether stress has been or will be suffered, what constitutes a sense of well-being, etc. The SIA equivalent of an EIA baseline study is the preparation of a social profile to establish what might be changed and what would probably happen if no development took place. Field research techniques can be divided into direct and indirect. Direct observation of human behaviour may be open or discreet (an example of the latter is the use of street videocameras), conducted during normal times or times of stress. Indirect observation includes study of: changes in social indicators, patterns of trampling, telephone enquiries directed at selected members of the public, historical records, property prices, suicide rates, etc.

Communities are a unit which can be monitored for changes using demographic, employment and human well-being data, so SIA often adopts a community focus. Alternatively, especially when aid donors commission an SIA, the focus is on target groups, typically the people(s) investment is supposed to help. An issues–oriented approach is another possibility, or a regional approach, or it is possible to make use of rapid rural appraisal and participatory rural appraisal methods (Gow, 1990). Given the complexity of identifying and assessing direct socioeconomic impacts, it is not surprising that much less progress has been made with cumulative impact assessment than is the case with EIA.

There are many variables of interest to SIA, including:

◆ assessment of who benefits and who suffers – locals, region, developer, urban elites, multinational company shareholders;
◆ assessment of the consequences of development actions on community structure, institutions, infrastructure;
◆ prediction of changes in behaviour of the various groups in a society or societies to be affected;
◆ prediction of changes in established social control mechanisms;
◆ prediction of alterations in behaviour, attitude, local norms and values, equity, psychological environment, social processes, activities;
◆ assessment of demographic impacts;
◆ assessment of whether there will be reduced or enhanced employment and other opportunities;
◆ prediction of alterations in mutual support patterns (coping strategies);
◆ assessment of mental and physical health impacts;
◆ gender impact assessment – a process which seeks to establish what effect development will have on gender relations in society.

The quest for sustainable development involves trade–offs that have adverse social and economic impacts, so it is desirable these are forecast and avoided. It is also vital to assess whether there are any social institutions or movements which could support or hinder sustainable development. Without supportive social institutions, sustainable development will probably fail. SIA can help develop these (Ruivenkamp, 1987; Hindmarsh, 1990).

Sometimes a multidisciplinary team deals with both EIA and SIA, or there may be separate specialists, or SIA is a modest sub-component of EIA or environmental auditing. Whichever is selected, SIA should be conducted by competent, professional social scientists. SIA has been most applied to road construction; boom towns; large projects; voluntary relocatees or refugees; and tourism development. Environmental management should make more use of SIA than is currently the case.

Strategic environmental assessment

Impact assessment should be better integrated into policy making, planning and administration (Htun, 1990; Hare, 1991; Jenkins, 1991; Pearce, 1992; Van Pelt, 1993:

99; Slocombe, 1993; Bowyer, 1994; Ortolano and Shepard, 1995: 16). Strategic environmental assessment (SEA) offers means of viewing and co-ordinating development from policy and programme levels down to project level through a tiered approach (Hill *et al.*, 1994; Sadler, 1994).

Assessing the potential for development and impacts of development: approaches other than EIA and SIA

Ecological impact assessment

This considers how organisms, rather than people, will be affected by activities (Westman, 1985: 86; Duinker, 1989). Recently the expression has been applied to the description and evaluation of the ecological baseline used by EIA. More accurately, ecological impact assessment is concerned with establishing the state of the environment, whereas EIA focuses on predicted and actual effects of change. Treweek (1995a; 1995b) has reviewed ecological impact assessment and reported it was a valuable support for EIA. An aspect of ecological impact assessment which is growing in importance is its application to biodiversity loss (Hirsch, 1993).

Ecological impact assessment may rely on selected ecosystem components as indicators or on ecosystem modelling. Ecosystem function can be complex and often is poorly understood, making accurate assessment difficult.

Habitat evaluation

Habitat evaluation seeks to assess the suitability of an ecosystem for a species or the impact of development on a habitat (Suter, 1993: 8). There may be more than one habitat affected by a development, in which case each is dealt with separately. This approach has been used by the US Fish and Wildlife Service, in assessments of the impacts of US federal water resource development projects, and by the US Army Corps of Engineers (Canter, 1996: 390).

Land use planning, land classification, land appraisal, land capability assessment, land suitability assessment, land evaluation and terrain evaluation

Land use planning is a process which may operate at local, regional or national scale; land capability assessment, land appraisal, land evaluation, land suitability assessment and terrain evaluation feed into that process. A land use survey indicates the situation at the time of study, and is not the same as a capability classification, which looks to the future. There are various approaches and methods for land use classification, e.g. the Ecological Series Classification or the Holdridge Life Zones System. Often the land use planning approach adopted depends on a country's politics. It is widely felt that land use planning is a valuable ingredient of EIA and in the quest for sustainable development and that EIA can feed into land use planning. In practice the two are often poorly integrated.

Land capability assessment, land evaluation and land appraisal generally follow a proactive approach similar to that of EIA (scoping, data collection, evaluation, presentation of decision) in the production of a land capability classification or land evaluation (Beek, 1978; Patricos, 1986). Some approaches consider a range of factors, which might include the concept of carrying capacity, others just soil characteristics and slope. The end product is a description of landscape units in terms of inherent capacity to produce a combination of plants, animals, etc.; it is also likely to reflect government development goals, market opportunities, labour availability and public demands (e.g. terraced agriculture may be possible but labour is not available).

Simple inventories of land use and, to a limited extent, capability were made in medieval times – notably the Domesday Book. Modern land capability classification was developed by the US Soil Conservation Service in the 1930s in response to problems like the US Dust Bowl. Linked to consideration of conservation and development, land capability classification can lead to a land suitability assessment (a rating of landscape units showing what development they might best support). Land suitability assessment may depend on overlay maps of various landscape or development attributes, or direct field observation of clues (something local people may traditionally do) – e.g. seek distinctive plants indicative of good soil. Geographical information systems (GIS) and remote sensing are increasingly applied to land capability assessment.

Universal Soil Loss Equation

The Universal Soil Loss Equation (USLE) is a predictive tool which uses data on a wide range of parameters to estimate and predict average annual soil loss. It was developed in the 1930s by the US Soil Conservation Service and was improved in 1954 and again in 1978 by the US Department of Agriculture. It is widely used by planners and consultants to check on existing and likely future soil loss and to select appropriate agricultural practices and crops to sustain production. Developed in midwestern USA, it has been modified to make it suitable for other environments, so there are numerous revised versions (Hudson, 1981: 258). The USLE should be used with caution: problems arise when data are imprecise or unavailable and it is best applied in situations where water rather than wind erosion occurs (although there are modified versions intended to cope with wind erosion). A typical form of the USLE is:

$$A = (0.224)\,RKLSCP$$

where:

A = soil loss;
R = rainfall erosivity factor (degree to which rainfall can erode soil);
K = soil erodability factor (soil vulnerability to erosion);

L = slope length factor;
S = slope gradient factor;
C = cropping management factor (what is grown and how);
P = erosion control practice factor.

Agroecosystem assessment

The agroecosystem zones concept was promoted by the FAO (1978) to provide a framework for considering a range of parameters over a limited planning term with the aim of promoting sustainable development. An agroecosystem is an ecological system modified by humans to produce food or commodities, which generally means a reduction in diversity of wildlife. Agroecosystem assessment (or analysis) evolved in Thailand and attempts rapid multidisciplinary diagnosis that includes ecological and socioeconomic concepts and parameters (Conway and Barbier, 1990: 162–193). It considers not only the farming system but also household characteristics, regional, national, even global factors likely to affect the local community. The area under consideration is zoned – often making use of a land use survey or land capability assessment. Agroecosystem assessment needs to be approached with some caution because it can lead to over-simple interpretation.

Farming systems research (FSR) is an open-ended, iterative, multidisciplinary, holistic, continuous, farmer-centred, dynamic process applied to agricultural research and development (it considers biophysical, social and economic factors and seeks to integrate their study) (Shaner *et al.*, 1982; Brush, 1986: 221). There is no single method but all approaches share five basic steps (Maxwell, 1986):

1   Classification – the identification of homogeneous groups ('target groups') of farmers.
2   Diagnosis – identification of limiting factors, opportunities, threats, etc. , for the target group.
3   Generation of recommendations – which may require field experiments, pilot studies and/or research station work.
4   Implementation – usually working with an agricultural extension service.
5   Evaluation – which may lead to revision of what is being done.

FSR is a systems approach applied to on-farm research, and is promoted as a way of increasing farmer participation in development, and of generating improved and appropriate approaches and technology. FSR includes study of factors which may be beyond control of the farming community – world trade issues, global warming, etc. Unless some 'off-the-shelf' input is available, FSR usually takes time – often two years, sometimes from five to 15 or more years.

Participatory assessment: rapid rural appraisal, participatory rural appraisal and rapid urban appraisal

There is considerable overlap between agroecosystem assessment, FSR and participatory assessment approaches. The latter place more stress on participation (by the local people or target group). Participatory assessment can be defined as qualitative research or survey work which seeks to get an in-depth understanding of a community or situation. Some impact assessment experts are promoting forms of participatory impact assessment and monitoring (Yar, 1990).

Rapid rural appraisal (RRA) is a family of approaches mainly focused on land capability assessment, which seek to incorporate (or involve) local people in the process and to reduce the time and costs of preparation. It is a systematic, semi-structured activity carried out in the field by a multidisciplinary team and designed to quickly acquire new information on, and new hypotheses about, rural life. RRA has rapidly evolved since the late 1970s and there is no single standardized methodology – for an introduction see *Agricultural Administration* vol. 8(6), special issue (1981); *IDS Bulletin* vol. 12(4), special issue (1991); Conway and McCracken, 1990; Chambers, 1992). A central thesis of RRA is 'optimal ignorance', the idea that the amount of information required should be kept to the necessary minimum (something some EIA practitioners should also bear in mind). Another central thesis is 'diversity of analysis' – the use of different sources of data or means of data gathering, and a range of experts, if possible, familiar with every aspect of rural life.

RRA, according to Conway and Barbier (1990: 177–178) is: iterative (i.e. processes and goals are not fixed and can be modified as an exercise progresses); innovative (it is adapted to suit needs); interactive (team members work to get interdisciplinary insight); informal (it often relies on informal interviews); and in contact with the community. RRA can be of variable character: exploratory – like agroecosystem analysis it seeks information on a new rural topic or agroecosystem; topical – with a specific output expected, often a hypothesis that can be a basis for research or development.

Participatory rural appraisal (PRA) approaches seek to enable local people to share, enhance and assess their knowledge of life and conditions, to plan and to act. PRA differs from RRA, in that the latter extracts information, whereas the former shares it and seeks rapport. Multidisciplinary-team studies and a stress on participatory public involvement also offer possibilities for better conduct of EIA. However, there has been a tendency to emphasize the strengths of RRA and PRA and understate the problems which might be encountered. Sometimes 'rapid' seems to refer to the speed of the assessors' fieldwork, rather than an approach designed to give useful results fast.

Rapid urban environmental assessment has been reviewed by Leitmann (1993). Given the tremendous growth of cities, and the misery and environmental damage this can cause, it is strange that rapid urban environmental assessment has been so little applied.

Predicting future scenarios

Forecasting and futures evaluation

Forecasting is an essential part of planning, programme and policy formulation. Forms of forecasting have been used by many peoples from prehistoric times to decide when, where and what to hunt, where to settle, to make agricultural decisions, embark on migrations or warfare, etc.

Since roughly the mid-eighteenth century western societies have based forecasting from rational observation, projection of trends and hindsight knowledge (Fortlage, 1990: 1).

By the 1930s in Europe, the USSR and the USA post- and in-project assessments of development were being conducted, and cautionary guidebooks, checklists, procedural manuals and planning regulations (and, in the UK, occasional public inquiries) were in use to improve decision making (Caldwell, 1989).

The banking, investment and insurance industries had developed hazard and risk assessment methods by the 1940s, and military tacticians were trying to predict war scenarios during the Second World War and the Cold War.

Environmental modelling, futures modelling and futures research

Models are used to understand complex situations, predict future scenarios, and assess the impacts of a wide range of developments such as: altered land use, effluent discharges, global climatic change, modification of river channels, estuarine conditions, coastal erosion, agricultural chemicals impacts, acid deposition, etc. Models include physical models (e.g. laboratory tests, scale models of estuaries or catchments), statistical models (e.g. principal components analysis), computer models, systems models (for a review of ecosystem models used for environmental management see Jorgensen and Goda, 1986; for a handbook see Jorgensen *et al.*, 1996).

Futures research makes use of modelling, e.g. for trend extrapolation and informed speculation. Futures modelling, futures research and 'futurology' attracted attention in the early 1970s following the publication of *The Limits to Growth* (Meadows *et al.*, 1972). A sequel reviewing how accurate the warnings had been appeared at the time of the 1992 Earth Summit (Meadows *et al.*, 1992).

Futures research is difficult and imprecise. It has to allow for both gradual and sudden changes that are due to new inventions, attitude changes, environmental alterations, and so on (Westman, 1985: 3). The further ahead one attempts to make predictions, the less accurate they are likely to be. The results of futures research are useful, but must be treated with caution.

Delphi technique

The Delphi technique was developed by the RAND Corporation in the late 1940s to try to obtain a reliable consensus of opinion about future developments from multidisciplinary panels of experts (Stouth *et al.*, 1993). These panel evaluations were used for Cold War purposes, and little was published for a decade until a report by Gordon and Helmer (1964). The approach is for expert assessors to be asked their views without communicating with each other. These are pooled, evaluated, and the assessors are allowed to see the result as a controlled feedback, and are given the chance to modify their opinions which are again fed back (a Gestalt approach); the feedback–pooled response process may be repeated three or more times to produce the final conclusions. The approach ensures anonymity for the assessors to prevent peer pressure or intimidation influencing results; and the controlled feedback helps to achieve a group viewpoint and an aggregate judgement.

The Delphi technique has been used in futures research on healthcare policy and innovations, gambling, tourism, marketing, management studies, resources allocation, technology innovation studies and war-games. The Environmental Evaluation Systems approach to EIA uses the Delphi technique; and the cross-impact matrix EIA approach has also been developed from it (Soderstrom, 1981: 20).

It is useful for short-range and for longer-range (over 15 years into the future) forecasting, especially if high degrees of uncertainty are involved and where there is a need to predict impacts on culture. The results are, of course, subjective and qualitative. Impact assessment asks what impacts may occur; the Delphi technique asks about the likelihood and date some impact will happen – it can thus complement impact assessment. It has become much easier to run with modern computers and may be done through a communications network such as the Internet, or even by mail without the need to gather expert assessors in one place. However, it can be slow.

Assessments of the technique suggest it is a valuable approach but one that has often been poorly applied. Careful selection of the experts is crucial to avoid gaps or bias, and it is also important to ensure that the questions they are asked are not too limited or their expertise could be constrained and lost. Bias can be introduced if assessors are allowed to suggest other assessors.

Hazard and risk assessment

The importance of hazard assessment and risk assessment hardly needs stressing in the wake of accidents like Seveso, Love Canal, Three Mile Island, Bhopal and Chernobyl, or natural disasters like floods or earthquakes.

Hazard assessment

A hazard is a *perceived* event or source of danger which threatens life or property or both. A disaster is the realization of a hazard (a catastrophe is a particularly serious disaster). Hazard assessment may be said to seek to recognize things which give rise to concern (Clark *et al.*, 1984: 501). Hazard assessment tends to deal with natural hazards: flood, storm, tsunami, locust swarm, etc. Human activities also pose threats (e.g. crime or technological innovation), and may initiate natural hazards and alter the vulnerability of the environment, wildlife or humans to them. Some people therefore divide hazards into into natural, quasi-natural and man-made.

One difficult problem faced by hazard or risk assessment, and to some extent EIA, is assessing what is 'acceptable'. Various groups, even within one society, may perceive and evaluate hazards and risks differently and often vary in their vulnerability. The perception of risk is often not based on rational judgements: people have gut reactions to or dread of certain things and little fear of other, perhaps more real, threats. There are likely to be different risk perceptions from class to class, age-group to age-group, and for different religions and sexes: much depends on previous exposure or awareness through the media (Douglas and Wildavsky, 1990; Krimsky and Goulding, 1992). Perception also varies from individual to individual, and for any given group through time – e.g. a youthful person may be more tolerant of risk than someone older; and the poor face and have to accept more risks. In general, people are more concerned about the short term rather than the long term, and by 'concentrated' hazards – an air crash which kills 300 rather than the same number of fatalities from household accidents dispersed over a country, or in time. Some risks tend to get more attention (e.g. radiation hazards compared with traffic accidents). If people think they are in control, as car drivers for example, they are probably less worried than as passengers in a train. Perception can be greatly affected by media and myth, and faced with a hazard or risk people's responses are diverse.

Risk and hazard perception has generated a growing literature from behavioural psychologists, health and safety specialists, anthropologists and specialist risk or hazard assessors. The assessor can categorize hazard or risk according to criteria like: minor/severe; infrequent/frequent; localized/widespread, and may resort to estimating the value of a life to weigh against risk probability and risk avoidance costs (the Bhopal tragedy in India raised the question of higher life valuations awarded to citizens of rich nations). Involvement of the public in risk and hazard assessment can pose problems: predictions may involve companies that wish to avoid giving away the fruits of their experience or research, or a government that wants secrecy concerning strategic information or activity they prefer the public or factions (e.g. terrorists) not to know about.

Risk assessment

One can define risk as the expression of the chance or probability of a danger or hazard taking place, and risk assessment as going beyond predicting probability to identifying objectively the frequency, likelihood, causes, extent and severity of exposure of people or things or activities. Put simply, risk is 'probability x consequence' (Suter, 1993). Risk assessment (appraisal or analysis) is a loose term – it considers hazard and vulnerability: how people react to risk and their pattern of exposure. Risk assessment has been defined as 'the process of assigning magnitudes and probabilities to the adverse effects of human activities (including technical innovation) or natural catastrophes' (P. Pritchard, 1993). It involves identifying hazards; estimating the probability of their occurrence; evaluating the consequences; using these findings to assess risk; presenting the conclusions, ideally with some indication of reliability of estimate. Hazard assessment and risk assessment are not precise arts: different assessments may assign different predictions to a risk. In the end the environmental manager must exercise judgement.

Risk assessment may go on to identify coping strategies or establish what people will pay to avoid a risk. Some recognize risk appraisal as the assessment of communities' attitudes to risks. Risk assessment can be divided into that concerned with risks to the environment or biota and that concerned with risks to humans. Risk assessment typically consists of risk identification, risk estimation (establishment of nature and levels) and risk evaluation (assessment of probability of occurrence, consequences, etc.) (P. Pritchard, 1993). Risk assessment studies effects, pathways or factors involved (e.g. laboratory experiments into toxicity). Often, risk assessment involves weighing dangers against benefits (e.g. the threat of asbestos-related illness versus its value in protection against fire).

Risk assessment is an analytical tradition, not a legal definition, with centuries-old roots in the actuarial, investment and insurance professions, which has spread to engineering, development of new materials (especially chemicals, pharmaceuticals and biotechnology innovations), economics, healthcare and criminology. Risk assessment may also take the form of screening a new product or activity, to ensure that it is safe for user and environment, before releasing it for general use – i.e. laboratory or test-bed assessments. Insurance companies and bankers need to know risks before providing cover or loans. Administrators use risk assessment to reduce the likelihood that they could be accused of negligence if something goes wrong and for contingency planning.

According to Suter (1993: 3), risk assessment can provide:

- a quantitative basis from which to compare and prioritize risks;
- a systematic means of improving understanding of risks;
- a means of making assessment more useful and credible by giving probabilities to predicted impacts.

Legislation like the US Toxic Substances Control Act 1976 (which requires regulation if there is a risk to human health or environment through use or release of a harmful chemical or biological agent) or the UK Environment Act 1995 (which requires local authorities to carry out risk assessment and maintain registers of contaminated land) makes it increasingly important for the environmental manager to commission and interpret risk assessments (Asante-Duah, 1998). Separation of 'natural' from 'man-made', industrial or technical hazard assessment, and general risk assessment, is maintained by practitioners and literature rather than reflecting different concepts.

Unlike EIA, risk assessment tends not to address development alternatives, and is at present less likely to be required by government policy or law (also true for technology risk assessment). Risk assessment is often better at estimating magnitude, certainty and timing of impacts than EIA. Risk assessment and hazard assessment are often applied where there is more uncertainty than EIA faces (Covello *et al.*, 1985: 16). Mainstream EIA differs from risk and hazard assessment in that it focuses on impacts caused by human actions (crime risk assessment also does so). EIA can increase planners' accountability to the public; risk assessment is likely to be more concerned with internal management or be applied by a regulatory agency.

Hazard and risk assessment usually use a template (to help order the process) to generate a statistical estimate of probability of occurrence of a certain level of impact (not a forecast but a statistical recurrence, e.g. a 1 in 100 year chance of a serious flood) and use it to produce a zoned map which can be used to determine land use or building regulations, prepare contingency or emergency procedures (e.g. provide hurricane shelters, tsunami protection walls and warning systems). Insurance companies often use risk assessment to determine premiums: for example, mapping risks against postcodes/ZIP codes.

Some threats appear suddenly, others creep up and for these it may be possible to give a warning forecast.

Well-developed areas of risk assessment include: ecological risks, health risks, technological and industrial risks. Like EIA, risk assessment is mainly applied at project level or to a particular process, although it is sometimes used at policy, plan and programme levels.

Environmental risk assessment is a sub-field of risk assessment which seeks to assess risks to the environment resulting from industrial activity and other develop-ments. Ecological risk assessment, another sub-field, seeks to define and quantify risks to non-human biota (i.e. assess the likelihood of adverse change in an ecosystem as a result of human activity). Since 1990 the EPA have promoted it in the USA.

Technology assessment, hazard, risk and impact assessment

Technology assessment (technical evaluation) seeks to establish whether equipment and techniques work. This can include assessment of use impacts to inform decision-making and clarify problems and opportunities (*Impact Assessment Bulletin* vol. 53, special issue, 1987). Technology assessment follows a broadly parallel path to EIA, and may involve evaluation of indirect and cumulative impacts (Kates, 1978; Kates and Hohenemser, 1982). It involves systematic study of the effects on environment and society that occur when a technology is introduced, extended or modified.

Technology assessment was widespread in the USA by 1967, so pre-dates EIA. In 1973 the US Congress created the Office of Technology Assessment to promote and oversee it. An International Society for Technology Assessment operated from the USA in the mid-1970s, developing into the International Association for Impact Assessment (IAIA), a body which promotes EIA, SIA, technology assessment, hazard assessment, risk assessment and related activities. The National Science Foundation in the USA also supports technology assessment, and Europe, Japan, Canada and Austria had established bodies to promote the field by the late 1980s. As well as having a warning function, technology assessment can, like EIA, aid decision making and planning in other ways. It may be initiated by government, international bodies, NGOs or the industries or agencies which plan to innovate.

Technology impacts can be a function of: technology failure; operator failure; poor maintenance; poor design; faulty installation; terrorism; natural or human accident; adaptations prompted by the innovation. Not surprisingly, assessment practitioners are often engineers, so socioeconomic issues may not be well covered. The tendency has been to concentrate on morbidity and mortality – but there is now increasing interest in civil liberties and social aspects of technology innovation. Technology assessment has an important part to play in the quest for sustainable development, identifying threats and promising development paths. (Social impacts of technology innovations are discussed in chapter 8 – e.g. the effects of TV broadcasting innovations.)

Technology risk may be posed by a known potentially dangerous activity like petrochemical processing or by new, untested technology, chemicals, biotechnology and pharmaceuticals (Ricci, 1981: 101). Technological innovation may relate to any aspect of life: attempts to improve agriculture, telecommunications, industry, transport, etc. Industrial hazard and risk assessment examines mainly established manufacturing practices, is less likely to deal with unknowns arising from technical innovation than technology assessment proper. There is increasing interest in using technology assessment to 'tune' new technology, and it is being applied to biotechnology, including genetic engineering. Europe is applying it to long-term strategic policy making and as a means of early warning.

Hazard and risk assessment increasingly demand international co-operation as global change and transboundary impacts from technology also grow because there is a tendency for technological hazard to be 'exported' to countries where laws, monitoring and enforcement may be less stringent and planners and regulators less well informed. Large sums of money may be involved in such exporting, making objective assessment a challenge.

Computers and expert systems

Impact assessment by computer

There have been attempts to computerize impact identification and assessment (see Guariso and Page, 1994; Benoît, 1995: 421–426). Canter (1996: 45) has argued that, as impact assessment gets more complex and laborious, in order to be more holistic and adaptive, computerization becomes more important. Computer techniques have also been used for interpreting impacts (Baumwerd–Ahlmann *et al.*, 1991). The development of better microcomputers and software has made it possible to run impact assessments, expert systems, environmental information systems, and models. There has been interest in integrating EIA, monitoring and GIS through computer use, and in applying computing to SIA (Leistritz *et al.*, 1995). Nevertheless, progress has still been limited by lack of user-friendly programs, and by the relatively low number of impact assessors who are skilled with computers (Guariso and Page, 1994).

The application of computing should be transparent, to reduce the risk of accidental or deliberate errors, unauthorized disclosure, etc. Accidents like the Chernobyl disaster have prompted a number of countries to co-operate and develop joint rapid impact assessment and data exchange systems. These are vital for coping with rapidly developing transboundary problems, like airborne pollution. The European Community has gone partway to developing such a system for radioactive fallout by establishing the EC Urgent Radiological Information Exchange (ECURIE) in 1987.

Expert systems

The expert systems (or 'knowledge-based systems') can be valuable once perfected, as an aid (not replacement) for skilled assessors. However, they may take a lot of research and time to develop (Loehle and Osteen, 1990; Geraghty, 1992; 1993). They are particularly useful when there is a shortage of expertise to conduct assessment and may have potential for improving public involvement (Schibuola and Byer, 1991). They are also used for environmental planning (Wright *et al.*, 1993; Tucker and Richardson, 1995), eco-audit and environmental management (Benoît and Podesto, 1995), and to apply EIA to regional planning (Burde *et al.*, 1994). The approach involves developing a computer program that stores a body of knowledge and with it performs tasks usually done by a human expert – for example, impact or risk assessment. These systems draw on heuristic (rule-of-thumb) reasoning to act as 'advisors', provide support for decision making, or aid data management.

Gray and Stokoe (1988) reviewed the potential and limitations of expert systems for impact assessment and environmental management, one of their hopes being that they could help achieve consistent quality of assessments. Mercer (1995), recognizing that impact assessment increasingly uses qualitative methods of assessment, tried to develop an expert system capable of coping with this.

Adaptive environmental assessment and adaptive environmental assessment and management

Impact assessment generally adopts a static, 'snapshot' approach, yet causal relationships are often not constant, e.g. monetary units may be devalued, the environment may alter, decision-making objectives may change, attitudes of people shift; such an approach can therefore be ineffective. There is also a risk that a one-off impact assessment could discourage planners from adequate monitoring. There is thus a need to ensure that assessment is continuous or repeated regularly (Holling, 1978; Gilmour and Walkerden, 1994). Two approaches have evolved: adaptive environmental assessment (AEA), and adaptive environmental assessment and management (AEAM). These are broader than mainstream EIA, and have a bias towards coping with uncertainty. In addition, AEAM seeks to integrate environmental, social and economic assessment with management.

AEAM was pioneered by Holling and colleagues (Holling, 1978), Environment Canada, the University of British Colombia, Vancouver (Canada), and the Austrian-based International Institute for Applied Systems Analysis (IIASA). The Holling approach was applied to the Obergurgl Valley (Austria), starting in 1974, by a UNESCO (Man and Biosphere Program)/IIASA/University of British Columbia team. It uses a series of carefully designed research periods followed by multi-disciplinary modelling workshops which include science and social science experts, planners, managers, resource users and locals. The workshops develop alternative scenarios and management strategies which are then compared to arrive at the best problem-solving approach. The workshops seek to ensure that the assessment team and participants continually review efforts to predict and model policy options for decision makers, and also provide a bridge for different disciplines and competing perceptions. The end result is a computer-based systems model that can be tested and tuned until it supports adaptive management and can help identify indirect impacts (Jones and Greig, 1985).

AEAM can be useful where baseline data are poor. It also encourages and facilitates multidisciplinary assessment. However, it can be demanding in terms of research expertise and time for completion. Some see AEAM as particularly sup-portive of sustainable development (Grayson et al., 1994).

Integrated impact assessment, comprehensive impact assessment, regional impact assessment, integrated environmental management, strategic environmental assessment and related approaches

The following approaches seek to cover more than just a restricted range of impacts, to do so over more than a snapshot of time, and at wider scales, or up through all project, programme and policy levels (or from local up to international). Some of the approaches seek to cope better with indirect and cumulative impacts than mainstream impact assessment (Nijkamp, 1986).

Integrated impact assessment is a generic term for the study of the full range of ecological and socioeconomic consequences of an action (Lang, 1986; McDonald and Brown 1990). It is difficult to predict the impacts of something if no account is taken of other current and planned developments. It also seeks to promote closer integration of impact assessment into planning, policy making and management, adopting a tiered approach (Parson, 1995).

To assess cumulative impacts a regional impact assessment approach can be an adopted (e.g. where successive tourism developments lead to regional problems or a number of irrigation projects combine to cause difficulties). It is also useful for establishing planning objectives, e.g. the impacts of a new shopping centre (mall) were considered by Norris (1990) using such techniques. It makes sense to assess developments in their spatial setting, rather than in isolation; it also allows the interfacing of planning and environmental management at the regional level and offers possibilities for assessing exogenous impacts on the region. Economists use econometrics and input–output analysis to explore economics and environmental linkages at regional level: for example, the impacts of an irrigation development on a region like Malaysia's Muda Scheme (Bell and Hazel, 1980; Isard, 1972; Bell *et al.*, 1982; Solomon, 1985).

Integrated regional environmental assessment is similar to the approach just discussed, having the following objectives:

♦ To provide a broad, integrated perspective of a region about to undergo or undergoing developments.
♦ To identify cumulative impacts from multiple developments in the region.
♦ To help establish priorities for environmental protection.
♦ To assess policy options.
♦ To identify information gaps and research needs.

There is no single methodology for doing this, and the approach is more difficult than mainstream EIA. A solution might be to subdivide regions into smaller units for assessment (perhaps ecosystems or river basins, although there may be situations where administrative regions offer better possibilities).

Integrated environmental management seeks to reconcile conflicting interests and concerns, minimize negative impacts, and enhance positive results. It is an approach which seeks to integrate impact assessment and evaluation into planning and decision making. For an example of an integrated environmental management procedure (proposed for South Africa), see Sowman *et al.* (1995).

While most EIA and SIA is applied at project level, it is also desirable to assess at programme and policy level, for example to improve:

♦ overseas aid provision;
♦ structural adjustment programmes;
♦ free trade developments;
♦ public transport policies.

It is not easy to find an effective and flexible, integrated approach that can be applied to, say, national energy policy, an industrial development zone, or to an extensive area of scenic value. The greatest promise probably lies with tiered assessments (Lee, 1978; 1982: 73–75; Wood, 1988; Harvey *et al.*, 1995). These adopt a sequential approach with broad assessment at policy level (tier 1), e.g. impact assessment of national road policy; followed by more specific assessment at the programme level (tier 2), e.g. regional road programmes; and even more specific assessment of individual (road) project(s) (tier 3), e.g. local road construction. Efforts are made to cross–reference broad and specific assessments. Events in tier 3 are conditioned by prior events or parallel events in higher tiers, so it is unsatisfactory to look at a lower tier without also considering higher ones (or vice versa). Tiered impact assessment can also adopt a multisectoral approach (horizontal tiers) – if sectors were considered in isolation cumulative impacts might be missed (or a sector might get missed). This requires a holistic approach to avoid missing interactive effects. Tiered impact assessment should acquire data that make subsequent or related impact assessments easier, faster and cheaper to conduct. Tiered impact assessments should complement each other and so avoid the duplication which might otherwise occur. It may be possible with some types of development to do broad impact assessments and dispense with a plethora of individual assessments, e.g. instead of factory-by-factory impact assessment it may be possible to do a single industrial estate assessment. The USA tries to encourage a tiered approach, and in other countries, such as The Netherlands, and more recently Europe as a whole, the trend is towards this.

Impact assessment experience at programme level and policy level is more limited than for project level, but it is growing. Such assessment differs from mainstream project-focused assessments, in that it must allow for the fact that other programmes and policies, cultural and other forces have considerable effect on what is being assessed (projects can usually be studied in relative isolation). To cope with these challenges strategic environmental assessment (SEA) (or programmatic EIA) has been developed. This is a form of tiered, nested, or sequential environmental impact assessment that seeks to provide a framework within which project, programme and policy impact assessment can take place (EIA can be used at the project level, tiered with SEA to link it to programme and policy levels or, as is increasingly the case, SEA is applied to all levels) (Wood, 1992; 1995: 266–288; Buckley, 1994; Partidário, 1996; Therivel, 1993; Therivel and Partidário, 1996; Horton and Memon, 1997; *Project Appraisal* 7(3), 1992 – special issue on strategic environmental assessment) (Figures 6.4 and 6.5).

SEA can be applied:

◆ with a sectoral focus (e.g. to waste disposal, drainage and transport programmes;
◆ with a regional focus (e.g. to regional, rural and national plans);
◆ with an indirect focus (e.g. to technology, fiscal policies, justice and enforcement, sustainable development). SEA can be applied at a higher, earlier, more strategic tier of decision making than project EIA.

Provision for SEA was made by NEPA in 1970 and in California's Environmental Quality Act of 1985, and it is now in use in various countries, including Canada, The Netherlands, the USA (especially California), Germany and New Zealand. The Netherlands has had a statutory SEA system in force since 1987 for waste management, drinking water supply, energy and electricity, and some land use plans, and its formal requirements were strengthened in 1991 under the National Environmental Policy Act. New Zealand has had SEA laws since 1991, under Part V of the Resource Management Act (1995). The EEC and the UK published proposals for SEA in 1991 (although Therivel *et al.*, 1992: 32 note that in the UK poor long-term strategic planning will probably make the adoption of SEA difficult). Since 1995 the EU has been moving towards requiring member states to adopt SEA procedures and the World Bank also supports it.

SEA is useful for site selection and by conducting such a 'higher order' assessment there may be less need for, and less depth required from, component

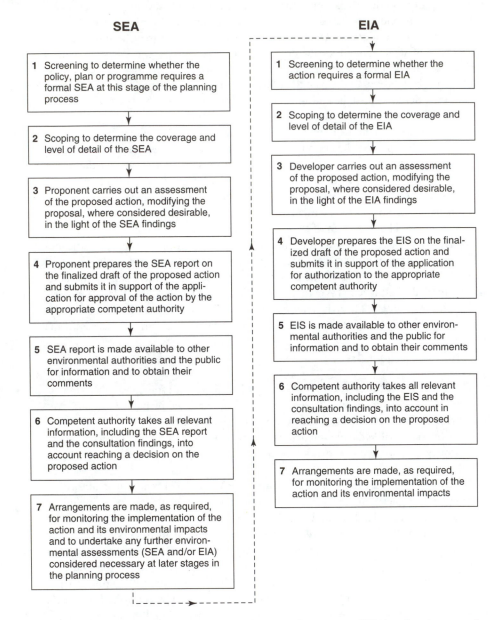

SEA

1　Screening to determine whether the policy, plan or programme requires a formal SEA at this stage of the planning process

2　Scoping to determine the coverage and level of detail of the SEA

3　Proponent carries out an assessment of the proposed action, modifying the proposal, where considered desirable, in the light of the SEA findings

4　Proponent prepares the SEA report on the finalized draft of the proposed action and submits it in support of the application for approval of the action by the appropriate competent authority

5　SEA report is made available to other environmental authorities and the public for information and to obtain their comments

6　Competent authority takes all relevant information, including the SEA report and the consultation findings, into account reaching a decision on the proposed action

7　Arrangements are made, as required, for monitoring the implementation of the action and its environmental impacts and to undertake any further environmental assessments (SEA and/or EIA) considered necessary at later stages in the planning process

EIA

1　Screening to determine whether the action requires a formal EIA

2　Scoping to determine the coverage and level of detail of the EIA

3　Developer carries out an assessment of the proposed action, modifying the proposal, where considered desirable, in the light of the EIA findings

4　Developer prepares the EIS on the finalized draft of the proposed action and submits it in support of the application for authorization to the appropriate competent authority

5　EIS is made available to other environmental authorities and the public for information and to obtain their comments

6　Competent authority takes all relevant information, including the EIS and the consultation findings, into account in reaching a decision on the proposed action

7　Arrangements are made, as required, for monitoring the implementation of the action and its environmental impacts

FIGURE 6.4 A comparison of strategic environmental assessment (SEA) and environmental impact assessment (EIA)

Note: EIS = environmental impact statement

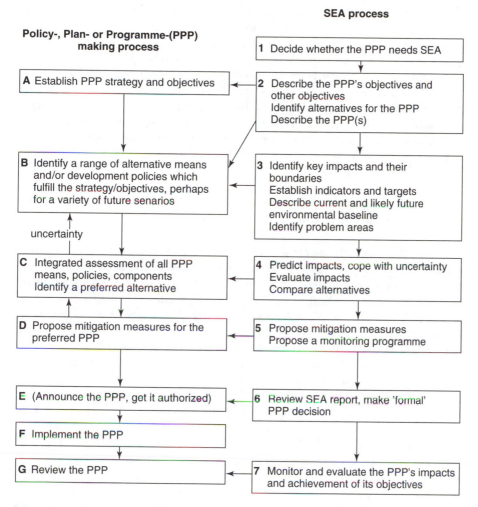

SEA process

Policy-, Plan- or Programme-(PPP) making process

1 Decide whether the PPP needs SEA

A Establish PPP strategy and objectives

2 Describe the PPP's objectives and other objectives
Identify alternatives for the PPP
Describe the PPP(s)

B Identify a range of alternative means and/or development policies which fulfill the strategy/objectives, perhaps for a variety of future senarios

uncertainty

3 Identify key impacts and their boundaries
Establish indicators and targets
Describe current and likely future environmental baseline
Identify problem areas

C Integrated assessment of all PPP means, policies, components
Identify a preferred alternative

4 Predict impacts, cope with uncertainty
Evaluate impacts
Compare alternatives

D Propose mitigation measures for the preferred PPP

5 Propose mitigation measures
Propose a monitoring programme

E (Announce the PPP, get it authorized)

6 Review SEA report, make 'formal' PPP decision

F Implement the PPP

G Review the PPP

7 Monitor and evaluate the PPP's impacts and achievement of its objectives

FIGURE 6.5 Stages in links between policy-, plan- and programme-making and strategic environmental assessment (SEA)
Source: Therival and Partidário (1996: Fig. 1.1)

project EIAs. The SEA approach may cope better with cumulative impacts, assessment of alternatives and mitigation measures than standard EIA. It is claimed that SEA can ensure that EIA is initiated at the correct point in the planning cycle and therefore makes it easier to pursue sustainable development by helping prevent problems that are difficult to reverse. Increasingly SEA is seen as a key approach for implementing the concept of sustainable development, because it allows the principle of sustainability to be carried down from policies to individual projects (Therivel *et al.*, 1992: 22; 126). SEA, at least in principle, can enable countries to work together on transboundary problems (see earlier discussion of transboundary EIA).

SEA is more demanding of data and expertise than mainstream EIA, but this is less of a problem if it overcomes many of the limitations of the latter. A difficulty faced by SEA is that programmes evolve in a subtle way, and at a given moment it may not be easy to see what actually constitutes a programme. Another problem is that policy makers may not want to give potential opponents or competitors a perspective of their strategy, so public involvement is a problem. Methodology is in need of development. SEA must make accurate assessments in spite of often vague proposals and policies (compared with the project-level situation), and it must cope with often uncertain system boundaries; limited information on existing and future developments; a large number of possible alternatives to consider; the involvement of a number of, possibly unco-operative, bodies; and possibly more political pressures than are felt by EIA.

Dealing with cumulative impacts

The systematic and comprehensive identification and assessment of cumulative impacts – cumulative effects assessment (CEA) (cumulative impacts assessment) is increasingly attracting the attention of researchers and practitioners. Mostly the focus has been on negative cumulative impacts. However, it can assess positive impacts as well. The USA, Canada, New Zealand and a number of other nations now have regulations requiring assessment of cumulative impacts (in the USA, it has been part of EIA legislation since 1979, but in practice progress has been slow).

Spaling (1994: 243) observed that environmental changes accumulate through many different processes or pathways:

◆ incremental (additive) processes (repeated additions of a similar nature a+a+a+a . . .);
◆ interactive processes (a+b+c+n . . .);
◆ sequential effects;
◆ complex causation;
◆ synergistic impacts;
◆ impact which occurs when a threshold is passed as a consequence of some trigger effect (e.g. chemical timebomb or biological timebomb);
◆ irregular surprise effects;
◆ impacts triggered by a feedback process (antagonistic – positive feedback which reinforces a trend, as opposed to ameliorative – negative feedback which counters a trend).

In practice CEA is difficult. Nevertheless, there are methods which are at least partially effective, for example the component interaction matrix and the minimum link matrix. There are also specific CEA methods (see Spaling and Smit, 1993; Smit and Spaling, 1995). Some have tried to assess cumulative impacts by adopting a regional or strategic stance (see earlier discussion of SEA), and others have tried CEA at the project level.

There are signs that global stability and even some of the Earth's life-support systems are increasingly shaped by cumulative impacts and global impacts can affect local and regional systems. Cumulative impacts may result in a runaway process which exceeds some critical threshold and may be difficult to remedy (e.g. global warming leads to uncontrollable releases of greenhouse gases from various sinks resulting in uncontrollable warming) – impact assessment has the potential to warn environmental managers of these.

Recommended reading

Journals which publish articles on impact, futures, risk and hazard assessment

Ecological Modelling
Environmental Assessment (IEA Magazine)
Environmental Impact Assessment Review
Futures
Global Environmental Change
Green Futures
Impact Assessment
Impact Assessment and Project Appraisal
Journal of Environmental Assessment Policy & Management
Long Range Planning
Risk Analysis
Social Impact Assessment
Technical Forecasting and Social Change

Environmental management and science

'. . . science carries us toward an understanding of how the world is, rather than how we would wish it to be, its findings may not in all cases be immediately comprehensible or satisfying' (Sagan, 1997: 31).

The environmental manager needs to understand the structure and function of the environment to be able to assess the effect of human activities. Such knowledge is incomplete and/or data collection has been inadequate so forecasting and decision making are often far from perfect. Nevertheless, compared with the situation before the International Geophysical Year (1957–8), there is much more knowledge on the structure and function of the environment, but reliable and comparable data on physical and human conditions are still often hard to come by.

Science has contributed enormously to western civilization: both material well-being and knowledge about the world and cosmos have been won through ordered, objective scientific study. With pressures for holistic approaches and popular interest in pseudo-science which is presented as objective truth, care is needed to ensure that support for science is not eroded. Another pressure is the growing demand, and funding, for applied research rather than pure science with no obvious practical outcome. Ironically, many of the benefits that have come from science were generated through pure, not applied, research.

Environmental science and environmental management

What can environmental science offer environmental management? 'Science', noted O'Riordan (1995: 7), 'involves theory building, theory testing and normative evaluation.' De Groot (1992: 8) felt it was better to talk of environmental sciences, because there were many fields: hydrology, geology, climatology, ecology, etc. When environmental management makes use of science there are two broad approaches: (1) multidisciplinary – which involves a communication between various fields of science but without much of a breakdown of discipline boundaries; (2) inter-disciplinary – the various fields of science are closely linked in an overall, coherent way. The interdisciplinary approach is widely advocated as a cure for the fragmentation of science (what some would see as unwelcome compartmentalization), but of the two it is much the more difficult to achieve (De Groot, 1992: 32). Environmental science often has to be problem-oriented, and this may help promote effective interdisciplinary study.

Environment can be defined as the sum total of the conditions within which organisms live. It is the result of interaction between non-living (abiotic) – physical and chemical – and living (biotic) components. Interest in the struggle of organisms, including people with one another and biota with their surroundings, was stimulated by the publication of *The Origin of Species by Means of Natural Selection* (1859) by Charles Darwin.

FIGURE 7.1 Cape Disappointment, South Georgia. A relatively simple flora and fauna, which, with the exception of larger marine mammals, has been relatively little disturbed by humans, and so offers opportunities for ecosystem studies

Ecologists, who study relationships between organisms and between organisms and environment, sometimes use 'natural environment' to indicate a situation where there has been little human interference and 'modified environment' where there has been significant modification or 'development' by people (see Figure 7.1). Increasingly, environmental management deals with environments that have been modified to varying degree, often considerably. Many organisms alter the environment: the change may be slow or rapid, localized or global.

At the roots of many of the world's environmental problems lie unsound concepts of development and modernization (Riddell, 1981; Adams, 1990). In the 1990s many people realize that there are growing problems caused by human activities and threats from nature; some argue there is a crisis – a point at which appropriate action must be taken to avoid disaster. Humans have the potential to recognize and to respond consciously to opportunities and to threats – natural or anthropogenic, perhaps to avoid or mitigate them. Whether humanity will successfully exploit that potential remains to be seen, but if there is a will to do so, environmental management offers the best means. For environmental management to develop strategies to avoid or mitigate problems and exploit opportunities effectively it must be much more than applied science, it requires understanding of human–environment interactions (Figure 7.2).

There has been huge growth of interest in environmental science since the 1960s, and today there are stronger links with social studies and politics.

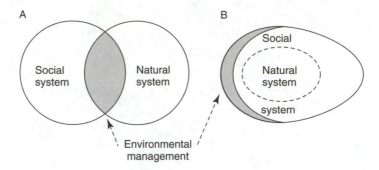

FIGURE 7.2 Natural system and social system relationship
Note: The social system is likely to affect the management of the natural system – usually the relationship of the two systems is visualized as in (a), with the shaded section representing the main field of activity for environmental management. However, few environments are 'natural': most are to some extent altered by human activity, so the social system and natural system are not largely independent – the pattern shown in (b) is more likely.
Source: Bormann *et al.* 1993: 3, Fig. 1.1

Environmentalism, a generic term for a range of moral codes directed at achieving better environmental management (see chapter 8), is widely used. It must be stressed that this is *not* a science, and while many environmentalists listen to scientific reason, others take little heed or oppose established science. Environmental management must work through science, often with environmentalists, and, if need be, control the errors that environmentalism is prone to. Some scientists are concerned by the tendency of certain environmentalists to present their activities as 'science', fearing this will degrade scientific rigour and truth. Environmental science must be done well and must withstand misapplication, the lobbying of special interest groups, and demands of policy makers; yet it has to be practised in a real world with time and funding constraints and demands for quick answers that may be difficult to come by.

Things are not especially promising; Carl Sagan (1997: 28) lamented the 'dumbing down' of the USA and the 'decay of substantive content' in its enormously influential media; for many people in the west, science is unimportant, mistrusted, or mixed up with pseudoscience and superstition. Environmental management must ensure that people and decision makers recognize and escape from the 'politics of polarized perception'.

The precautionary principle

All those involved in environmental management have world-views, which affect how they proceed (see later in this chapter and in chapter 8). Environmental managers, whatever their world-view, are likely to face: (i) data problems; (ii) modelling difficulties; (iii) analytical difficulties; (iv) insufficient time for adequate research. For example, there may be little baseline data, and what there is may be inaccurate or have gaps or may be in an unsuitable form; models may not have been developed or may have deficiencies; analysing random processes presents problems, or the process may be complex and difficult to understand. Increasingly, scientists are asked to provide advice before they have proof (Funtowicz and Ravetz, 1993). Faced with uncertainty, environmental management often follows the precautionary principle (see chapter 1), making recommendations that are adaptive, leaving leeway for change as research finds new information, building in ways of responding to the unforeseen. The precautionary principle generally means that the burden of proof is shifted to the developer, who must use science to show a proposal is safe before proceeding. O'Riordan (1995: 9) argued that

'... prevention is simply a regulatory measure aimed at an established threat. Precaution is a wholly different matter. It introduces the duty of care on all actions, it seeks to reduce uncertainty simply by requiring prudence, wise management, public information and participation, and the best technology.'

Ecology and environmental management

One might argue that 1960s and 1970s ecologists triggered interest in environmental management and helped establish environmentalism. While some of the environmental activism has been more messianic than scientific, it stimulated government and public concern for nature (Bailey, 1993). There continues to be an input from ecology into environmental management (Troumbis, 1992; Underwood, 1995). However, this may pose difficulties: one problem is that ecologists are often unable to make precise predictions; another is that there has been debate amongst ecologists over sacrificing universality for utility and practicality in environmental management (Shrader-Frechette and McCoy, 1994: 294–295).

In addition to the knowledge of present conditions, reconstruction of past conditions (palaeoecology) is valuable. Information about what happened in the past may warn of future change and hazards, establish trends that can be extrapolated into the future, or generate possible future scenarios. The expression 'backcasting' has been applied to such studies (Mitchell, 1997: 99). It is also likely that study of other planets may yield knowledge useful for managing Earth's environment.

A holistic approach to environmental management

The concept of holism was proposed in the 1920s by Smuts (1926). Modern holism is often poorly defined, although it implies acceptance of the concept that the whole is greater than the sum of the parts and the idea that modern science has unwisely tended towards excessive reductionism, empiricism and compartmentalization (isolation of fields of study from each other). In short, holistic research seeks to understand the totality of problems, rather than their components. Not everyone is happy with these trends – science has yielded much through reductionism – for example, Atkinson (1991a: 154) warned of risks involved in adopting a wholly holistic approach.

Many recognize a postmodern period, beginning in the early 1960s, characterized by a collapse of 'normality', increasingly post-industrial activity and a holistic worldview (Capra, 1982; Risser, 1985; Savory, 1988; Cheney, 1989; Warford and Partow, 1989; Cosgrove, 1990: 355; Kirkpatrick, 1990; Stonehouse et al., 1997). In the last two decades some mathematicians and fundamental physicists have shifted from approaches based on cartesian order and systematic, reductionist analysis, to trying to understand chaotic complexity using postmodern holism that embraces chaos theory or fractals (Lewin, 1993). A number of processes of concern to environmental management appear to be best explained by chaos theory (which may mean there will always be problems in predicting future outcomes accurately) (Cartwright, 1991). The holistic approach may also prove useful because it is increasingly difficult to maintain a separation between science and politics. Bond (in *New Scientist* 30 May 1998: 54) noted: 'science without the bigger picture is simply bad science'. (In 1998 the University of Plymouth, UK, launched an M.Sc. in holistic science.) Holism is valuable as a support for established reductionist science and must not be seen as a replacement.

Structure and function of the environment

Living organisms, including humans, and non-living elements of the environment interact in often complex ways. The study of these interactions – ecology – was founded as an academic subject (oecology) in 1866 by Ernst Häckel. By 1914 *The Journal of Ecology* had been established. Charles Elton in 1927 described ecology as 'scientific natural history'; modern definitions would include: the study of the structure and function of nature; the study of interactions between organisms (biotic) and their non-living (abiotic) environment; the science of the relations of organisms to their total environment, and the interrelationships of organisms inter-specifically and between themselves within a species (Fraser-Darling, 1963; Odum, 1975; Park, 1980). Since the early 1970s 'ecology' has also come to mean a viewpoint – typically a concern for the environment – as much as the discipline (O'Riordan, 1976). The science of ecology should guide environmental management, environmentalism and environmental ethics.

People's behaviour and culture are partly a consequence of physical surroundings and partly human genetics (just how much of each is debated). Humans either adapt to, or seek to modify, their environment to achieve security and well-being. In making modifications people create a 'human environment' (Treshow, 1976). Human ecology developed in the early twentieth century to facilitate the study of people and their environment, expanding in the 1960s and 1970s, and then dying back (Sargeant, 1974; Richerson and McEvoy, 1976). A field that currently seems to be expanding, and which can be very useful for environmental management, is political ecology. Political ecologists seek to build foundations for sustainable relations between society and the environment (Atkinson, 1991b; Blaikie, 1985) (see chapter 13).

The global complex of living and dead organisms forms a relatively thin layer, the biosphere. The term 'ecosphere' is used to signify the biosphere interacting with the non-living environment, biological activity being capable of affecting physical conditions even at the global scale. The global ecosphere can be divided into various climates, the pattern of which has changed in the past (a world map of climate for, say, 20,000 years ago would be very different from today's) and will doubtless do so in the future. Climate might be affected by one or more of many factors, e.g.:

◆ Variation in incoming solar energy due to fluctuations in the Sun's output or possibly dust in space.
◆ Variation in the Earth's orbit around or change in its rotation about its axis.
◆ Variation in the composition of the atmosphere or in the quantity of dust, gases or water vapour present (biological activity may alter atmospheric composition).
◆ Altered distribution of continents, changes in oceanic currents or of sea-level that may expose or submerge continental shelves.
◆ Formation and removal of topographic barriers.

Environmental managers must not assume climate is fixed and stable – even if there is no significant threat of change through pollution (Figure 7.3).

The ecosystem

The biosphere is composed of many interacting ecosystems (ecological systems), the boundaries between which are often indistinct, taking the form of transition zones (ecotones) where organisms from adjoining zones may be present (it is possible for organisms to be restricted to an ecotone only). Large land ecosystems or biomes (synonymous with biotic areas) can be recognized. These are areas with a prevailing regional climax vegetation and its associated animal life, in effect regional-scale ecosystems. Biomes usually reflect climate but are also likely to be shaped by the incidence of fire, drainage, soil characteristics, grazing, trampling, etc. (e.g. desert biomes or grassland biomes). The biome concept seeks to extend the ideas of community among vegetation and animal populations to cover the patterns of life within both (Watts, 1971: 186). The term 'ecosystem' was coined by Tansley in 1935, and has become the basic functional unit of ecology (Tansley, 1935; Park, 1990: 107). It is an assemblage of organisms living and interacting in association under certain environmental conditions, with, according to Miller (1991: 112), six major features: interdependence, diversity, resilience, adaptability, unpredictability and limits. An ecosystem boundary can be defined at organism, population, or community level, the crucial thing being that biotic processes are sustainable within that boundary. It is possible to have different physical and functional boundaries to an ecosystem. No two ecosystems are exactly the same, but one may recognize general rules and similarities. There are two ways of viewing ecosystems: (1) as populations – the community (biotic) approach, in which research can be conducted by individuals; (2) as processes – the functional approach (energy flow studies), best investigated by a multidisciplinary team.

FIGURE 7.3 A glacier calving into the sea, Cumberland Bay, South Georgia. Evidence shows considerable change in extent of glaciers on this island over the last 10,000 years. Climate is not static.

Ecosystems can be subdivided, according to local physical conditions, into habitats (places where an organism or group of organisms live) populated by characteristic assemblages of organisms (e.g. a lake ecosystem may be composed of gravel bottom habitats rock bottom habitats, and mud bottom habitats). Biomes and habitats may be subdivided into communities, which may consist of several populations of different species that live and interact together in a particular place.

In a stable ecosystem each species is assumed to have found a position, primarily in relation to its functional needs: food, shelter, etc. This position, or niche, is where a given organism can operate most effectively. Some organisms have very specialized demands and so occupy very restricted niches (e.g. the water-filled hollow of a particular bromeliad plant, itself with a restricted niche), others can exist in a wide range of niches. A species may be using only a portion of its potential niche; or alteration of a single parameter affecting competition with other organisms may suddenly open, restrict or deny a niche for an organism.

The ecosystem concept

The ecosystem concept may be applied to natural or human-modified conditions. The latter include urban ecosystems and agroecosystems, although these are not true, discrete units in terms of energy flows, function and so on. Ecosystem management is the application of the ecosystem concept (Golley, 1993). Slocombe (1993) was optimistic that the ecosystem concept might offer a route to integrating environmental management and development planning that would lead to sustainable development (the value of the ecosystem approach is discussed in chapter 9).

Biodiversity

Ecological diversity refers to the range of biological communities that interact with each other in a given environment. Biodiversity (biological diversity) refers to species diversity plus genetic diversity within those species. Loss of biological diversity occurs when species extinctions exceed the rate of species creation. Extinction is a natural process, sometimes sudden, perhaps catastrophic, otherwise an ongoing, gradual process. However, humans have greatly accelerated the rate of extinctions. Loss of biodiversity is one of the most serious problems facing environmental managers.

Biogeochemical and biogeophysical cycles

Within the biosphere, cyclic processes move and renew supplies of energy, water, chemical elements and air. These cycles affect the physical environment and organisms, and some are affected by life forms. Although upset by occasional catastrophic events (e.g. volcanic eruptions, planetesimal strikes), biogeochemical and biogeophysical cycles are assumed to reach a state of dynamic stability. Nevertheless, environmental managers must not assume an unchanging natural environment, and human activity is affecting global cycles and might trigger serious runaway problems (i.e which are difficult to solve).

There are cycles which are crucial for the nutrition of organisms: the maintenance of atmospheric gas mix and maintaining global temperature within acceptable limits, including water, oxygen, carbon dioxide, nitrogen, phosphorus, sulphur (there are over 30 known biogeochemical cycles). Some involve gases and have a turnover of as little as a few days; some involve sediments, and are so slow (with turnovers of perhaps millions of years) that the material is non-renewable as far as humans are concerned. Biogeochemical and biogeophysical cycles are not fully understood, for example, there is much to learn about the cycling of carbon. Without better insight, accurate modelling and prediction of global change is very difficult.

Biogeochemical and biogeophysical cycles can be classified as: (1) natural, (2) upset by humans and (3) recycling (managed by man and sustainable) (Chadwick and Goodman, 1975: 4). Many of the first group have already been converted to the second and the threat of this grows; conversion of these to the third group is an important goal for environmental managers.

Environmental limits

Von Liebig's Law of the Minimum states that whichever resource or factor necessary for survival is in short supply is the critical or limiting one which restricts population growth of a species – for example, lack of water, space, nutrients, or harsh climate, noise, recurrent fires, a predator, disease, etc. A population of organisms will tend to grow until it encounters a resource limit or limiting factor. The outcome may then be gradual or sudden, limited or catastrophic, or cyclic boom and bust but whatever course is taken there will be a cessation of growth. Solar energy drives most of Earth's ecosystems: few are not ultimately dependent on sunlight. Exceptions include deep ocean hydrothermal vent communities and bacteria deep underground (Cann and Walker, 1993). Photosynthesis is thus a major parameter, and few of the world's agricultural strategies function at anything like potential maximum efficiency, so improvement of food and commodity production without further expansion of farmland should be possible.

There has been much debate as to what the maximum global human population could be without causing serious disruption of the Earth's life-support systems. Miller (1991: 138) suggested that, with technology and foreseeable economic development, global population might reach 10 or even 30 billion (thousand millions). The global population is already more than halfway towards the lower of those two estimates so humanity would be advised to treat the problem with urgency. Caution is necessary when dealing with estimates of the population the Earth might support as they are often speculative. It may be possible to produce 40 tonnes of food per person for the 1990 global population, but will there be investment, environmental and social conditions allowing that production to be maintained in the future, let alone be expanded? Meadows *et al.* (1992) have argued that the limits have already been exceeded, but that there is still hope of human survival and ultimately stabilization at a level offering reasonable quality of life.

Resources

A resource can be defined as: 'something which meets perceived needs or wants'. A resource is the expression of appraisal, a subjective concept (Zimmermann, 1993). Resources become available through a combination of increased knowledge, improving technology, changing individual and social objectives. Mitchell (1993: 2) noted 'In summary, natural resources are defined by . . . perceptions and attitudes, wants, technical skills, legal, functional, and institutional arrangements, as well as by political customs'. Economic and non-economic criteria determine utility. Non-economic criteria include: aesthetic quality, sense of moral duty to conserve wildlife, cultural importance, religious beliefs, etc. An economist might subdivide resources into those with actual value, those with option value (possible use perceived), and those with intrinsic value (no obvious practical value, but there is a will to maintain them). Resource demand changes as human perceptions alter, new technology is developed, fashions vary, and new materials are substituted. There are some who wish to develop environmental management with non–utilitarian goals (part of the postmodern trend), so that resources are valued for their own sake and, if need be, utilization forgone; how this will be done in practice is not clear.

A rough classification of resources which may be useful to environmental management is:

- ◆ those that can be safely stretched by humans;
- ◆ those that can be stretched with care;
- ◆ those which cannot or should not be stretched.

Stretching of resources might be achieved through strategies like the alteration of natural vegetation to agriculture; the conversion of slow-growing woodland to fast-growing plantation; farming of fish rather than fishing wild stocks, etc.

The amount of a particular resource believed to exist is the total resource; the term 'identified resource' is applied to that which has actually been mapped and assessed. A reserve or economic resource is that which is extractable, given current technology, economic conditions and civil order. Undiscovered resources are those deemed by specialists to be likely to exist but are unproven. Resources vital to a country are termed critical resources and those needed to ensure national security are strategic resources. A comparison of known resource supplies and rates of use yields a depletion rate, typically the time it takes for 80 per cent of known reserves to be used.

Assimilative capacity

Discussion of resources usually focuses on inputs. As population increases and people over-stress the land, congregate in urban areas, demand manufactured goods, and are fed with the produce of modern farming, these all lead to outputs – pollution. Ecosystems can render a certain amount of a pollutant harmless – their assimilative capacity. This varies from ecosystem to ecosystem, requires time, and is affected by the types and quantities of pollutant received. Where biotic processes cope with pollution this capacity can be seen as a *renewable resource*. However, the sudden arrival of a very toxic compound, large quantities of the usual pollutants, or unusual weather conditions may cause a breakdown of assimilative capacity that is difficult to repair and means undiminished pollution until it is restored. Environmental management must consider outputs as well as inputs.

Trophic level and organic productivity

Organisms in an ecosystem can be grouped by function according to their trophic level (the level at which they gain nourishment). Each successive trophic level's organisms depend upon those of the next lowest for their energy requirements (food). The first trophic level, primary producers or (autotrophs), in all but a few cases convert solar radiation (sunlight) to chemical energy (the exceptions include hydrothermal-vent communities and some micro-organisms deep below ground). Seldom are there more than four or five trophic levels because organisms expend energy living, moving and in some cases generating body heat – and transfer of energy from one trophic level to the next is unlikely to be better than 10 per cent efficient. Given these losses in energy transfer, it is possible to feed more people if they eat at a low rather than high trophic level – put crudely, a diet of grain supports more people than would be possible if it were used to feed animals for meat, eggs or milk (it has been calculated that only about one part in 100, 000 of solar energy makes it through to a carnivore).

The sum total of biomass (organism mass, expressed as live weight, dry weight, ash-free dry weight or carbon weight) produced at each trophic level at a given point in time is termed the standing crop. This needs to be treated with caution; if taken at the end of an optimum growing period it indicates full potential; if taken during a drought, cool season, period of agricultural neglect or insect damage, it is an underestimate of possible production. Primary productivity can be defined as the rate at which organic matter is created (usually by photosynthesis, although in some situations by other metabolic processes) at the first tropic level. It can be established in several ways. The total energy fixed at the first trophic level is termed gross primary production. Minus the estimated respiration losses, this gives net primary productivity (in $g\,m_{-2}\,d_{-1}$ or $g\,m_{-2}\,y_{-1}$). Net primary productivity gives a measure of the total amount of usable organic material produced per unit time. Most cultivated ecosystems, i.e. efforts to stretch food and commodity production, are well below the net primary production of more productive natural ecosystems. There is thus, *in theory*, potential for the improvement of existing agriculture.

Thus, ecologists have developed a number of concepts and parameters, some of which have been adopted (sometimes modified) by those seeking to manage the environment. The most widely used are: maximum sustainable yield, and carrying capacity (Box 7.1). These should be treated with caution. Maximum sustainable yield may be correctly calculated, but if environment changes a 'reasonable' resource exploitation strategy leads to over-exploitation. Maximum sustainable yield calculations can thus give a false sense of security. A given ecosystem can have more than one carrying capacity, depending on the intensity of use, the technology, etc. Some organisms adjust to their environment through boom and bust, feeding and multiplying during good times, and in bad suffering population decline, migrating or hibernating; calculating carrying capacities for such situations can be difficult. Biogeophysical carrying capacity may differ from the behavioural carrying capacity, such that a population could be fed and otherwise sustained but feel crowded and stressed to a degree that limits their survival. Ultimately, the more people the Earth supports, the lower the standard of living they are likely to enjoy, and the more conflict and environmental damage are probable (although there may be situations where human population increase does not exacerbate environmental degradation or result in lower standards of living: see discussion of Boserüp in chapter 2). With foreseeable technology, adequate standards of living and satisfactory environmental quality probably demand that human population on Earth be less than today's 5,000 million plus. We are told by the media that world-wide much more is spent on golf than on family planning aid; the golfer environmental manager should reflect on this!

BOX 7.1 Ecological concepts and parameters which are useful for environmental management

Maximum sustainable yield.
The fraction of primary production (as organic matter) in excess of what is used for metabolism (net primary production) that it is feasible to remove on an ongoing basis without destroying the primary productivity – i.e. 'safe harvest'. Under US law, maximum sustainable yield would be defined as: maintenance in perpetuity of a high level of annual or regular periodic output of renewable resources.

Carrying capacity.
Definitions vary and can be imprecise. Examples include: the maximum number of individuals that can be supported in a given environment (often expressed in kg live weight per km^2); the amount of biological matter a system can yield, for consumption by organisms, over a given period of time without impairing its ability to continue producing; the maximum population of a given species that can be supported indefinitely in a particular region by a system, allowing for seasonal and random changes, without any degradation of the natural resource base.

Assimilative capacity.
The limiting resource may not be an input like food or water, it may be inability to deal with outputs (waste products). A given environment has some capacity to purify pollutants up to a point where the pollutant(s) hinder or wholly destroy that capacity – this is termed the assimilative capacity.

Carrying capacity can be stretched by means of trade, technology and military power (the latter ensures tribute from elsewhere – assuming it is available to be taken). Often net primary productivity increases at the cost of species diversity. The timing of resource use may be crucial: for example, rangeland might feed a certain population of livestock, provided grazing is restricted for a few critical weeks (at times when plants are setting seed, becoming established or are otherwise temporarily vulnerable). If this is not done, or a disaster like a bushfire strikes, land degradation occurs and far fewer livestock can be supported in the future.

Within even the simplest ecosystems there are complex relationships among organisms and between organisms and environment: intertwined chains forming a food web; complex pathways along which energy (food) and perhaps pollutants are passed; subtle interdependencies for pollination, seed dispersal, etc. Pesticides, radioactive isotopes, heavy metals and other pollutants can become concentrated in organisms feeding at higher trophic levels: apparently harmless background contamination could, through such biological magnification (bio–accumulation), prove harmful to man and other organisms without assimilative capacity having obviously broken down (Carson, 1962). Today it is known that pollutants like PCBs and DDT, which are present globally at low levels get concentrated by the food web to such a degree that birds of prey and other predators suffer serious poisoning, and there may be other unpleasant discoveries to be made.

Holdridge Life Zone Model

The Holdridge Life Zone Model is a widely used eco-climatic classification system, based on the relationship of current vegetation biomes to three general climatic parameters: annual temperature, annual precipitation and estimated potential evapotranspiration. It is an approach often used in land use classification. The model predicts eco-climatic areas but does not directly model actual vegetation or land cover distribution (Holdridge, 1964).

Ecological stability

Ecosystems adjust to perturbation through regulatory mechanisms. When the relationship between input and output to the system is inverse (e.g. increased sunlight causes more cloud, which reduces the impact of that sunlight on the surface), it is termed a negative feedback. The opposite is a positive feedback, whereby an effect is magnified (e.g. global warming might release methane hydrates trapped in the ocean causing increased warming). There is a risk that a positive feedback could result in an uncontrollable runaway reaction affecting a critical biogeochemical or biogeophysical cycle, so one of the tasks of environmental management should be to warn of such threats.

The environmental manager needs to know whether the environment and ecological processes are stable (Smith, 1996). It is widely held that, given long enough, a steady state will be reached by an ecosystem because a web of relationships will allow it to adjust to serious localized or moderate widespread disturbances. Such an ecosystem should remain in steady state unless a critical parameter alters sufficiently. If change then occurs, it is termed 'ecological succession' or 'biotic development'. Over a very long period of time organisms may evolve to an evolutionary maturity; over a shorter period a successional maturity may be reached before such evolution can occur (Johnson and Steere, 1974: 8)

The concept of ecological succession, pioneered by Clements (1916), is complex and still debated. According to the concept, organisms occupying an environment may modify it, sometimes assisting others – a birch wood may act as a nursery for a pine forest, which ultimately replaces the birch – thus birch is a successional stage *en route* to a pine stage. These transitional stages leading to a mature climax community are known as seres. Each vegetational stage or sere will have a characteristic assemblage of macrofauna and micro-organisms. Two types of succession are recognized: (1) primary succession and (2) secondary succession. The former is the sequential development of biotic communities from a bare lifeless area (the site of a fire, volcanic ash, newly deglaciated land, etc). The latter is the sequential development of biotic communities from an area where the environment has been altered but has not had all life destroyed (cut forest, abandoned farmland, land that has suffered a flood or been lightly burnt, etc). Where succession is taking place from a bare area, the first stage is known as the pioneer stage, although in practice the expression may be applied to growth taking place in areas that do have some life – such as regrowth after logging (natural forests may be assumed to maintain maturity, rather than becoming senile and degenerating, through 'patch and gap' dynamics – clearings caused by storms, etc., that allow regeneration). Pioneer communities have a high proportion of plants and animals that are hardy, have catholic niche demands, and disperse well (weeds with wind-carried seeds, insects which can fly, etc). Mature, climax communities are supposed to have more species diversity, recycle dead matter better, and be more stable.

Many communities do not reach maturity before being disturbed by natural forces or humans. It is often argued that an ecosystem with greater species diversity is more stable than one with less. In practice many variables are involved in determining ecosystem stability, and in a given situation the path of succession can be unpredictable (Figure 7.4).

Until quite recently, the world population was non-urban; now, after rapid urbanization since the 1800s, over 50 per cent of people live in cities, and the

FIGURE 7.4 Abrupt boundary between cleared lowland tropical rainforest and young oil-palm plantation, Peninsular Malaysia. A contrast between rich diversity of plant species in the forest, and the oil-palm/ground-cover species (planted to try to reduce erosion and weed growth) of the plantation

percentage is increasing. Many of the largest, fastest growing cities are in poor countries and pose severe environmental problems. Even in developed countries urban growth is a challenge for environmental management. In recent years there has been a shift in interest from just coping with city problems to seeking strategies for 'sustainable cities' – however, there is a long way to go before there are practical solutions in most, if not all, countries. Engineering and institutional developments alone will not provide solutions for urban transport, water supply, sanitation, control of crime, improving social cohesion, etc. For effective environmental management there must be better understanding of urban and peri-urban environments, societies and economies and how they interact with rural surroundings.

Environmental crisis?

Warnings that the Earth's environment faces a 'crisis' have blossomed since the 1960s (Ehrlich, 1970; Eckholm, 1976; White, 1993). The cause is usually identified as one or a combination of the following: people's cavalier use of nature; over-population; misapplication of technology; faulty development ethics. 'Crisis' is a turning-point, a last chance to avoid, mitigate or adapt. One may recognize several categories of perceived crisis (these are not arranged in order of importance, do not represent a comprehensive list, nor are they all wholly separate and discrete):

1   Renewable resource depletion (especially shortfall in food production and problems with water supplies) and degradation;
2   Global environmental change;
3   Pollution;
4   Nuclear or biological warfare;
5   Biodiversity loss;
6   Increasing hunger and poverty;
7   Increasing human repression, marginalization and disempowerment;
8   Rapid, often poorly planned, urban growth.

'Crisis' has become an overworked word. People's perceptions differ, so not all agree on the circumstances that constitute a crisis – 'crisis' for one may be normal to another, an opportunity to another. The term is also prone to emotive, journalistic usage (Blaikie, 1988). Some, mainly on the political left, suggest that the idea of a crisis is a 'liberal cover-up' to divert attention from doing anything about 'real problems' like social injustice and poverty (Young, 1990: 142–143). Others feel that environmental problems are mainly due to social problems, that there is a social or ethical crisis behind any environmental crisis (e.g. Weston, 1986: 4; Caldwell, 1990; Merchant, 1992: 17).

Identification of large-scale crisis may be a mistaken response to a patchy problem, reflecting inadequate observation. Science is vital, providing the environmental manager with the means for objective and careful monitoring (Blaikie, 1989; Blaikie and Unwin, 1988: 7; Thompson *et al.*, 1986). Writing on 'rural poverty unperceived', Chambers (1983: 13–27) noted a range of social science research errors which lead to false impressions (physical science can make similar errors), e.g. a researcher's tendency to view roadside areas and miss the 'interior'; the fact that the majority of studies are made during dry seasons; interviews with unrepresentative groups of people; research that is too short term. Ives and Messerli (1989), in discussing the Himalayas, which many identify as in environmental crisis, indicated little firm evidence that this is so. Indeed, some records show areas markedly worse several decades ago that have now improved. Blaikie and Unwin (1988: 13) cited an example of gully erosion in Zimbabwe identified as constituting a crisis, where careful study revealed that only about 13 per cent of total soil loss was from the spectacular gullies, while 87 per cent was from insidious inter-gully sheet erosion. Funds could easily have been spent treating gullying (a symptom of the problem) rather than sheet erosion (the actual problem).

Another danger in adopting a crisis orientation is that decision makers suddenly respond to a problem (crisis management or 'fire-fighting') rather than make sustained efforts to avoid or solve it (Henning and Mangun, 1989: 3). It should be stressed that infrequent or random events can suddenly cause considerable environmental change with no sign of an approaching crisis.

The growing number of environmental problems has been seen as indicating a 'progressive loss of ecological stability' (Simmonis, 1990: 26) – it might also reflect more research and awareness. A wise comment was made by Sir Crispin Tickell: 'We can remove one, two, or ten rivets. But at a certain point – it could be the eleventh or the thousandth rivet . . . things fall apart' (*The Times*, 27 April 1991: 4). With any complex system there may be failure of component parts, the breakdown of one of which is relatively insignificant, but it might, alone or in combination with other factors, contribute to overall collapse. The global environment is a complex system. Environmental managers need to recognize significant thresholds, and act to avoid problems. An area of mathematics, catastrophe theory (which is concerned with the way in which systems can suddenly change by passing a crisis point), may aid the identification of critical environmental thresholds before they are reached. However, even with adequate knowledge of the structure and function of the environment and of human behaviour, and using tools like impact assessment and catastrophe theory (see later), advance warning may be difficult to provide.

Another aid to threshold identification is ultimate environmental thresholds assessment. This is derived from threshold analysis, which is based on the assumption that there are final boundaries which may be broken by direct or indirect (including cumulative) impacts. Kozlowski (1986: 146) defined these thresholds as: 'stress limits beyond which a given ecosystem becomes incapable of returning to its original condition and balance'. It is possible to recognize temporal, quantitative, qualitative and spatial dimensions of these thresholds (Kozlowski, 1986: 18–30), and to assess their present and future status. The approach has many things in common with EIA, and possibly some advantages, including a chance of better integration into the planning process.

There have been regional catastrophes which ultimate environmental thresholds assessment might have helped avoid, e.g. the ruination of the Aral Sea or the recent forest fires in Brazil, Venezuela, Mexico and South East Asia.

The Brundtland Report rekindled crisis warnings made in the 1960s and 1970s, and suggested a rough timescale: 'Most of today's decision-makers will be dead before the planet feels the heavier effects of acid precipitation, global warming, ozone depletion. . . . Most of the young voters of today will still be alive' (World Commission on Environment and Development, 1987: 8). At present global warming is generally seen to pose the greatest threat. Other threats are: projected population growth rates set against projected per capita availability of key resources: land, water, food and fuelwood, and there can be little doubt that pollution with hazardous compounds, soil degradation and loss of biodiversity are serious problems world-wide.

In roughly one generation from now human population will probably have doubled, and might use 80 per cent of primary production. Even if climatic change and pollution do not depress photosynthesis, and if agricultural productivity improves, the limits are getting close (Holmberg, 1992: 27).

There is still wide disagreement over strategies to counter problems. Questions often asked are:

◆   Are the environmental problems faced by developed countries and the developing countries the same?
◆   Are some or all of the developing countries' problems caused by the developed countries (or vice versa)?
◆   Are developing countries suffering more environmental damage than the developed countries?
◆   Are the developing countries more vulnerable to problems?

Countries have tremendous diversity of environment, government, administration, historical background, etc. However, two things are widely shared by developing countries: poverty and environmental degradation. Whether poverty reflects accidents of history or special handicaps associated with the tropics has been debated (Huntington, 1915; Adams, 1990: 6–8; Kates and Haarmann, 1992). Developing countries' populations are growing more than those of the developed. However, they consume far less per capita of the world's resources. In an inter-dependent world both developed and developing countries will have to co-operate, or conflict and failure to resolve problems will probably follow. Whether global environmental change will disadvantage developing countries more than developed is difficult to predict. For example, climatic change may have very different effects on even closely neighbouring countries.

Africa is frequently singled out as having or being close to an environmental crisis, a development crisis or both (Watts, 1989; Davidson *et al.*, 1992). Blaikie and Unwin (1988: 20) were sceptical, noting that soil erosion was not really serious. Others feel things seem to be getting worse, especially in the Maghreb and south of the Sahara (excluding South Africa). Many refer to a crisis in sub-Saharan Africa (Harrison, 1987: 17–26, 56), caused by:

1   a decline in per capita food production;
2   increasing poverty;
3   a debt crisis;
4   civil unrest (Africa, with less than 10 per cent of the world's population had almost 50 per cent of the world's refugees in the late 1980).

Drought is often cited as a cause of a sub-Saharan African crisis, yet there is no conclusive evidence that rainfall is less or receipts more variable in recent decades than during the past few thousand years (Holmberg, 1992: 225). More likely drought in Africa exposes other weaknesses – a 'litmus of development'.

Often it is possible to recognize what might cause a crisis, but tracing *why* these things happen is less easy. It has been suggested that shortcomings in western ethics are frequently the root cause. However, non-western countries also have environmental problems. Population growth cannot be blamed where, despite very low settlement density, certain activities (e.g. ranching) lead to severe damage. Population growth projections are therefore not a certain indicator that environmental problems will occur. Livelihood strategies which have long served people, often in harsh environments, have often broken down in recent years. The reasons are diverse, including: population increase; structural adjustment; spread of commercial agriculture; adoption of new crops; restrictions on movement of people or livestock. Environmental management must look carefully at physical, social and economic factors before drawing conclusions – false impressions are easily gained.

How stable are environments?

Environmental management is likely to want to know whether an ecosystem is stable, and what would happen if it were disturbed. As discussed earlier, the concept of ecosystem stability has provoked much debate and is not fully resolved (Hill, 1987). Natural ecosystems are rarely static: the best environmental management can expect is a sort of dynamic equilibrium, not a fixed stability. Equilibrium is in part a function of sensitivity and resilience to change. Sensitivity may be defined as the degree to which a given ecosystem undergoes change as a consequence of natural or human actions. Resilience refers to the way in which an ecosystem can withstand change. Originally it was proposed as a measure of the ability of an ecosystem to adapt to a continuously changing environment without breakdown. It would be misleading to give the impression that these concepts, stability and resilience, are straightforward.

There is disagreement as to whether an ecosystem evolves in the long term towards a steady-state with equilibrium of its biota through slow and steady evolution of species (phyletic gradualism) or generally steady slight and slow evolution punctuated by occasional sudden catastrophes and extinctions, after which there may comparatively rapid and considerable biotic change (punctuated equilibrium) (Gould, 1984; Goldsmith, 1990). Whatever the process, the end result is held to be a 'climax stage', reached via more or less transient successional stages (at any of which succession might be halted by some parameter) (Clements, 1916).

Stability (some prefer to use 'constancy') is often invoked by those interested in establishing whether conditions will remain steady or will return via a predictable path to something similar to the initial steady-state after disturbance. It is widely held that ecosystem stability is related to biological diversity: the greater the variety of organisms there is in an ecosystem, the less likely is there to be change in biomass production, although population fluctuations of various species may still occur

(Tilman, 1996). However, it is quite possible that a change in some parameter could have an effect on all organisms. Thus diversity may help ensure stability, but does not guarantee it. An ecosystem may not be stabilized when disturbed: it may be close to a starting-point, or it could be undergoing cyclic, more or less constant or erratic change. Return to a pre-disturbance state is therefore uncertain.

Resilience is often measured by the speed of recovery of a disturbed ecosystem, but can refer to how many times a recovery can occur if disturbance is repeated (Holling, 1973). Topsoil, for example, has little resilience; easily lost, it may well take centuries to develop a new cover. An ecosystem may return to stability after several disturbances but fail to after a subsequent upset for various reasons. The concept of resilience has been applied to human ecology: some societies absorb or resist social change and continue with traditional skills and land uses or develop satisfactory new ones; other societies fail and their resource use and livelihood strategies degenerate.

Referring to sensitivity and resilience, Blaikie and Brookfield (1987: 11) suggested a simple classification of land, which may be modified to apply to ecosystems in general:

1 *Ecosystems of low sensitivity and high resilience*
   These only suffer degradation under conditions of poor management or natural catastrophe. Generally these are the best ecosystems to stretch to improve production of food or other commodities.

2 *Ecosystems of high sensitivity and high resilience*
   These suffer degradation easily but respond well to management and rehabilitation efforts.

3 *Ecosystems of low sensitivity and low resilience*
   These initially resist degradation but, once a threshold is passed, it is difficult for any management and restoration efforts to save things.

4 *Ecosystems of high sensitivity and low resilience*
   These degrade easily and do not readily respond to management and rehabilitation efforts. It is probably best either to leave such ecosystems alone or to alter them radically – for example, forest might be converted to rice paddy-field and suffer less ongoing degradation than if it were converted to tree crops.

Managers or researchers often wish to establish in advance, or sometimes after a disturbance, what the consequences will be:

(a) Will the ecosystem re-establish its initial state?
(b) Will there be a shift to a new state?
(c) If (a) takes place, how rapid will the recovery be and how complete?
(d) What path does the recovery take?
(e) How often can recovery occur?
(f) Will the same recovery path always be followed?
(g) Will successive, similar disturbance have the same effect?
(h) Would change still occur if there were no disturbance?

Some ecosystems are in constant non-equilibrium or frequent flux, rather than in a stable state at or near carrying capacity. The behaviour of an ecosystem (physical or human) can be modelled. However, there is often such complexity that the outcome is difficult to predict reliably with simple systems analysis. Succession may not be as reliable and useful a concept as some would like. In particular, ecological change may not be as predictable as might be wished. For example, in some environments heavy grazing leads to increased scrub cover; a reduction of grazing might be expected to lead to a reduction of the scrub because it sometimes causes a thickening of the woody vegetation. Some plant communities do not exhibit succession as a directional change but follow a cyclic fluctuation about a mean (the classic case being bog or tundra hummock formations) (Kershaw, 1973: 65–84).

The Gaia hypothesis

Since the 1860s Darwin's concept of evolution – adaptation of organisms to the environment – has held sway (Goldsmith, 1990). The Gaia hypothesis, proposed in 1969 by James Lovelock, calls for some modification of evolutionary theory. Similar views were expressed by James Hutton as early as 1785: he, and later Pierre Teilhard de Chardin, suggested that the biosphere acted as a self-evolving homeostatic system. The Gaia hypothesis received little support before the late 1980s, and is still much-debated. However, there have been recent suggestions that there is a biologically credible mechanism. If proven, this would be a strong argument for a holistic approach to environmental management (Hunt, 1998).

There are several variations of the Gaia hypothesis (Lovelock and Margulis, 1973; Schneider, 1990: 8) but, whichever variant is accepted, it runs counter to the prevailing attitude in the west that humans can exercise what controls they want over the Earth (Lovelock, 1979; 1988; 1992; Watson, 1991). Whether or not they accept the hypothesis, many have been stimulated by it to think carefully about environment and development issues. For example, it has helped provoke valuable research into the global carbon cycle. The Gaia hypothesis also provides a framework for people–environment study that is holistic (Levine, 1993).

Broadly, the hypothesis suggests that life on Earth has not simply adapted to the conditions it encountered, but has altered, and controls the global environment to keep it habitable in spite of disruption from things like changes in solar radiation or occasional planetesimal strikes. The hypothesis seeks to explain the survival of life on Earth by treating the organic and physical environment as two parts of a single system ('Gaia') in which biotic components act as regulators that so it can control and repair itself (this is not a conscious process, nor is there implied a design or purpose). Temperature and composition of the Earth's atmosphere, according to the hypothesis, are regulated by its biota, the evolution of which is influenced by the factors regulated. Without Gaian regulation, the suggestion is that average global temperatures would be more extreme, and atmospheric oxygen would probably be locked up in rocks.

In effect, the Earth is seen as a superorganism, a single homoeostatic system with feedback controls maintaining global temperature, atmospheric gases and availability of nutrients. The controls involve a number of biogeochemical cycles, notably those of carbon dioxide, nitrogen, oxygen, sulphur, carbon and phosphorus. The system functions in the 'interests' of the whole physical environment and biota: the whole is greater than the sum of the parts. The implications are that humans are part of a complex system and must fit in, obey the limits or be cut out. If humans upset Gaian mechanisms, there could be sudden, possibly catastrophic, runaway environmental changes. Environmental management must assess the reality of this threat and, if it is significant, monitor for and prevent runaway changes.

Environmental catastrophes and changes

The scale of catastrophes varies from local to global. They may happen every few years or be millions of years apart, and they may or may not have a predictable pattern of recurrence. Catastrophes may be sudden, obvious and gradual, or of the creeping form (where a system is stressed and changes virtually imperceptibly until a threshold is reached, whereupon there may be sudden drastic alteration). Given long enough, chance events probably affect the survival of organisms at least as much as evolution – the process has been described as 'contingency' (Gould, 1984). Events which challenge life but give insufficient time for adaptation would allow some organisms to prevail for quite fortuitous reasons (rather than 'survival of the fittest').

Early earth scientists invoked catastrophic events to explain erosive land forms, prehistoric extinctions and geological unconformities (Thomas Huxley probably coined the term 'catastrophism' in 1869). With the publication of *The Principles of Geology* in 1830, Charles Lyell helped uniformitarianism (the idea of continuing gradual change, involving processes operating in the past that operate today) to prevail over catastrophism, but since the mid-nineteenth century there have been various attempts to revive it (Smith and Dawson, 1990; Ager, 1993).

A number of scientists recognize mass extinctions, perhaps 15 significant events in the last 600 million years, the four major ones being: ca. 440 million years BP, ca. 390 million years BP, ca. 220 million years BP, and (the K/T boundary event) ca. 65 million years BP (Raup, 1988; 1993). The cause of mass extinctions is debated, and some question whether there really is adequate evidence, suggesting instead more gradual loss of species.

In the early 1980s Walter Alvarez noted the widespread occurrence of iridium (a rare metal), glass spherules and 'shocked quartz' grains in a thin clay layer of K/T boundary age (Alvarez and Asaro, 1990). This and tsunami beds around the Gulf of Mexico have been interpreted as evidence of a planetesimal (of roughly 10 km diameter) impacting with the Earth (Kerr, 1972). Others suggest that a very large sheet-lava eruption, possibly the outpouring of the Deccan Plateau Basalts of India caused the extinctions. These are by no means the only causes suggested by supporters of the K/T mass extinction. Others include: climate change, sea-level falls, reduction of atmospheric oxygen levels, disease, etc.

Whether or not a planetesimal strike caused the extinction of the dinosaurs or caused earlier and subsequent disruptions, there is enough evidence of impacts to indicate a threat that environmental managers should seriously consider. Over 100 ancient craters, a few of more than 100 km diameter, are known on Earth and some are as recent as 1500 BP (Huggett, 1990). A small body (estimated 100 metres diameter) probably exploded about 8 km up at Tunguska, Siberia, in AD 1908, flattening 1200 to 2200 km² of *taiga* forest. A similar strike may have occurred in South Island, New Zealand, ca. 800 BP (Hecht, 1991), and a blast (of about 100 kilotons yield) in the South Atlantic in 1978 may have been caused by a planetesimal (Lewin, 1992). The impact of a 1-km diameter body would probably endanger civilization.

Volcanic eruptions can be locally devastating (e.g. Pompeii and Herculaneum – AD 79; Hekla, Iceland – AD 1636; Tambora, Indonesia – AD 1815; Krakatoa, Indonesia – AD 1883), and large outpourings of lava or eruptions of ash, gases and aerosols into the stratosphere could alter climate and cause acid fallout. Smaller eruptions like El Chichon (Mexico – 1982) and Mt Pinatubo (Philippines – 1991) caused temporary slight lowering of global temperatures. Palaeoecologists and archaeologists have correlated past eruptions, acid deposition in Greenland ice and alteration of climate affecting human fortunes in Europe.

The recurrence of catastrophic events may not be random: planetesimal strikes, variation in Earth's solar radiation receipts and perhaps vulcanicity and seismic activity might be more likely at certain alignments in the orbits of the planets or perhaps as the solar system passes the galactic plane every 26 to 33 million years. Velikovsky (1950; 1952; 1955) suggested that planetary alignments within the solar system could be blamed for catastrophic events. However, this, and a modern variant, the 'nemesis' hypothesis have won only limited support. The nemesis hypothesis, suggests that a hidden companion star to the Sun in an eccentric orbit periodically affects the solar system enough to alter climate and possibly trigger volcanicity.

Unstable climate

'Ice ages', cold glacial phases alternating with warmer interglacial or less cold interstadial phases, have happened at several points during the Earth's history. During glacials ice extended further from the poles and to lower altitudes on high ground. The most recent cooling began roughly 40 million BP, became more pronounced from about 15 million and reached glacial maximum in the last 1.8 to 2.4 million years (the Quaternary Era). The Quaternary 'ice age' has so far comprised over 20 major glacial/interglacial oscillations. The major interglacials each lasted between 10,000 and 20,000 years and the glacials spanned roughly 120,000 years. The peak of the last interglacial was about 132,000 to 120,000 BP and the last glacial maximum was about 18,000 BP. The postglacial seems to have begun quite fast, around 13,000 BP in Europe, and ice had retreated to broadly its present limits world-wide by around 10,000 BP (between 7000 and 3000 BP average conditions may have been as much as 2°C warmer than today). One might ask whether there is a threat of natural global cooling and, if so, whether possible anthropogenic warming is such a bad thing?

Many causes have been suggested for natural climatic changes (Broecker and Denton, 1990; Rudderian and Kutzback, 1991; Paterson, 1993). While their causes may be disputed, glacials and interglacials clearly occurred. There are well-established links between glacial conditions and low levels of carbon dioxide in the atmosphere (approximately 25 per cent reduction compared with the present), low levels of methane in the atmosphere, and low sea-levels (which may drop to perhaps 140 metres lower than those of today during glacials). During warm interglacials, carbon dioxide and methane in the atmosphere were higher than now and sea levels perhaps 40 metres above today's.

Drought in Africa, the Americas, South East Asia and other parts of the world and the patterns of monsoonal rainfall have been linked to atmospheric and oceanic changes which show some periodicity or quasi-periodicity. Particular attention has focused on the El Niño – Southern Oscillation (ENSO) (and related El Niña events). ENSO is believed to function in the following manner: a low-pressure, high-temperature weather system lies over Indonesia; thousands of miles away over the southwestern Pacific is a related high-pressure, low-temperature system. It has been established that if pressure in one increases, it falls in the other. These pressure differences cause the southeast trade winds to blow steadily and move water away from the western coast of South America. This causes upwelling of nutrient-rich cold seawater. Every year in spring and autumn there is a weakening, even cessation of the trade winds, peaking in the middle of the austral summer (around Christmas – hence El Niño – 'the Boy-Child') and, if it is fully manifest, the eastern tropical Pacific can warm markedly (Diaz and Markgraf, 1992). ENSO events cause increased rain along the Pacific coast of South America and, later, drought in Brazil, Australia and Australasia and reduced austral summer rainfall and cloud cover in South Africa. The USA and Central America also feel the effects (Diaz and Markgraf, 1992; Hamlyn, 1992). Study of the phenomenon enabled prediction of recent weather shifts in some of the aforementioned regions nine months or more in advance.

Infrequent events pose a threat to humankind and it is advisable to devote resources to providing early warning, defence and mitigation measures. Environmental management should plan for infrequent as well as more everyday threats and ongoing processes.

Recommended reading

Journals which publish articles on science and environmental management

Ambio
Environment and Ecology
Environmental Management
Journal of Environmental Management

Note: So many sources cover this field that it is difficult to recommend a fair and brief selection.

Chapter 8

Environmental management, environmentalism and social science

'When the history of the twentieth century is finally written, the single most important social movement of the period will be environmentalism' (Nisbet, 1982: 10).

Growing environmental concern (1750 to 1960)

Some societies protect certain plants and animals for reasons of religion or local economy (e.g. baobab trees are protected by people in most of Africa), and here and there rulers established reserves (for example, in parts of India before the fifteenth century). From the late seventeenth century European and American geographers, explorers and naturalists popularized natural history (mainly for the leisured classes), stimulated academics to seek better understanding of it, and encouraged policy makers to legislate for better treatment of nature. By 1700 the forests and wildlife of colonies like Mauritius had been degraded, the timber had been cleared on Madeira, the Cape Verde and several other islands. By the 1760s there was legislation to try to protect forests, e.g. on Tobago, Mauritius and St Helena (Grove, 1992; 1995).

Two broad groupings of environmentalists evolved in Europe and America:

1   Utilitarian environmentalists
In the late nineteenth century the British sought assistance from German foresters to sustain timber production in Burma and India. In South Africa, other African colonies and India, legislation was passed to try and reduce soil erosion, control hunting and conserve forests and outstanding natural beauty. By 1900, reserves had been established in Kenya and South Africa, often by hunters or ex-hunters (Fitter and Scott, 1978).

In North America by the 1850s, damage to forests, wildlife and soil was evident. Some feared the open frontiers were closing and that limitless land and resources were a thing of the past. One of those who was concerned was George Perkins Marsh, who in 1864 published an influential, if somewhat deterministic, book on environment and development, *Man and Nature*. This and publications by others prompted action – essentially two groups concerned for the American environment formed in the late nineteenth century: 'preservationists' and 'conservationists'. The former included John Muir, who wished to maintain unspoilt wilderness areas; the latter included Gifford Pinchot, and were prepared to see environmental protection combined with careful land use (McCormick, 1989; Barrow, 1995: 8). Environmental managers still face this preservation or conservation choice today (in the UK National Parks have chosen to allow controlled resource exploitation).

During the 1860s the US National Parks Service and the US Forest Service were established. Pinchot, Chief of the US Forest Service between 1890 and 1908, was a major force in establishing parks and reserves (and probably coined the term 'conservation' in 1907, although the British already had conservancies in India) (Kuzmiak, 1991). John Muir has been hailed as 'High Priest of the Sierras' and 'Father of the US conservation movement'. In 1892 he founded the Sierra Club in California – still an influential NGO, it played an active role in promoting popular environmental concern between the mid-1960s and mid-1970s; it also gave rise to Friends of the Earth, one of today's foremost environmental NGOs (for a history of the American conservation movement, see Kuzmiak, 1991). Political theorists, like Pyotr Kropotkin in Russia, professed forms of 'utilitarian environmentalism' by the 1890s, which aimed to improve man through better working and living conditions (Kropotkin, 1974). Kropotkin, an anarcho-communist, argued for small, decentralized communities, close to nature and avoiding industrialization and the division of labour – something quite similar to what many environmentalists seek nowadays.

Conservation bodies began to spread in America, Europe and colonies before the First World War (Dalton, 1994: 25). After 1917 divergence of development paths between Russia (and later other socialist economies) and the free-enterprise west made little difference – both had and have serious environmental problems (Gerasimov *et al.*, 1971; Komarov, 1981; Smil, 1983; De Bardeleben, 1986) (see chapter 12). The eastern bloc has, however, played an active part in international conservation and environmental protection activities, and the former USSR and China have established many national parks and reserves.

2   Romantic environmentalists

Eighteenth- and nineteenth-century industrial revolution led, especially in Europe and North America, to overcrowded, filthy cities, damaged countryside, loss of commons, and misery. A diverse group of intellectuals questioned capitalism, agricultural modernization and industrial growth. Some were anarchists most were dubbed 'romantics', and saw nature as a source of inspiration. They include poets like Wordsworth, Blake and Coleridge, writers like Henry Thoreau (1854), artists like Holman Hunt and John Turner, 'utopian liberals' and proto-socialists such as William Morris (1891), and social reformers like John Ruskin and Robert Owen (the latter founded utopian colonies, with limited success, in the UK, Ireland and the USA in the 1820s). These romantics have certainly inspired twentieth-century environmentalists, but their contribution is 'more escapist than visionary' (for a review of romantic environmentalism see Bate, 1991).

Environmental concern between the First and Second World Wars

There was serious drought in the USA midwest Dust Bowl, especially between 1932 and 1938. The soil eroded, and wind-blown dust was visible as far away as Chicago and Washington DC. Large numbers of farming families were displaced. The folksinger Woody Guthrie and novelist John Steinbeck (1939) were among those who publicized the degradation and misery. At first seen as subversives, they helped provoke public and government concern. To counter these problems President Franklin D. Roosevelt promoted integrated development of natural resources, and in 1933 established the US Soil Erosion Service, and in 1935 its successor, the US Soil Conservation Service, to fight land degradation.

The 1939–1945 war hindered the growth of concern for the environment, accelerated the development of resources and led to the production of new threats like DDT and atomic weapons. During the first decade or so after 1945 efforts focused on economic and industrial reconstruction, on raising agricultural production, and on the Cold War. A few publications on the environment began to appear from the late 1940s (Dale and Carter, 1954; Osborn, 1948; Leopold, 1949; Thomas, 1956; Vogt, 1948). Of these it was especially Aldo Leopold (1949) who stimulated many of the 1960s–1970s environmentalists. In 1949 the UN held one of the first post-war environmental meetings, the Conservation Conference at Lake Success, New York State, and during the early 1950s helped establish the International Union for the Protection of Nature, which in 1956 changed its name to the International Union for Conservation of Nature and Natural Resources (IUCN).

Environmental concern in the 1960s and 1970s

NGOs began to speak out on environmental issues in the late 1950s. By the mid-1960s there had developed what has been variously called an environmental(ist) movement, environmentalism, the ecology movement, an environmental revolution, the conservation movement. In the 1960s and 1970s, particularly in California, public interest law firms (e.g. the Environmental Defense Fund or the Natural Resources Defense Fund), supported by grants or foundations, acted on behalf of citizens or groups of citizens (previously action had to be undertaken by individuals) to protect the environment (Harvey and Hallett, 1977: 62). Understanding of the structure and function of the environment was improved by initiatives like the International Geophysical Year (1957–1958), the International Biological Program (1964–1975) and the International Hydrological Decade (1965–1974), plus expanding research. The USA Civil Rights movement, hippies, the anti-Vietnam War movement, European anti-nuclear weapons protests and the 1960s–1970s 'pop culture' in general encouraged people to ask awkward questions about environment and development (McCormick, 1989). After a peak of interest in the early 1970s media coverage and public interest declined after 1974 until the mid-1980s (Sandbach, 1980: 2–6; Simmons, 1989: 6; Atkinson, 1991b).

In the 1970s, environmentalists, although active in publication, litigation and protest, were relatively non-political (in New Zealand, Germany and the UK politically active Green Movements were developing) (McEvoy, 1971; Morrison, 1986; Dunlap and Mertig, 1992). The focus was on over-population (Ehrlich), conservation of wildlife, and problems associated with technology (Farvar and Milton, 1972). Many of the publications between the mid-1960s and mid-1970s were dogmatic: warning of coming crisis, so that some environmentalists became known as 'prophets of doom' or 'ecocatastrophists' (White, 1967; Commoner, 1972).

In 1965 the US Ambassador to the UN, Adlai Stevenson, used Buckminster Fuller's metaphor Spaceship Earth in a speech; Boulding (1971) also used it, and the catch-phrase spread the idea that the world was a vulnerable, effectively closed system. The International Biological Program, and later the UNESCO Man and Biosphere Program, helped establish an awareness that global-scale problems were real and the Earth's resources were finite. By 1970 some identified population growth as the primary cause of environment and development problems – neo-Malthusians (Ehrlich, 1970; Ehrlich *et al.*, 1970). The more extreme neo-Malthusians went so far as to discuss the possibility of triage (withholding assistance from over-populated countries with little chance of improvement, to concentrate resources on recipients who might with help achieve control).

Hardin (1968; 1974a; 1974b) published an essay on the fate of common property resources in the face of population growth. His 'tragedy of the commons' argument was that people will tend to over-use commonly owned resources, in all probability destroying them, because without overall agreement each user seeks to maximize short-term interests and does not assume sufficient responsibility for stewardship (see Box 8.1). Hardin's views have been widely attacked on several grounds, one being that he was describing more of an open-access resource situation than common property resource exploitation. (Open-access resources are not managed, and so might be damaged.) Harrison (1993) noted that seldom is use of commons a free-for-all; communities do generally have some controls and manage things. Neo-Malthusian views have been criticized as simplistic and invalid (Boserüp, 1990: 41; Todaro, 1994: 339). There were, however, more moderate critics of western neglect of the environment, like Maddox (1972) or Ward and Dubois (1972).

Two early 1970s publications helped shake the west's complacency: *Blueprint for Survival* (Goldsmith *et al.*, 1972) and *The Limits to Growth* (Meadows *et al.*, 1972). The latter was intended to promote concern and further research, and explored a range of possible future scenarios which depended on how population and other key development parameters were managed (McCormick, 1989: 75). A second Club of Rome report was published by Mesarovic and Pestel (1974) and a heated futures debate developed, with some advocating slow or even zero (economic) growth and others, like Kahn *et al.* (1976) or Simon (1981), of the view that a free market would overcome environmental difficulties before limits were met, making it unnecessary for zero growth (Freeman and Jahoda, 1978; Hughes, 1980). Critics have termed excessive optimism about limits 'cornucopian' (Cotgrove, 1982). A sequel to *The Limits to Growth* appeared 20 years later: *Beyond the Limits* (Meadows *et al.*, 1992) – its message: that the world has already overshot some of the limits flagged in 1972 and, if present trends continue, severe problems are virtually certain within 50 years. However, Meadows *et al.* (1992) still felt catastrophe could be avoided, provided the right approaches were adopted soon.

In *Small Is Beautiful* Schumacher (1973) warned that the west had promoted giant organizations, increased specialization, economic inefficiency, environmental damage and inhuman working conditions. The remedies he offered included 'buddhist economics', 'intermediate technology' (technology using smaller working units, local labour and resources) and respect for renewable resources.

BOX 8.1 Common property resource: the relationship between the returns to labour on a given resource (e.g. cropland or a fishery) and the number of labourers exploiting it

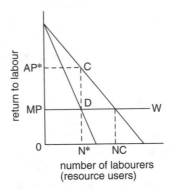

Under private ownership for any additional employee hired beyond N*, the cost to the producer W will be greater than the employees marginal product, and the difference will represent a net loss to the owner. To maximize profit requires the hire of N* workers, with a total output equal to AP* multiplied by the number of workers, N*.

Under a system of common property each worker is able to appropriate the entire product of their work, which is equivalent to the average product of all workers. Worker income will continue to exceed the wage (W) until enough workers are attracted to cause the average product to fall to the level of the wage, at which point the labour force = Nc. The implication is that aggregate welfare will fall and resource use is inefficient (and causes degradation).

Sources: Drawn from several sources, including Todaro, 1994: 338–339

Environmental concern in the 1980s and 1990s

Two seminal publications of the 1980s were the *World Conservation Strategy* (IUCN, UNEP, WWF, 1980) and the Brandt Report (Independent Commission on International Development Issues, 1980). The Brandt Report stressed that many world problems would be solved only if it was recognized that rich and poor countries had a mutual interest – the solution of developing countries' problems was not just a question of charity but of global interdependence. The *World Conservation Strategy* promoted conservation for 'sustainable development' (the first time the latter phrase was widely publicised). The World Commission on Environment and Development set out in 1984 to re-examine environment and development problems and to formulate proposals for solutions. The Commission's findings (the Brundtland Report – World Commission on Environment and Development, 1987) highlighted the need for sustainable development and urged a marriage of economics and ecology. The Brundtland Report may be said to have initiated a new relationship between social science, natural science, economics and policy making, and is probably one of the most important publications of the twentieth century.

By the late 1980s the World Bank had adjusted its policies to give greater support to environmental management (Warford and Partow, 1989), oil prices had fallen, and a Green Movement had emerged, particularly in Europe, and embarked on policy advocacy. By 1988 environmental matters were on the agendas of politicians and decision makers with a higher public profile than ever before. Although green activity in politics has declined from a peak in the early and mid-1980s (Bramwell, 1994), it is by no means weak.

Environmentalism, ecologism and the Green Movement

By the mid-1980s, many environmentalist groups had developed, the members of which were willing to alter their lifestyles and encourage (or even force) others to do so, in order to try and halt environmental damage (Buttel, 1978). It is difficult to give a precise coverage: what follows is intended to serve as a brief introduction.

Environmentalism

'Environmentalist' was not used before the 1970s, but has been applied retrospectively to those involved in environmental matters long before that (Grove, 1990; 1992; Pepper, 1984). Environmentalism has been described as a moral code or a set of mediating values to manage human conduct (O'Riordan, 1976: viii) or a concern for environment elevated to a political pursuit (McCormick, 1989: ix; Fox, 1995; Sessions, 1994). Dobson (1990: 13) argued that environmentalism is more managerial than ecologism and makes less demand for fundamental changes in human values. Environmentalism calls for 'a managerial approach to environmental problems, secure in the belief that they can be solved without fundamental changes in present values or patterns of production and consumption' (Dobson, 1995: 1). It is not an ideology, according to Dobson.

It is pointless seeking a precise definition, especially because the term 'green' has appeared and overlaps environmentalism. However, all share a concern for the environment and seek sustainable development, even if their ideologies and exact objectives differ (O'Riordan, 1991) (see Box 8.2).

From the 1960s to mid-1970s environmentalists operated with what Rees (1985: 2) called 'messianic fervour'; they stimulated popular interest but did not venture from advocacy to real solutions or political activism (Lewis, 1992). That changed by 1980,

157

BOX 8.2 Some common green characteristics

The 'four pillars of green':

1 ecology
2 social responsibility
3 grassroots democracy
4 non-violence

The 'six values of green':

1 decentralization
2 community-based economics
3 post-patriarchal principles
4 respect for diversity
5 global responsibility
6 future focus

Green characteristics:

◆ Holistic approach
◆ Disillusionment with modern unsustainable development paths
◆ Non-violence
◆ A shift in emphasis away from philosophy of means to ends
◆ A shift away from growth economics
◆ A shift toward human development goals
◆ A shift from quantitative to qualitative values and goods
◆ A shift from impersonal and organizational to interpersonal and personal
◆ Commonly a feminist interest
◆ A decentralized approach – 'think globally, act locally'

Sources: Spretnak and Capra, 1985: xx; Porritt, 1984: 10, 15;
Merchant, 1992: 15

---

with environmentalism increasingly involved with politics, commerce, law and business (Wilson, 1994). Some environmentalists are willing to embrace technology, biotechnology and the free market; many will not (Anderson, 1993; Narveson, 1995). There are also those on the side of science and rationalism who challenge environmentalism and the Green Movement (Brick, 1995).

Environmentalism and green spirituality

Spiritual ecologists include those who focus on established western religion, for example Piere Teilhard de Chardin (1959; 1964), and Matthew Fox (Fox, 1983; 1989;

Merchant, 1992: 124; Kimmins, 1993; Kearns, 1996); and those who look to pre-Christian religions of Europe, America or the orient for inspiration to transform human consciousness so that it will have reverence for nature. In 1986 the World-Wide Fund for Nature held its 25th annual meeting at Assisi, where leaders of Buddhist, Christian, Hindu, Islamic, Judaic and other faiths established an International Network on Conservation and Religion, and published the Assisi Declarations on Man and Nature. Religious beliefs play a significant role in environmental management; for example, in some countries sacred groves are often the last remaining forest sites (Singh, 1997).

Postmodern, and post-industrial environmentalism

Environmentalism, it has been suggested, is a rejection of modernism (Pepper, 1996). Modernism can be defined roughly as 'seeking to fulfil human needs through the development of technology and the creation of wealth'. Unfortunately, this has caused problems, and led to calls for postmodern alternatives (for a discussion of modernity see Giddens, 1991; and for postmodernism Harvey, 1989). While 'postmodern' is widely used, the concept is confused (Funtowicz and Ravetz, 1992). Many recognize an ongoing postmodern period, beginning during the early 1960s (Bell, 1975; Frankel, 1987; Cosgrove, 1990: 355), characterized by the collapse of 'normality' and increasingly post-industrial or post-material activity and a holistic worldview (Bell, 1975; Roszak, 1972; 1979).

A postmodern and holistic approach might offer better understanding of cultural and environmental phenomena, especially when circumstances demand multidisciplinary study of problems (Young, 1990; Kirkpatrick, 1990; Warford and Partow, 1989; Capra, 1982; Cheney, 1989). There are also signs that maths and fundamental physics are moving from cartesian order (the systematic, reductionist approach to understanding chaotic complexity) toward postmodern holism, for example, by embracing chaos theory and fractals (Peat, 1988: 341; Lewin, 1993). Some have gone beyond postmodernism to advocate what they call post-environmentalism as the best approach to environmental management (environmentalism is a reformist philosophy which tends to maintain a distinction between human affairs and nature; post-environmentalism seeks to reduce that separation in developing environmental ethics) (Pearce *et al.*, 1989; 1990; 1991; Barde and Pearce, 1990; Pearce and Turner, 1990; Gare, 1995).

The postmodern concept may prove useful, given that it is increasingly difficult to maintain a separation between science and politics, etc. The concept of holism was used long ago by Smuts (1926) (see chapter 7), and implies that the whole is greater than the sum of the parts, and that modern science tends toward excessive reductionism, empiricism and compartmentalization (isolation of fields of study from each other). In short, postmodern researchers seek to understand the totality of problems, rather than their components. Not everyone is happy with these trends: Atkinson (1991b: 154), for example, warns of the risks involved in adopting a holistic approach.

'Ecologism' is a generic term for an ideology that argues for care of the environment and a radical change in human relationship with nature to get it (put crudely, ecology is the science and ecologism is a worldview that draws upon it (Kirkman, 1997; Dobson, 1994). Dobson (1990: 36) described ecologism as 'the ideology of political ecology' (see chapter 13). Ecologism, Dobson (1995) argues, is a political ideology, which holds that a sustainable, fulfilling existence 'requires radical changes in the human relationship with the natural world, and in the mode of social and political life' (most deep greens would support this).

The Green Movement

The Green Movement is a social or cultural movement, of considerable diversity, that shares a common environmental concern and which often embarks on political action, mainly of a reformist or radical nature. 'Green' roughly means 'environmentally friendly'; 'greening' roughly means 'environmental improvement'. Reich (1970), writing about the possibilities for a new development ethic after the demise of the corporate state, was probably first to use 'greening'. The use of green terminology increased after the mid-1980s in politics and as a popular alternative to 'environment', soon becoming common in media discussions.

There is little about green philosophy which is new (Hill, 1972; Weston, 1986). Although 'green' often implies politicized environmentalism, many groups are not politically active, and indeed eschew politics. Greens are essentially mounting a cultural attack on the ills of modern society and economics, a sort of parallel to the economic attack by socialists (Redclift, 1984; Adams, 1990: 71). What would probably have been called Gandhian in the mid-1970s is now likely to be called green. Greens may be socialists, conservatives, intellectuals, poor people, Bhuddists, Christians, Muslims, or humanists. Most share a fear that industrial nations are pursuing an unsustainable, dangerous development path (Porritt, 1984: 15). North (1995: 3) noted that greens often overlook the fact that they are the 'flowering of a science-based industrial society', and that unreasoning opposition to scientific progress, business and so on may not achieve useful environmental progress.

Greens can be roughly subdivided into: romantic, anarchistic and utopian; or simply into 'light' or 'dark' greens. They may be said to have grown from partially American roots and draw upon the writings of Henry Thoreau, Theodor Roszak, Ivan Illich, Aldo Leopold, Martin Luther King and others (Roszak, 1979; Spretnak and Capra, 1985: xvii; Devall and Sessions, 1985) (see Box 8.2).

The Green Movement has tended to develop a schism between light-green (or shallow) and deep-green (or deep) ecology. The division was largely initiated by the Norwegian philosopher Arne Naess (Naess, 1973; 1988; 1989). It might be more accurate to talk of deep and shallow ecologies, as there is a wide spectrum of interpretation of what 'ecology' means.

Deep ecology seeks to replace the existing social, political and economic status quo with new environmentally appropriate bioethics and supportive politics. Supporters blame many environmental problems on the anthropocentric nature of modern development, and adopt a biocentric (ecocentric) outlook, granting all life (human and non-human) intrinsic value (Evernden, 1985; Grey, 1986; Devall, 1988; Sessions, 1994). In general, deep ecology is synonymous with radical ecology and extends beyond the approach proposed by Naess, to include perspectives like social ecology and eco-feminism, and some incorporate Taoist or Gandhian philosophy. It can be argued that deep ecology gives non-scientific input similar to (if not greater than) the importance scientific, and in some cases may be hostile to science. This rejection of science may well prove a serious barrier to effective environmental management. One of the most radical groups of deep ecologists, Earth First!, is prepared to use violence to support its environmentalism – 'monkeywrenching' or 'ecotaging' (ecological sabotage) if need be (Abbey, 1975).

Shallow ecology seeks to apply ecological principles to ensure better management and control of the environment for human benefit – i.e. it is anthropocentric (Jacob, 1994). There is far less of the rejection of established science characteristic of most deep ecologists. Shallow ecology is more inclined to try to work with existing economics and ethics (Fox, 1984; 1995); it is more likely to be concerned with solutions than efforts to avoid problems in the first place.

Social ecology was largely initiated (in the USA) by the anarcho–socialist Murray Bookchin, who was critical of deep ecology (Bookchin, 1980; 1990). In some camps it is seen as separate from deep ecology; others view it as an offshoot. Social ecology supporters see environmental problems as basically the result of social problems, and adopt an anthropocentric, decentralized, co-operative approach – a sort of eco-anarchy (Devall and Sessions, 1985; Tokar, 1988; Devall, 1991). The main difference from mainstream deep ecology is that social ecology is humanist rather than ecocentric.

If decisions have to be made to protect the environment without adequate proof, deep ecologists are more likely to give support because they require no obvious human advantage. Jacob (1994) explores the potential of deep and shallow ecology as routes to sustainable development. It seems unlikely that either extreme – deep or shallow – alone can effectively serve environmental management. Indeed, they form a continuum and so some sort of blend of both their ethics and approaches is required (Norton, 1991; Jacob, 1994). However, environmental management must also make use of science.

The value of the social sciences and environmentalism to environmental management

The social sciences provide information for one side of the human–environment interrelationship which environmental managers seek to understand and steer (Burch *et al.*, 1972). The potential inputs to environmental management from the social sciences are:

◆   to provide information on social development needs and aspirations;
◆   to explain present and predict future human attitudes, ethics and behaviour;

◆   to study and develop ways of focusing the activities of social institutions, non-governmental organizations, groups of consumers, etc., to achieve better environmental management;

◆   to show the environmental manager social constraints and opportunities;

◆   to unravel the often complex and indirect social causes of environmental problems – e.g. deforestation may have roots in social changes;

◆   the articulation and fulfilment of the shared interests of people (so far mainly at the local, regional or national level). National governments have mainly been reactive rather than forward-looking: social science will be needed to clarify how people think, nations relate to each other, and institutions behave if a more proactive approach is the goal;

◆   to cut through 'technological determinism' so that the voice of social science can be heard (Redclift and Benton, 1994).

Environmentalism is playing a vital role in the evolution of better environmental ethics but some of it is radicalism of limited practical value. Adams (1990: 83) warned: 'it is necessary to move outside environmental disciplines, and outside environmentalism, to approach the problem from political economy and not environmental science . . . to the understanding of environmental aspects of development which uses both natural science and social insights'. An example of such an integrated approach is that applied by Blaikie (1985) to the problem of soil erosion (see discussion of political economy – chapter 13).

The delay before social scientists began to study human–environment issues in the 1980s might have been because there were separate academic traditions. However, other factors may also have been at work, in particular, suspicion of empirical research, and many concepts like environmental determinism and social Darwinism (Chappell, 1993) (see Box 8.3). There has been a huge increase in the interest taken by social science in the environment since the late 1970s, with a shift from mainly enlightened activists at first to more widespread interest since 1992. There has been some borrowing of concepts and jargon by social science, mainly from ecology, but sometimes things become distorted when they have been borrowed. This is common with environmentalists who do not derive their concepts by a process of logic, but bolt on scientific justification to values they already hold.

To anyone reading the literature it soon becomes clear that there is inconsistency and imprecision of terminology, so it may be better to try to understand the stance of those involved. For example, some adopt an ecocentric, others an anthropocentric viewpoint (Moghissi, 1995). Box 8.4 offers a broad subdivision of green stancea.

So far, social science seems to have been concerned more with the social impacts of environmental problems and less with establishing the causes of the problems (McDonagh and Prothero, 1997: 21), or has examined social aspects of management. The field of social impact assessment has established itself (chapter 6). Social science has also contributed in a practical way to environmental management, for example, social forestry management; agricultural development (e.g. participatory research, advice on extension and project implementation); irrigation extension and

---

BOX 8.3 Concepts dealing with human–environment relations which might have discouraged social scientists from taking an interest in environmental management

Environmental determinism

From the 1870s a number of environmental determinists argued the human–nature relationship was such that physical factors (like climate) influence, even substantially control, behaviour and thus society and development. For the last half-century these views have attracted condemnation. Some, like Pepper (1984: 111–112), recognize 'crude' and 'scientific' environmental determinists. Crude environmental determinism, and associated concepts, like comparative advantage, were expressed by intellectuals like Richter, Kant, Ritter, Ratzel, Semple (1911) and List. Scientific environmental determinists like Ellsworth Huntington (1915) were a little more objective (Simmons, 1989: 3).

There can be no doubt that human fortunes often reflect natural events. However, much of what has been written by environmental determinists ignores that humans can make different choices under similar environmental conditions, and often modify the environment. Nevertheless, environmental determinism is not dead and debate about its value continues, especially among social scientists, geneticists and psychologists concerned with inheritance of traits, deviant behaviour and upbringing, culture and anthropology (Milton, 1993; 1996). Supporters of the Gaia hypothesis could be said to accept a type of neo-determinism, and the interpretations of human development history put forward by Diamond (1997) are distinctly deterministic (Stout, 1992; Frenkel, 1994; Mannion, 1996).

Social Darwinism

Closely allied to environmental determinism is the concept of social Darwinism. At its core was the idea that humans are fundamentally controlled by nature – competition and struggle, rather than co-operation and mutual aid, were seen as natural and justifiable ways to behave, and the group best able to adapt to environment would become dominant (Pepper, 1984: 134; Chappell, 1993). By the 1920s eugenics was supported by many as a way of improving a particular human group's genetics and thus their long-term survival and achievements. Eugenicists encouraged the breeding of 'desirable' people and suppressed 'undesirables' – the approach was embraced in Nazi Germany. By the 1950s it was accepted in most quarters that social and economic development could overcome environmental factors and determine evolution, so social Darwinism fell out of fashion.

Environmental possibilism

A concept put forward by Vidal de la Blanche, and later by Febvre (1924) – environmental possibilism – holds that the environment constrains human

continued . . .

endeavour and sets limits, but that choices between courses of action for man are possible within those limits; the same environmental opportunities may be used differently by the various cultures.

BOX 8.4 Broad groupings of greens (avoiding deep and shallow categorization)

Conservationists/traditionalists heirs to the nineteenth-century romantic liberal rejection of industry and materialism. Less interested in drastic change of attitudes and lifestyle than some greens. Includes traditional conservationists like members of the UK Royal Society for the Protection of Birds or the Council for the Protection of Rural England and in the USA of the National Audubon Society or Sierra Club.

Reformists no particular tradition, midway between the previous and following groupings. Tend to be single-issue groups with problem-orientated aims, for example: a group opposed to construction of a new airport or road or rail route.

Formal political parties and political groupings e.g. Die Grunen, UK Green Party, Greens in the European Parliament, SERA, etc. These produce regularly revised manifestos of wide-ranging policies. Green thinking has also been incorporated into the policies of a range of political institutions and has prompted new perspectives.

Academic responses to green issues marxist/structuralist and market (mainstream) economics tend to be hostile or dismissive of many green paradigms (including New Economics and some aspects of sustainable development).

Radical environmentalists draw ideas from sources like Kropotkin, Henry Thoreau, Theodor Roszak, Aldo Leopold, Godwin, etc. Recognize need for considerable change of attitudes and lifestyles because environmental problems arise. They seek to alter other people's outlook, the economic system, social inequalities, etc. Often holistic, multi- issue approach. Considerable range, from moderates like Friends of the Earth to extremists like Earth First! who espouse militant tactics like 'ecotage' (sabotage of things and people they see as a threat to the environment), 'ecovangelists'(who profess reverence for environment, not just stewardship) and even shamanists. (A schism has opened between practical and spiritual factions of Earth First!)

Eco-feminists believe women need to organize to achieve sustainable development and blame male-centred approaches to development rather than anthropocentric approaches, so can be hostile to deep ecology (see chapter 12).

Cornucopians place faith in technology and science as a solution for environment and development problems (e.g. Fuller, 1969).

Rational seek to use science, social science and technology with care to achieve sustainable development. For example, non-cornucopian techno-fixers (e.g. work by the Rocky Mountain Institute – http://www.rmi.org/newsletter /97fwn/index.html).

Mystics a wide diversity, who turn to their inner voices for inspiration and guidance. This grouping would include those who derive their inspiration from Teilhard de Chardin, Buckminster Fuller, Taoism, Zen and paganism. The label 'New Age' was coined in the late 1960s by journalists to incorporate a hotchpotch of greens who rely on astrology, the occult, Gaianism, non-mainstream religions, etc., as a guide to their relationship with the environment – in effect those with a postmodern spiritualist worldview. Many New Age supporters look towards the change from the present solar age of Pisces to Aquarius early next century as a moment of opportunity and possibly crisis (Henderson, 1981b). Certainly, there are greens who might be dismissed as 'cranky'.

Sources: Porritt (1984: 4–5); Weston (1986: 20); Taylor (1991)

management; pastoral development and range management; involvement of indigenous peoples in conservation; fisheries management and conservation; human resources management.

Sociologists have studied relationships between society and the environment (Albrecht and Murdock, 1986; Yearley, 1991). Various social science disciplines focus on behavioural fields (risk perception, hazard avoidance, consumerism, property rights, etc.) (Shankar, 1986). Historians have explored past attitudes and approaches to environment; political studies specialists and economists consider the politics and economics of environmental usage; theologians and philosophers explore the human–environment relationship. Anthropology and human resources management is increasingly used to inform the environmental manager about human behaviour, attitudes and beliefs, institutions and organizational capacity (Wehrmeyer, 1996). Environmental management has also been aided by the development of participatory research and management, monitoring and appraisal (Burton *et al.*, 1986; Brokensha, 1987; Montgomery, 1990a) (see chapter 13). Anthropologists have been less aloof from environmental studies than sociologists, possibly because of their involvement with indigenous peoples and livelihood strategies and with archaeologists, palaeo-ecologists and ecologists helping to reconstruct past scenarios. Anthropological input has been especially strong in the fields of relocation and resettlement, pre-development appraisal, SIA, conservation area management planning, and in studies of resource use, hazard perception and survival strategies adopted by land users (Jull, 1994; Blackburn and Anderson, 1995). Ethnobotany involves anthropologists and ethnographers assessing indigenous peoples' use of plant and animal resources with the hope of identifying useful crops, pharmaceuticals, etc. Anthropologists have also played a role in helping governments and environmental managers understand and reach working arrangements with indigenous peoples, and in assessing social and cultural impacts of development on them (Snipp, 1986; Dale, 1992). Much has been published on the potential contributions of social science to environmental management, most from social scientists, rather than from environmental scientists (Freudenburg, 1989; Herberlein, 1989). Some natural scientists are sceptical, even hostile, to these contributions. However, at the very least they act as catalyst where progress might otherwise have been slow.

A late-twentieth-century paradigm shift?

Different social groups and individuals vary in outlook, and often alter their views as time passes. This has been the case over the last few decades to such an extent that many recognize an ongoing paradigm shift, whereby a wide diversity of political groups, religious persuasions, old and young, share concern for the environment to a greater extent than has been the case in western nations in the past. There was some environmental concern around the turn of the century, but this was limited to individuals, and mainly directed toward conservation of wildlife and natural treasures; since the 1960s public attention has focused on environmental problems and human survival. What were desirable goals in the past are being questioned; the way forward is far from clear and the environmental manager is charged with finding the best path. Social science must clarify issues for environmental management: warn of changing attitudes, advise on human institutions that will work for ecologically sound development, and help identify policies that will work.

It seems unlikely that development, as practised so far, will enable the world's poor to reach standards of living achieved in rich countries. It may also be difficult to maintain the quality of life in rich countries. Changed attitudes and new approaches are needed, and humankind probably has limited time to acquire them. Social science will play a vital part in managing the stresses societies will probably undergo in the coming decades.

Many organisms alter the environment: the changes they bring about may be slow or rapid, localized or global. Humans are unique in that they have the potential to recognize and to make a conscious response to opportunities and to threats – natural or anthropogenic – perhaps to avoid or mitigate them, for example through technology. Recognition of problems and reaction to them depends on what individuals and communities think of themselves and how they relate to their environment. At the roots of many of the world's environmental problems lie unsound concepts of development and modernization. A widespread problem is that people tend to make Faustian bargains – decisions which sacrifice long-term well-being for short-term gains. Another is that people can react in an emotive way to questions which require careful investigation. Environmental managers weed out unreliable advocacy and ensure that rational enquiry is not discouraged.

Social science and environmental management in practice

Social forestry

Social forestry deals with the establishment and management of forest, woodlots and hedges by or for local people. The focus is on establishing tree cover, where it is needed, in the most appropriate manner, with minimal dependency on outside help (Lee *et al.*, 1990). The social forester may also be interested in why people destroy trees and in ways of countering such behaviour – e.g. finding substitute fuels, or establishing alternative livelihoods. In some regions there has been NGO activity, some of it more or less spontaneous, whereby local people have come together to improve forest conservation or to support reafforestation and woodlot planting.

There has been strong support for social forestry in India since the 1980s (Tiwari, 1983; Arnold, 1990; Chatterjee, 1995). Whether the approach is farm-based, community-based or focused on women's groups, the key feature is people's participation in planting and management. Getting effective participation may require careful encouragement, perhaps manipulation of people, which demands guidance from applied social scientists.

Indigenous peoples and conservation

Indigenous people can make ideal guides, managers, and police for conservation areas, and they may be able to use conservation as a way of maintaining an adequate livelihood in their traditional environment (Wesche, 1996). Conservation efforts have often been insensitive to local people, which has alienated them and sometimes triggered poaching and other destructive activities. The conservation planner must avoid alienation and get effective involvement.

An understanding of people's attitudes, capacities and needs is vital for managing fisheries, pastoral development, or anything involving land users.

Recommended reading

Journals which publish articles on environmental management, environmentalism and social science

Alternatives: Perspectives on Society, Technology and Environment
Annual Review of Sociology
Appropriate Technology
Ecologist
Ecumene
Ekistics
Environment
Environment & Behavior

Environmental Ethics
Environmental Values
Human Organization
Inquiry
Journal of Agricultural & Environmental Ethics
Journal of Environmental Education
Journal of Social Issues
Pan Ecology
Progress in Human Geography
Resurgence
Rural Sociology
Science of the Total Environment
Society & Natural Resources

Ecosystem
management

'. . . ecosystems provide the best paradigm for the integration of the biotic and abiotic parts of the biosphere, and for the solution of real problems, as well as giving an adaptable theoretical base' (Dickinson and Murphy, 1998: x).

The first step taken by most planners and managers is to determine the limits of their task so that they can do an effective job, given the time and resources available. For environmental management a stable unit is needed which reflects the structure and function of nature, but which as far as possible goes beyond being a biogeophysical unit to facilitate consideration and management of social, economic, cultural and other aspects of human–environment interaction.

For those seeking in-depth treatment of these issues, there are books in the Routledge Environmental Management series:

> G. Dickinson and K. Murphy (1998) *Ecosystems: a functional approach*
> P. French (1997) *Coastal and Estuarine Management*
> R. Clark (1999) *Countryside Management*

Ecosystems: definitions, values and function

People have long recognized functional environmental units, e.g. *maquis* scrubland of southern France; the *taiga* forests of Siberia; Norfolk's brecklands. Many would view these as landscape units. Environmental managers have an alternative – the ecosystem (ecological system), which is a basic functional unit of ecology (Golley, 1991). The term was coined by Sir Arthur Tansley (1935), and there are various definitions, which include: 'an energy-driven complex of a community of organisms and its controlling environment' (Billings, 1978); 'a community of organisms and their physical environment interacting as an ecological unit' (Dickinson and Murphy, 1998); 'an integration of all the living and non-living factors of an environment for a defined segment of space and time' (Golley, 1993).

A system is a set of linked components, where the linkages may not be direct – a network or web with organisms as nodes within it (Figure 9.1). Table 9.1 suggests two ways of classifying environmental systems, by function or degree of disturbance. A naturalist might map the ecosystem of an animal, say a bear, by reference to the resources it uses (i.e. as a function of the organism), so the area might alter with seasons, differ according to the age or sex of the animal, or from individual to individual; such an ecosystem would incorporate a number of distinct components (valley, mountain forest, coastlands, etc., each of which could itself be recognized as an ecosystem) (Gonzales, 1996). Alternatively, delineation could be by ecosystem function (i.e. as a sort of landscape unit). The latter form is often selected as a working unit by those concerned with environmental protection, the former by, for example, a game warden.

TABLE 9.1 Classifications of environmental systems

(A) BY FUNCTION

Isolated systems	Boundaries are closed to import and export of material and energy.
Closed systems	Boundaries prevent import and export of material, but not energy. For example, 'Biosphere 2' receives sunlight but is supposed to function with no other exchanges. The Earth is largely a closed system, although it receives dust, meteorites and solar radiation.
Open systems	Boundaries allow free exchange of material and energy. Many of the Earth's ecosystems are of this form and may actually be interdependent.

(B) BY DEGREE OF HUMAN DISTURBANCE

Park (1980: 42) suggested environmental systems could be classified as:

Natural systems	Unaffected by human interference.
Modified systems	Affected to some extent by human interference.
Control systems	Human interference, by accident or design, plays a major role in function (includes most agricultural systems).

Note: Biosphere 2 is an enclosed environment experiment constructed some years ago in the Sonoran Desert, USA

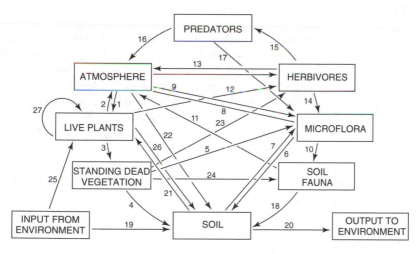

FIGURE 9.1 The relations between ecosystem components
Source: Van Dyne (1969: 83, Fig. 3)

Ecosystems may be recognized across a great range of spatial scales: one may cover 10,000 km^2, another less than 1 km^2 (one could argue the half-litre of water trapped in a pitcher-plant, or a clump of lichen on a tombstone are ecosystems). In a stable ecosystem each species will have found a position, primarily in relation to its functional needs for food, shelter, etc. This position, or niche, is where a given organism can survive most effectively. Some organisms have very specialized demands and so occupy very restricted niches; others can exist in a very wide niche. Niche demands are not always simple: in some situations a species may be using only a portion of its potential niche, and alteration of a single environmental parameter may suddenly open, restrict or deny a niche for an organism. Competition for the niche with other organisms is one such parameter.

Ecosystems can be subdivided, according to local physical conditions, into habitats (places where an organism or group of organisms live), populated by characteristic mixes of plants and animals (e.g. a pond ecosystem may have a gravel bottom habitat and a mud bottom habitat). Within an ecosystem change in one variable may affect one or more, perhaps all other variables.

There are few ecosystems where there are no complex energy flows and exchanges of materials across their boundaries. Even something as well-defined as a cave may exchange water and nutrients with regional groundwater or capture debris blown from outside (Bailey, 1986). To simplify study, ecologists have attempted to enclose small natural ecosystems, create artificial laboratory versions (e.g. phytotrons and growth chambers), and study very simple types (such as those of the Antarctic 'dry valleys'). A huge hermetically sealed greenhouse complex with a crew of eight, designed to study the function and interaction of several ecosystems, was established in Arizona, USA, in 1991. Named 'Biosphere 2' (to emphasize its separation from the Earth's biosphere, and to reflect one motive of the experiment, which was to test the feasibility of such facilities for life-support on Mars), it maintained a more or less breathable atmosphere and provided almost enough food for the crew for two years (Allen, 1991).

Ecosystems are commonly investigated by systems analysis (Watt, 1966; Odum, 1983). In the late 1940s, systems diagrams were constructed to show energy flows between components of ecosystems. Soon similar approaches had been adopted by many social scientists and business managers as frameworks for study and as means of prediction (a systems approach was used by the Club of Rome to try to model global limits) (Smith and Reeves, 1989). Applied systems theory and systems modelling have been steadily improved and are used by environmental managers (Perez-Trejo *et al.*, 1993). While the ecosystem approach may not give precise results, it does provide a valuable framework for analysis.

Adaptive environmental management approaches often adopt an ecosystem approach. However, use of an ecosystem approach is not without problems: it can be difficult to recognize boundaries; measurement of what goes in and comes out can be difficult; establishing whether an ecosystem is natural, rather than modified, can be difficult, and it is possible for organisms to migrate in or out. Also, the assumption that an ecosystem will behave in a linear, predictable manner may be over-optimistic; in practice ecosystem predictions are often inaccurate. Nevertheless, it is often possible to get some idea of an ecosystem's energy and material distribution. Without understanding all of the complex interactions one could model the behaviour of an ecosystem, although with complex ecosystems this becomes difficult (Figure 9.2). There is also a chance that some of the processes that are operating work at random, and therefore cannot be modelled satisfactorily.

It is important for the environmental manager to integrate ecology and policy in order to manipulate ecosystems to meet human needs and desires (Brown and MacLeod, 1996). Ecosystems researchers must therefore ensure that they are looking at realistic assumptions, not over-simple abstractions or misconceptions. According to systems theory, changes in one component of a system will promote changes in other, possibly all, components. As subsystems may interact in different ways, the ecosystem approach is essentially holistic. A concise critique of the ecosystems approach may be found in Pepper (1984: 107–110).

Given time, natural, undisturbed ecosystems theoretically reach a state of dynamic equilibrium (steady state). Regulatory mechanisms of (checks and balances) of positive and negative feedbacks counter changes within and outside the ecosystem to maintain the steady state. However, since each ecosystem has developed under a different set of variables, each has a different capacity to resist stresses and to recover.

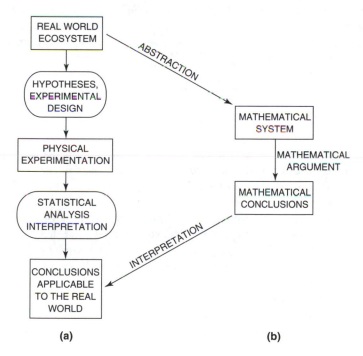

FIGURE 9.2 The conventional approach to studying ecosystems (a); a second approach (b) involves abstraction of the system into a model leading to interpretation of mathematical conclusions
Source: Adapted from Van Dyne (1969: 337, Fig. 7)

Also, humans often upset regulatory mechanisms of natural ecosystems, so response is distorted. When ecosystems are exposed to stress, some responses may be immediate, others delayed, perhaps for decades. To manage ecosystems effectively it is necessary to know longer term behaviour as well as short-term response. This means palaeoecology and historical records have a part to play, as has long-term monitoring.

Ecosystems adjust to perturbation through regulatory mechanisms. When the relationship between input and output to the system is inverse (e.g. increased sunlight causes more cloud which reduces the impact of that sunlight on the surface), it is termed a negative feedback. The opposite is a positive feedback, whereby an effect is magnified. There is a risk that a positive feedback might result in a runaway reaction affecting crucial biogeochemical or biogeophysical cycles – environmental management must watch for such threats.

Prompted by Darwin's work on evolution, it was hypothesized (notably by W.M. Davis) that, under conditions of constant climate and sea-level, geomorphological processes would slowly evolve a steady-state landscape (geomorphologists now argue that similar earthforms in comparable environments might not follow so predictable an evolution, given the complexity of other factors which operate). A similar reasoning was adopted by Clements (1916), that vegetation evolves to a steady-state – climax via ecological succession (or a regression) of communities (Johnson and Steere, 1974: 8). The ecosystem should remain in such a steady state unless a critical parameter alters sufficiently; if change occurs, the process of ecological succession or biotic development will try to return to the steady-state. This concept of ecological succession is debated: change may be directional or random, and climax communities are not as common as textbooks suggest.

How stable are ecosystems?

Ecosystems are subject to natural and anthropogenic changes, some catastrophic and sudden, but often gradual and less marked. Ecologists, botanists and geomorphologists have argued that ecosystems tend towards a steady state achieved through adaption to changes (Hill, 1987; Stone et al., 1996). Some economists and political studies specialists have suggested economics, politics and social development follow a predictable evolutionary path to a steady-state. 'Stability' can have a number of meanings, including: lack of change in structure of an ecosystem; resistance to perturbations; or speedy return to steady-state after disturbance (Troumbis, 1992: 252). Mitchell (1997: 51) felt that basic concepts of ecosystem diversity and stability did not adequately describe complex reality: ecosystems were inherently complex, there were unlikely to be simple answers, and environmental managers must accept that they could not just manage ecosystems, but that they were managing human interactions with them.

The ecosystem concept and ecosystem management

The ecosystem concept became a widely used conceptual tool for research after 1945; for example, it has been adopted in the studies of the International Biological Program (Myers and Shelton, 1980). Nowadays, ecologists often adopt an ecosystems approach when seeking to understand and monitor a given situation. The approach focuses on energy flows or nutrient transformations. Biotic activity within an ecosystem can be divided into that of producers, consumers and decomposers, and efforts to study these may focus on population dynamics and productivity, predator–prey relations, parasitism, and so on. Study of non-biotic aspects of an ecosystem may focus on estimation of biomass or micrometeorology. In the last three decades there has been a shift from description of the structure of ecosystems to a focus on trying to understand function, processes, mechanisms and systems behaviour. There is a much better understanding of the structure and function of ecosystems than was the case in the 1960s, but there are still gaps in knowledge, leading to strong criticisms of lack of scientific rigour and vagueness (Armitage, 1995: 470).

The ecosystem concept allows the environmental manager to look at portions of complex nature as an integrated system (Van Dyne, 1969: 78; Holling, 1987). The concept may be applied to cities or agriculture (urban ecosystems and agroecosystems respectively), although these are not actually true, discrete units in terms of energy flows or function. An ecosystems approach allows a holistic view of how components work together, i.e. it can incorporate human dimensions into biosphere functioning. This requires interdisciplinary teamwork that includes consideration of science and social science issues (Darling and Dasmann, 1969; Roe, 1996; Yaffee, 1996). Environmental managers may treat an ecosystem rather like a factory: they seek to improve and sustain output and reduce costs but, unlike a factory, there are often several different 'products' (agricultural produce, tourism, water supply, conservation, etc).

A precise, universal definition of ecosystem management is impossible, partly because it depends on the stance and outlook of the definer, partly because it is still evolving, and also because it involves a diversity of actors – scientists, policy makers, commerce, citizens, etc. It is not a science, nor it is a simple extension of traditional resource management; rather it seeks a synthesis of ecosystem science and ecosystem approaches, to provide a framework that links biophysical and socioeconomic research and practice in a region or ecosystem through a holistic ecological and participatory methodology (although *how* it might achieve these goals is usually less than clearly stated) (Grumbine, 1994; 1997). Many of the principles used by ecosystem management are normative, i.e. moral and ethical rather than strictly scientific, which has attracted criticism (Likens, 1992; Haeuber, 1996). Concern has been voiced at the lack of satisfactory established principles for ecosystem management (Brunner and Clark, 1997). It is not always clear how ecosystems management differs from environmental management, although the former involves application of the ecosystem concept and use of an ecosystem boundary.

Increasingly, the emphasis is on sustainable ecosystem management, the goal of which is to maintain ecosystem integrity and, if possible, produce food and other commodities on a sustained basis. The ecosystem approach helps define the temporal and spatial scale of management. This requires a multidisciplinary or, better, an interdisciplinary approach in order to deal with complexities of ecosystem function and usage. Mitchell (1997: 62) voiced concern that ecosystem management may lead to a broad and possibly superficial approach in the effort to break down an over-sectoral treatment; therefore he suggested that ecosystem management should be integrated with organizational structures that continue along sectoral lines. Other problems of ecosystems management include: the need to address complex problems (di Castri and Hadley, 1985); that experience gained in one ecosystem may be of limited value for other, even similar, ecosystems; the character of natural ecosystems may be difficult to establish where there has been disturbance, so it is difficult to agree what conservation or land restoration should aim for.

O'Neil (Cairns and Crawford, 1991: 39) suggested the ecosystem approach could be seen as methodology (with models to simulate the ecosystem) and mindset (with a focus on function and properties of ecosystems) the strength of the approach being synthesis of the complexity of problems faced, enabling assessment of consequences. In practice there has been a good deal of fragmentation, for example: ecosystem studies of risk; ecosystem quality management; assessment of ecosystem potential; ecosystem conservation, and so on.

It is not only ecologists and environmental managers who have adopted an ecosystems approach: many other disciplines frequently do so, including human ecology (perhaps the first to do so – see chapter 13), cultural anthropology (Moran, 1990), political science, planning, management and urban studies. These users generally seek to define a workable 'ecosystem' for study, and then apply ecological concepts. Slocombe (1993: 294) pointed out that the 'ecosystems' that are selected as management and planning units are often larger than true ecosystems, and may have considerable human activity affecting them.

It has been argued that an ecosystems approach should consider humans as part of, not separate from, nature and incorporate human values and traditional knowledge (Watt, 1969; Samson and Knopf, 1996; Vogt et al., 1997).

The ecosystems approach means different things to various disciplines, so it is a useful generalization rather than a precise term. Even if widely agreed that an ecosystems approach demands a holistic perspective, that can be interpreted in either a comprehensive or an integrated manner. The integrated approach does not try to research all ecosystem components, only those deemed crucial by planners (Barrett, 1994; Bocking, 1994; Margerum and Born, 1995). A comprehensive approach seeks to research in much greater depth with wider focus, taking time and costing more, so it may be less practical for planning and management.

The decision to adopt an ecosystems approach will usually be based on an assessment of whether its advantages outweigh its disadvantages (see Box 9.1). An eminent ecologist, having weighed integrated and comprehensive approaches, stressed how important it was that planners and analysts had a clearly thought-out interpretation of what an ecosystem approach means before using it. As many institutions are commodity or service orientated, rather than ecosystem orientated, data collection and personnel training may need changing. A commodity or service orientation may be

BOX 9.1 Advantages and disadvantages of the ecosystem approach

Advantages	*Disadvantages*
Comprehensive, holistic approach for understanding whole systems.	May neglect sociocultural issues such as politics, power and equity.
Different view of science that recognizes diversity of cause and effect, uncertainty, and probabilistic nature of ecosystems.	Ecological determinism: danger of generalizing from biophysical to socioeconomic systems.
Draws on theory and methods from different fields to generate models and hypotheses.	Nebulous: a vague, superorganismic theory of poor empirical foundation, that relies on analogy and comparison.
Contributes to understanding limits, complexity, stresses and dynamics.	Non-standard definition of 'ecosystem'.
Encourages preventive thinking by placing people within nature.	Reification of analytical systems; in some approaches linked to reductionist and equilibrium views.
Facilitates locally appropriate, self-reliant, sustainable action.	Narrow spatial focus on local ecosystem structures and processes.
Facilitates co-operation, conflict reduction, institutional integration.	Functionalist and/or energy analysis are overemphasized.
Requires recognition of mutual dependence on all parts of a system: e.g. natural/cultural, person/family.	Duplicates and/or overlaps other disciplines without a special contribution of its own.
Results in criteria for management actions.	If ecosystem approaches can apply to everything they may be meaningless.
Facilitates studies that integrate a range of disciplines (holistic).	

Source: Slocombe, 1993: 298, Table 3 (with modification)

BOX 9.2 How the ecosystem approach can advise the environmental manager – three selected situations

Range management
what type of stock;
stocking rate;
the state of the range;
how to manage grazing rotation;
whether to augment with seeding or fertilizer;
potential threats;
parallel usage opportunities (recreation, conservation, forestry, etc).

Forest management
whether the forest trees are healthy and regenerating;
whether the mix of species is steady or in decline;
whether there are threats;
what harvesting is possible and how;
parallel usage opportunities (forest products, conservation, tourism, etc);
whether forest can be established/re-established in currently unforested areas.

Conservation management
whether conservation is viable in the long term;
what mix and number of species can be carried;
whether a cull or improvement in breeding is needed;
whether there are threats;
what parallel uses are possible (ecotourism, etc);
whether there are alternative ecosystems to provide back-up.

---

fine if the goal is to maximize production of a single product or service; it is less satisfactory where the ecosystem yields several 'products' and it is important to know hazards, limits and opportunities (see Box 9.2).

Two themes emerge from the literature: the first is a search for ways of integrating environmental and socioeconomic planning, and the second to define and bound areas (ecosystems) of interest and value to managers and planners. Sometimes ecosystem boundaries coincide with clear physical features, e.g. an island or a forest, but often they are less well delineated. Gonzalez (1996) noted the need to define an ecosystem in 3-D, not just mapping area, but also 'top' and 'bottom'. The quest is for an ecosocioeconomic planning unit which is stable, clearly defined and likely to support sustainable development. Comprehensive regional approaches began to evolve in the 1930s and 1940s (mainly based on river basin ecosystems), and there was interest into the 1970s. There have been attempts to integrate ecological concern into regional planning and policy making (McHarg, 1969; Isard, 1972; Nijkamp, 1980).

Ecosystems analysis, modelling and monitoring

Ecosystems can be analysed using systems theory, which enables complex, changing situations to be understood and predictions made. Systems theory assumes that measurable causes produce measurable effects. There have been attempts to combine ecological and economic models in systems analysis. For example, a systems analysis approach to environmental assessment and management was used in the Oetzertal (Valley of the River Oetz, Austria) from 1971, as part of the UNESCO Man and Biosphere Program. This alpine valley ecosystem has experienced great change as a consequence of tourism, especially skiing, and, with the help of the modelling, managers now have a clear idea of what is needed to sustain tourism and maintain environmental quality (Moser and Peterson, 1981). In the early 1990s the USA established a nation-wide Environmental Management and Monitoring Program (EMAP) to aid ecological risk analysis by assessing trends in condition of ecosystems – so far a controversial and expensive exercise.

Ecosystem planning and management – biogeophysical units

The environmental management of specific ecosystems is considered in chapter 10. Here a number of ecosystem-based frameworks are considered.

Ecozones

Various researchers have attempted to divide the Earth into ecozones or life zones for study, planning and management (Schultz, 1995). One of the best-known and most widely used systems for land use classification is the Holdridge Life Zone Model. This is based on the relationship of current vegetation biomes to three parameters (annual temperature, annual precipitation, potential evapotranspiration) (Holdridge, 1964; 1971).

Ecoregions and ecodistricts

The Netherlands National Institute of Public Health and Environmental Protection has developed a framework for hierarchical ecosystem classification to try to overcome the confusion resulting from the use of many different geographical regionalizations by various bodies. This is known as 'standardized regionalization', a hierarchical mapping of nested ecosystems started in 1988 (Table 9.2), and is used for regional environmental policy. It ties in with GIS, is useful for state-of-environment reporting, and has been quite successful. Similar approaches have been tried or adopted in several countries, such as Canada, the USA and Belgium (Omernik, 1987).

TABLE 9.2 Hierarchical ecosystem classification used in The Netherlands

Unit	Area (km^2)	
Ecozone	< 62,500	
Ecoprovince	2,500–62,500	
Ecoregion	**100–2,500**	⎤ best suited
Ecodistrict	**6.25–100**	⎬ to most needs
Ecosection	0.25–6.25	⎦
Ecoseries	0.015–0.25	
Ecotope	0.0025–0.015	
Ecoelement	< 0.0025	

Source: Based on Klijn *et al.* (1995: 799, Table 1)

Coastal zone planning management

There has been growing interest in coastal zone management (Carter, 1988; OECD, 1993; Brower *et al.*, 1994; Viles and Spencer, 1995; Clark, 1996; Prestcott, 1996; a journal is dedicated to the field: *Coastal Zone Management*). In many parts of the world it is in the coastal zone that most human activity is concentrated and environmental management is required, especially for coastlands subject to flooding or erosion, and regions where mangrove forests are being exploited. With the threat of global warming and rising sea-levels coastal zone management is likely to grow in importance (for further coverage see French, 1998).

Marine ecosystem planning and management

An ecosystems approach has been explored for managing the Baltic Sea (Figure 9.3) (Jansson, 1972), the Mediterranean (and more especially the Aegean), the North Sea and the Japanese Inland Sea. Although not strictly marine, but with similarities, are the Great Lakes of North America, the Aral, Caspian, and Black Seas, and Lake Baikal). These ecosystems involve several countries, and in order to control pollution management must extend inland to incorporate regions which pollute, control riverflow, etc.

River basin planning and management

In a river basin flowing water acts as an integrative element. Using watersheds as a management unit (see following section), there is more attention given to moisture and soil conservation. River basins have been used for integrated or comprehensive regional development planning and management since the 1930s. The river basin

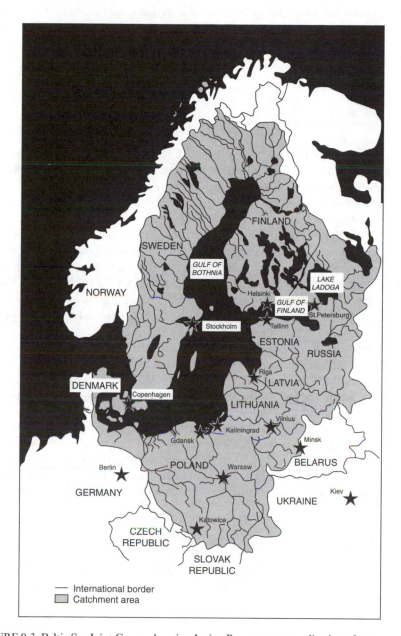

FIGURE 9.3 Baltic Sea Joint Comprehensive Action Programme – application of an ecosystem approach for management of a sea bordered by several countries. Note catchment area to ensure jurisdiction over things which affect the ecosystem (or might be argued to be part of it)
Source: Mitchell, 1997: 64, Fig. 3.2 – which was based on material from the Helsinki Commission (1993) *The Baltic Sea Joint Comprehensive Action Programme.* Government Printer, Helsinki.

biogeophysical landscape unit is suitable for applying a holistic, ecosystem approach, and is useful when several states share a river system (Briassoulis, 1986; Barrow, 1997). There is probably more experience with the use of river basins as a means for integrated environmental–socioeconomic planning and management than with any other ecosystem approach and much debate about its effectiveness.

Watershed/catchment planning and management

A watershed ('catchment' is often used in the UK) offers a biogeophysical unit usually with well-defined boundaries and within which agroecosystem use, human activity and water resources are interrelated. Researchers and environmental managers have made use of watersheds or subdivisions (micro-watersheds) to study how land use changes affect hydrology, etc., since the 1930s (starting with the US Forest Service Coweeta Experimental Forest, North Carolina) (Vogt *et al.*, 1997: 40). Watershed experiments seek to establish the effects of disturbing vegetation or soil, monitoring inputs to the basin (measuring sunlight, rainfall, etc) and outputs (by measuring quantity and quality of flows from streams or material removed as produce). One of the best known of these is the Hubbard Brook Experimental Watershed, New Hampshire (USA) (Van Dyne, 1969: 53–76). Watersheds are useful for forestry, agricultural development, erosion control, water supply, pollution and fisheries management.

Armitage (1995: 470) felt that integrated watershed management, like soil erosion control, had focused mainly on technical issues (Easter *et al.*, 1986; FAO, 1988; Pereira, 1989). Recently there has been interest in using watersheds as units for integrated biophysical and socioeconomic management to promote better community development or land husbandry and sustainable development, and a number of major agencies have published guidelines or handbooks (Bouchet, 1983; FAO, 1986; Naiman, 1992). In India participatory watershed development has been used to try and improve rural livelihoods and counter environmental degradation (Turton and Farrington, 1998). Hufschmidt's (1986) model has attracted particular attention as an integrative methodological framework, although it is not really ecologically focused.

Bioregionalism

This is an approach which argues for human self-sufficiency at a local scale. Sometimes advocates have been somewhat naive, on occasion verging on eco-fascist.

Agroecosystem analysis

Basically this is a form of rapid rural appraisal (Conway, 1985a; 1985b; Conway and Barbier, 1990: 162–193) and a type of ecosystem approach. An agroecosystem is an ecosystem modified by humans in order to produce food or other agricultural. Four agroecosystem properties were recognized by Conway (1985b):

1   *Productivity* – output, yield or net income from a valued product per unit of resource input. This can be measured as yield or income per hectare, total production per household or farm, or at a regional or even national scale. Alternatively, it may be expressed as calories.

2   *Stability* – the constancy of productivity in the face of climatic fluctuations, market demand, etc.

3   *Sustainability* – the capacity of an agroecosystem to maintain productivity in the face of environmental challenges and degradation arising from its exploitation.

4   *Equitability* – the evenness of distribution of the productivity benefits among humans.

The agroecosystem can be managed in ways that give optimum levels of each of these properties: maximizing productivity is likely to reduce agroecosystem sustainability; ensuring sustainability might reduce productivity.

Agroecosystem management

This demands an understanding of ecosystems and of how natural processes are modified by agricultural objectives. To manage agroecosystems effectively requires application of knowledge from a range of disciplines, and the approach supports this (Risser, 1985; Gliessman, 1990). Because the main goal is to improve socioeconomic conditions, some feel the agroecosystem approach is more socioeconomic than ecological in orientation (Armitage, 1995).

Landscape ecology approach

The landscape ecology approach focuses on spatial patterns at the landscape scale (Vink, 1983; Forman and Godron, 1986; Vos and Opdam, 1993; Ze'ev, 1994). The response of an ecosystem to disturbance frequently depends on its neighbouring ecosystems: for example, organisms may escape if there are suitable nearby ecosystems and recolonize after disturbance ceases; also, energy or materials may be transferred between ecosystems. An ecosystem seldom functions in isolation and its ability to withstand stress may depend on how a nearby ecosystem is being managed, or on whether the boundaries are altered – a road or cleared area of forest may prevent animal or plant dispersal to a favourable alternative site. The landscape ecology approach extends ecosystem management to a group of more- or less neighbouring or linked ecosystems (Jensen *et al.*, 1996). An International Association of Landscape Ecology (UK-based) was founded some years ago to help advance the field.

GIS and quantitative techniques have been applied to the landscape ecology approach (and it has also been applied to agroecosystems management and to conservation) (Hassan and Anglestam, 1991; Turner and Gardiner, 1991; Bunce *et al.*, 1993; Haines-Younge *et al.*, 1993). Interesting applications of landscape ecology and GIS have been: the prediction of the occurrence of Lyme Disease, a growing public health problem in the USA (*New Scientist* 15 November 1997), and the spread of Chagas Disease in South America. In the UK the Countryside Commission has been exploring the value of landscape character mapping.

Ekistics

Ekistics is described as the 'science of human settlements': it draws upon human ecology and regional planning and treats urban territory as a living organism, adopting an interdisciplinary, problem-solving approach – in some respects similar to an ecosystems approach, especially in its focus on networks (Doxiadis, 1968; 1977). Although the journal *Ekistics* is widely read, the approach is now mainly of academic interest, and is little used in practice.

Applying the ecosystem concept to tourism and heritage management

The application of environmental management to tourism and heritage features has grown since 1970s. It has mainly involved the application of impact assessment, eco-auditing and the exploration of sustainable development strategies (Edington and Edington, 1986; Butler, 1991). Two themes appear frequently: sustainable tourism development, and avoidance or mitigation of tourism impacts. Tourism and heritage features management can be divided into: (1) natural history-oriented tourism; (2) eco-tourism (tourism based on visits to areas of unspoilt natural beauty or rich wildlife; (3) tourism actively involved in assisting conservation and/or gathering environmental information (e.g. tourists pay to assist on a survey or archaeological dig).

Tourism often takes place in a sensitive environment: coastal zones; alpine skiing; coral reefs; and where walkers or off-road vehicles cause damage. The value of the ecosystems approach is that it can highlight vulnerable features and threatening human behaviour, which may be easily overlooked if ecosystem structure and function are not considered. For example, in parts of Australia and South Africa, there have been calls to cull sharks. Before doing so it would be wise to study their behaviour and role in the ecosystem to see whether their value outweighs their threat, and also to see whether they move about so much that local removal is pointless. Similar situations may arise in tropical rainforest environments where apparently minor disturbance of bird or bat roost sites might have serious regional effects, through reduced pollination, seed dispersal or insect predation. Where Alpine farmers turn to tourism and relax their management of summer grazing, the under-grazed grass may fail to anchor winter snow and increase the threat of avalanche.

Tourism may become even more important as a means of financing and encouraging respect for conservation, and of generating income for local peoples. Ecosystem management can help ensure that tourism provides optimum support for conservation. Heritage sites can be established to conserve cultural and natural features, including wildlife and old crop varieties in arboreta and the gardens of large estates. In many parts of the world some of the last remaining stands of ancient trees are found as sacred groves, around burial areas, and in temple gardens. There is a need to apply ecosystem studies to determine how such refuge areas can be sustained and augmented. Caves are especially vulnerable: visitors can introduce moulds and other organisms which damage delicate structures or fauna, and ecologists can advise to help reduce these problems (Cigna, 1993).

Applying the ecosystem concept to urban and peri-urban management

More than half the world population now live in conurbations and the effects of urban settlement, in the form of fuelwood demand, air pollution and contamination of watercourses, are increasing and are felt at growing distances into the surrounding regions (White, 1994). As with tourism, there is a growing literature on urban environmental management. An ecosystem approach can help to identify strategies that can reduce pollution, aid safe disposal of pollutants and production of food, together with some provision of employment – through activities like urban agriculture. At a regional or national scale it may be possible to understand the linkages that have driven people to settle urban areas, often abandoning once sustainable rural livelihoods (Dorney and McLellan, 1984).

Applying the ecosystem concept to conservation management

Forest management and wildlife conservation make extensive use of the ecosystem approach (Lajeunesse *et al.*, 1995; Bailey, 1996; Samson and Knopf, 1996; Boyce, 1997; Weeks, 1997). Biosphere reserves are essentially islands in a sea of disturbance (whether terrestrial ecosystems or aquatic, such as coral reefs), so the study of island ecosystems by biogeographers like David Simberloff, Edward Wilson and Robert McArthur (McArthur and Wilson, 1967; di Castri and Robertson, 1982) provides key information on rates of extinction and evolution; minimum size of habitat and linkages between habitats necessary for sustained conservation; whether to conserve selected species or a whole ecosystem; assessment of likely impacts of climate change or acid deposition; clarification of vital pollination and seed dispersal needs; information on predator–prey relationships, and so on (Miller, 1978; Goeden, 1979; Higgs, 1981; Mueller-Dombois *et al.*, 1981). Caution is needed, for some of the island bio-geographic theory which conservation managers draw upon is incomplete, imprecise, or has been little tested (Shrader-Frechette and McCoy, 1994).

Once established, a conservation area may fail to sustain biodiversity because it is too small for species to breed and feed, or because disruptive edge effects penetrate too far (Soule, 1987). Studies have been in progress for some years in the Amazonian forests of northern Brazil to improve understanding of the impact of various intensities of forest disturbance and ecosystem fragmentation on biodiversity survival using different sizes and patterns of forest fragments (for an introduction to island biogeography, and a discussion of the Minimum Critical Size of Ecosystem Study undertaken in Amazonia see Quammen, 1997). These studies, and similar ones elsewhere, are vital for establishing what are viable locations, ideal size and pattern of conservation areas (whether several smaller reserves offer greater security and hold more or fewer species than one larger, and whether multiple reserves should be linked by corridors to facilitate movement of flora and fauna).

Recommended reading

Journals which publish articles on ecosystem management

BioScience
Conservation Biology
Ecological Applications
Ecological Modelling
Environment and Urbanization
Environmental Management
Human Ecology
Journal of Environmental Management
Journal of Environmental Planning and Management
Journal of Range Management
Landscape Ecology

Chapter 10

Environmental management in sensitive, vulnerable and difficult situations

There are many reasons why an environment may be sensitive or difficult to manage: harsh climate; remoteness; the impact of natural disasters; as a consequence of easily damaged vegetation or soil; because of insularity; as a result of excessive human demands. Excessive demands may be made in rich and poor countries, causing environmental degradation sometimes at low human population densities (as in parts of Australia, Amazonia, or Siberia). Certain parts of the world are more likely to suffer natural disasters: seismically and volcanically active areas, those subject to hurricane or tornado, tsunami, avalanche, landslide, sudden frost, etc. These risks can be mapped by hazard and risk assessment, for insurance companies, civil defence, etc. It is also possible to map things that are vulnerable to disruption, by say frost or pollution or erosion. Hazardous sites, like chemical plants, and potential military targets can also be mapped. Various assessments and maps can be overlaid or combined in a GIS-type system to assess combined risks. Unfortunately, there may be no efforts to make such assessments.

Are there areas of the world particularly prone to environmental problems?

Given long enough, even the safest area could be subjected to natural or anthropogenic problems. Environmental managers must be alert for situations where risk and likely severity of problems may be altered by human activity – for example, land may be sensitized to drought or soil erosion by misuse. The effects of storms can be magnified if people remove vegetation cover from watersheds or coastal land. Development may drive people, or they may be attracted into areas where they trigger natural processes to cause environmental problems. People often evolve strategies of environmental use – nomadic grazing, shifting cultivation, etc. – which minimize environmental problems and risks to their well-being, but these strategies may break down as a result of development. Ideally, environmental management would monitor for such changes. However, there is a limit to resources, so such wide-ranging study is seldom possible. The solution may be for international agencies to monitor.

Particularly in developed countries people are becoming more dependent on technology, which increases their vulnerability, manifest in two ways: (1) hazards posed by malfunction; (2) hazards posed by system breakdown, through mismanagement, accident, obsolescence, civil unrest or war. The way to reduce this vulnerability is to have better regulations and controls to ensure safe equipment and fail-safe systems. Insurance companies and public opinion may help provide such safeguards. However, the poor often have to make do with poor inspection, weak regulations and inadequate technology – disasters like the Bhopal pollution accident result (Barrow, 1995a: 270). Generally the rich can buy their way out of risk.

Countries which have complex, interlocking technology and economics are vulnerable. Complex systems are easily disrupted and need skilled specialists to maintain them. They are difficult to run in times of stress and may be a challenge to salvage. Natural disasters or terrorism could have marked effects on complex computer systems needed by government and banking; a poor country may have few difficulties if it is still using robust card-indexes, decentralized services, etc. There are currently fears that the millennium bug or some computer virus could wreak havoc with electronic systems. If so, it may prompt governments not to rely so much on vulnerable and centralized systems.

How sensitive and vulnerable are ecosystems?

The concept of ecosystem stability was discussed in chapter 9 (Hill, 1987; Stone *et al.*, 1996). Mitchell (1997: 51) felt that basic concepts of ecosystem diversity and stability were too simplistic adequately to describe reality; so, as ecosystems were inherently complex, environmental managers would need to accept that often they could not manage ecosystems, although they might manage human interactions with them.

On the whole, biogeochemical and biogeophysical processes tend to resist change and are self-regulating within limits, so one can expect a sort of dynamic equilibrium. However, some global cycles, environments and organisms (and groups of people) are more sensitive to change than others. Stability is in large part a function of resistance to change and resilience following it. Resistance (or sensitivity) may be defined as the degree to which a given ecosystem undergoes change as a consequence of natural or human actions or a combination of both. Resilience may be used to refer to the way in which an ecosystem can withstand change. It is widely held that ecosystem stability is to a significant degree related to biological diversity: the greater the variety of organisms there are in an ecosystem, the less likely is there to be instability (Pimm, 1984). However, it is quite possible that a change in some parameter could have an effect on all organisms regardless of diversity: thus diversity may help ensure stability but does not guarantee it. Resilience is often used as a measure of the speed of recovery of a disturbed ecosystem but can refer to how many times a recovery can occur if disturbance is repeated (Holling, 1973).

What the environmental manager seeks to avoid is environmental degradation – a rough definition of which is: the loss of utility or potential utility or the reduction, loss or change of features or organisms which may be difficult: costly or impossible to replace. Recognizing degradation can be difficult: it may be slow and gradual, or it may take place long after disturbance. People may fail to notice change which may sometimes be too imperceptible for a single generation to see. Nowadays it is rare for an environment to be 'natural'. The chances are that there has been degradation by humans, e.g. development in southern France may degrade the *maquis* scrubland, but that is already much degraded compared with the prehistoric forest cover. The present condition of the an ecosystem may not indicate what has been lost, or show if there has been improvement. An ecosystem may not be stabilized when disturbed: it could already be much degraded or improved compared with its natural state, or it could be undergoing cyclic, more or less constant or erratic change (Kershaw, 1973: 65–84). Return to a pre-disturbance state when disturbance ceases is by no means certain (Burton *et al.*, 1977; Blaikie and Brookfield, 1987; Goldsmith, 1990). For example, grazing can lead to increased scrub cover; a reduction in grazing might be expected to lead to a reduction of the scrub – but that sometimes causes a thickening of woody vegetation.

Areas of the world prone to natural disasters

Certain parts of the world are more likely to suffer natural disasters: seismically and volcanically active areas, those subject to hurricane or tornado, typhoon or tsunami, drought, flooding, avalanche, landslide, sudden frost or intense storms. There are probably areas more likely to be affected by warfare and social difficulties. These threats can be recorded on a hazards map or database. It is also possible to map things that are especially vulnerable to disruption by, say, pollution damage, frost, or erosion. Hazardous industry or power generation and potential military targets can also be mapped. These maps can be overlaid or fed into a GIS to assess cumulative risks.

Environmental problems and developing countries

At the 1972 Stockholm Conference on the Human Environment problems of the environment were widely regarded in poor countries as matters for developed nations, as they were too poor to afford the luxury of worrying, and anyway 'the rich were to blame'. Until roughly 1985 it was common for developing countries to suspect calls to protect the environment of being a ploy to hold back their development and continue their dependency or to withhold aid. Virtually all developing countries would now accept that there are environmental problems which require attention (Schramm and Warford, 1989). The nature and causes of the problems and the cure for them are often less than clear.

Developing countries have tremendous diversity of environment, style of government, administration, historical background, degree of poverty, etc. Many have handicaps associated with being tropical: e.g. no season cold enough to kill pest organisms; soils that are often infertile and difficult to manage without causing environmental degradation; intense storms (Huntington, 1915; Ooi, 1983: 2; Kates and Haarmann, 1992). Adams (1990: 6–8) suggested developing countries faced a double crisis: a crisis of development and a crisis of environment. The first of these involves debt, falling commodity prices and poverty. The second is the result of global environmental change, the impacts of resource exploitation.

Marginalization

People who are marginalized – forced or attracted onto poor-quality, perhaps easily degraded land, or in some other way live close to the edge – become progressively more disadvantaged and vulnerable (a vicious spiral). The reasons for marginalization are diverse and include: loss of common resources; efforts to escape unrest; the hope of employment or access to farmland; eviction from conservation areas or from the estates of large land users; altered trade opportunities; economic impacts of structural adjustment and national debt; changes in labour costs and availability; widowhood; and reservoir flooding. Environmental or socioeconomic change or technological innovation can cause people to become marginalized (or demarginalized) *in situ*; for example, drought; disease or pests; pollution; decline in demand for produce due to change in fashion, economic slump, or substitution; warfare; rising labour costs; changes in communications; altered land-user attitudes; introduction of new crops; labour migration.

There is considerable support for the view that there are growing environmental problems in developing countries, often caused by the disempowerment of local people, i.e. locals can no longer participate in resource management and are losing access to resources (Ghai and Vivian, 1992: 72; The Ecologist, 1993; Harrison, 1992: 126; Bromley, 1994). A widespread cause of loss of access to common resources is the penetration of capitalism (Tornell and Velasco, 1992). In India, Thailand or Brazil it may be companies seeking land to grow eucalyptus, or large landowners seeking land to grow soya for export, that acquire common land; elsewhere it may be ranchers looking for more grazing land for export-orientated beef production.

What tends to happen through marginalization is that the marginalized over-stress the resources they still have access to, and with nowhere to move to, or no means of moving, they become unwilling agents of damage and their own ultimate demise. Marginal land is likely to demand inputs and be less forgiving to users but is least likely to get such investment.

People forced to move often end up in difficult environments, and are also likely to be disorientated. Together with many of those who have willingly relocated, they probably lack the necessary local experience and resources to establish sustainable livelihoods. Many of those who practise degenerate shifting cultivation are thus 'shifted cultivators', people who have relocated.

Sustained resource exploitation strategies may be disrupted, those disturbed may adapt their activities, cause environmental problems and suffer hardship. Disruption can be caused by quite minor changes, for example in attitudes, trade, weather, and so on, particularly if the resource or land use was poised on a knife-edge. The terms of trade can be a root cause of poverty which may drive people to damage the environment and which also starves governments of funds to counter problems.

Studies of poverty and environmental degradation suggest that three factors often combine to cause marginalization: (1) rapid population growth; (2) land consolidation and agricultural modernization in fertile agricultural areas; (3) prevailing inequalities in land tenure (Leonard *et al.*, 1989: 5).

Population growth and environmental problems

Many developing countries struggling to maintain living standards in the face of growing poverty have little to spend on countering environmental problems. The growing populations of developing countries presently consume far less per capita of the world's resources and cause less pollution than do the populations of rich nations. Nevertheless, demographic increase puts some regions under stress. Population growth does not automatically mean environmental degradation: it can stimulate agricultural production and improvement of technology (e.g. population growth in Europe probably drove farmers to farm fertile but difficult clay-lands and shift from long fallow to annual cropping). It is simplistic Malthusian or neo–Malthusian determinism to say that population growth inevitably leads to problems; environmental impact is a function of population and standard of living, the technology practised and attitudes. Devastation can occur at low population levels and it is probably fair to say that, up to a point, population increase becomes a socioeconomic problem only if food production technology fails to keep up.

Caution is necessary when examining population–environment relationships – for example, there has been little study to check a common assumption that the presence of poor people correlates with environmental degradation (Kates and Haarmann, 1992) (for an introduction to Malthusian and Boserüpian views see Harrison, 1992: 11–19).

Urbanization

Cities have grown rapidly in the last half-century, and relatively recently humankind has become more than 50 per cent urbanized. Rapid growth has led to environmental problems: pollution of air and water, refuse disposal, demand for fuelwood, and large poverty-stricken slums (mainly in developing countries) (Barrett, 1994). In the twenty-first century urban environmental management is going to become much more important as those problems develop.

An African crisis?

Africa is frequently singled out as having or being close to an environmental crisis, a development crisis or both (Ravenhill, 1986; Commins *et al.*, 1986; Watts, 1989; Davidson *et al.*, 1992), although there are some who feel this is exaggerated (Blaikie and Unwin, 1988). Things look grim for a large portion of sub-Saharan Africa. Harrison (1987: 17–26) has concluded that there was a crisis, particularly an environmental crisis, and that, unlike the rest of the world, most of the African continent was not developing but was regressing, because:

1   there was a food supply crisis, manifest as a decline in per capita food production;

2   poverty was increasing;
3   there was a debt crisis which got worse as Africa's exports fell in value and
     imports rose in cost;
4   there was an environmental crisis, getting worse, as vegetation and soils become
     degraded.

To these difficulties may be added unrest (sometimes an important factor): Africa, with less than 10 per cent of the world's population, had almost 50 per cent of the world's refugees in the late 1980s (Harrison, 1987: 52). Another problem, the disease AIDS, seems to have taken a particular hold in parts of sub-Saharan Africa and increasingly contributes to the continent's problems by depleting agricultural labour.

The trends for food production are worrying: in the 1950s most of Africa was self-sufficient, but now many states import, and it is the only continent to show a per capita decline in food production. By AD 2000 it has been predicted that 65 of the world's 117 nations will be unable to feed their populations, and at least 30 of those will be in sub-Saharan Africa. Food security for Africa would probably demand a 4 per cent per annum increase in the continent's food production, plus a similar increase in export crops to provide foreign exchange for inputs. Over the last 30 years the average growth rate for food production has been ca. 2 per cent and export crop production has shown a decline (added to which the prices for these crops have fallen, making it difficult to buy inputs and to encourage producers). There is widespread acceptance that Africa has a food problem but little agreement on why (Rau, 1991), although suspicions have been voiced that it reflects widespread traditional communal or state land ownership, and that a move towards individual land ownership or improved communalism might help.

Environmental management in developing countries

There has been growing interest in applying environmental management to developing countries, partly stimulated by large funding agencies which since the late 1970s have established environment departments and adopted policies of environmental assessment and EIA. By the 1990s most aid agencies and funding bodies had policies seeking to improve environmental management and many published guidelines which have influenced a wider spectrum of companies and consultants.

From the late 1970s developing countries have established environmental agencies, so that by 1992 virtually all had such bodies (although their powers vary enormously). In parallel with these developments international and in-country NGOs were spreading. Nowadays NGOs maintain a network of contacts and command considerable funds and power. Environmental management may therefore have to work with government agencies, international agencies and NGOs. In developing countries a major task is often one of co-ordination, hindered by lack of funds and trained manpower, diverse goals, poor infrastructure, sometimes difficult environmental conditions, inefficiency and corruption. (For an introduction to developing country environmental management see Little and Horowitz, 1987; Montgomery, 1990b; Koninklijk Instituut voor de Tropen, 1990; Eröcal, 1991).

Environments which challenge environmental management

There are environments which require especially careful management because they are easily damaged, are prone to excessive human demands (often both), or demand a specialist approach (the following section is only a brief overview).

Environments used as common resources

The problem of over-exploitation of common resources and the 'tragedy of the commons' model have already been discussed (Berkes, 1989; Bromley and Cernea, 1989). Interest recently has been renewed (Feeney *et al.*, 1990; Vandermeer, 1996; Elliott, 1997). An environment subjected to use as a common resource need not be particularly sensitive to suffer damage: an inappropriate resource development approach can easily cause stress.

Where common resources have sustained livelihoods for a long time, thanks to local people developing social controls, exploitation may break down as a consequence of changing attitudes. For example, in certain traditional fisheries in Amazonia, fishermen left areas undisturbed, or only occasionally fished, allowing stock to recover. The enforcement was through superstition and tradition, but this has broken down as outsiders have been seen to break the rules without mishap.

Islands

A recurrent problem has been the decimation of endemic island flora and fauna, by accidental or deliberate introduction of alien organisms, e.g. the decimation of native songbirds of the main Hawaiian islands, partly because of the introduction of disease-carrying mosquitoes (Elton, 1958). Woodcutting, overgrazing, building, and more frequent fires have also caused damage. Island biogeography can assist those developing sustainable management strategies for islands (Mueller-Dombois, 1975; Gorman, 1979; Troumbis, 1987; Beller *et al.*, 1990; D'Ayala *et al.*, 1990). Managers of island environments must consider dispersal of biota as well as on-island conservation; for example, disturbance of migrant birds on a particular island may have a much wider impact if they are denied that island stepping-stone. Study is vital to uncover situations where the degradation of an island environment may have causes elsewhere; Margaris (1987) reported the breakdown of terrace agriculture in the Aegean Islands as a consequence of the falling demand for dried fruit and olives caused by European women entering full-time employment and changing to ready prepared or frozen food, and to large-scale mainland production which floods the market with cheaper produce.

Alpine and high latitudes

In both the Old and New Worlds there has been considerable development of high-altitude environments. World-wide, mountain (or alpine) environments have attracted tourism. High-altitude and high-latitude ecosystems are subject to extreme conditions, not just low temperature but also high winds. Mountains experience marked diurnal temperature fluctuations, high levels of UV radiation, wind exposure and drought; high latitudes suffer all three, plus they may have permafrost soils which impede drainage of summer melt and are prone to cryoturbation (frost movements), and daylength varies by season, with prolonged winter darkness (Bliss *et al.*, 1981). These areas cover a considerable portion of the Earth's land surface and their vegetation and soils are sensitive to disturbance, are likely to be slow to recover, and may have a relatively low species diversity. With vegetation and soils under stress, mountain and high-latitude areas are vulnerable to transboundary pollution, especially acid deposition (Figure 10.1).

A number of mountain environments have experienced considerable population increase in recent decades, leading to forest, pasture and soil degradation. In Europe and the Rockies of the USA, cross-mountain highways spread vehicle exhaust emissions into high passes where it may directly cause pollution or produce (tropospheric) ozone which damages vegetation – some countries have tried to force traffic off mountain roads to try to halt damage to alpine forests. Disturbance of

FIGURE 10.1 Alpine resort of Cervinia (Matterhorn mid-background). The slopes are subject to pressures from winter ski activity, car traffic reaches as high as 2,300 m above sea-level (foreground), and there is considerable hotel and chalet construction

FIGURE 10.2 Overgrazed land and poorly maintained terraces, High Atlas Mountains, Morocco. As vegetation is degraded at higher altitude, landslides, silted streams and erratic streamflow disrupt farmland and irrigation at lower altitudes

mountain ecosystems may impact on lower altitudes through avalanches, landslides and altered streamflow (see Figure 10.2). In mountain ecosystems managers tend to adopt a valley, watershed or micro-watershed approach to ensure an integrated view of higher and lower slopes (livelihood strategies often operate at several altitudes).

There has been less population growth in high latitudes than mountains, although there are cities in Canada, Alaska, Norway, Finland and Russia, and military and resource development activity. Any traffic across permafrost during the summer is likely to result in damaged vegetation and soil that will be slow to mend. In winter, alpine and tundra regions are less likely to suffer soil compaction and ground vegetation damage. However, plants emerging from the snow, such as young trees, are easily damaged by skiers and skidoos, and snow compaction may delay spring thaw and cause problems for wildlife.

At high latitudes pollution may break down slowly, so oil spills are a problem. Radioactive fallout can become concentrated in lichens and bryophytes, affecting grazing animals. Alaska, Canada, Scandinavia, Greenland, Spitzbergen, Iceland and Russia have oil and gas, and other mineral development in tundra regions (e.g. the Trans-Alaska Pipeline) and so far have managed environmental impacts quite well (Williams, 1979; Copithorne, 1991).

Northern high latitudes have experienced considerable social and technological change: the hunting and transport practices of indigenous people have altered, notably with the adoption of motor boats, skidoos and firearms. There has also been pressure from some NGOs for change in traditional hunting practices (Berg, 1969). The end of the Cold War and better scientific equipment and vehicles have facilitated study, monitoring and exchange of data, assisting northern high-latitude management (Perkins, 1995).

Disposal of waste presents problems at high latitude and in alpine areas. In Antarctica regulations now strictly control waste disposal and most is returned to lower latitudes for disposal (Harris and Meadows, 1992). Some mountain areas have growing waste problems, mainly associated with tourism and climbing activity, notably the Himalayas. Polar seas are vulnerable to pollution because of the slow growth of organisms and slow decay of pollutants and also as a consequence of ice cover, which can restrict mixing of water masses and trap pollutants; the risk of spills is increased by the movement of icebergs, which can damage oil extraction and other infrastructure.

There have been marine oil spills near Antarctica and Alaska, e.g. the *Exxon Valdez* disaster. The CIS has a problem with radioactive waste dumping in the Barents Sea and other Arctic waters, and with radioactive contamination from military facilities along the northern seaboard. These are likely to be expensive to manage and are strategically sensitive.

There are virtually no tundras in the high southern latitudes, but there are extensive peat bogs and swamps in southern South America, the Falkland Islands, and on some sub-Antarctic islands. These peatlands and the southernmost forests of Tierra del Fuego share many of the vulnerabilities of northern tundra and alpine areas. Sub-Arctic and sub-Antarctic islands have some of the problems of both high-latitude environments and island isolation.

Drylands

Like alpine and high-latitude regions, dryland (i.e. seasonally dry as opposed to arid environments) vegetation, soils and fauna are under stress, and so are easily damaged, can be slow to recover and difficult to rehabilitate. Drylands are areas where agricultural productivity is limited by periodic shortage of moisture and where fire damage may be common. Roughly 20 per cent of the world's people live in drylands and many of these are suffering as a consequence of the breakdown of traditional livelihood strategies and land degradation. Some drylands have had marked human and livestock population increases. The reasons for this are diverse, and include: provision of medical and veterinary services, improved water supplies.

Drylands degradation ('desertification') has attracted much attention and has generated many misinterpretations (Mainguet, 1994; Thomas and Middleton, 1994). Since the 1960s problems with drought and desertification have prompted interest in environmental management (Beaumont, 1989; Dixon *et al.*, 1989; Stiles, 1995), improved rangeland management, savanna management (Mott and Tothill, 1985; Werner, 1991; Young and Solbrig, 1992), rehabilitation of degraded drylands, sustainable development of drylands, and coping with fire. There has been limited success in countering dryland environmental problems. This may partly be because these areas have experienced considerable unrest and warfare, but also because governments have neglected these areas or intervene in a heavy-handed way with inappropriate strategies. In drylands care must be taken to be sure of the cause of problems and of the environmental and socioeconomic parameters.

Areas with sensitive and vulnerable soils

There are areas of sensitive and vulnerable soil in many different environments (Figure 10.3). Some soils dry out quickly, some lose their organic matter easily through oxidation if disturbed (a problem in drylands) or drained (a problem with peatlands). There are soils which shrink, crack, develop crusts or concretionary layers. Infertile, acid-sulphate soils may develop on drainage, and there are areas where aluminium and boron deficiency pose an immediate or potential threat (especially if there is acid deposition). Loess soils and similar fine-grained loams wash and blow away easily if disturbed and require skilled land husbandry if production is to be sustained. Soils which are fine-textured allow salt-carrying groundwater to rise and evaporate leaving a saline crust unless there is enough rain or irrigation to leach salts away.

The key needs are for environmental managers to understand the soils they deal with and to promote appropriate soil and water management – put simply, to ensure good land husbandry (Hudson, 1992). To some extent global warming and other fashionable development issues have sidelined concern for soil degradation, which is unwise, for without good soil, food production cannot be sustained. In a number of countries soil degradation disasters have galvanized interest, notably in the USA midwest Dust Bowl during the 1930s. Many agencies warn that soil degradation is bad in developed and developing countries and it rates as one of the world's major environmental threats. Nevertheless, soil conservation and land husbandry are not attracting priority attention and funding. Many countries are spending too little to counter soil degradation, and some have even cut back on their efforts. The growth of interest in environmental management in the UK, Europe and the USA has not been matched by stronger support for soils research and extension services. Indeed, in the UK quite a number of geography or earth sciences courses at universities now have little or no coverage of soils! A historian looking back on the late twentieth century may well be puzzled by this obvious weakness.

Coral reefs

Throughout the world coral reefs have suffered as a consequence of collection for building and cement manufacture, the souvenir trade, from damage by anchors, and the use of dynamite for fishing. Pollution, and perhaps disease related to it, are taking a toll (Wells, 1992; Gray, 1993). The loss of sediment-filtering mangroves, plus more turbid river flow caused by land development may be to blame for some reef damage. There has been suspicion that anti-foul paint may be causing coral damage. A number of reefs have been damaged by the spread of the crown-of-thorns starfish. There seems to be a correlation between agrochemical use on Northern Australian sugar plantations

(a)

(b)

FIGURE 10.3 Vegetation damage leading to soil degradation. Deforested landscape in the High Atlas Mountains, Morocco. Note the pollarded trees (a) (goat grazing and fuelwood collection); gullying and sparsity of groundcover vegetation (b)

and damage to the Great Barrier Reef. Fears are voiced that background pollution of the world's oceans, UV damage from stratospheric ozone thinning, and possibly the effects of global warming, are damaging coral (Pernetta, 1993; Wilkinson and Buddemeier, 1994).

Damaged reefs means loss of biodiversity, nursery and feeding areas for fish and other commercially important species, and reduced storm protection for low-lying islands and coastlands. One proposal is to establish artificial reefs, perhaps with scrap cars or old tyres.

Forests

Forests are being degraded and lost world-wide. In the humid tropics there has been tremendous loss of lowland rainforest. Forests in the seasonally dry tropics have also suffered, as has tree cover in drylands and in temperate and cold environments. There has been some recovery of forest area in North America and the UK since 1900, although species diversity has been reduced; in Scandinavia, western and central Europe and some other areas acid deposition and other pollution has started seriously to damage conifer and, more recently, broad-leaved forests. Within the last few years large-scale logging has become a serious threat to the boreal forests of the CIS.

The cause of forest damage and loss varies from area to area, although there may be shared factors (Barrow, 1995: 138). The causes are often difficult to identify precisely and may be multiple: sometimes logging is to blame, sometimes land clearance by small farmers or governments, pollution may play a role, or ranchers may be responsible. Clearing is usually facilitated by road building or the opening of trails for power cables. The former may in part be for strategic reasons or to facilitate mineral prospecting and development. Ironically, there have often been areas of biodiversity-rich natural forest cleared for monoculture plantation cropping, usually of eucalyptus or fast-growing pine species.

There have been efforts to improve environmental management of forest ecosystems, often linked with local people's participation, agroforestry or 'tolerant forest management' (the extraction of products, leaving as much of the natural forest as possible intact) (Anderson, 1990; Barrow, 1995: 172). Sustainable logging has been more difficult and is less common than some foresters care to admit, and few manufacturers claim 'product of sustainable forestry' on their labels. It is more likely to be 'product of a managed forest' – what 'managed' means is often not clarified.

Wetlands

Wetlands comprise a wide range of ecosystems, the functioning of which depends on water. They include marshes, fens, bogs, peatlands, swamps, delta areas, mangrove forests, floodlands, coastal marshlands and man-made wetlands – irrigated land, reservoir drawdown areas. Roughly 6 per cent of the Earth's land surface could be classed as wetland (Maltby, 1986: 41). Some of the world's most productive habitats are wetlands: they may be breeding and feeding areas for fish and other fauna, and potentially very sustainable cropland. Some wetlands are rich in biodiversity and merit better conservation. Wetlands often play a vital role in regulating streamflow and river flooding, and may help cleanse runoff of pollution and excess sediment.

People often depend on wetlands for food, fuel or building materials and there is potential for domesticating wetland plant and animal species for aquaculture. Some of these areas are heavily populated, like the deltalands of Bangladesh or Egypt. Unfortunately, there are many ways in which wetlands can be damaged: by drainage; by dam or barrage construction; by canal building or channel improvement; by pollution; by over-exploitation of plants and animals; through climate or sea-level change; and by reduction or diversion of inflow.

Mangrove swamps have suffered world-wide as a consequence of land development for real estate, aquaculture ponds, oil-spills, logging and clearance for agriculture. By 1990 it is likely that the world's mangrove forests had decreased by about 79 per cent and the loss is accelerating (Kunstadter *et al.*, 1989: 8). Global warming might cause even greater losses, leaving tropical coastlands more exposed to storm damage, resulting in serious loss of biodiversity and of habitats where a wide variety of marine animals, including commercially valuable species, breed and feed. The costs of mangrove damage have been realized and there is some interest in conservation and reafforestation, and in sustainable management (Kunstadter *et al.*, 1989).

Around the world, coastal wetlands, marshlands, peatlands and floodlands are being converted to agriculture or cleared for building at an alarming and accelerating rate. For example, in southern Iraq extensive wetlands are drying out as a consequence of river diversion, in South America there is a chance that the huge Pantanal wetlands could be damaged by river navigation and canal projects, and things look gloomy for the Mekong Delta and many other wetlands. Often the benefits of 'development' are short-lived and land is left degraded. Where peats are drained the oxidation adds to global atmospheric carbon (Barrow, 1991: 117–128; Turner and Jones, 1991; Mitsch and Gosselink, 1993; Roggeri, 1995).

Estuaries and enclosed or coastal seas

World-wide, marine environments with restricted circulation have suffered from pollution and overfishing. The Baltic, Caspian, North Sea, Aegean and Japanese Inland Sea have suffered. Effective commercial management demands control over the catchment areas that contribute pollution and in many cases international co-operation (see chapter 3).

Rivers

Failure to take proper care of the environmental management of river systems can have severe consequences for the riverine ecosystem, adjoining floodlands, estuaries and nearby seas. Enclosed seas and lakes are especially vulnerable to poor river management. The Aral Sea is a clear example of the environmental degradation and socioeconomic misery which result from failure to co-ordinate and control developments within a river drainage basin (Kotlyakov, 1991).

The main issues of concern to the environmental manager are pollution within the drainage basin which contaminates the river, and regulation of flow by dams or barrages. Dams pose a greater threat than barrages because they alter downstream flow and water quality far more and pose a greater barrier to migration of fish and other organisms. Dams are also more likely to impound an extensive reservoir, which has significant environmental impacts on an area and may force the relocation and disruption of livelihood for large numbers of people (Barrow, 1995a: 221–241).

Lessons the environmental manager can learn from study of sensitive environments

A number of common points can be recognized in the environments just discussed:

- Damage often progresses covertly to become serious before the problem is accepted and action is taken (sometimes too late – as for the rainforests of West Africa).
- Adopting a careless approach to researching problems, often exacerbated by inadequate data and time, can lead to misassessment. Consequently, symptoms rather than causes of problems are focused upon and treated. It is sometimes convenient for those in power to make such mistakes: better for them to blame nature or the peasantry than admit misguided, perhaps personally profitable, policy decisions.
- Local resource users tend to be overlooked in favour of national interests, large companies and their investors. Worse, local people may be marginalized – rural folk are less likely to riot or vote out a government than their urban cousins.
- Long-term effects are overlooked as a consequence of pressure to maximize shorter-term gains.
- Each situation is special. It is dangerous and often difficult to generalize.
- A problem may be realized, but a ministry or other responsible body may lack power, funds or trained personnel to make a satisfactory attack on it.
- Crucial issues, like soil degradation, may fail to attract enough support.
- A number of the problems just listed, plus many others, are, at least in part, due to lack of adequate co-ordination and overview.
- Problems are increasingly transboundary, making it difficult for environmental managers to have jurisdiction or powers to enforce solutions (or even to assess the threat).

There are clearly things which could be done to reduce, avoid or mitigate damage to vulnerable environments:

1   As far as possible leave them alone and find less damaging ways of getting the same resources (or, at the very least, ensure that some examples of the ecosystem are conserved). Environmental managers might do more to prompt those considering development to look at technology, or better use of areas already developed, or rehabilitation of degraded resources.

2   The environmental manager should pay attention to the local conditions, not generalize. (A point stressed by Johnson and Lewis (1995: 303) is that it is important to build on local knowledge and local traditions and be aware of local constraints and opportunities.) However, co-ordination is needed to ensure that each local activity does not cause wider difficulties.

3   Planning tools like strategic environmental assessment could help to highlight risks where there are complex environmental and socioeconomic linkages.

4   Impact assessment can encourage policy makers and planners to check what they propose more carefully, and should identify most risks, so that they can be avoided or the development be modified or abandoned.

5   Risk and hazard assessment can encourage the timely development of contingency plans.

6   Better monitoring of environments and of socioeconomic conditions is important.

7   A problem is to achieve more willingness to consider long-term impacts, and to take preventive or remedial action. That is as much a problem for governments, NGOs, international agencies, the media and the public as for environmental managers, although the latter should be catalysts.

8   One of the key inputs from the environmental manager is to co-ordinate and to encourage and facilitate a thorough (holistic) overview of proposed developments and monitoring of the state of various ecosystems, even if they are not obviously being altered.

Vulnerable environments (assuming they are recognized) deserve particular attention from monitoring bodies, more care from planners and greater vigilance from NGOs, media and international bodies. There are agencies or NGOs which focus on particular problem environments, or threatened organisms. Unfortunately, many lack sufficient funds and other resources to intervene effectively, and may find it difficult to tackle transboundary problems.

Biodiversity conservation has generated a lot of debate, but not everybody supports it: marginalized people may clear forest to survive; businessmen may develop areas of scientific interest for profit (and generate employment in doing so); a government may be forced to weigh aid for the poor against protecting the environment; deer may fare better when hunted with hounds but public opinion finds the practice abhorrent; the ethics of conservation can be far from straightforward (for a discussion of the ethics of biodiversity conservation see Blench, 1998).

Preservation of the environment is often not practicable, given commercial forces and a growing human population. Johnson and Lewis (1995: 228) make the important point that human use of the Earth has two faces: 'creative destruction, the process by which the natural world is modified and sustainable land-use systems are developed'. The second is 'destructive creation' characterized by 'a failure to achieve long-term sustainability and by the initiation of progressively more serious patterns of land degradation'. An environmental manager has to accept that there will usually be environmental changes (good husbandry involves making changes). The crucial thing is to decide when 'destructive creation' has begun, or is likely, and to act to stop it or prevent it.

Recommended reading

Journals which publish articles on environmental management of difficult and vulnerable environments

Arctic and Alpine Research
Desertification Control Bulletin
Journal of Arid Environments
Journal of Range Management
Journal of Tropical Geography (Singapore)
Land Degradation & Development
Mountain Research & Development
Savannah
Society & Natural Resources

Chapter 11

Pollution and

waste management

This chapter gives a broad introduction to pollution and waste management. The following Routledge Environmental Management Series text offers further coverage:

A. Farmer (1998) Managing Environmental Pollution

Pollution can be defined as the introduction by humans, deliberately or inadvertently, of substances or energy (heat, radiation, noise) into the environment – resulting in a deleterious effect (O'Riordan, 1995). Contamination is the presence of elevated concentrations of substances in the environment, food, etc., which may not necessarily be harmful or a nuisance. Pollution involves contamination, but contamination need not constitute pollution. Nature can generate toxic or nuisance compounds (e.g. volcanic ash). Waste can be defined as movable material that is perceived, often erroneously, to be of no further value. Once discarded, it may be no problem, or a nuisance or a hazard (Hill, 1998).

As waste may indirectly give rise to pollution, it is necessary to view both together. Pollution and waste management can focus on (1) prevention, or (after escape or release), (2) collection and disposal, or (3) treatment/mitigation (which sometimes may be difficult and costly or impossible). There are thus three pollution and waste management strategies:

1   Prevention
2   Reclamation
3   Disposal

In an ideal situation, where environmental management has full support, one might add a fourth:

Avoidance (elimination at source, by using longer-lasting construction materials; avoiding dangerous and problematic materials; better processes and machines) – prevention may involve catching waste or pollution before release while avoidance seeks elimination from the outset. Ideally, environmental management seeks a shift from (2) and (3) to (1) (Young, 1990; Bradshaw *et al.*, 1992). A hierarchy of desirability can be agreed. The following is that favoured in the USA (Middleton, 1995: 217):

(a)   reuse;
(b)   waste reduction;
(c)   recycling;
(d)   resource recovery;
(e)   incineration;
(f)   landfill.

Pollution can be 'primary', having an effect immediately on release to the environment, or 'secondary', the product of interaction after release with moisture, other pollutants, sunlight, etc. Pollution may be local, regional, transboundary, or global. The effects may be direct, indirect or cumulative, felt intermittently or constantly, immediately or after a delay; affecting the atmosphere, soil, oceans, water bodies, groundwater or be restricted to certain organisms, produce or localities. The effects of pollution may be short term or longer term; pose a hazard or a nuisance; be toxic or non-toxic; take the form of a chemical, biological, radiation, heat, light, noise, dust, or smell problem.

The environment may render pollution and waste harmless until a threshold (the absorptive capacity) is exceeded, after which, if there is no effective control, there will be gradual or sudden problems. Loss of absorptive capacity may be very difficult to recover from, so it is important that environmental managers model or monitor to avoid exceeding thresholds.

The risks from pollution and wastes are far from fully understood, and available standards and monitoring techniques need improvement. What was considered safe twenty years ago is often no longer accepted, and what is acceptable today may not be in the future. A 'safe' background level of a pollutant may become dangerous to organisms near the top of a food web (through bioaccumulation or biomagnification), as food organisms concentrate it by feeding or absorption. Some pollutants become concentrated in certain tissues of higher organisms: e.g. DDT and polychlorinated biphyenyls (PCBs) in the fat; radioisotopes like strontium-90 in the bone and radio-iodine in the thyroid. This can damage the affected and surrounding tissues (Odum, 1975: 103). Wastes and pollutants can also be concentrated by tidal action, sudden rain-out by storms, chemical bonding to certain soil compounds, localized inter-ception of contaminated rainfall, etc., to form hot spots. Some pollutants change little after release, some decay or disperse and become harmless, others are unstable and may be converted into harmful compounds.

Pollutants or wastes initially discharged into water or the atmosphere may exchange between these two systems, for example airborne dust may settle on water and sink or polluted water may form aerosols or contaminate groundwater which surfaces at a different time and place. Monitoring and modelling can consequently be difficult and costly. Pollution sources may be: a point (e.g. an explosion), linear (e.g. a road) or extensive (e.g. dust from a desert). Releases can be: continuous, single, brief, random events, or periodic emissions.

The distance pollution and waste disperses depends on its qualities and how it is released. Gases or dust are affected by the height of the release, their temperature relative to the air, weather conditions (especially windspeed), and their density or particle size, presence of inversion layers, whether any obstacle is encountered and the texture of that obstacle, and many other factors. Dispersal in water is affected by an equally diverse set of factors. Larger particles may be scattered by natural or artificial explosions, especially if material is projected into a jet-stream, storm or ocean current. It is not uncommon for a temperature inversion in the atmosphere effectively to put a lid over an area, trapping pollution. Water bodies (the sea, lakes, etc.) may also be stratified, with only the upper few metres mixing. Generalization is unwise so environmental managers must model and check each situation.

A brief history of pollution and waste problems

Humans have always polluted their environment: even wandering hunter-gatherers or those living in scattered hamlets or small towns contaminated water supplies and faced health risks as a consequence of slaughtering animals and living in smoke-filled dwellings. Real problems followed urban development, population concentration, industrial activity and applied chemistry. In London the smell from tanning, the operation of lime-kilns, and the shift from wood to coal burning polluted the air enough for Edward I to legislate in AD 1306 (Brimblecombe, 1987). There is evidence of smoke and heavy metal (especially lead) pollution by Roman times; the shift in Europe from wood to coal burning has shown up as soot in Greenland ice cores (Wellburn, 1994).

Chemists have developed man-made compounds, especially since the 1940s, some of which have serious effects on the environment, such as pesticides, radioactive isotopes, PCBs, and chlorofluorocarbons (CFCs). These and other modern pollutants can be toxic, carcinogenic, mutagenic, or harmful in a variety of other ways, even at very low concentrations, and some persist, posing a danger for organisms or bio-geophysical cycles for a long time. Losses of marine mammals in the Baltic and elsewhere might be due to viral infections triggered as background levels of compounds like PCBs reduce the victims' immunity.

Before the 1960s it was common for industry and government bodies to ignore or hide harmful on-site or off-site impacts. There were wide gaps in health and safety laws and it was often difficult for workers, consumers or bystanders to seek damages. The authorities seldom reacted unless there were obvious health threats or severe nuisance. When action was taken it was cleaning up after rather than preventive. Consequently, the burden of pollution and wastes have not necessarily been borne by those who benefit from development, and sometimes people far removed and unrewarded are disadvantaged. The impacts may also be indirect in time, with effects felt and clean-up costs suffered even generations after pollution occurred or waste was discarded.

Pollution and waste happens world-wide: both socialist modernism and western capitalism have neglected environmental management (Feshbach and Friendly, 1992; Mnaksakanian, 1992). Gradually governments, international agencies and NGOs have increased monitoring and control of pollution and waste, and there is a shift towards making the polluter pay and to encouraging prevention. This shift is far from complete, and for some activities progress has been poor. Changing technology, expanding industrialization and growing urban populations mean that provision for pollution control and waste disposal must continue to be improved.

Many sites where pollution and waste have accumulated have not been recorded yet pose a hazard, especially if dangerous material in containers is released when seals deteriorate or if acid deposition makes compounds in soil more mobile (chemical time-bombs). Pollution and waste are increasingly transboundary problems, sometime affecting the global environment. Before the 1970s such transboundary threats were largely unrecognized, now increasingly the environmental manager must seek pollution controls that can be applied to more than one country or the global environment.

Over the last few decades pollution and waste management has been aided by:

- growing adoption of the polluter-pays principle (Box 11.1);
- a trend towards more proactive planning and management (e.g. use of EIA);
- increased release of information on pollution and waste risks and nuisance – as a result of government, NGO, media and international agency activity;
- improved legislation to define, monitor and control pollution and waste;
- spread of better environmental quality standards more widely applied – which aids monitoring and exchange of information, and provides yardsticks for legislators and enforcement;
- development of better policing, and of self-regulation and joint agreements between regulators and potential polluters;
- better methods and equipment for monitoring and assessment;
- some shift to treating pollution before discharge;
- the end of the Cold War and improved international co-operation and exchange of information (Young and Osherenko, 1993).

Regulatory authorities, industry, etc., have to balance costs of pollution control and waste management against the value of environmental quality or human

---

BOX 11.1 The polluter-pays principle, NIMBY and NIABY

Polluter-pays-principle
This principle aids pollution and waste control by ensuring that manufacturers, agriculture and public realize and pay the full costs for goods and services, i.e. incorporating pollution damage and pollution control costs into prices. However, even within one country people hold different values so its adoption involves complex sociopolitical and economic interactions, and implementing it on a wider front, like the EU or internationally, is a challenge (O'Connor, 1997).

The agricultural sector is a major source of pollution in many countries but has lagged in adopting the principle (Baldock, 1992; Seymour *et al.*, 1992; Tobey and Smets, 1996).

NIMBY and NIABY
The public are becoming better informed on environmental issues, and may object to real or imagined pollution and waste hazard or nuisance. Special-interest groups or the public can adopt a not-in-my-backyard (NIMBY) attitude. NIMBY is often invoked when authorities are proposing to site a hazardous or 'nuisance' waste or pollution treatment plant (Hunter and Leyden, 1995). The reaction may not just reflect local views: some proposals are opposed by environmental activists and NGOs *wherever* they are to be sited (for example, deep underground storage of high-level nuclear waste) – a not-in-anybody's-backyard (NIABY) response.

well-being. Too strict a control and business suffers and may relocate or go bankrupt; too lax and people and environment suffer. The goal is therefore the best possible environmental option (BPEO) (O'Riordan, 1995). Pollution and waste control are now a significant force in politics (Weale, 1993), and ideally should be integrated with economics, social and political policies (Haigh and Irwin, 1987).

Pollution and waste associated with urbanization

The term 'urban' broadly means 'the concentration of people in cities and towns'. Some urbanized areas are the most altered, unhealthy and contaminated of Earth's environments. Cities affect other, often distant environments, and rapid urban expansion, especially in poor countries, often stresses services and infrastructure to the point of breakdown. Many cities, even in developed nations, have dangerous levels of atmospheric pollution, and sewage and waste pose problems.

Heat-island effect

Built-up land has a different albedo, heat storage characteristics, and roughness than non-urban, and there may also be considerable waste heat from homes and industry – these combine to cause a heat-island effect. This means that city areas are warmer than their surroundings, causing local airflows that may recycle pollution.

Urban sprawl

Spreading cities destroy farmland, biodiversity and amenity areas. Between 1958 and 1974 the USA lost an estimated 5.1 million ha to urbanization and transport land use. The FAO estimated that world-wide between 1980 and 2000 about 1,400 million ha of arable land would be lost through urban sprawl (WRI, IIED, UNEP, 1988: 42). Most cities have considerable areas of derelict land which could be used to reduce demand for new land, but to decontaminate and rehabilitate it for settlement can be costly, although it can be relatively cheaply converted to amenity areas by tree planting and landscaping (which reduces the heat-island effect).

Urban storm run-off

Drains and sewers speed up run-off of sewage, silty and contaminated storm water from cities. Leaking sewerage contaminates groundwater beneath a city – London has such a problem, which means that it cannot be exploited and alternative supplies must be taken from surrounding areas, reducing streamflow ('sewerage' refers to the infrastructure/pipework concerned with conveying sewage).

Before the late nineteenth century sewage was only a problem in urban areas, which depended on cess-pits, latrines, street collection by nightsoil carts, or open-channel sewerage systems that emptied without treatment. Cities in Europe and North America began to install water-borne sewage disposal systems in the 1850s, following rising incidence of faecal–oral diseases and smell.

Urbanization shifted sewage management from reclamation to disposal, from resource use to resource waste. Some parts of the People's Republic of China are an exception to this trend, in that much human waste is still collected and returned to farmland. Many of the world's sewerage systems are becoming overtaxed by waste disposal that consumes large amounts of water that might be used for other purposes. Sewers in cities which grew before the 1930s are often crumbling and need costly refurbishment. Modern sewerage design can reduce silting up, for example by installing stepped or ovoid cross-section pipes but there are still many problems associated with water-borne sewage disposal:

- The cost of installing, extending and maintaining sewerage.
- Failure to separate storm water, sewage and industrial waste, which makes treatment and disposal more difficult.
- Waste of often scarce water.
- Treatment of sewage before discharge, which is seldom satisfactory.

Many of the world's rivers, lakes and seas are so polluted that they pose a health risk and have begun to affect adversely the tourist trade and wildlife. Where long sea-outfalls were once satisfactory, population increase and anti-discharge regulations mean raising treatment costs a great deal. More appropriate alternatives to established water-transported sewage disposal should get more attention (composting latrines, etc.).

Most sewage treatment generates phosphate and sludge contaminated with pathogens and often rich in toxic heavy metals. In the past this was sent to landfill sites, spread on agricultural land or dumped out at sea. The last option has been outlawed in the USA since 1993, and will be illegal in the EU from late 1998. In Europe and the Americas sludge is increasingly pumped onto farmland. In the USA and Europe treatment reduces the pathogen content, but in the UK about 25 per cent (in 1998) was disposed of as raw, untreated sludge – mainly onto farmland (and is unlikely to be reduced in the immediate future). Disposal of raw sewage sludge onto farmland risks contaminating agricultural produce, groundwater, streams and ultimately, perhaps, domestic water supplies with problem micro-organisms like *Cryptosporidium* or especially harmful strains of *Escherichia coli*. These disposal options are increasingly outlawed, which leaves high-temperature incineration as the only viable option. Europe and the USA increasingly de-water sewage and incinerate the solids.

Village- or household-scale biogas production can offer safe, cost-effective sewage disposal and also supply gas-fuelled heating, cooking and lighting. Unfortunately, even cheap systems may be too costly for very poor communities and there needs to be an optimum mix of sewage and farm or household waste, which is not always to be found.

There are a number of 'waterless' sewage disposal systems: low-volume water flush to septic tank, earth-fill latrines, household or village composting toilets, electric incineration and chemical digestion toilets (from which safe waste can be periodically removed and spread on the land or safely disposed of in some other way). Septic tanks (limited sewerage systems) are widely used and are effective *provided* the soil and groundwater conditions are suited and the operation and regular solids removal and treatment are well supervised. At the village, large farm or small town scale composting sewage mixed with agricultural waste like straw may prove an effective method of disposal, yielding a safe, useful end-product.

Domestic refuse

Refuse (trash or garbage) disposal can be based on self-help, which cuts the cost and may benefit poor people. Such an approach includes street corner skips which are collected and taken to the tip or recycling plant by a rota of local people. An alternative is to offer an incentive to people to collect waste and bring it to a recycling plant, composter or incinerator. Recycling waste can provide employment, and local authorities or aid agencies could assist by providing protective clothing, supervision, healthcare and refuse handling and processing equipment (where informal and less healthy garbage picking would probably develop anyway).

Cities generate large quantities of refuse: in developed countries this can be 500 to 800 tonnes per day per million people. This may be landfilled, incinerated, dumped at sea, recycled or composted. Domestic waste is a mixture: in the UK it is typically (approximately): 7 per cent plastics; 8 per cent metals; 10 per cent glass; 10 per cent fines (dust); 12 per cent miscellaneous textiles; 20 per cent waste food and other easily decomposed material; and 33 per cent paper products (*The Times* 14 June 1993: 32). The trend in developed countries has been towards a greater proportion of packaging materials, much of it non-degradable plastics and metal foil, and a decline in the use of reusable glass bottles since the 1960s, matched by an increase in plastic disposable bottles. This mixture can make sorting and treatment a problem. Tin and steel can be recovered with magnets, and aluminium cans are fairly easy to recycle, but plastics are more of a challenge.

In developing countries refuse is likely to contain less packaging and more organic matter, so it may be easier to compost or generate methane from, but more difficult to compress or incinerate.

Over 90 per cent of UK refuse was disposed of by landfill in the mid-1990s (North, 1995: 164); at the same time in the USA over 70 per cent was similarly disposed of. Landfill sites should be located to avoid nuisance and the risk of contaminating streams or groundwater: a minimum of a layer of clay should be put in place before tipping, and after completion used to cap and seal the tip (Figure 11.1). Many redundant tips and some of those at present in use meet none of those standards and present a serious future hazard because they are poorly sealed. Sometimes

FIGURE 11.1 Landfill refuse disposal site in Belgium. This is a state-of-the-art facility with geosynthetic clay and high-density polyethylene lining to prevent leaching. Each pit can hold ca. 250,000 tonnes of waste. The gas generated during decomposition will be captured for electricity generation
Source: Press release photo from Bitumar N.V. Belgium, 1998

domestic refuse is mixed with industrial wastes (co-disposal), power-station flue-ash or sewage for convenience or in the hope that it will assist breakdown of harmful materials. Whether it is wise is debated.

It is important to locate landfill sites to avoid nuisance to surrounding areas, to reduce the risk of ground and surface water contamination, to minimize damage from escaping methane or underground fires, and to ensure that vermin are not a problem. Houseflies and rodents can cause difficulties some distance from landfill sites if they are allowed to breed, and scavenging birds may pose a serious threat to airports within a few miles (Clark *et al.*, 1992).

Provided that decomposition of organic matter is vigorous, a refuse tip should generate enough heat to kill most harmful organisms. However, 'tip archaeology' in the USA suggests that paper products may be a major source of contamination of groundwater, streams and surrounding environments because of the printing inks, waxes and sealants used on them. Landfill generates methane, which presents an explosion and fire risk for decades after tipping. Methane, heat from spontaneous combustion, toxic compounds and subsidence limit the future land use of tip sites, although in some cases the gas can be collected and used for power generation or combined heat and power (biotechnology might improve methane production). (For an objective discussion of waste disposal and recycling see North, 1995: 164–186.)

Plastic waste is a problem in landfill, as litter on land and adrift in the oceans. Some plastics degrade slowly and can cause considerable harm to wildlife (for example marine turtles are injured by eating floating polythene bags) and equipment like pumps. Phantom fishing – lost or discarded plastic nets and long-lines – do tremendous damage to wildlife. This might be reduced if biodegradability could be built in. Unfortunately, fishermen do not want equipment to deteriorate before it is lost. What is needed are degradable plastics which quickly rot once lost or discarded. There has been some progress, and laws in the USA, Sweden and Italy insist on biodegradable plastics for certain types of packaging.

Germany requires *manufacturers* to arrange for proper disposal of the packaging materials around their products, and The Netherlands has a covenant with manufacturers which aims to reduce and simplify packaging to aid recycling. About 60 per cent of the world's shipping *should* be covered by a 1989 treaty requiring no dumping of plastics at sea (Annex V of the International Convention for the Prevention of Pollution from Ships). However, a glance at any strandline confirms that compliance is lax, and much plastic also gets into the sea from rivers and sewers.

Lead pollution

High lead levels in the air has been a problem for six or seven decades in some cities. About 90 per cent of the atmospheric lead is probably from leaded petrol. Ice cores from Greenland clearly show the pattern of pollution rising after the 1750s and accelerating from 1925. Lead reduces birthweights and children are vulnerable as they accumulate the metal and may suffer retarded mental development, especially if exposed in the early years of life. Atmospheric lead may be compounded by drinking water contaminated by old plumbing, and ingestion of white lead from old paint. The poor are likely to suffer greater contamination. Some countries, starting in 1972, have insisted on the use of non-leaded petrol. Such controls are not universal or always enforced. Nevertheless, atmospheric lead in the UK has fallen from a peak in 1974 (and similar patterns can be seen in countries that banned leaded fuel).

Smogs

Between the 1860s and 1950s many UK and European cities had sulphur dioxide-rich winter smog problems caused by domestic coal-fires. That problem has been much reduced; however, there has been a world-wide increase in warm weather nitrogen dioxide-rich (photochemical) smog, mainly caused by petrol-engine vehicles. The 1956 Clean Air Act, the 1968 Clean Air Act, the 1974 Control of Pollution Act, and a consumer shift to less polluting natural North Sea gas cured UK smogs (British Medical Association, 1991: 11).

Photochemical smogs are likely where there are sunny and still weather conditions and traffic pollution, especially at high altitudes where there is less shielding from UV (e.g. Mexico City or Madrid). Other emissions are caused by vehicles in urban areas – partially burnt hydrocarbons including the dangerous volatile organic carbons (VOCs) (which include toluene, ethylene, propylene, benzines, etc.), toxic dust, heavy metals (notably lead), and noise. VOCs are formed mainly from diesel exhausts, cause respiratory diseases and may be carcinogenic; they also play a part in tropospheric ozone production and acid deposition.

Pollution continues downwind of cities or busy road systems. A common problem is tropospheric (the lower few kilometres of the atmosphere) ozone formed from partially burnt hydrocarbons in vehicle exhaust or power-station flue-gases. The WHO consider 60 ppbv of ozone to be dangerous to humans (the UN suggests 25 ppbv as a 'safe limit') – in 1992 Mexico City exceeded 398 ppm on more than one occasion. Many other cities exceed safe ozone levels in hot still weather. Crop damage from tropospheric ozone throughout the USA may amount to a 5 to 10 per cent depression of harvest. A car manufacturer has recently introduced a radiator catalyser which it hopes reduces ozone in the air passing the car, utilizing waste heat to do so.

Air pollution from combustion-engine vehicles can be reduced by exhaust catalysers, cleaner fuel (especially reduced sulphur and lead content), lean-burn and direct-injection petrol engines, capture of evaporated fuel, non-polluting vehicles (driven by electricity, natural gas, hydrogen, or fuel-cells), restrictions on use of polluting private cars, such as road tolls for city driving or high parking charges and other vehicle use restrictions, and improved public transport (Association of County Councils, 1991). (Note that exhaust catalysers do not reduce carbon dioxide emissions.)

In some countries (including the UK) total mileage travelled by car has increased and markedly reduces the effect of better emissions controls. One or two cities have tried restricting car use (environmental management goals may be pursued through enforcement), for example by restricting cars with odd-numbered licence plates to alternate days (the risk is that some will buy old cheap, polluting, even-number-plate cars and increase emissions). Paris and some other French cities recently banned car use in certain areas for days to encourage alternative transport use.

The problem of ocean pollution has been helped by new emission standards for marine engines. It is also important to control disposal of lubricants, hydraulic fluid and other harmful transport-related pollutants. What is needed in many countries, including the UK, is a more foresighted and integrated approach to planning and managing land use, transport and manufacture.

Public health-related pollution

Pesticides are widely used by city health authorities to control mosquitoes, flies, lice, ticks, rats, etc. There are safer alternatives that might be used more widely to reduce pesticide applications: net screens on windows, application of small quantities of oil or kerosene to standing water to prevent mosquitoes reaching maturity, stocking water bodies with mosquito- or snail-eating fish, trapping rodents, enforcing laws that prevent pest-breeding sites.

Industrial waste and pollution (non-radioactive)

Pollution and wastes are produced during extraction and processing of raw materials, transportation, manufacture, product use and disposal. The pollution or waste may be gaseous, particulate, liquid, debris, radiation, heat, light or noise (see Figure 11.2).

Fine particles and gas, radiation and noise are difficult to counter once released and dispersed (and are better managed before release); water-borne waste and solid waste (large particles) are more easily intercepted and managed. Effluent may be moved via pipes and sewers, by road or rail tanker or ship to chemical treatment plant, recycling plant, incinerator, landfill site, deep underground repository, injection borehole, or the ocean.

FIGURE 11.2 Sungai Besi tin mine, south of Kuala Lumpur, Malaysia. This is one of the world's largest holes in the ground (a large lorry mid photo gives an idea of scale). Once worked out, the pit will flood. Spoil (sandy tin tailings) from mines in this region has caused considerable nuisance, choking streams and lying as an infertile layer over large areas

Management should be an ongoing process: landfill may contaminate ground-water or streams years after burial, through poor site choice, inadequate sealing, bad management, disturbance by burrowing animals, erosion, earth movements, acid deposition, or human interference.

Wastes and pollutants are often disposed of in the sea, in the hope that dilution will neutralize them. Unfortunately, in shallow marine environments (estuaries, enclosed seas and continental shelf shallows) this may not happen. These waters also receive pollution from rivers and atmospheric fallout (dust, acid deposition, etc.). Waste sealed into containers and dumped in ocean deeps may escape through corrosion, the activities of marine organisms, trawlers, anchors or undersea landslides. Once it has been dumped into the deep ocean, inspection and remedial action is difficult (Clark, 1989).

Waste motor-tyres are abundant and, if they are dumped, waste space, may accidentally ignite to cause air pollution, or be leached, releasing effluent to ground-water and streams. The best treatments are: remoulding (only possible for some worn tyres); combustion in district combined heat and power plants and cement kilns, provided these are designed to minimize pollution; or dumping at sea. Tyre 'reefs' reportedly attract fish, become encrusted with marine organisms, do not leak pollu-tants, and could offer storm protection and sites for wildlife conservation (Mason, 1993: 5). Another possibility is to shred waste tyres for road-surfacing material.

A lot of land contaminated by industry is abandoned or resold, and could cause serious health problems (Syms, 1997). Known contaminated land presents a rehabilitation challenge. However, in many countries unknown contamination has been built upon. Infamous cases include: Love Canal (USA) and Lekkerkirk (The Netherlands). The solution is legislation, adequate record-keeping, rehabilitation and land-use restrictions.

Sulphur dioxide and acid deposition

Pollution from thermal power stations and industry can affect the environment at considerable distances off-site, one impact being acidification. Acid deposition can be in the form of snow, mist or cloud droplets (wet deposition), or as dust, aerosols or gases, especially sulphur dioxide (SO_2) (dry deposition). Uncontaminated precipitation is usually slightly acid (pH above about 5.6). Acid deposition is generally recognized when pH falls below 5.1 (Elsworth, 1984: 5). (Note that pH 4 is 10,000 times more acid than pH 8.)

Acid deposition may:

- damage plants and animals directly;
- alter soil chemistry or structure;
- alter plant metabolism;
- alter metabolism or species diversity of soil micro-organisms, leading to change in fertility or soil chemistry;
- damage man-made and natural structures;

◆ mobilize compounds in soils, waste dumps and water (notably, phosphates, heavy metals, aluminium).

The impact varies: some localities may be exposed to prevailing winds, others get localized storms of acid rain, some receive sudden snowmelt carrying the accumulated deposition of a whole winter. Some soils or water bodies can withstand more acidification than others (certain soils may become more fertile): they are said to 'buffer' the pollution, through alkaline material within or reaching them from underlying basic (alkaline) rocks. In temperate and colder environments soils over slow-weathering, non-alkaline bedrocks are more likely to be affected; in warmer climates already acidic, aluminium-rich soils are vulnerable. Soils which receive a dressing of ammonium-rich fertilizer may suffer acidification whether or not there is acid deposition (Eriksson, 1989; Kennedy, 1992). Agricultural practices deserve as much attention as causes of acidification as acid deposition has attracted.

Volcanic eruptions, sea spray, weathering of gypsum and gas emissions from forests, grasslands and marine plankton can lead to natural acid deposition. Anthropogenic acid deposition has been recognized in the UK since the 1850s, but the significance was only realized after diatom analysis of lake sediments in the 1970s showed serious acidification of water bodies. In the Pennine uplands of the UK, blanket peat's acidification since the 1750s has damaged plants vital for continued peat formation, notably *Sphagnum* spp. Land has eroded and the moorland is now dominated by only two species: *Eriophorum vaginatum* and *Vaccinium myrtilius* (Usher and Thompson, 1988).

During the 1960s acidification of Scandinavian water bodies was linked to acid deposition from Europe and the UK, and in Germany die-back of conifers was noted by the 1960s. At the 1972 UN Conference on the Human Environment in Stockholm, concern was voiced, but was met with some scepticism. By the mid-1980s precipitation of pH 3.0 was not uncommon in central Europe. Five years later western Europe, parts of North America, and several other countries were suffering serious damage to acid-sensitive plants and animals, and increased maintenance costs for infrastructure. Gradually the problem was accepted as real. Acidification may make pollutants in soil more mobile and hazardous, and cause aquatic systems to suffer mercury methylation (release of harmful levels of mercury from sediment or bedrock).

Most years volcanoes vent less SO_2 than the UK's power stations did in 1987, but some eruptions release huge amounts, and affect winter temperatures for a few years. Human SO_2 emissions have more significance in terms of acid deposition than climatic cooling. Elsworth (1984: 6) suggested that roughly 70 per cent of acid deposition was due to SO_2 pollution (much produced by combustion of coal), and roughly 30 per cent due to nitrogen compounds – nitrogen dioxide (NO_2) and nitric oxide (N_2O) mainly. Greenland ice cores show a two- to threefold increase in sulphate and nitrate deposition during the last ca. 100 years, mainly attributable to acid deposition. By 1988 about half of the sulphur in the Earth's atmosphere could be attributed to human activity. The distribution is not uniform: over Europe the anthropogenic component would probably have been about 85 per cent and over the USA about 90 per cent (Rodhe and Herrera, 1988: 11).

Even in regions which generate little pollution, wildlife, agriculture and buildings can suffer acid deposition – an infringement of the polluter-pays principle. Until recently, acid deposition was a problem for Europe and northeastern America. It is now spreading because of increasing combustion of coal by industries in developing countries (Park, 1987: xii; Rodhe *et al.*, 1992).

Northern polar regions receive acid deposition mainly in the spring (visible as atmospheric 'Arctic haze' and as soot particles in the snow), along with aerosols, dust, pesticides, heavy metals and radioactivity (Heintzenberg, 1989). The sources are Eurasia, Europe and North America. There is concern that this haze will trap solar radiation and warm the Arctic enough to cause problems. Another difficulty is that slow-growing Arctic lichen and mosses may accumulate pollution and die, or grazing animals get heavy doses of pollutants (Soroos, 1993). Tundra vegetation appears to be vulnerable to acid deposition damage.

It is possible to map areas of vulnerable soil, vegetation and water bodies, and to superimpose forecasts of future acid deposition. Large areas of Southeast Asia, Asia, Africa and Latin America have soils already acidic and with high concentrations of aluminium and other heavy metals which mobilize to damage plants if the soil is further acidified. Upland cloud forests which intercept precipitation are vulnerable to acidification, as are epiphytic plants and acidic tropical rivers.

By the time there are obvious signs of acid deposition there will have been damage to sensitive ecosystems. How acid deposition damages vegetation can be difficult to unravel and impacts vary even from plant to plant of the same species. Plants may not be damaged directly: it may be that symbiotic bacteria or fungi and other soil micro-organisms are affected and a plant then has less support in its quest for nutrients or resistance to disease and pests. Vulnerability of trees may be affected by position, altitude, soil, moisture availability, etc. (Park, 1987: 110).

Conifers suffer first, possibly because they often grow in exposed positions and trap pollution effectively so are under stress and vulnerable. Broad-leaved trees appear less susceptible, although in Europe and North America they are increasingly showing die-back. In Europe beech (*Fraxinus* spp.) and oaks (*Quercus* spp.) are generally the first broad-leaved trees to show damage. The process can be slow, taking up to 40 years, so is probably under way in many areas without having become manifest. In 1988 the cost of acid deposition to Scottish foresters was estimated to be roughly UK£25 million (Milne, 1988: 56). By the mid-1980s probably over half of Germany's coniferous forests were showing signs of die-back, and about 560,000 ha were 'devastated' (Elsworth, 1984: 18). In addition to serious forest damage and loss of fisheries, if acid precipitation is not checked, soil may suffer which would damage agriculture and wildlife. Wellburn (1988: 52) reported that cereals and grasses might benefit from *slight* acid deposition (but once levels rose above 60 ppmv SO_2 productivity fell). Some wild and crop species suffer, including: rye, salad vegetables, barley, oats, wheat, tomatoes, apples and pears. McCormick (1988: 5) estimated the value of crop losses to acid deposition in Europe at US$500 million a year.

With acidification environmental managers must deal with a threat that is episodic, complex and insidious. There is a need for sensitive, effective monitoring.

For this the presence or absence of lichen species have been used as indicators of increased acidity. In general lichen species diversity decreases as SO_2 levels rise.

Radioactive waste and pollution

Natural radon emissions can damage human health; production of uranium, plutonium and other (unnatural) radioactive materials has contaminated miners, enrichment plant workers and the global environment, especially through atomic weapons testing, military and civil nuclear power plant accidents, and contamination from industrial and medical isotope sources. Between 1945 and 1978 there were at least 1,165 nuclear test explosions (ca. 130 above-ground in the atmosphere, the rest mainly underground). The 1963 Limited (or Partial) Test Ban Treaty ended test explosions in the atmosphere, under water and in space, by its signatories. However, tests continued below ground. The 1967 Nuclear Weapons Test Ban ('Test Ban Treaty') much reduced above-ground testing although some non-signatory nations still do it.

Some underground test sites are failing to offer complete containment of radioactivity which seeps into groundwater and thence to rivers or the sea. There are a number of weapons test-contaminated areas: in the deserts of southern USA, in the Soviet Arctic around Nova Zemlya, in what was Soviet Central Asia, the Gobi Desert (PRC), near Muroroa Atol (French Pacific), Montebello Is. (Indian Ocean), Maralinga (South Australia), in Pakistan and India. Accidents have led to the loss of several nuclear submarine reactors at sea, and there have been at least 54 re-entries of nuclear isotope-powered satellites, some of which scattered radioactive debris above or upon the Earth's surface. Nuclear weapons have been lost at sea, and a few have broken open on land. Gourlay (1992: 62–64) has estimated that there have been at least 50 such accidents.

Radioactive wastes can be highly hazardous and very long-lived (with half-lives of thousands of years). Stored high-level wastes generate heat and gas pressure that damage their containment and radiation may also corrode containers. There must also be adequate radiation shielding and protection against hazards like earthquakes. Radioactive materials are also attractive to terrorists, so their management is expensive, difficult and a very long-term demand.

Nuclear waste can be stored in shallow or deep repositories, landfilled, discharged into rivers or the sea, pumped down deep boreholes, dumped in containers in deep ocean, or reprocessed (Berkhout, 1991). Most of these options are imperfect, and some are now felt to be inadvisable or illegal. Low-level waste is generally disposed of by shallow landfill. World-wide nuclear installations hold huge quantities of often high-level waste in temporary storage awaiting long-term disposal. For ten years there has been a moratorium on dumping nuclear waste at sea (Japan, the UK, the USSR, France and some other nations failed to observe this fully up to 1993), so managers of high-level waste are tending to focus on underground storage or reprocessing. Underground storage demands thick, non-fissured, impermeable rocks which are not prone to earthquakes – even where the geology is suitable there is likely to be NIMBY resistance, and the costs are high.

There is still a lot to be learnt about safe levels of exposure to gamma, beta and alpha radiation. Concern has been voiced about alpha-particle-emitting tritium (often released from atomic power stations and other nuclear installations in the belief that it poses little hazard), because research suggests it might be a risk to health, and is difficult to keep in containment (Fairlie, 1992). Low-level waste containing caesium, strontium and plutonium has in the past been pumped into the sea, and in some countries there are now signs of hot spots or contaminated wildlife.

Obsolete or failed nuclear power stations, weapons production plants and military reactors pose problems. Disassembly of nuclear facilities using robot equipment will probably be needed, and when completed much of the waste still has to be disposed of. Like Chernobyl, which suffered a meltdown of one of its reactors and release of radioactivity in 1986, it seems likely that many contaminated sites will be buried under a mound of concrete, clay or pumped sand to save money. Whether such containment is effective for long enough remains to be seen, Chernobyl's concrete sarcophagus is already breaking up.

Decommissioning the UK's obsolete nuclear stations may cost £30 billion (Pasqualetti, 1990; *The Times*, 3 May 1993: 5) and the country will also have to dispose of ten nuclear submmarines by AD 2000. In late 1989 there were at least 356 nuclear power-generation reactors in 31 countries, operating or under construction. By late 1988 world-wide 239 units had been shut down and 100 were being decommissioned. Japan, South Korea, the PRC and the USA were still building atomic power stations in 1993. Sweden will cease to use atomic power, no easy decision, given that 52 per cent of Swedish electricity came from nuclear generation in 1992. Other countries will continue to depend a great deal upon it for decades: in 1989 the former USSR got roughly 14 per cent of its electricity from nuclear reactors, France 73 per cent, Japan 27 per cent , Belgium 59 per cent, the UK 23 per cent, Germany 28 per cent, Switzerland 40 per cent, Spain 40 per cent – overall, roughly 17 per cent of the world's electricity is generated by nuclear reactors (Gourlay, 1992: 59).

There are dangers in nuclear generation, but burning natural gas oil and coal is a waste of valuable industrial feedstock and a source of greenhouse gas emissions – until good alternatives are developed the true costs of various energy sources need to be weighed before nuclear power is blindly opposed (North, 1995).

Electromagnetic radiation (non-ionizing)

Electromagnetic force (EMF) emissions are produced by microwave ovens, radar transmitters, household power cables, radio and TV broadcasting, telecommunications equipment, computers and high-voltage transmission lines. Stray EMF can cause difficulties with legitimate radio and TV broadcasting, hospital equipment, research activities, control systems in cars, aircraft, weapons, etc., and measures are taken to shield against it and to legislate to control sources.

Epidemiological studies in the USA and by the Swedish National Board for Industrial and Technological Development suggest high-voltage power cables might cause childhood leukaemia, cancer and brain tumours; worries about portable-telephone emissions are so far unproven. But so far there is no convincing proof that

EMF of less than 100,000 hertz is dangerous to humans (Hester, 1992). However, until proven completely safe, EMF should be treated seriously. It may prove necessary to shield equipment much more carefully and to zone land use to keep transmission lines and housing apart.

Coping with pollution and waste

Pollution and wastes are deemed hazardous if they threaten human health or environment by virtue of their toxicity, ability to cause cancer or genetic disorders, or because they transmit disease or pest organisms. Less hazardous material may be a nuisance or unsightly.

Hazardous pollution and waste

Hazardous pollution and wastes can be grouped as chemical hazards, bio-hazards, radiation hazards. In addition, emergency services and health and safety planners usually recognize explosives and fire hazards. Chemical hazards include organo-chlorine compounds and PCBs, which, once released, pose a long-term threat even at low concentrations. At very low concentrations PCBs can mimic hormones: one effect of this is to cause cancer, another is to disrupt reproduction in fish, reptiles, birds and mammals. Nicknamed 'gender benders', these, and possibly other background pollutants, have already disrupted fish and alligator stocks in various countries, and there are fears that they might be reducing human sperm counts. Unfortunately, these compounds are utilized in the manufacture of plastics and other widely used materials.

Hazardous materials must be effectively labelled, carefully handled, stored and used. They must either be securely isolated from the environment (sealed containment) and after use treated chemically or biologically, or incinerated to render them safe. Pumping material into rivers, the sea or the ground is widespread but unsafe and so is increasingly being stopped. Containment is effectively storing material, often without reducing its threat, and hoping time will reduce the danger. Treatments seek either to neutralize a material chemically or biologically or to bind it to something (e.g. vitrification) to prevent its escape or destroy it by heat.

To avoid emission of dangerous fumes or dust, incinerators must achieve complete combustion at high temperature – to treat PCBs effectively requires over 1200°C for at least 60 seconds (British Medical Association, 1991). Even with back-up filtration of flue gases and oxygen injection things can go wrong, so it might be better to site hazardous waste incinerators in remote areas or on board ships that can move to a suitable place. However, there has been criticism of shipboard hazardous waste incineration (it may be difficult to oversee, and an accident means widespread and untreatable contamination); in EU and North Sea waters a moratorium is in force. America has companies which offer mobile (trailer-mounted) high-temperature incinerators which can be taken by road to where decontamination is needed. However, some countries like Canada are hesitating to rely on incineration.

In the future particularly dangerous compounds may be treated in incinerators at over 9000°C using solar power or plasma-centrifugal furnaces. Present treatments can be expensive – PCBs, incineration or bioremediation (treating with micro-organisms) cost US$2,000 to 9,000 per tonne of soil/waste treated (in 1995). Many countries export hazardous waste for such treatment, either because they do not have the expertise or facilities, or because it is cheaper, or a way in which commerce can avoid tight environmental controls at home.

At present there is no cheap, effective way to decontaminate fissured rocks or clays that have been deeply infiltrated by materials like PCBs or dioxins. Some soils can be ploughed up and formed into banks, treated with bacteria and left for bioremediation or could be transported for treatment at a decontamination facility. Fermentation and oxidation may be sufficient to treat many pollutants. Bacteria and yeasts are being bred to neutralize more effectively hazardous compounds (including toxic chlorinated hydrocarbons and waste oil) in bioreactors, yielding a safe and ideally useful end-product. For organic wastes, composting or fermentation can be suitable strategies, yielding useful compost and methane. There has been considerable interest in some of the bacteria found deep underground or around deep ocean hydrothermal vents, in the hope that they might be used to effectively convert heavy metal pollution to recoverable sulphates.

Chemical treatment of wastes ranges from simple disinfection (e.g. maceration and chlorination or ozone treatment) to complex detoxification plants that chemically convert materials like nerve gases. The environmental manager's dream is a treatment that gives a safe end-product of enough value at least to pay for treatment.

Asbestos, widely used for construction (e.g. roofing panels or cement-pipe manu-facture), insulation, fireproofing, and in vehicle brake and clutch linings, poses health problems during manufacture, through dust generated when it is in use, and when it is disposed of. Blue and white asbestos present the greatest threat; brown asbestos is less of a hazard. Inhalation or ingestion, particularly of white or blue asbestos, causes asbestosis, a chronic, debilitating, often fatal respiratory disease that can manifest itself decades after exposure. The dust can be carried on the wind and workers using the material may contaminate people downwind, and their families and friends through dust on clothes. In developed countries controls have been greatly tightened in recent years but in many developing countries they are still woefully inadequate.

Illicit dumping and export of waste and pollution

Illegal waste disposal is a problem. Within most countries fly-tipping poses health threats, and damages the landscape and wildlife. It is one of the most widespread means of sidestepping the polluter-pays principle. Fly-tipping may be by house-holders, traders or manufacturers, or by a dishonest contractor whom a client has paid for proper disposal. The solution is surveillance and checking waste for clues to its origin, then enforcement of severe penalties.

Transporting waste or a pollutant does not solve the problem of disposal, it merely shifts it. As pollution controls are tightened in developed countries there is a temptation for the export of hazardous substances to where regulations, labour costs and public resistance are more favourable. There are two ways of doing this: (1) a factory can be relocated in a developing country, or a subsidiary company can be established; (2) waste or pollutants can be shipped for 'disposal'. If hazardous processes are transferred to a less developed country, employees and local people may not appreciate the risks, or may be forced by circumstances to accept them in return for employment.

Companies may make inadequate declarations about the materials they are using for fear of regulations or loss of trade secrets (Ives, 1985: 76). There is a need for better labelling of materials, inspection of sites and carriers, so that all involved know what is present, whether there is risk, and what safety measures are needed.

Efforts have been made to improve controls on the export of hazardous waste. The EEC introduced regulations in 1988 which, like similar legislation in the USA, aimed at improving access to information so that monitoring cargoes would be easier for governments and NGOs. The Basle Convention, which came into force in 1993 (amended 1995), is intended to regulate international trade in hazardous waste and especially to ensure that hazard is not exported to developing countries. Unfortunately, although it was signed by 105 countries, it has gaps, and a number of European and other developed countries did not ratify the convention.

Less hazardous pollution and waste

A lot of 'less hazardous' waste is sent to shallow landfill. Choice and supervision of these sites has become more strict in recent years, at least in developed countries. In developing countries controls are still often lax. Suitable landfill sites are getting difficult to find in many countries and their selection must be integrated into land-use planning (Clark *et al.*, 1992). With disposal at sea increasingly outlawed, the alternatives are composting, recycling and incineration. Landfill is widely used to cope with sewage sludge, domestic refuse and agricultural wastes. Leachate control is better planned for newer landfill sites. However, there are many old sites where contamination is likely to remain a problem for decades: the nature of the compounds involved is uncertain and retrospective treatment is difficult. Switzerland and Denmark incinerate a large proportion of their wastes (in 1990 the UK had only four domestic waste incineration facilities). A problem (discussed earlier) is that 'less hazardous' waste may develop into something threatening after burial as packaging, inks, etc., decompose, mix, react, and perhaps leach to the groundwater or streams. At present there is essentially a choice: well-engineered, carefully sited and managed landfill with the risk of leachate; or incineration with risk of air emissions.

Agricultural pollution and waste

Intensification of agriculture may lead to pollution and waste from agrochemicals, livestock manure, livestock feedstuffs, crop residue and crop processing. Pollution can result from unwise subsidies, farmers' ignorance, marketing pressures and fears of crop damage. Those responsible for pollution and waste may not perceive it or bear the costs and this can hinder remedial measures.

Chemical fertilizers

Once agriculture relied on livestock and human manure, compost, bonemeal, dried blood, green manures, marl, agricultural lime and crop rotation. Work in the UK by Lawes, Gilbert and others, and in Germany by Von Liebig, led by the 1840s to the development of superphosphate artificial fertilizer. Between 1885 and 1985 the UK, one of the earliest countries to adopt artificial fertilizer widely, increased applications 25-fold (Briggs and Courtney, 1985: 34, 101). After 1945 combined nitrogen-potassium-phosphate (NPK) fertilizer use in the UK increased considerably. The same period also saw changing agricultural practices, leading to reduced use of animal manure and agricultural lime, more mechanization and less input of manual labour. In the 1930s UK agriculture could not feed the population; between 1952 and 1972 UK agricultural output rose by about 60 per cent and now feeds a much larger population, largely thanks to artificial fertilizers, although changes in the crops grown make it difficult to assess how much.

On a world scale, fertilizers, particularly N-fertilizers, have played a key role in increasing crop production (Pinstrup-Andersen, 1982: 148). Because of the diversity of factors involved, it is difficult to be sure how much is attributable to improved crops. In 1950 the world used about 14 million tonnes of N-fertilizer; by 1985 this had risen to about 125 million tonnes (Saull, 1990). In the late 1970s on average the developing countries used 28 kg ha^{-1} and the developed countries 107 kg ha^{-1}. Most of the fertilizer used in developing countries is for large-scale grain and export crop production. Boserüp (1990: 40) noted that in 1970 80 per cent of India's chemical fertilizer was used by only 15 per cent of districts; it is therefore probably reasonable to say that most developing country farmers use little or no chemical fertilizer. Japan's success in modernizing its agriculture and the roughly one-third increase in food production in China between 1970 and 1985 are attributed largely to fertilizer use (Allen, 1977; Wolf, 1986: 12).

The world's food and commodity production is clearly dependent on chemical fertilizers, and their use is likely to increase, but unfortunately they can be a serious source of pollution. In addition, there are uncertainties about the long-term impact of chemical fertilizers on farmland. There is some indication that where year-round use of monocrops and fertilizer has replaced crop rotation and use of livestock manure, fertility problems arise, in particular a net loss of organic matter from the soil, and in some areas zinc or sulphur deficiency.

Some countries have moved away from mixed agriculture for commercial reasons so that arable and livestock farming are no longer integrated – the former must rely on chemicals and the latter have an animal waste disposal problem. The costs of disposing of agriculture waste may one day bring agriculture full circle, to recycling livestock manure and crop residue, possibly together with domestic refuse and human sewage.

But to do so will require composting facilities and distribution. An alternative is to incinerate these wastes and recover electricity and district heating (as in Denmark).

Artificial fertilizers offer the following advantages over organic fertilizers:

◆ They can be easier to store, handle, apply and transport than most natural fertilizers in use at present.
◆ There is less smell, lower risk of pathogenic contamination (although well-composted organic material is virtually pasteurized).
◆ Land spread with manure cannot be properly grazed for some time due to the risk of disease transmission and because cattle dislike unclean pasture. Artificial fertilizers allow intensive use of grazing land more rapidly after treatment.

If they are not applied with caution, artificial fertilizers cause contamination (fertilizers are contaminants rather than pollutants) and fail to give their full potential (Mellanby, 1970; Gunn and Stevens, 1976). Both organic manures and artificial fertilizers can cause eutrophication of water bodies and increased nitrates in groundwater.

Phosphates have been accumulating in soils, river and lake sediments for decades, as a consequence of the use of phosphatic fertilizers, spreading of livestock manure, disposal of sewage and leaching of poorly sealed landfill sites. This poses a threat, particularly in Europe and North America. Studies in Europe suggest that, even if application of phosphates is controlled, steady leaching and possibly more rapid mobilization if there is soil acidification or global warming will lead to a six- to ten-fold increase in river and groundwater contamination. Such levels would raise problems for domestic water supply and for the ecology of rivers, lakes, the Baltic, the North Sea and other seas (Behrendt and Boekhold, 1993).

Excessive levels of nitrates (NO_3) in groundwater and surface water are increasingly a problem in Europe, the USA and other parts of the world. The indications are that it is N-fertilizers which are responsible for a good deal of contamination, which may also be caused by more deep ploughing, use of detergents, sewage pollution, conversion of pasture to arable or land drainage. In parts of the USA irrigation using N-fertilizers seems to be a major cause of groundwater nitrates. In the UK borehole studies suggest correlations between conversion of pasture to arable with N-fertilizer use and high groundwater nitrate levels (Conway and Pretty, 1991: 186). In 1991 between 30 per cent and 35 per cent of the UK population depended on groundwater, which in some areas is increasingly contaminated.

There are ways of controlling nitrate fertilizer use: reduction of price supports for crops; regulation of crops grown; quotas or permits which seek to limit expansion of an activity; set-aside – the withdrawal of land from production; taxation of nitrate fertilizers (Clunies-Ross, 1993). Even if such controls were adopted, improvement would come slowly because nitrates may take up to 50 years to reach groundwater, depending on the geology (Hornsby, 1989). Conversion of farmland to some other use could, because agricultural liming ceases, lead to increasing soil pH and greater releases of nitrates, phosphates and heavy metals. Costly slow-release liming treatment may be needed. In temperate environments, planting winter wheat with white clover might help to reduce nitrate leaching, and would cut costs of fertilizer inputs and discourage pests. Authorities will be forced to treat domestic water to remove nitrates, blend contaminated and pure supplies or store water in surface reservoirs for long enough to reduce nitrate content.

Pesticides

Pesticides are compounds used to kill, deter, or disable pests, for one or more of the following purposes:

◆   to maximize crop or livestock yields;
◆   to reduce post-harvest losses to rodents, fungus, etc.;
◆   to improve appearance of crops or livestock;
◆   for disease control (human health and veterinary use);
◆   for preservation and maintenance of buildings, clothing, boats, furniture;
◆   to control weeds which hinder transport and access (road and railway use, control of weeds and other organisms on boat hulls, in pipes and canals);
◆   for aesthetic or leisure reasons, lawn-care, garden flowers, golf courses.

Some natural pesticides are available. However, natural compounds ('organics') are not necessarily harmless alternatives to synthetics: some are very toxic or carcinogenic.

DDT was one of the first synthetic organic compounds (mainly organochlorines or chlorinated hydrocarbons), initially synthesized in 1874, rediscovered in 1939 and adopted for louse and mosquito control during the Second World War and from the 1950s for agricultural use. The second main group of synthetic pesticides, the organo-phosphates, were discovered in the 1930s. After the 1940s other synthetic organic compounds were developed and widely used for agriculture and public health measures. There has been a trend to replace many of these pesticides with 'safer' organophosphate (e.g methyparathion), and pyrethroid insecticides and synthetic herbicides and fungicides. Organophosphates can be more toxic than organochlorines but are less persistent (Conway and Pretty, 1991).

The benefits claimed for pesticides are considerable, in terms of improved harvest, reduced storage losses, human and livestock disease control. Successful pest control commonly reduces crop and produce losses by 20 per cent or more and improves security of harvest and storage. But it is difficult to quantify the benefits and the risks of pesticide use – for example, in developing countries a large proportion of what is used is applied to luxury export crops, not staples; there may also be off-site pollution that is difficult to trace back to the pesticide use. Pests may flourish if predators are poisoned and they survive. Pesticides are also used because consumers demand blemish-free produce, and growers seek to ensure ripening of the bulk of a crop at a given moment to assist gathering and processing. There have been suggestions that, in spite of pesticides, crop losses have increased in the last few decades – but would things have been worse without pesticides?

Recognition that 'safe' pesticides caused environmental problems came by the early 1960s, the public being alerted by by Carson (1962). DDT was found to concentrate in the fat of higher organisms through 'biological magnification'. By 1972 its use in the USA was banned (but not manufacture and export). Weir and Shapiro (1981: 4) publicized how the export of pesticides banned in the USA still had an impact there through contaminated food imports. The problems associated with pesticide use can be summarized as:

◆ poor selectivity of compounds (not narrow-spectrum, i.e. not very specific in terms of what is killed or injured);
◆ over-use;
◆ toxicity and slow breakdown;
◆ tendency to be concentrated by foodweb;
◆ misuse or unsafe methods of application;
◆ the effects of long-term usage of pesticides on soil fertility is little known;
◆ the impact of cumulative effects on the global environment is not known.

Ideally, a pesticide should be specific, i.e. kill, disable, or deter a pest and affect nothing else. Unfortunately, most compounds are far from specific: non-pest organisms may be directly or indirectly affected. There are other possible impacts: on-farm (contamination of workers, livestock, crops, soil, wildlife and groundwater); off-farm (contamination of nearby woods, hedges, housing, streams); and global contamination. The impacts may be short term or long term, are often indirect, and may have cumulative (synergistic) effects. Tracing impacts (and proving liability) from pesticide use back to the point of application can be difficult.

Much pesticide is used pre-emptively and may not be necessary. Usage increased rapidly from roughly 1950, partly reflecting the green revolution and the spread of modern crop varieties. About 50 per cent of all pesticide is applied to wheat, maize, cotton, rice and soya. Most used in developing countries goes onto plantation crops like cocoa, coffee and oil palm. Japan is probably the most intensive user; the largest user is the USA followed by western Europe. Roughly half of known pesticide poisonings and at least 80 per cent of fatalities have occurred in developing countries, yet these use only 15–20 per cent of world's pesticides (Pimbert, 1991: 3).

As pesticides are costly to develop, even those acting with the best of motives and care may be unable to test them fully, and could be reluctant to withdraw a compound if there is some fault; they may resist developing specific pesticides (i.e those that act on just one or a few types of pest) because it restricts sales; they may resist giving safety advice that could cut sales; they may promote use (or the middlemen may do so) in inappropriate situations to maximize profit. Side-effects may only become apparent after extensive use, and pesticide developers may neglect important pests if there are limited profits to be made from their control.

Pesticide problems can be reduced by:

◆ banning dangerous compounds;
◆ developing alternatives like biological control or integrated pest management;
◆ restricting trade of pesticide-contaminated produce;

- controlling pesticide usage by monitoring, inspection and licensing to ensure sensible procedures;
- developing less dangerous pesticides;
- controlling prices of pesticides to discourage excessive use;
- education to discourage unsound strategies;
- rotation of crops to upset pest breeding and access to food;
- hand- or non-chemical weeding;
- encouraging agencies to cut funds for pesticides;
- treating drinking water to remove pesticides.

Most countries have established departments responsible for reviewing pesticide use which have powers to initiate controls, but there are still problems in disseminating information about pesticides and their effects, in monitoring, and with political and economic aspects of control (Ghatak and Turner, 1978; Boardman, 1986). In 1986 the FAO issued an International Code of Conduct on the Distribution and Use of Pesticides and in 1990 got 100 countries to sign a code of conduct on pesticides. The UNEP, WHO, OECD, ILO, EC, the Pesticides Action Network (PAN) and other international bodies and NGOs make efforts to improve pesticide use and controls, but in practice there is a long way to go before controls are satisfactory. Various databases and networks are now established to assist with monitoring and control. The FAO and WHO have set up the Codex Alimentarius Commission ('Codex System') to establish food standards. One of its tasks is to check on pesticide residues in produce (and each year to publish information to assist in this). Under GATT agreements the Codex has increased influence over the way countries set their food and agriculture standards (Avery *et al.*, 1993).

Integrated pest management (IPM) should reduce the use of pesticides and make pest control more focused. IPM involves study of the pest(s) and the context, using approaches like participatory rural appraisal, to diagnose the best mix of crop and pest control techniques to use. IPM must be co-ordinated with conservation, land and water management, social and economic development, public health, etc., and uses pesticides only as a last resort in a judicious manner.

As with chemical pesticides, there is a need for caution over biological controls. History has taught that control organisms may become a problem. Genetic engineering may also be a double-edged sword. It offers alternatives to chemical pesticides but also threatens serious problems if a dangerous trait were passed to another species, or a modified organism 'misbehaves'.

Agricultural wastes

These include: animal dung and urine; silage effluent; cereal straw and other crop residue. Agricultural waste problems can be countered by:

- quotas – limits on quantities a farm may produce;
- incineration or composting (discussed earlier), ideally linked to electricity or district heating or used to reduce use of chemical fertilizers.

◆　　set-aside – withdrawal of land from production A risk is that remaining agricultural land will be more intensively used.

Livestock wastes

In Europe and the USA livestock waste has become a major problem because farms have increased in size and arable and livestock production have tended to be separated spatially. Livestock waste is a major cause of nitrate pollution of ground and surface waters in Europe, North America and some other parts of the world. The dependence of developed country livestock producers on imported feed should be noted. Forest clearance and land degradation in some developing countries may, at least in part, be driven by the market for feedstuffs like soya and cassava.

Manure, once a resource used to sustain cropping and pasture, is now often a problem. A UK farm of 40 ha with just 50 cows and 50 pigs can present waste disposal problems equivalent to a town of nearly 1,000 people. UK livestock produce 2.5 times the total human sewage; in the USA about ten times (Conway and Pretty, 1991: 276). In 1993 The Netherlands had a ca. 40 million tonne manure mountain – more than twice that which could be safely disposed of onto all the farmland. Consequently The Netherlands (and Denmark) have established waste processing plants (some contributing to district heating or greenhouse heating) and some manure is returned to farmland or sold in composted form to gardeners.

Stored in pits or lagoons, livestock waste generates methane, ammonia and hydrogen sulphide, which cause nuisance smells, damage vegetation downwind (because of the ammonia) and act as greenhouse gases. If slurry escapes, as it often does, it can cause serious stream, lake or groundwater pollution (through chemical oxygen demand – COD, biological oxygen demand – BOD, harmful bacteria and parasites, excreted antibiotics or growth-promoting hormones, steroids and some-times heavy metals – especially copper and zink added as growth accelerators to pig feed). Disposal by spraying onto farmland is impractical as it may transmit diseases, and the heavy metals from feedstuffs can concentrate in the soil, and nitrates and phosphates leach to contaminate surface and groundwaters – de-watering, composting or incineration are needed.

Silage effluent

Silage has become popular in Europe over about the last 25 years as livestock feed. When it is made moisture is released, the amount depending upon how dry the grass or other crop was on collection and on the mode of production. It is common for 330 litres of effluent to be formed for each tonne of silage made. This means farmers must store and dispose of large quantities of acidic (often pH 3.4) effluent. Escapes damage soil, aquatic life and groundwater. Stored in lagoons or pits, the effluent gives off ammonia and hydrogen sulphide, both active as greenhouse gases. The solution may have to be de-watering and incineration or composting.

Straw and crop residue

Around the world farmers burn off coarse vegetation to encourage new growth or to clear land for cultivation. Cereal straw burning has been a problem in Europe for some years until recently when legislation began to curb it. In Brazil, Mauritius, parts of Australia and the Caribbean sugar fields are burnt before harvesting. Crop residue burning helps control weeds and pests but also destroys harmless or useful wildlife, damages soil, causes accidents through smoke affecting visibility, and generates soot and greenhouse gases. Modern cereal straw may not be as strong as in the past (because of rapid growth due to fertilizer use), and thus less useful for thatching, but there is still potential for manufacturing strawboard, paper, cardboard, or for on-farm or district heating. The problem has been the cost of collection and transport.

Brush clearance

Clearing land for agriculture is often done with fire, which each year generates vast amounts of soot and greenhouse gases, damages soil and kills wildlife. The problem has recently got seriously out of control in South East Asia, northwestern Amazonia, and Venezuela and Mexico. In Europe, Australia and the USA fires are more likely to be accidental or set by arsonists, rather than be intended for agricultural clearance. In some situations regular brush burning may be vital as part of land management to prevent occasional serious fires.

Agricultural products processing waste

Processing rubber, sugar, meat, fish, coca (for cocaine) and many other products generates effluent. In West Malaysia and Sabah palm-oil processing takes place in local factories, to ensure that treatment takes place without delay to get a high-quality product. Consequently few major streams have escaped pollution in spite of legislation since the late 1970s. In Brazil the processing of sugar, cassava and yams to produce alcohol for automobiles results in about 13 litres of high-BOD effluent for each litre of fuel produced; rivers, especially in the northeast, have suffered.

Crop processing often demands fuelwood and large areas can be deforested for tobacco curing, tea drying, and preparing many other crops. Leather tanning with oak bark, wattle bark or other natural compounds produces acidic, high-BOD effluent, smell and nuisance from flies. Toxic chemicals are increasingly adopted for tanning: some contain chromium or mercury, and can cause damage to aquatic ecology and contaminate groundwater.

Recycling and re-use of pollution and waste

Waste recovery and waste recycling are terms that can lead to misunderstandings: a country might recover 80 per cent of its waste paper but recycle little, instead using it for district heating; another may recover 10 per cent but recycle/reuse most of it. There is usually a need to sort, transport and treat recovered waste. Sorting can be done by the state, companies, householders, individual 'scavengers', the waste producers. In the USA 'reverse vending' has been tried – a waste-skip credits a company for return of cans, bottles, etc.

Plastics and non-ferrous metals are at present difficult to recover: estimates suggested about 5 per cent of Japanese, 15 per cent of European and 10 per cent of USA plastics were recycled in the late 1990s. Even if plastics or metals of the same general type can be recognized, pieces vary in subtle ways and may be attached to other materials or have an unwanted coating or contamination that is difficult to remove. Some plastics absorb chemicals, reducing their value for recycling. Crude sorting is sufficient if the aim is just to recover a limited range of materials like aluminium, glass, low-grade plastics, iron and combustible material for fuel.

Developed countries can learn about refuse recycling and reuse from the informal sector of developing countries (Bouverie, 1991). Alternatively, they might export waste (mixtures of plastics packaging) to where cheap labour can sort it. Unless recovery ensures that there are few contaminants, plastics have a low value, making it difficult to pay for collection, sorting, washing, etc. Plastics, and some metals, are difficult to sort into various types, and a less than pure mixture may prevent recycling. Recovered material is often bulky for a given weight, making transport and storage costly (Engstrom, 1992; Fairlie, 1992).

Recycling may not be as environmentally desirable as it first seems. Virtanen and Nilsson (1993) suggested that waste paper processing may generate more pollution than burning it for electricity generation and district heating (Kurth, 1992; Pearce, 1998). Controlling packaging materials and ensuring they are labelled should reduce the cost of recycling (Johnson, 1990; Gourlay, 1992: 185).

Glass can be recycled indefinitely and each time saves on energy compared with production of new material (but, at the time of writing Europe recycled only about 49 per cent of its glass, and some individual countries far less). Reuse, of soft-drinks- or milk-bottles, requires a decentralized network of manufacture. Centralized supermarket retailing in the UK, USA and Europe is unlikely to encourage a return to reusable bottles which are heavier, and so cost more to transport than plastic. Reusable bottles also get damaged and many are not returned, which reduces the value of recycling (North, 1995). If a manufacturing firm arranges to recycle its products, it might be able to restrict sales of salvaged second-hand parts, and so profit.

Steel and aluminium can recovery can be worthwhile: the latter saves ca. 95 per cent of the electricity used in making fresh aluminium. Paper can be recycled up to four times before the fibres are damaged too much (*The Times*, 14 June 1993: 33). The increasing use of disposable nappies (diapers), which may also pose health hazards for those working in refuse disposal, might be countered by establishing laundry delivery and collection services – but for this to work consumers need to be assured of very high, standards of hygiene.

Organic matter such as human sewage, livestock manure, food waste, straw, paper packaging could be disposed of by fermentation or composting (possibly aided by earthworms). There has been some development of these strategies in China and

India, linked to biogas production. But of the developed countries it has mainly been Denmark and The Netherlands which have developed these facilities. The viability of biogas production largely depends on the quality of refuse or other waste, and it may be necessary to legislate or subsidize to support composting or fermentation. There are also problems with biogas production and refuse incineration for heat or power in ensuring reasonably consistent energy output.

Recommended reading

Journals which publish articles on environmental management of waste and pollution

Ambio
Archives of Environmental Contamination and Toxicology
Atmospheric Environment
Biogeochemistry
Environment and Planning (C)
Environmental Monitoring and Assessment
Environmental Pollution
Environmental Science and Technology
Environmental Toxicology and Chemistry
Geochimica et Cosmochimica Acta
International Journal of Environment and Pollution
Journal of Cleaner Production
Journal of Environmental Quality
Journal of Environmental Management
Journal of the Water Pollution Control Federation Science
Land Degradation & Development
Science of the Total Environment
Waste Management
Water Air and Soil Pollution
World Wastes

Participants in environmental management

This chapter explores the groups involved in environmental management.

Adams (1990) identified two groups involved in environment and development: 'the blind' and 'the dumb'. The 'dumb' may include people or governments who are uninformed of the implications of development, or are unable adequately to voice their views and affect change. The 'blind' may include consultants, scientists, economists, bankers, those bent on riches or blinkered by concern for sovereignty, religion, or national security. The 'dumb' are often marginalized people, victims of disaster or unrest, underclasses, or simply those without enough influence or power to realize what the 'blind' are doing and to lobby them to act when change is needed. The environmental manager has to try to disseminate information to the 'dumb', and possibly protect or empower them and, if need be, inform and control the 'blind'.

Modern development has focused on yield increase, often for the benefit of individuals or special-interest groups. It is only in the last few decades that appropriateness, sustainability, equity, participation and security have also started to become goals. Traditional resource users often seek sustainability, equity and security, and much can often be learnt from them. Before the 1970s only a minority of development agencies asked whether a proposal was 'appropriate', or made any effort to seek indigenous knowledge, or involve local people in decision making and management.

In any given environmental management situation there are likely to be a number of different perspectives, and hence various possible responses. The environmental manager has to grasp the sum total of perspectives and try to avoid conflicts between participants and minimize damage to the environment (Box 12.1) (Bowander, 1987). In this there are parallels with the role of the state. Like a state, environmental management deals with policy, planning, legislation, and control, implementation and management (Cooper, 1995).

Existing users

Those using an environment or resources usually evolve rights and develop management skills. Problems arise where unwritten traditional strategies and rights break down or get usurped, typically by incoming migrants and settlers, urban elites or powerful commercial organizations. World-wide, the expropriation of common resources from traditional users has become a problem (The Ecologist, 1993). The politics of exclusion appear to be expanding – states license companies to exploit an area or resource used by people without documented rights and they are evicted to degrade marginal land or to settle in urban slums.

BOX 12.1 Participants in environmental management

◆ *Existing users*: land or resource users (males and females may make different demands); there may well be multiple users.

◆ *Groups seeking change*: government (may be conflicting demands from various ministries or policy-makers); commerce (national, MNCs/TNCs), individuals seeking personal gain or to change the situation, international agencies, NGOs, media, academics, 'utopians').

◆ *Groups pressed into making changes*: the poor with no option but to over-exploit what is available without investing in improvement; refugees, migrants, relocatees, eco-refugees (forced to move or marginalized so that they change the environment to survive), workers in industry/mining/etc., who face health and safety challenges while carrying out changes.

◆ *Public* (may not be directly involved): may be affected as bystanders; may wish to develop, conserve or change practices (if aware of what is happening); expatriate or global concern.

◆ *Facilitators*: funding bodies, consultants, planners, workers, migrant workers (latter two groups affected by health and safety issues), Internet exchanges of environmental data.

◆ *Controllers*: government and international agencies, traditional rulers and religions, planners, law, consumer protection bodies and NGOs (including various green/environmentalist bodies), trade organizations, media, concerned individuals, academics, global opinion, and the environmental manager.

Note: for a given issue there is often more than one participant, some involved at different points in time and with varying degrees of involvement. As time progresses a group may become more aware of developments and/or empowered and act more effectively. There are subtle differences between 'involvement' and 'participation': the former may imply simply telling people what is happening or what will happen. Participation means that there is some degree of consultation and involvement (often far short of influencing whether a development takes place).

Indigenous groups

There has been a growing practice of seeking to consult and involve local people in environmental management, and to understand and make wider use of indigenous knowledge (Klee, 1980). Environmental management can learn a lot from study of people's livelihood strategies; Geertz (1971) was one of the first to try to understand the process of exploitation and ecological change in the real world, focusing on Indonesia. There is now a growing field of study of traditional knowledge. For an overview see IUCN Inter-Commission Task Force on Indigenous Peoples (1997).

Women and environment

There has been a growth of interest in this field, especially since the 1975–1985 UN Decade for Women. Some have attempted to subdivide studies according to the perspective adopted:

(1) *women, environment and development* – focusing on women as having a special relationship with the environment as its users and managers;

(2) *gender and development* – with gender seen as a key dimension of social difference affecting people's experiences, concerns and capabilities;

(3) *women in development* – focusing on reasons for women's exclusion or marginalization from decision making and receipt of the benefits of development (Rao, 1991; Leach *et al.*, 1995; Ngwa, 1995).

(Gender can be defined as a set of roles. For a review of gender and development from an environmental management standpoint see Mitchell, 1997: 199–217.)

Women are often adversely affected by environmental degradation: for example, they are often the poorest sector of society and depend on common resources, loss of access to which may well hit them harder than the menfolk. Women and children are commonly gatherers of fuelwood and water, so shortages mean more work for them. Exposure to environmental hazards like insect pests and pesticide contamination may differ from that of the men, reflecting divisions of labour, different diets and routines (Sachs, 1997). In Burkina Faso studies discovered that productivity was better if men and women were given separate plots of land, rather than having women work on men's land (Zwarteveen, 1996). The two genders are likely to respond to opportunities in a different way as well as being differentially marginalized – so to think of even a single citizen social group as uniform is probably mistaken (A. Agarwal, 1992; B. Agarwal, 1997).

There have been suggestions that women are more likely than men to be concerned for local environmental issues (e.g. in the USA Love Canal pollution case women recognized the problem and campaigned for a solution; in India the Chipko and related forest protection movements started with largely female memberships). Women often benefit more from environmental improvements because they are often the fuel and water collectors – afforestation and improved water sources reduce the distance they have to walk and the risks they face (Dankelman and Davidson, 1988; Shiva, 1988; Momsen, 1991; Sontheimer, 1991; Jackson, 1993). In a number of periurban areas it has been the women who have organized to practise gardening and tree planting. Gender differences in ownership can be important; if women are seen by men to be improving their crop yields or tree-cover and they do not own the land, they will probably have it taken from them. To get participation in soil conservation, tree planting and other environmental improvements it is necessary to ensure that women enjoy the full fruits of their labour.

Eco-feminism (ecological feminism) is a broad field, but in the main it recognizes parallels between oppression of women and oppression of the natural world. Men dominate both, so 'greening of the Earth can only begin with the empowerment of women' (Diamond and Drenstein, 1990; Spretnak, 1990; Rodda, 1991; Mies and Shiva, 1993; Wells-Howe and Warren, 1994). Eco-feminism has made attacks upon radical environmentalism, including the deep greens and social ecologists, arguing that these are still androcentric, and gender-neutral attitudes are not enough to control male domination of women and nature (Mies, 1986; Merchant, 1992; 1996; Warren, 1997). The role of women in attempts to achieve sustainable development has been explored by Braidotti *et al.* (1994) and Harcourt (1994).

There is also a more romantic debate on the contribution of women to environmental care, based on the perception that women (through reproduction and the nurture of children) are more closely attuned to nature, and are in a position to influence future behaviour by virtue of educating the young. In developed countries women seem to have been at the forefront of raising environmental awareness, e.g. various pioneering conservation NGOs were founded by women; permaculture/ organic farming was initiated by a woman; Rachel Carson and Barbara Ward were among the first to raise public awareness of environmental issues in the 1960s and 1970s, and women played a central role in the formation of green politics in Germany and elsewhere in Europe from the 1970s (notably the late Petra Kelly) (Seager, 1993). A move towards establishing new environmentally friendly and more socially appropriate producer-to-market networks was taken by Anita Roddick's Body Shop chain of stores in the 1980s. In many countries women play an important part in the consumption of manufactured goods, are targeted by advertising, and can set trends and alter buying patterns, which can have significant environmental implications.

Groups seeking change

It is probably the exception to the rule for special-interest groups not to control policy making and development, although a few do so with the aim of improving environmental care (e.g. the Club of Rome). The environmental manager should be vigilant for such control, and seek to reduce it if it acts against environmental quality. When environmental management involves more than one country, which is often the case, negotiation skills are at least as important as access to technology, knowledge and management strategies (Vogler and Imber, 1995).

Groups with little control

The poor

Many identify two challenges for those in charge of development at the end of the twentieth century: poverty alleviation and environmental care. The two issues are sometimes closely related, although linkages are often unclear and complex. The poor, it is often claimed, degrade their environment in the effort to survive – a trap of poverty. Poor people are vulnerable to environmental problems and the accusation that they cause environmental damage. In reality they are usually part of a process not the cause, and blame lies with trade issues, government policies, faulty land rights, etc. Getting people out of poverty may be important for protecting the environment, but the environmental manager must consider each local case to be sure of causes. For example, the causes of environmental degradation in urban areas may lie with policies affecting agriculturalists hundreds of kilometres away, causing them to migrate and swell city populations.

There are situations where there is likely to be poverty–environment stress: cities where population growth is outstripping employment and infrastructure; marginal, often vulnerable land where people have relocated, areas where traditional livelihood strategies are degenerating (Leonard *et al.*, 1989: 19).

There is also national or institutional poverty: nations may be unable to afford adequate environmental management or they may have misspent funds. Aid may assist, and there have been efforts to establish means of paying that would improve environmental management in poor countries. For example, the Montreal Protocol has tried to set up funds to assist with ozone protection, and the UN Conference on Environment and Development tried to establish a Global Facility (initially set up by the World Bank in 1990) to channel aid to assist developing countries with environmental issues. The Earth Increment (established 1992) is supposed to support developing countries seeking to implement *Agenda 21*. So far progress has been hindered by squabbles over allocation and the failure of many signatories of the agreements to pay up enough to support the funds (Holden, 1991; Patlis, 1992).

Displaced people

People relocate for a variety of reasons, some willingly, some reluctantly. Many are economic migrants who do not have the same legal status as refugees, and may be less welcome in the areas they settle. The distinction between refugee and economic migrant is likely to be blurred where displacement has been caused by structural adjustment or other economic causes of marginalization. World-wide there were over 15 million, possibly as many as 50 million refugees in 1998. Eco-refugees are probably the largest category of displaced people and their numbers could increase considerably. People may be forcibly displaced from their familiar surroundings and livelihoods, or they may be tempted to move. Displacement can be through dam construction and reservoir flooding, persecution, land-grabbing, civil unrest or warfare, accidental pollution like that of Chernobyl, market or communication changes which make cash crop agriculture less viable, social or economic changes that trigger abandonment or neglect of traditional livelihoods, irrigation schemes, large-scale cropping or ranching development, political expediency or planners' desire to provide services for scattered populations (e.g. the concentration of villages together in Tanzania under the *ujamaa* scheme) (Parasuraman, 1994).

Those forced or tempted to move may relocate within national boundaries (relocatees) or move to another country (refugees) (as discussed above there is debate concerning whether refugee status includes those who move seeking better livelihood, i.e. economic migrants). Migrants share some of the characteristics of these groups but retain their roots, returning home seasonally, from time to time, or at the end of an extended period of employment, and in all probability remitting cash between visits. Migrants can cause environmental degradation in the areas they have *left* as a consequence of labour depletion which then leads to unsustainable livelihood strategies. However, there are situations where migrants are able to earn enough funds to finance improved land husbandry, or simply by leaving prevent excessive sub-division of landholdings and over-exploitation of resources.

Government relocation and land development schemes sometimes support voluntary migration of those seeking employment or new land. In Amazonia and many other regions of the world, the bulk of relocation is undertaken by unassisted voluntary migrants. Displaced people, even when officially aided, may have difficulty in sustaining new or recovering their old livelihoods. Even if they are compensated and supported, the unassisted are likely to fare worse. Displaced people may face conflict with host populations in the areas they move to, may have problems with other refugee groups and frequently adopt short-termist strategies for survival which damage the vegetation, soil and other resources (Black, 1994).

There can be beneficial effects of relocation: selective migration of skilled and resourceful people contributes to a host country; depopulation of an area by relocation of people may lead to nature conservation and tourism benefits. The Scottish Highlands (UK) are such an example – a region of scenic beauty in large part because of the eighteenth-century Highland Clearances (forced relocation of peasant settlers).

Movements of people can spread diseases and organisms affecting humans, crops and wildlife (Prothero, 1994), and may have a serious impact on food security in the host region (Döös, 1994). In Malawi in the early 1990s displaced persons outnumbered the host populations in some regions. Some displaced persons may return to their original homes once the reason for their move has been resolved, or if their hopes for better conditions have failed, but there are camps which have become virtually permanent features. There have been a few cases where refugees have brought in skills which have benefited host populations (McGregor, 1994: 123).

Refugee camps may hinder and exacerbate problems by concentrating people together, causing dependency and deterring people from drifting back. Large numbers of people restricted to a camp and its surroundings can have a serious impact on flora and fauna as people desperate for fuel or food can collect virtually everything. Water bodies and streams may also become depleted and polluted. In a number of countries the influx of refugees has caused serious environmental impacts – for example, Pakistan's Northwest Frontier Province received over 3,500,000 refugees in the late 1980s and suffered serious forest and pasture damage (Young, 1985; Allan, 1987).

One of the best-researched aspects of human displacement is dam and reservoir-related resettlement (Figure 12.1). Numerous studies have been undertaken since the late 1950s and a number of agencies have developed resettlement guidelines (Barrow, 1981; Cernea, 1988; Gutman, 1994). A number of large reservoir projects are currently in construction or are at advanced stages of planning. With the accumulated hindsight of four decades environmental management *should* be able to combat problems, but

FIGURE 12.1 Tucuruí Dam, across the Tocantins River, Amazonian Brazil, ca. three years before completion. The reservoir flooded about 2,300 km² and led to the forced relocation of a large number of smallholders and their families, some settled only a decade or so earlier by offical land development programmes!

real-world development situations make it difficult (Thukral, 1992). There is also a tendency to consider the disruption to people in the area flooded by a reservoir. Downstream of a dam many people may suffer changes in livelihood as river flows are altered and may have to relocate but are often largely ignored (Horowitz, 1991).

Refugees and migrants often follow road construction into less settled areas and it should be possible to monitor and control these dispersal routes. To reduce refugee camp impacts it may be possible to provide alternative fuel and stoves to discourage wood collection. Where camps seem likely to remain for a long time, their inmates should be educated and supported to establish treecover, sustainable horticulture and adequate water supply and sewage disposal (UNHCR, 1992).

Various countries have used planned resettlement schemes to relocate people from areas of high population or environmental degradation (sometimes to settle a given area and strengthen sovereignty). In Malaysia the Federal Land Development Authority (FELDA) has opened up large areas of forest for resettling small farmers from land-hungry states (Fong, 1985; Sutton, 1989); Indonesia has an ongoing transmigration programme, settling people from Java on other islands. Similar state-supported land development and resettlement programmes can be found in Latin America (e.g. Bolivia, Ecuador), Kenya, the Sudan, Ethiopia, and several other countries (Collins, 1986; Pichon, 1992). These schemes often cost a lot, move relatively few people, may fail to sustain the settlers, and frequently degrade the environment (Scholz, 1992). Studies have shown why settlers may fail to get established and resort to damaging the environment and re-migrating (Moran, 1981). Much depends on there being adequate incentives for sustainable land use (e.g. enough return for labour, secure landholdings) and upon the attitude of settlers, things which environmental management may be able to control. Resettlement planning should benefit from adoption of a participatory approach (Hall, 1994).

Eco-refugees are people displaced by natural or human–induced environmental disaster or environmental degradation (El–Hinnawi, 1985; Ramlogan, 1996) (Figure 12.2). Natural disasters such as floods, storms, volcanic eruption, soil degradation, drought, or the arrival of a disease like malaria can cause people to move. In the future the trigger to move may increasingly be one or more of the following: global environmental change due to pollution, land degradation through poor land husbandry, pollution, and non-conventional warfare. Eco-refugees could becomes a major challenge for environmental managers in the future (Sinclair, 1990). There is also a risk they might become a significant threat to global peace (Homer-Dixon, 1991; Westing, 1992; Myers, 1993; Ramlogan, 1996). Döös (1997) noted that the countries receiving most refugees so far have tended to respond by tightening border controls, and there was a need to look beyond this and to address causes. Some developed countries are seriously concerned about the possibility of an influx of eco-refugees in the future (Nolch, 1994).

It has been claimed that the world's poor are tending to be displaced to disaster-prone areas by the 'politics and economics of exclusion', and so the numbers of

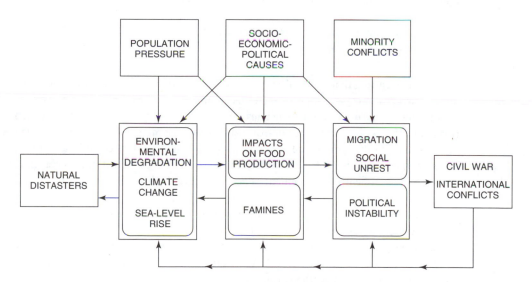

FIGURE 12.2 Schematic illustration of the links between the major factors that can have an influence upon, or reinforce, environmental degradation, resulting in an increased risk of environmental migration (eco-refugees)
Source: Döös (1997: 43, Fig. 1)

refugees is likely to increase. There are regions prone to recurrent disasters, yet people still settle them; for example, coastal Bangladesh, or Northeast Brazil, where recurrent drought is blamed for hardship and relocation of poor people (although in reality lack of land reform may be as much to blame) (Hall, 1978).

Some 'natural' catastrophes have an anthropogenic component – excessive grazing makes land vulnerable to droughts, and global warming may raise the incidence of severe weather events (Woehlcke, 1992). People displaced by 'elemental forces' may have little warning; those shifted by gradual environmental degradation should be better prepared, although the poor have little chance to adapt.

Often environmental causes are merely a trigger for relocation because the poor have become more vulnerable or less able to recover from environmental problems. A number of international agencies, notably the UN High Commission for Refugees (UNHCR), have expertise on eco-refugees, and those concerned with global environmental change have tried to predict likely future scenarios (McGregor, 1993; Myers, 1993; Döös, 1997).

The public

The public usually consists of more than one group of people who probably have different, perhaps conflicting, views and goals. Powerful groups tend to dominate, so the environmental manager may have to establish the needs of the weak, and ensure that they are not ignored, yet work with the influential.

Participatory environmental management

One way of ensuring that the weaker are heeded is to give them a say in what should be done. Participation and empowerment have become important for most western nations and many international agencies. However, there are some countries which prefer not to pass on too much control to the public: some are simply authoritarian regimes, but in others the people seem to prefer to have the state co-ordinate firmly, and sometimes authorities feel the public are not ready for participation. Increasingly effective environmental management is seen as that which deals with people at the local or community level.

Sustainable development strategies need to be designed to fit local conditions and be co-ordinated to ensure that one locality does not conflict with another. Environmental management should act as mediator and catalyst to develop collaborative approaches (Selin and Chavez, 1995). And in this, public support can be crucial (Box 12.2). For example, it is pointless promoting tree planting if people later fail to take care of the growing saplings. Environmental problems are often a sum total of individuals' actions, so people may have to change their attitudes to ensure a solution. Working with local people can inform environmental managers of threats, limits and opportunities they might otherwise have missed (Lise, 1995; Park, 1997).

BOX 12.2 Why the public should be involved in environmental management

- The public may be able to provide advice that would be missed
- Open planning and management should be more accountable and more careful
- Fears and opposition to management may be reduced if people are informed
- If people identify with management they may well support it
- It reduces risk of a communication gulf between 'experts' and 'locals'

Note: The *public* is often a mixture of different groups: local people of differing age, sex, etc.; regional, national, or global groups.

    Involved may mean minimal information; adequate information; active input to management before and during development; or involvement after management decisions.

Sources: Author; Wilkinson, 1979

Participatory approaches to data gathering, problem solving and development implementation have been developed by anthropology, agricultural extension, public administration and development agencies, and have been adopted for environmental management (Messerschmidt, 1986; Cumberland, 1990; Chambers, 1994a; 1994b; 1994c). If the environmental manager does not understand society and history as well as ecology, then serious difficulties can arise – Fairhead and Leach (1996) note the past misinterpretation of the nature of forest 'islands' in the savannas of Guinée. Similar warnings are given by Leach and Mearns (1996), that received wisdom is not enough, and that local knowledge, and objective multidisciplinary or interdisciplinary study are needed.

Facilitators

There are so many bodies and individuals who promote and assist environmental management that it is impossible to give a complete review; in the following section sources of funds, research bodies and channels of communication are singled out.

Funding bodies

Funding bodies can support environmentally desirable developments or withhold money until proposals are modified to meet required standards. Starting with the World Bank in the early 1970s, most funding bodies have developed environmental management units, guidelines and manuals (Turnham, 1991). There have been cases where failure to carry out environmental management measures has led to withdrawal of funding from large projects already well under way (e.g. the Narmada Dam in India).

Research bodies

There is a huge diversity of bodies conducting research aimed at improving environmental management: universities, private research companies, independent international research institutes, and UN or UN-related agencies. Most research is applied and in response to perceived needs, but some is anticipatory and warns of possible threats and potentially useful strategies.

Communications

The Internet is playing an increasingly important role in environmental protection and management (Anon., 1995; Anon., 1996; McDavid, 1995; DeRoy, 1997). NGOs can exchange information, report problems beyond a national boundary (before they can be prevented by a state), and are able to co-ordinate activities. For individuals involved in environmental management the Internet has become an important source of information and means for dissemination and discussion (Schuman, 1996). The media are also playing an important part in improving public awareness of environmental issues, although unfortunately it is not always objective or accurate. Improved telecommunications make monitoring easier as instruments can radio information back (often in real time) via satellite and phone lines to research or administrative bodies. Development of computers, software and GISs make data handling and analysis far more powerful than was dreamed possible even ten years ago.

Controllers

Traditions and spirituality

Traditional societies commonly control resource use through local rulers, who may allocate land for cultivation, decide whether to move a village, etc. Religion and superstition can also effectively regulate resource usage. Unfortunately, these controls may lose effect as contact with the outside world increases.

Religion and spirituality also play a part in shaping environmentalist approaches (Hallman, 1994; Gottleib, 1996), and in nations where religion is widespread environmental management policies will need to be adjusted to the constraints and opportunities that result. In a number of countries religious bodies are in the front line of action to protect indigenous peoples and the environment, in promoting improvements of slum areas, and in poverty alleviation.

Environmental ethics and green spirituality alone are not enough: they do not guarantee adequate environmental management co-ordination, generate data, or monitor things closely enough. The skills of environmental managers and ecologists are vital to determine the best strategies for the survival of fauna and flora and to organize sustainable land and resource use. Having said that, it is valuable for the public to have environmentally sensitive ethics.

NGOs

NGOs have become important watchdogs of corporate, government and special-interest group activities. They have a multifaceted role: lobbying at international meetings and at national government level; media campaigning to increase public awareness and empowerment; fund-raising for environmental management, conservation and environmental education; researching environmentally sound strategies and approaches; acting as ginger groups to identify environmental problems and fight for their control. Between 1909 and 1988 international organizations (bodies like IUCN, UNEP, etc.) increased from around 37 to 309 and NGOs (e.g. Oxfam, Friends of the Earth, Greenpeace, etc.) expanded from 176 to 4,518 (Princen and Finger, 1994, provide a list of environmental NGOs).

An important role for the NGOs is to act as a link between local, national and international activities. Many NGOs have a tiered local-to-international structure (e.g. Friends of the Earth), and command huge resources in terms of funding and expertise. There is growing networking by NGOs, and increasing numbers of coalitions and, with compact satellite telephones and the spread of the Internet, it is becoming increasingly difficult for governments or other powerful groups to keep issues hidden or to subdue opposition.

NGOs involved in environmental issues are a very diverse group: some are catalysts, some key actors; they promote, condemn, empower, expose and monitor; some are politically orientated and some apolitical; there are also scientific NGOs (bodies like the Scientific Committee on Antarctic Research – SCAR, which deals with Antarctica). At the 1992 UN Conference on Environment and Development environmental NGOs played both official and parallel roles (in the Global Forum) and were active in promoting sustainable development. Unfortunately, some NGOs promote misguided policies which project their polarized perceptions, and others act in a careless or obstructionist manner.

Environmental management problems can be difficult to solve with existing inter-state regulatory and scientific approaches. It is in these situations that NGOs can perform a crucial linking role. Princen and Finger (1994: 221; 223) felt that NGOs are especially valuable for linking knowledge from science with the grassroots (i.e. to people and real-world politics). Often they are swifter to respond to environmental problems and challenges than other organizations or governments, and in many cases grow from the grassroots in response to issues (Ekins, 1992b; Zeba, 1996). Some grassroots NGOs are somewhat ephemeral. However, large NGOs may have wide experience and command more resources than some countries or corporations.

There is a risk that NGOs may be pressured to find neat, comprehensive solutions to complex problems; their supporters expect to see 'magic bullet' solutions and sometimes lose interest or withdraw support if these are not quickly forthcoming. This limits the staying-power of such an NGO faced with a problem (Vivian, 1994).

Recommended reading

Journals which publish articles on participation in environmental management

Alternatives: Perspectives on Society, Technology and Environment
Community Development Journal
Development & Change
Ecofeminism
Environmental Ethics
Feminist Studies
Journal of Peasant Studies
Society & Natural Resources
Technology and Environment

Chapter 13

Environmental

management approaches

Environmental management involves the application of a mixture of objective scientific and more subjective, often qualitative approaches. It is a blend of policy making and planning, with greater implementation, control and management; but it still does not have a well-defined, widely adopted framework to shape its application, although there are guides to policy and procedures, and standards and systems – like ISO 14001 (Croner Publications Ltd, 1997). Each situation faced by an environmental manager is to some extent unique. The approach adopted reflects the attitudes of those involved, the particular situation, time and funding available, and many other factors. Even synthesizing information is often hindered by the sheer volume of material.

Although 'environmental management' is sometimes little more than a catch-phrase, when seriously undertaken it is a process of decision-making about the allocation of natural and artificial resources that will make optimum use of the environment to satisfy at least basic human needs for an indefinite period of time and, where possible, to improve environmental quality. Newson (1992: 259) noted that a large part of environmental management was 'decision-making under uncertainty'. There is often more than one route to a goal: perhaps one is the best all-round solution, one the best practical, one is that favoured by the government, another is favoured by a company – the environmental manager generally tries to pursue the best all-round solution. Another core role of environmental management is environmental arbitration. This can be attempted by an individual acting as a 'czar', by a democratic body, or through 'green anarchy'.

Much of what has just been said is difficult to separate from environmental planning. In the past planners often neglected environmental issues, were insuffi-ciently aware of the dynamic nature of Earth processes, and failed to identify natural limits, hazards and potential. Today it is hard to comprehend that before the 1970s bodies like the World Bank or the United Nations had few, if any, established environmental advisors, and that often environmental quality was seen as an optional extra by teams of decision makers dominated by economists and lawyers. Planners nowadays are much more aware of environmental issues, and differ from environ-mental managers mainly in that they are more concerned with forward decision making.

Environmental planning might be defined as efforts to strike a balance between resource use and the environment, the primary objective of planning being to make decisions about the use of resources. Landscape planning has a long tradition and runs parallel with environmental management, focusing on aesthetic issues (Ashworth and Kivell, 1989; Foder and Walker, 1994; Kivell *et al.*, 1988). An important aspect of environmental planning which overlaps with environmental management is *implementation*.

The Netherlands adopted a National Environmental Policy Plan (NEPP) in 1989, the first serious attempt by a national government to develop an integrated environmental policy based on explicit control principles and clearly formulated long-term objectives (Bennett, 1991). This is in sharp contrast to the more usual incrementalist (step-by-step) approach by most environmental planning and management. The Netherland's NEPP environmental planning and management approach gives serious consideration to the concept of sustainable development and the polluter-pays principle. Although NEPP is behind schedule for its implementation, it has already influenced several other governments to develop similar approaches.

At one time the main, if not only, means of trying to consider environmental issues in planning and management was to use cost–benefit analysis (CBA). For environmental management to be a significant improvement on CBA or cost-effectiveness analysis (which are inadequate because they require monetary valuation, which can be difficult, and they fail to consider social and environmental issues adequately), it must view things from social, economic and environmental perspectives. To do that effectively demands a multidisciplinary (or interdisciplinary) approach (Spash, 1996). However, a functional grouping approach is often adopted in practice: e.g. a pollution control agency; a conservation body, and this may hinder multidisciplinarity.

As if it is not enough to have to deal with complexity and uncertainty, the environmental manager often has to cope with situations where the development objectives and strategy have already been decided by others (politicians, special-interest groups, aid agencies, etc.). Environmental management may also have to proceed in a piecemeal manner, with inadequate jurisdiction, poor data, insufficient time to act effectively, public and administrative mood swings (Trudgill, 1990). Environmental managers may be faced with a crisis-management (reactive, short-term response) situation even though one of their principles is anticipatory planning (Scher, 1991).

There are three main focuses an environmental manager can adopt (in a given situation a mix of more than one will probably be used):

1   *Advisory*
    ◆ advice, leaflets, phone help-line;
    ◆ media information (which can be covert i.e. hidden in entertainment or open);
    ◆ education;
    ◆ demonstration (e.g. model farm).

2   *Economic*
    ◆ taxes;
    ◆ grants, loans, aid;
    ◆ subsidies;
    ◆ quotas.

3   *Regulatory/Control*
    ◆ standards;
    ◆ restrictions;
    ◆ licensing of potentially damaging activities.

Environmental management can adopt three distinct stances:

1   preventive management – which aims to preclude adverse environmental impacts;
2   reactive or punitive management – which aims at damage limitation or control;
3   compensatory management – mitigation of adverse impacts through trade-offs. One trade-off is to protect some habitats of conservation or aesthetic value, and develop other localities. The goal is to prevent an overall slow decline of environmental quality. Montgomery (1995: 186) suggested the environmental manager might be better advised to focus on: (a) modifying anthropogenic inputs (input management – controlling use); (b) responding to ecosystem attributes (output management – driven by assessment of resources). Ideally an environmental management framework will integrate (a) and (b) to control environmental degradation most effectively.

While co-ordination of environmental management approaches is desirable, it is difficult to see how too rigid a framework can help, given that each situation is to some degree unique. Companies, funding agencies, NGOs and governments have developed codes, manuals and guidelines to guide environmental management (Forrest and Morison, 1991; Nash and Ehrenfeld, 1997); Europe is adopting codes which will shape practices in all member countries, and in the USA the Environmental Protection Agency sponsors new environmental management programmes.

There are demands for environmental planning and environmental management to act to strengthen the drive for achieving sustainable development (Costanza, 1991; Blowers, 1993). One means is to use covenants, which offer a means of providing companies with a stable regulatory environment, and act as incentives to encourage development of pollution control plans and environmental management systems (a government can focus its attention on companies and bodies that have not signed covenants). The Netherlands has one of the most innovative and best-developed approaches to environmental management, and covenants are one of its two primary components: (1) National Environmental Policy Plans (NEPPs); (2) covenants (Beardsley et al., 1997). NEPPs were adopted by the Dutch Parliament in 1989 and 1994, set targets for pollution reduction, and are a relatively integrated approach. The covenants are voluntary agreements between the Dutch Government and various sectors of industry to facilitate the improvement of environmental management objectives and keep down enforcement costs. The Dutch approach has apparently been quite effective in achieving environmental management goals (mainly pollution control, but also sustainable development initiatives).

Before long there should be environmental management system standards widely in use. These, together with eco-auditing and environmental management system standards, will provide internationally recognized foundations for environmental management to draw upon in any given situation.

Adaptive environmental management

Adaptive environmental management can mean different things to different people; it is seen by some as a tool or approach that can be quickly modified to suit a particular situation; systems modellers may see it as meaning the ability to explore various 'what if?' scenarios; or it can be an approach that is flexible and able to cope with poor data availability, and respond to new challenges as they arise. The latter is the most common interpretation and involves a continuous learning process that should not be separated from research and ongoing regulatory activities. The latter approach probably never reaches a state where there is fully satisfactory knowledge for environmental management (Walters, 1986; McLain and Lee, 1996). A related field – adaptive environmental assessment and management (AEAM) – has been developed by those concerned with EIA – see chapter 6).

Adams (1990) complained of widespread 'juggernaut' development which was too inflexible and clumsy, and so caused environmental and socioeconomic problems. The best response to such development is an adaptive one which can alter to match challenges, a strategy championed by natural resource managers in the 1970s who borrowed ideas from operational management and management science (Holling, 1978). Mitchell (1997: 82–85) outlines 'hedging' and 'flexing' strategies for decision making where there is severe uncertainty. Hedging is a process of trying to avoid the worst consequences, and flexing is a continuing search for other possible options even after a decision has been taken.

Adaptive management is far better than the disjointed incrementalist approach often adopted, i.e. just muddling through. However, it is not perfect – McLain and Lee (1996) reviewed three adaptive environmental management case-studies and found 'serious flaws', mainly in relation to how environmental management decisions were made. They also noted a risk of ignoring non-scientific knowledge.

GIS and environmental management

GIS is a powerful aid for environmental management, in practice and for training environmental managers (Woodcock et al., 1990; Gumbricht, 1996) (see chapter 9).

Expert systems and environmental management

Expert systems are computer programs that rely on a body of knowledge to perform a difficult task usually performed only by a human expert. They are increasingly used where there is a shortage of skilled experts. Costly to establish, the systems should improve with use. There have been applications to environmental management (Moffatt, 1990; Fitzgerald, 1993; Warwick et al., 1993).

Decision support for environmental management

One of the problems faced in environmental decision making is complexity, with limited time and difficult-to-trace webs of interrelationships. Tools that can clarify data are useful (data visualization for decision support is reviewed in *Landscape and Urban Planning* 21, no. 4 – published 1992). Decision support systems are derived from operational research and management science, they deal with complexity by 'playing' to learn fast. Usually they take the form of interactive computer-based systems which help the decision-maker model and solve problems (some would argue that anything that aids decision making is a decision support – even a cup of coffee) (Janssen, 1995).

Whether complicated approaches like the multiple criteria method (Paruccini, 1995) are of practical value is unclear. There is also a need for approaches that can help the environmental manager weigh goals against costs and risks, and structure strategies in the best way. Operational research or management and multi-objective decision support methods can provide useful help for the environmental manager (Bloemhofruwaard *et al.*, 1995).

The use of computer-based systems in support of decision making in environmental management has increased over the last decade. Some systems integrate the use of GIS and modelling as well as aiding decision making (Zhu *et al.*, 1998).

Systems or network approaches

Systems and ecosystems approaches have been discussed in chapter 7. Systems analysis and network approaches have been applied to environmental management since the 1970s (Bennett, 1984; Carley *et al.*, 1991). These can be demanding of research, and slow to perfect, but are useful for ongoing management of particular situations, and as a way of making sense of complexity.

Local, community, regional and sectoral environmental management

The value of local participation was discussed in chapter 12, and environmental management has frequently been tackled on a local, a community, or regional scale (Kok *et al.*, 1993; Welford, 1993). Wilson and Bryant (1997: 141) argue that Amazonian rubber-tappers, farmers, etc., could be classed as grassroots environmental managers; they also stress that environmental management is a multi-layered process: there may well be different tiers involved from local up to state and even international levels, all interrelating.

Smith (1998) found in the USA that, for pollution discharge control, decentralization did seem to improve environmental management performance, the key factor being access to local knowledge. The social sciences offer a pool of experience on community development aspects of natural resource management which the environmental manager should draw upon (Smith *et al.*, 1994). Regional planners have often worked closely with environmental managers.

A number of sectors have developed approaches, standards and pools of expertise – for example, the petrochemicals, paper–pulp production, mining, oil, cement, sewage treatment and power generation industries. Tourism is also beginning to develop environmental management approaches and standards, e.g. for ski resorts (Williams and Todd, 1997). This expertise can greatly assist and speed up further environmental management in the same sector.

The state and environmental management

Environmental management has in part evolved separately from environmental science and is a politicized process (Wilson and Bryant, 1997). Is the process of environmental management, then, controlled by the state, NGOs, international agencies, or what? Ultimately, with global interdependence and shared world systems there has to be some element of international co-ordination and control. Below that, the majority of environmental management is in state hands but, like medicine or economics, the profession should be able to steer the state towards certain goals. Hopgood (1998) has examined US policy on international environmental issues since 1972, seeking to establish whether the state had retained or lost control of policy making to environmental groups and international agencies. The answer was not clear.

A decentralized approach might prove less robust against special-interest groups, large companies, etc., than a centralized and state-supported approach (Walker, 1989). It is not uncommon for states in a federal system to come into conflict amongst themselves or with central government over environmental issues. One reason for the formation of the EPA in the USA was to co-ordinate and integrate efforts under a federal system.

Transboundary and global environmental management

The need for transboundary and global environmental management is growing. Local, regional, national and corporate environmental management can draw upon established social institutions, the market, law and, ultimately, the power of the state to force a resolution of conflicts. However, transboundary and global environmental management must rely on building international co-operation. In practice honouring agreements is often more difficult than achieving them. There is also the question of who or what body should foster international co-operation to search for solutions to transboundary and global problems, oversee implementation and, if environmental management is to be anticipatory, identify potential problems and conflicts before they develop too much (Davos, 1986; Agarwal, 1992). Some see UN bodies as able to fulfil these roles, others suggest it should lie with internationally respected research centres. At present both these types of institution play a part, but overall co-ordination and enforcement is too weak.

With the spread of free trade as a consequence of the General Agreement on Tariffs and Trade (GATT) (which became the World Trade Organization – WTO – a few years ago), the North American Free Trade Agreement (NAFTA), and similar undertakings, environmental management must cope with problems caused if controls can be interpreted as a 'trade barrier'. Efforts are being made to improve environmental management provisions in free trade agreements, but there are still problems – like the USA–Mexico yellow-fin tuna debacle (Mumme, 1992; Seda, 1993).

Integrated environmental management

Much environmental management and planning has been reactive, narrow in focus, piecemeal and poorly co-ordinated. Integrated approaches have been explored to try to counter these problems, and to ensure that environmental management yields socio-economic benefits. Environmental problems cross political border and boundaries between air, water and land; they also involve different disciplines and actors, so can be difficult to deal with without integrated environmental management.

There has been considerable interest in integrated environmental management in recent years, from industry, academics, politicians and professional planners (Müeller and Ahmad, 1982; Cairns and Crawford, 1991; O'Callaghan, 1996). However, it has been difficult to put into practice, and there is lack of agreement as to what exactly it is (Barrett, 1994; Margerum and Born, 1995). Terminology is a little vague; for those involved in corporate environmental management 'integrated' means the development of an environmental management system that combines health, safety and environmental quality issues. Alternatively, the Dutch government, concerned with the environmental management of the North Sea, would see 'integrated' as implying the assessment of all relevant environmental factors: pollution, fisheries, erosion, etc., and resolving issues in an integrated way (Wolters, 1994).

As with a number of other environmental management approaches, there is a risk that academics and professionals become too involved and forget that it is a means to an end: achieving sustainable development; better resource use for the general good; reduction of environmental problems, and so on (Born and Sonzogni, 1995). In spite of these problems, improvements may soon make it possible to adopt effective integrated environmental management (Rabe, 1996).

The roots of integrated environmental management lie in integrated area development approaches and comprehensive regional planning and management, including comprehensive river basin planning and management. There are also similarities shared with areas of management science, such as total quality management. The key elements of integrated environmental management are, according to Born and Sonzogni (1995: 168):

◆ co-ordinated control, direction, or influence of all human activities in a defined environmental system (such as a river basin or a watershed) to achieve and balance the broadest possible range of long- and shorter-term objectives;

◆ a process of formulating and implementing a course of action involving human and natural resources in an ecosystem, taking into account the social, political, economic and institutional factors operating within the ecosystem in order to achieve specific societal objectives;

◆ an inclusive approach that takes into account the scope and scale of environmental and human issues and their interconnections. A strategic and interactive process is used to identify key elements and goals which need attention.

Strategic environmental management

The formalized, systematic and comprehensive process of evaluating the environmental effects of a policy, programme, or plan and alternatives (leading to publication of a report) is known as strategic environmental assessment. This has been applied to things like aid programmes, structural adjustment, changes in public transport policy, etc. (Partidário, 1996). Overlapping a little with strategic environmental assessment is strategic environmental management (SEM), which can be defined as the preparation and implementation of policies that seek sustainable development of the environment (Nijkamp and Soeteman, 1988). SEM should ensure a long-term view and adequate monitoring of local, regional and global issues. The Netherlands has gone further than most countries towards adopting SEM as part of national policy (Ministerie VROM, 1989), and Europe is committed to adopting it (Figure 13.1).

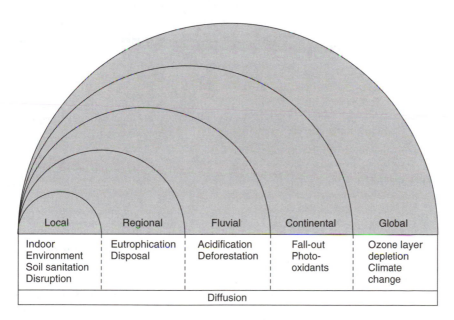

FIGURE 13.1 Linkages of levels in sustainable development tasks (based on the approach adopted by the National Environmental Policy Plan of The Netherlands
Source: Carley and Christie (1992: 199, Fig. 9.2)

It has been argued that there are situations where SEM may not be the best option, especially for some companies, in spite of pressure for its adoption (Vastag *et al.*, 1996).

Stance and environmental management

Political and ethical stances play an important part in determining environmental management goals and the strategies used to achieve them. An environmental manager can follow a textbook scientific approach or, more likely, socioeconomic and politically aware approaches (Boehmer-Christiansen, 1994), and is influenced by his or her own outlook. Those who profess concern for the environment have a wide spectrum of viewpoints and usually frequently revise their ideas, so stance is usually rather elastic (Parkin, 1989). (O'Riordan and Turner, 1983: 1–62 give an overview of environmentalist ideologies.) There are 'light-greens', prepared to make use of science and technology to improve human well-being and environmental quality, and who are aware of limitations in doing this; there are 'cornucopians', who probably have excessive trust in the capacity of science and technology to cure all environment and development problems; there are 'deep-greens', who mistrust science and technology and seek social changes and altered attitudes as a strategy; there are deep-greens who adopt a romantic approach, and some who profess a 'holistic' approach; and some who favour spiritual development or New Age values (Naess, 1989). Some environmentalists are ecocentric and give nature greater priority than human needs, while others are anthropocentric and place human needs first. Many greens adopt a decentralist, slightly anarchistic stance; others support established political parties (Pepper, 1984; Dalton, 1994; Dobson, 1995). The question is, with which group(s) does environmental management have sympathy?

Many deep-greens believe that ecological awareness is spiritual and that new ethics, vital for satisfactory environmental management, must be grounded in spirituality (Sessions, 1994: 21). Those who profess deep ecology also seek a paradigm shift, to a philosophy which aims at a sustainable society based on material simplicity and spiritual richness (Dobson, 1995).

Supporters of social ecology advocate a decentralized, co-operative, anarcho-socialist lifestyle (claiming that if people are in harmony with one another they are more likely to be in harmony with nature – a far from established assumption) (Bookchin, 1972; 1982; 1986). Eco-feminism (see chapter 12) has been critical of deep-green and social ecology viewpoints, arguing that gender neutrality is not enough, and anti-androcentric approaches are needed to end paternalistic behaviour which leads to exploitation of women and the environment (Zimmerman, 1987; Cheney, 1987; Merchant, 1992).

Extreme eco-radicals or 'eco-warriors', such as the Earth First! groups, put environmental welfare before human welfare and may resort to eco-terrorism ('monkey-wrenching'), even violence in pursuit of their goals. Some animal rights groups take a similar line.

Ecosocialism involves more than redefinition of human needs and redistribution of resources: it also seeks new forms of production which reject private ownership in favour of social justice and new forms of social order (Pepper, 1993). Environmental issues have been underplayed by Marxism and socialist theorists; the German die Grünen ('greens') boasted in the 1970s: 'we are neither left nor right, we are ahead!' and the lead seems not to have been challenged much. Socialist and communist utopian development efforts, say in the former USSR, have generated as severe environmental problems as western capitalism – both use industrialized manufacture and agriculture and have exploited resources with little concern for nature (Pryde, 1991). There are significant differences between socialism and green orientations (Bahro, 1982; 1984); to address the environmental gap in socialism, 'green socialism' has appeared (Ryle, 1988).

An environmental manager working for a company or a government will probably have to liaise with a number of environmentalist groups, some co-operative, others difficult to work with or downright hostile. Without some form of co-ordination and, if need be, restraint a plethora of different environmental groups is unlikely to achieve much, but, guided by good environmental management, they may become powerful and useful allies. However, initially at least, there is a need for caution in dealings, to avoid misinformation, the risk of one group trying to gain advantages over another, over-powerful alliances, etc. Corporate environmental managers are generally aware of these risks and have developed guidelines.

Political ecology approach to environmental management

Political ecology is the study of the relationships between society and nature (Bell *et al.*, 1998; Bryant and Bailey, 1997; Low and Gleeson, 1998). Political ecology holds that radical changes in human social habits and practices are required in order to counter environmental degradation and achieve sustainable development (Dobson, 1995: 17). The political ecology approach implies an interest in cause–effect relationships, study of the different interest groups involved in using the environment, of their economy, habits and livelihoods (Chapman, 1989; Atkinson, 1991b; Hershkovitz, 1993; Oliver, 1994). Scientific study is not enough: social, economic and political issues must be considered, for example the struggle against logging in Sarawak can only be understood in the light of the history of local peoples and present politics and economics (Colchester, 1993); the process of environmental degradation in Honduras only becomes clear through studying the political ecology of poverty (Stonich and Browder, 1996).

Political economy approach to environmental management

An understanding of human–environment interactions can be gained through examination of how the social relations of power relate to the control and use of resources and nature – the political economy approach.

There are likely to be different perceptions of environmental needs and problems between planners, policy makers, government ministers, various sections of the public, etc. To deal effectively with environmental management demands an awareness of political economy. Blaikie (1985) adopted a political economy approach to examine soil erosion and its control in developing countries. Urging small farmers to control soil erosion for the national good is unlikely to have much effect if it brings them no significant benefit. It may require people far removed to pay and alter attitudes so that environmental management can be supported at the local level.

Human ecology approach to environmental management

Human ecology is the study of relations between humans or society and nature, through a multidisciplinary approach (Begossi, 1993). An alternative definition is the study of ecosystems that involve humans (Garlick and Keay, 1970; Hardin, 1985; Catton, 1994). There has been interest in human ecology since the 1920s or earlier (Barrows, 1926). The scale of approach may be local to global, and it supports holistic study (Sargeant, 1974; Steiner and Nauser, 1993).

The best approach?

To a considerable extent the ends are more important than the means; the approach really doesn't matter, provided environmental and other goals are attained, and that it is not done in a draconian manner. Environmental management usually has two choices: (1) where time and funds are short, the 'quick-and-dirty' approach; (2) a more thorough, slower and usually more expensive approach. The former sacrifices depth of assessment and reliabilty for speed and cheapness. The latter is often too slow to be practical. The ideal is a quick, thorough, adaptable and transparent (i.e. the public and other onlookers can see what is being done) approach – and nothing quite fits that.

Recommended reading

Journals which publish articles on environmental management approaches

Ambio
Environment
Environmental Conservation
Environmental Management
Environmental Progress
Human Ecology
Green Futures
Journal of the Chartered Institution of Water and Environmental Management
Journal of Environmental Management
Journal of Environmental Planning and Management
International Journal of Environment and Pollution

The way ahead

'We have to understand that we can never control Nature. Nature's systems are far, far too complex. But we *can* manage them'
(Charles Secrett, Director, Friends of the Earth:
The Times, 28 April 1998: 8).

Key challenges and new supports

Some of the problems faced by environmental managers are reasonably clear: population increase, pollution, urbanization, and rising consumption (consumerism) and globalization (Kiely and Marfleet, 1998). A consequence of some of these are: possible greenhouse warming, worsening soil degradation, and loss of biodiversity. For some of these problems remedial action has been much too limited, and necessary future responses may have to be 'quick and dirty' with no time to wait for adequate data, better technology, change of public opinion and effective legislation. It is fair to say that environmental management is increasingly running-on-the-spot, trying to keep up with growing environmental problems, and some fear that cumulative/ synergistic problems may be emerging to make it even more difficult. North (1995: 105) warned of 'a blizzard of cliché and prejudice' surrounding environmental challenges. However, he was able to present a rational, often optimistic and readable assessment of the challenges being faced by environmental management. North felt that, though the world may have to support 10 billion people within a couple of generations, it might be possible to do so and still care for the natural world.

Not all challenges faced by environmental management are about human survival and conservation of biodiversity. Many concern aesthetics. For example, windfarms make sense as a means of supplying clean sustainable electricity, but siting them in countries like the UK is proving controversial. Often environmental management will be invoked to give scientific respectability to government or public preferences, rather than to ensure sound research and rational choice (North, 1995: 119).

There is a need to better integrate physical and social sciences, and to get a more problem-oriented problem-solving form of environmental science (de Groot, 1992, has discussed such issues). Some of these issue are familiar to geographers, and perhaps human geography and environmental management can be usefully linked. Both environmental management and geography stress the importance of multi-disciplinarity or interdisciplinarity. There are difficulties in seeking this – Marion (1996) warned of 'infoglut', the flood of data that has to be constantly sifted and made sense of. To be effective, environmental management must have mastery of 'infoglut' and effectively develop a clear overview of development scenarios.

Environmental management can draw upon palaeoecologist and historian to 'backcast', i.e. from an understanding of past events obtain warning of possible future challenges and of how environments and people might respond to various changes in the light of past responses. Environmental managers might benefit from two popular books which also use backcasting to try explain the present and suggest future situations: Diamond (1997) provided an interesting insight into how human fortunes might be affected by environmental factors and past history; and Kennedy (1993) tried to produce an objective assessment of likely future scenarios using the approach of a historian. Environmental managers must have a broad and long-term view, which can bring them into contact with the field of futures study and 'futurists'. These may often (if not always) be speculative, but they provide ideas, warnings, and prompt contingency planning (e.g. futures debates in the 1960s and 1970s helped prompt concern for limits and the concept of sustainable development).

Environmental management must deal with a diversity of stakeholders – ministries, NGOs, various groups among the public, international agencies, etc. That demands an ability to cope with complexity and conflicting demands. Environmental management must not be pursued in isolation from issues like growing poverty, resource degradation, etc.

There has been progress in understanding and monitoring the world's structure and function, the development of environmental management standards and systems, accessible computing systems, tools like remote sensing, automatic instrumentation and GIS which permit much better data gathering, information storage, retrieval and processing. The tools used for risk, hazard and impact assessment have also improved a lot since the 1970s. The improvement and spread of telecommunications, especially the Internet, makes contact between the environmentally concerned easier and cheaper, and should help prevent planners, governments or special-interest groups from hindering dissemination of information to the public, NGOs and various other bodies. The Internet has made it easier for people to blow the whistle on environmentally ill-advised activities, share information and promote environmental issues.

Sustainable development and coping with global environmental change

One of the key goals for environmental management is to achieve sustainable development. Although the concept of sustainable development is increasingly dominating environmental management, it still needs clarification, and tried and tested practical strategies are scarce (Carley and Christie, 1992; Barrow, 1995). The literature is choked with cliché and wishful thinking about paradigm shifts to a sustainable society, and the need for eco-ethics, but little of this is of practical value for the near future. Academic publications overflow with management, decision-making and planning proposals, only a fraction of which are likely to be adopted by practitioners – what is needed are practical solutions.

To improve environmental care and make a transition to sustainable development more likely will demand a change from current reliance on GNP and GDP as measures of national performance, to something more green (Henderson, 1994) (see state-of-the-environment accounts in chapter 4). *Agenda 21* signatories committed themselves to improving national accounting to include environmental costs, benefits and values. Environmental management approaches need to be developed and tuned for practical use: more effort could be spent on this. One such study, by Auty (1995: 262–271), made a comparison between strong green and weak green approaches to environmental management.

Environmental management makes decisions which affect future generations as well as the present generation. There is a need for better rules and ethics to guide environmental managers: what trade-offs between present and future are acceptable; should as little as possible be done to reduce options for those in the future (a part of the concept of sustainable development)? Cooper and Palmer (1992: 135–146) have examined the ethics of likely future environmental challenges.

Biodiversity conservation

With respect to biodiversity conservation the responsibility of present-day environmental management is relatively clear. Living species are being lost at an alarming rate; once extinct, they are not recoverable; their value for ensuring environmental stability and providing benefits for humans is largely undetermined. Even excluding philosophical and moral beliefs that causing extinction is wrong, it makes sense to conserve biodiversity to keep open future options. Without the bark of one tree (for quinine) much of the settlement, trade and progress of the last few centuries would have been impossible; without access to one yam species in the 1950s modern oral contraceptives would probably not have been discovered and synthesized. E.O. Wilson (1992: 335) suggested that, regardless of a person's beliefs, 'the ethical imperative should therefore be, first of all, *prudence*. We should judge every scrap of biodiversity as priceless' (my italics).

In biodiversity protection and, I would argue, most other aspects of environmental management, prudence (the precautionary principle) should underpin all decisions. Biodiversity conservation is not just about establishing and managing reserves, gene banks, zoological and botanical collections – it requires environmental management to ensure that there are no transboundary or global threats that endanger such collections, and to try to ensure that there are safeguards (duplicated collections well apart, secure as possible sites, etc.).

Biotechnology – double-edged sword?

Biotechnology is of great value for developing new crops, pest control methods which reduce reliance on chemical pesticides, bioremediation of pollution, biological nitrogen fixation, etc. (Hector, 1996). The value of biotechnology to improve food and commodity production, to offer alternatives to agrochemicals (fertilizers, pesticides and herbicides), aid healthcare and treat pollution must be weighed against risks. The main risks are the escape of genetically engineered organisms carrying recombinant DNA material and causing a serious environmental problem, or the use of biotechnology for commodity substitution. There have already been cases of substitution which have had severe economic and social impacts, for example: the adoption of high fructose corn syrup by the food and drinks industries in developed countries hit some developing country sugar producers badly (between 1983 and 1984 America cut sugar imports by US$130 million). When export markets collapse, farmers may be forced to produce other crops or to abandon land, both of which can cause serious environmental degradation. Biotechnology might make it possible for large companies to produce things like cocoa butter substitutes or naturally de-caffeinated coffee, or even alternatives to palm-oil, which would severely upset countries that rely on these exports.

There is little disagreement that biodiversity is a world resource that all should benefit from. But in practice, seed companies, biotechnology companies and other commercial interests seek to profit and recoup their research and development costs if they develop genetic material. The call for patent rights by developers of biodiversity is growing as biotechnology develops (global free trade allows holders of rights to control huge markets for their products). In response, developing countries, indigenous peoples and NGOs have started to campaign for free access to 'raw material' for biotechnology (i.e access to biodiversity), and some reward for and control over products developed from their indigenous biodiversity. Biodiversity conservation and development is thus a sensitive issue. Some governments have accused MNCs and TNCs and developed countries of 'bio-piracy', taking genetic material from poor nations, producing something from it with biotechnology, and then selling it back at huge profit (Fowler and Mooney, 1990; Shiva, 1993).

The 1992 UN Conference on Environment and Development, Rio de Janeiro, *Agenda 21*, and follow-up meetings

One commentator felt that the main achievement of the Rio Earth Summit was to 'put the world's nose against the window'; i.e. it made environmental issues matters of serious interest for administrators, commerce and the Earth's public (Thomas, 1994). The Earth Summit produced a programme of action, *Agenda 21*, which published goals and targets enunciated in the Earth Charter. It has already had some influence on policy making in Europe, North America, many other countries, and a number of international agencies (Young, 1994; Henry, 1996; Voisey *et al.*, 1996). It is not an exaggeration to view the Earth Summit and *Agenda 21* as an important and effective catalyst for environmental management and sustainable development.

What the 1992 Earth Summit agreed was a Convention on Climate Change; a Statement of Principles on Forests; a Biodiversity Treaty (which the USA would not sign, largely because it threatened biodiversity patent rights); *Agenda 21*; the establishment of a UN Commission on Sustainable Development (possibly the most important achievement); and a Declaration on Environment and Development (Holmberg *et al.*, 1993; Dodds, 1997). Since Rio, the UN General Assembly has held (in 1997) a Special Session in New York, dubbed 'Earth Summit II' (or 'Earth Summit + 5'). This was intended to take stock of what progress had been made in meeting the commitments made at Rio (Osborn and Bigg, 1998). The next Earth Summit is scheduled for AD 2002. (Before and during Rio and for the 1997 session NGOs held their own meetings to develop and contribute their views.)

Post-Cold War environmental management

Not only has the Iron Curtain fallen, making it easier to exchange information and to co-operate on environmental care, but the capitalist system seems likely to become dominant. To have much effect, environmental management will probably have to work with and manipulate commercial interests. With growing populations and limited resources, developing countries should be targeted for environmental aid to spread better environmental management (Colby, 1990; Erocal, 1991; UNDP, 1992).

In many countries over the last decade there has been a trend towards privatization, decentralization and economic restructuring. The private sector has taken on much of what the public sector once did, so that private companies, non-profit-making bodies and NGOs are playing and will in future probably play greater roles in things like environmental management and resource management (Carney and Farrington, 1998).

Sovereignty is a problem: states have the right to exploit their own resources, but this can affect other nations. Nation states are here for the foreseeable future and ruling elites will continue to influence their political decisions and development policies. There also appears to be a shift towards supranational controls (Stoett, 1995: 12). Current western thinking on the global environment is dominated by a faith in the essentially compatible nature of humanity, rationality and enlightened self-interest.

Since the late 1940s unity and co-operation between the nations of Europe have grown. The European Economic Community (EEC) evolved into the European Union (EU) in 1957, and is still gaining members and developing links with non-EU countries. The EU consumes a significant part of the world's resources and plays a strong and increasing role in shaping the modern global economy, influencing the world's environmental agreements and providing aid to poor countries. As the EU expands and becomes more integrated it offers environmental policy makers opportunities for wider co-operation and enforcement. (For an overview of EU environmental policy and country eco-profiles see Hewett, 1995.)

The Cold War may have ended (at least for the near future between western nations and the former Soviet Union), but conflicts with serious environmental impacts continue – the Iraq–Kuwait conflict caused serious pollution through burning oilfields. With nuclear, chemical and biological armaments spreading, fears of economic stagnation or slump, and a growing underclass of poor, often disenfranchised people means that, while the Cold War may have ended, there are still abundant threats.

How can nation states be prevailed upon to adopt good environmental management? Stoett (1994) examined these issues and expressed hope that international bodies could be instrumental, arguing that the UN had already established a

Commission on Sustainable Development (in 1992), and that the Intergovernmental Panel on Climate Change (established 1988) had brought scientific legitimacy to global warming predictions. There has also been some progress since the 1994 (Cairo) International Conference on Population and Development in dealing with human population growth, plus some signs that there may be the start of a fall in birthrates in some countries. Unfortunately, even if there is establishment of relevant international bodies, and assuming most nations sign agreements, there remains the problem of enforcement – signing a treaty, convention or agreement is no guarantee the signatory will abide by it or contribute to funding.

Some hope the market will drive environmental management; others are looking beyond that (Redclift, 1992). Perhaps novel and relatively painless new taxation measures could be developed by the UN to pay for environmental management: levies on use of geosynchronous orbits for satellites, eco-tax on all air travellers, or golfers? Compared with expenditure on armaments at the height of the Cold War, or even at present, the cost of curing the most pressing environmental problems is relatively affordable (see Figure 14.1).

The politics and ethics to support environmental management

Environmental management is, as has already been stressed, a politicized process (Wilson and Bryant, 1997: 85); it is much affected by politics and ethics. There has been considerable debate about the most supportive forms of politics for environmental management: is it better to seek centralized or decentralized, citizen-led or state-managed, liberal or authoritarian control? Goldsmith *et al.* (1992: 23) suggested there were two groups of future strategies (which may be of value to environmental management): (1) those that counter destructive trends; (2) those that help foster more positive objectives. The precautionary principle should prompt the latter.

Some argue that democracy of some form is necessary for effective environmental management. Environmentalism and green politics developed in western democracies and has so far been more democratic in outlook than authoritarian, but it has been mainly reactive to problems, whereas environmental management needs to be anticipatory. A democratic system may allow public involvement and some degree of scrutiny of development, but it may also slow decision making (for a discussion of ecology and democracy see the 1995 special issue of *Environmental Politics* 4(4), 1–321) (Figure 14.2). The People's Republic of China recently announced a nationwide shift of labour to reafforestation and controls on logging, prompted by growing land degradation and flooding, illustrating that non-democratic governments are perfectly able to take proactive environmental measures.

Popular concern for posterity and people in other countries may not be strong and could need shaping, i.e. environmental management will sometimes have to go beyond the will of the people, or continue in spite of loss of interest or fashion changes. How, then, can environmental management deal with popular self-interest, inertia or

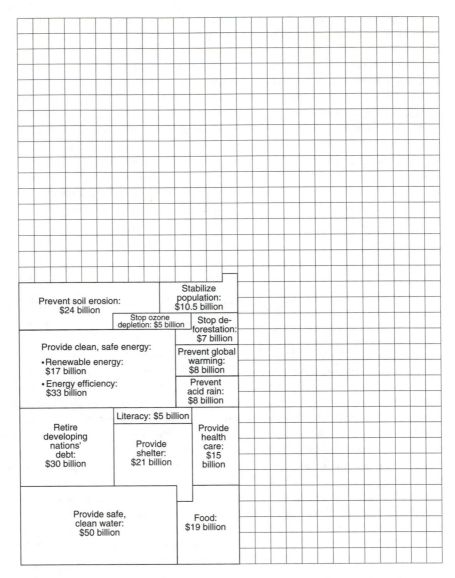

Total chart denotes total annual world military expenditure ($1 trillion); each square denotes 0.1% of annual world military expenditure ($1 billion)

FIGURE 14.1 What the world wants – and how to pay for it

Source: Henderson (1994: 128, Fig. 2)

Note: Figure shows annual costs of various global programmes. Each programme is estimated to be sufficient to accomplish its goal world-wide. The combined total cost of all these programmes is about 25 per cent of the world's total military expenditure in 1994 (in US$, US billion and trillion).

FIGURE 14.2 Singapore, a city state which, in spite of a dense population and a challenging humid tropical environment, has made impressive progress with urban environmental management. In a number of fields the city is among world leaders, notably in efforts to control car traffic and provide adequate public transport. The approach adopted has been quite 'top–down'

misguided hostility without resort to authoritarian 'eco-fascist' powers? If a liberal democratic approach is favoured, should it be moral, popular or pragmatic in outlook? Appealing to a people's sense of decency or altruism is probably too much of a gamble, and anyway liberalism tends to be anthropocentric. One way of countering the environmental inertia of democracy might be to adopt a World Charter on the Rights of Nature (efforts to do so at the 1992 Earth Summit failed).

Global environmental problems are apparent now and will probably increase in future. Already national energy needs have led to conflict over resources and transboundary pollution. Environmental problems can lead to political conflicts and vice versa. To be anticipatory environmental management will have to involve political analysts as well as ecologists, social scientists and economists. Science can be used by environmental management to reduce the polarization and squabbling that can be generated in negotiations (Brenton, 1994).

There are situations which demand a large-scale approach to their solution, for example vital investment in research may be beyond the level a single region or country could afford. The dictum 'think globally, act locally' is wise. Most sustainable development strategies will have to be tuned to local conditions, but need co-ordination at a higher level. EIA has moved towards a tiered approach, as have some environmental management systems (like SEM). With such a tiered approach, environmental management could be applied to local conditions, so that adjoining areas may have quite different approaches, yet somewhere else there may be shared similarities. Overall co-ordination, probably tiered at regional, national and global levels, would look for conflicts, ideas that might be shared, resources (notably biodiversity, crop varieties and knowledge) that should be duplicated far enough apart for security, so that if one locality suffers a disaster there are possibilities for recovery. The overall pattern would be like mosaic tiles, a global picture with considerable local diversity and simplicity of organization and duplication of units at different locations to give security against loss of infrastructure, skills, biodiversity, etc., if there is a disaster. Switzerland manages its environment and other affairs with a canton system of government which is similar.

Noting that environmental management is a multi-layered process, Wilson and Bryant (1997) suggested that it could be undertaken by international, state and non-state bodies. At present environmental management is under central, state control in some countries, while in others it is decentralized. There are also grassroots environmental managers (e.g. peasants seeking to protect their forests), MNCs and TNCs which have global environmental policies, NGOs (often with a sectoral focus – e.g. active in protecting whales and dolphins), and individual activists/scholars (e.g. Vandana Shiva, Anil Agarwal, Ignacy Sachs). The future probably lies with ensuring that environmental management operates as a multi-layered process dealing with human–environment interaction, as suggested by Wilson and Bryant (1997). Co-ordination of such a multi-layered process, involving social and physical science co-operation will be a challenge.

Concluding note

In 1952 few people expressed concern that there was an environmental problem. In 1962 environmentalists began to publish 'messianic' warnings. In 1972 the UN Conference on the Human Environment (Stockholm), one of the first world gatherings on environmental issues, closed with many of the delegates, especially those from developing countries, seeing environmental management as a luxury (some even suspected environmental concern might be a new type of green imperialism), with only a handful of nations having environmental ministries, and with few in the media or public interested. In 1992 the UN Conference on Environment and Development attracted a huge attendance, and there were few delegates willing to state publicly that environmental care was not a vital component of development: virtually every country had an environmental ministry or agency; most newspapers and television channels had environmental correspondents; and the public were following events.

It is likely that better environmental management will be realized through the evolution of present patterns of international organizations and agreements, the co-operation and coercion of commerce, local peoples, etc. Unthinking opposition to modern agriculture or commerce will not counter many of the environmental challenges, and may exacerbate some problems. There is a need for ways for the various layers involved in environmental management to communicate and arrive at decisions. Hildyard (1992: 154) called for a 'Liberation Ecology' which would empower local people to counter pressures from MNCs and TNCs or goverments and promote better environmental management and improved livelihoods.

Practical, binding agreements and an adequate Earth Charter may not all have been achieved at Rio. Nevertheless, there has been considerable progress in four decades – with no serious global crisis yet felt to prompt such changes, so there are grounds for optimism.

There is a need for environmental management to ensure that it does not neglect 'blue-sky research' and slight but worrying risks, issues which state governments might argue they could not afford to waste funds upon. There was, for example, reluctance to fund the studies which gave warning of a growing stratospheric ozone loss; funds for maintaining checks on atmospheric gas levels were hard to come by in the 1950s, yet without long-term monitoring carbon dioxide and methane changes would be difficult to understand and extrapolate. Luckily those areas of research found support. In 1991 asteroid 1191B narrowly missed the Earth. There were subsequently other interesting events, including the collision of fragments of comet Shoemaker Levy-9 with Jupiter, and the discovery of the 2-km-diameter asteroid 1997xf11, which it is hoped will narrowly miss in AD 2028. Such astronomical warnings, together with the debate about possible planetesimal strikes in the past which may have caused mass extinctions (notably at the close of the Cretaceous Period), should alert environmental management to the need for some measure to warn of and react to exogenous threats (Huggett, 1990; Ahrens and Thomas, 1992; Lewin, 1992; Chapman and Morrison, 1994; Steel, 1995; Gribbin and Gribbin, 1996). Some people feel that current technology (or technology that could be reasonably easily developed) would give some protection (for the first time in roughly 4,000 million years of Earth history); unfortunately, there may be some planetesimals which approach 'out of the Sun' or too fast for much warning. There are other slight but worrying threats: geologists suspect that massive outpourings of flood lavas in the past may have had serious impacts on the atmosphere and climate; nationally and regionally. Flooding, tsunamis, earthquakes and drought demand better long-term planning measures be undertaken.

Space research at present seems to be purely academic to most of the public. However, it is giving interesting insight into Earth processes and is helping unravel issues like global warming, natural periodic climate change, vegetation changes, patterns of pollution, etc. One day environmental managers as well as science fiction writers may have to worry about terraforming Mars, Europa or other planets (Robinson, 1992) (terraforming is the alteration of entire planetary conditions towards something more suited to human needs). Terraforming – interfering in the fate of worlds, prompts the question: what are environmental managers driven by? A referee who read the draft of this book commented that environmental managers may be in the position of selecting one of many possible alternative futures, and in so doing preventing the other possibilities. The profession should bear in mind the old adage 'those whom the gods wish to cast down, they first inflate with pride'. The practice of environmental management – developing policies, collecting data, implementing developments, co-ordinating, trouble-shooting, etc. – must all be guided by principles that are based on prudence and sound ethics.

Recommended reading

Journals which publish articles on environmental futures

Future Generations Journal (Valetta, Malta)
Future Survey
Futures
Futures Research Directory
Futures Research Quarterly
Futurist
Speculations on Science and Technology
Terra Nova
World Future Society Bulletin

References

Abbey, E. (1975) *The Monkeywrench Gang*. Avon, New York.

Acharya, R. (1991) Patenting of biotechnology: GATT and the erosion of the world's biodiversity. *Journal of World Trade* 25 (6), 71.

Adams, P. (1991) *Odious Debt: loose lending, corruption and the Third World's environmental legacy*. Earthscan, London.

Adams, P. and Solomon, L. (1985) *In the Name of Progress: the underside of development aid*. Earthscan, London.

Adams, R., Carruthers, J. and Haml, S. (1991) *Changing Corporate Values*. Kogan Page, London.

Adams, W.M. (1990) *Green Development: environment and sustainability in the Third World*. Routledge, London.

Agarwal, A. (1992) Towards global environmental management. *Social Action* 42 (2), 111–119.

Agarwal, A. and Narain, S. (1991) *Global Warming in an Unequal World: a case of environmental colonialism*. Centre for Science and Environment, New Delhi.

Agarwal, B. (1992) The gender and environment debate: lessons from India. *Feminist Studies* 18 (1), 119–158.

Agarwal, B. (1997) Environmental action, gender equity and women's participation. *Development and Change* 28 (1), 2–44.

Ager, D. (1993) *The New Catastrophism: the importance of the rare event in geological history*. Cambridge University Press, Cambridge.

Ahmad, Y.-J., El Serafy, M. and Lutz, E. (eds) (1989) *Environmental Accounting for Sustainable Development*. World Bank, Washington.

Ahrens, T.J. and Thomas, A.W. (1992) Deflection and fragmentation of near-Earth asteroids. *Nature* 360 (6403), 429–433.

Albrecht, D.E. and Murdock, S.H. (1986) Natural resources availability and social change. *Sociological Inquiry* 56 (3), 380–400.

Alfsen, K.H. and Bye, T. (1990) Norwegian experiences in natural resource accounting. *Development* 1990 (Nos. 3–4), 119–130.

Allan, N.J.R. (1987) Impact of Afghan refugees on the vegetation resources of Pakistan's Hindukush-Himalaya. *Mountain Research and Development* 7 (3), 200–204.

Allen, G.R. (1977) The world fertilizer situation. *World Development* 5 (5–7), 526–536.

Allen, J.P. (1991) *Biosphere 2: the human experiment*. Penguin, New York.

Allenby, B.R. and Richards, D.J. (eds) (1994) *The Greening of Industrial Ecosystems*. National Academy Press, Washington.

Alpert, P. (1993) Conserving biodiversity in Cameroon. *Ambio* XXII (1), 44–9.

Alvarez, W. and Asaro, F. (1990) What caused the mass extinction? An extraterrestrial impact. *Scientific American* 263 (4), 76–84.

Amin, A. (ed.) (1994) *Post-Fordism: a reader*. Blackwell, Oxford.

Anderson, A.B. (ed.) (1990) *Alternatives to Deforestation: steps toward sustainable use of Amazon rainforests*. Columbia University Press, New York.

Anderson, I. (1992) Can Nauru clean up after the colonialists? *New Scientist*, 135 (1830), 12–13.

Anderson, K. and Blackhurst, R. (eds) (1992) *The Greening of World Trade*. Harvester Wheatsheaf, London.

Anderson, W.T. (1993) Is it really environmentalism versus biotechnology? *Bio-Technology* 11 (2), 236.

Anon. (1990) Draft convention on environmental impact assessment in a transboundary context. *Environmental Policy and Law* 20 (4–5), 181–186.

Anon. (1992) Where should GATT go next? *Nature* 360 (6401), 195–196.

Anon. (1993) Cakes and caviar? The Dunkel Draft and Third World agriculture. *The Ecologist* 23 (6), 219–222.

Anon. (1995) Environment information systems in sub-Saharan Africa: an Internet resource. *Bulletin of the American Society for Information Science* 21 (4), 24.

Anon. (1996) Environment – plastics waste trading on the Internet. *Chemical Week* 158 (19), 17.

Armitage, D. (1995) An integrative methodological framework for sustainable environmental planning and management. *Environmental Management* 19 (4), 469–479.

Arnold, J.E.M. (1990) *Social Forestry and Communal Management in India* (Overseas Development Institute, Social Forestry Network Paper No. 11b). ODI, Agricultural Administration Unit, London.

Aronsson, T., Johansson, P.-O. and Löfgren, K.-G. (1997) *Welfare Measurement, Sustainability and Green National Accounting: a growth theoretical approach*. Edward Elgar, London.

Asante-Duah, D.K. (1998) *Risk Assessment in Environmental Management: a guide for managing chemical contamination problems*. Wiley, Chichester.

Ashworth, G. and Kivell, P. (eds) (1989) *Land, Water and Sky*. Geopers, Groningen.

Association of County Councils (1991) *Towards a Sustainable Transport Policy*. ACC, London.

Atkinson, A. (1991a) *Green Utopias: the future of modern environmentalism*. Zed Press, London.

Atkinson, A. (1991b) *Principles of Political Ecology*. Belhaven, London.

Auburn, F.M. (1982) *Antarctic Law and Politics*. Indiana University Press, Bloomington; World Bank, Washington.

Auty, R.M. (1995) *Patterns of Development: resources, policy and economic growth*. Arnold, London.

Avery, N., Drake, M. and Lang, T. (1993) Codex Alimentarius: who is allowed in? Who is left out? *The Ecologist* 23 (3), 110–112.

Baarschers, W.H. (1996) *Eco-Facts and Eco-Fiction: understanding the environmental debate.* Routledge, London.

Bahro, R. (1982) *Socialism and Survival.* Heretic Books, London.

Bahro, R. (1984) *From Red to Green: interviews with 'New Left Review'.* Verso, London.

Bailey, R.G. (1986) Delineation of ecosystem regions. *Environmental Management* 7 (3), 365–373.

Bailey, R.G. (1993) *Eco-scam: the false prophets of ecological apocalypse.* St Martin's Press, New York.

Bailey, R.G. (1996) *Ecosystem Geography.* Springer, New York.

Baldock, D. (1992) The polluter pays principle and its relevance to agricultural policy in European countries. *Sociologia Ruralis* 32 (1), 49–65.

Ball, S. and Bell, S. (1991) *Environmental Law.* Blackstone, London.

Barbier, E.B. (ed.) (1993) *Economics and Ecology: new frontiers in sustainable development.* Chapman and Hall, London.

Barde, J.-P. and Pearce, D.W. (1990) *Valuing the Environment.* Earthscan, London.

Barrett, B. (1994) Integrated environmental management: experience in Japan. *Journal of Environmental Management* 40 (1), 17–23.

Barrett, B.F.D. (1995) From environmental auditing to integrated environmental management: local government experience in the United Kingdom and Japan. *Journal of Environmental Planning and Management* 38 (3), 307–332.

Barrow, C.J. (1981) Health and resettlement consequences and opportunities created as a result of river impoundment in developing countries. *Water Supply and Management* 5 (2), 135–150.

Barrow, C.J. (1991) *Land Degradation: development and breakdown of terrestrial environments.* Cambridge University Press, Cambridge.

Barrow, C.J. (1995a) *Developing the Environment: problems and management,* Longman, Harlow.

Barrow, C.J. (1995b) Sustainable development: concept, value and practice. *Third World Planning Review* 17 (4), 369–387.

Barrow, C.J. (1997) *Environmental and Social Impact Assessment: an introduction.* Arnold, London.

Barrow, C.J. (1998) River basin development planning and management: a critical review. *World Development* 26 (1), 171–186.

Barrows, H. (1926) Geography as human ecology. *Annals of the Association of American Geographers* 13 (1), 1–14.

Barton, H. and Bruder, N. (1995) *A Guide to Local Environmental Auditing.* Earthscan, London.

Bate, J. (1991) *Romantic Ecology: Wordsworth and the environmental tradition.* Routledge, London.

Baumol, W. and Oates, W. (1988) *The Theory of Environmental Policy* (2nd edn). Cambridge University Press, Cambridge.

Baumwerd-Ahlmann, A., Jaschek, P., Kalinski, J. and Lehmkuhl, H. (1991) Using KADS for generating explanations in environmental impact assessment, pp. 866–876 in H.J. Bullinger (ed.) *Human Aspects in Computing* (Proceedings of the HCI International, 1–6 September, 1991, Stuttgart). Elsevier, Amsterdam.

Baxter, M. and Bacon, R. (1996) Which EMS? – your questions answered. *Environmental Assessment* 4 (1), 5–6.

Beardsley, D., Davies, T. and Hersh, R. (1997) Improving environmental management: what works, what doesn't. *Environment* 39 (7), 6–9; 28–38.

Beaumont, J.R. (1992) Managing the environment: business opportunity and responsibility. *Futures* 24 (2), 187–198.

Beaumont, P. (1989) *Environmental Management and Development in Drylands*. Routledge, London.

Beck, P. (1986) *The International Politics of Antarctica*. St Martin's Press, New York.

Beek, K.J. (1978) *Land Evaluation for Agricultural Development*. International Irrigation Research Institute (IIRI), Wageningen.

Begossi, A. (1993) Human ecology: an overview of the relationship man–environment. *Interciencia* 18 (3), 121–132.

Behrendt, H. and Boekhold, A. (1993) Phosphorus saturation of soils and groundwater. *Land Degradation & Rehabilitation* 4 (4), 233–243.

Bell, C.L.G and Hazel, P. (1980) Measuring the indirect effects of an agricultural investment project on its surrounding region. *Australian Journal of Agricultural Economics* 62 (1), 75–86.

Bell, C.L.G., Hazel, P. and Slade, C. (1982) *Project Evaluation in Regional Perspective: a study of an irrigation project in northwestern Malaysia*. Johns Hopkins University Press, Baltimore.

Bell, D. (1975) *The Coming Post-Industrial Society*. Basic Books, New York.

Bell, D., Keil, R., Fawcett, L. and Penz, P. (eds) (1998) *Political Ecology: global and local*. Routledge, London.

Bell, S. (1997) *Ball and Bell on Environmental Law: the laws and policy relating to the protection of the environment* (4th edn). Blackstone Press, London.

Beller, W., D'Ayala, P. and Hein, P. (eds) (1990) *Sustainable Development and Environmental Management of Small Islands*. UNESCO, Paris.

Bello, W. and Cunningham, S. (1994) Dark victory: the global impact of structural adjustment. *The Ecologist* 24 (3), 87–93.

Bennett, G. (1991) The history of the Dutch National Environmental Policy Plan. *Environment* 33 (7), 6–9, 31–33.

Bennett, G. (1992) *Dilemmas: coping with environmental problems*. Earthscan, London.

Bennett, R.J. (1984) System analysis and environmental management: development and future trends. *Mitteilungen der Österreichischen Geographischen Gesellschaft* 126 (1), 29–49.

Benôit, R. (1995) Current and future directions for structured impact assessments. *Impact Assessment* 13 (4), 403–432.

Benôit, R. and Podesto, M. (1995) Environmental assessment: transition of a decision support system to the environmental management of projects. *Impact Assessment* 13 (2), 117–133.

Berg, G. (1969) *Circumpolar Problems: habitat, economy, and social relations in the Arctic: a symposium for anthropological research in the north, September, 1969*. Pergamon Press, Oxford.

Berkes, F. (ed.) (1989) *Common Property Resources: ecology and community-based sustainable development*. Belhaven, London.

Berkhout, F. (1991) *Radioactive Waste: politics and technology*. Routledge, London.

Billings, W.D. (1978) *Plants and the Ecosystem* (3rd edn). Wadsworth Publishing Co., Belmont.

Birnie, P.W. and Boyle, A.E. (1992) *International Law and the Environment*. Clarendon Press, Oxford.

Black, R. (1994) Forced migration and environmental change: the impact of refugees on host environments. *Journal of Environmental Management* 42 (3), 261–277.

Blackburn, T.C. and Anderson, K. (eds) (1995) *Before the Wilderness: environmental management by Native Californians* (Anthropological Papers No. 40). Ballena Press, Menlo Park.

Blaikie, P.M. (1985) *The Political Economy of Soil Erosion in Developing Countries*. Longman, Harlow.

Blaikie, P.M. (1988) The explanation of land degradation in Nepal, pp. 132–158 in J. Ives and D.C. Pitt (eds) *Deforestation: social dynamics in watersheds and mountain ecosystems*. Routledge, London.

Blaikie, P.M. (1989) The use of natural resources in developing and developed countries, pp. 125–150 in R.J. Johnston. and P.J. Taylor (eds) *A World in Crisis? Geographical perspectives* (revised edn). Basil Blackwell, Oxford.

Blaikie, P. and Brookfield, H. (1987) *Land Degradation and Society*. Methuen, London.

Blaikie, P.M. and Unwin, T. (eds) (1988) *Environmental Crisis in Developing Countries* (IBG Developing Areas Research Group, Monograph No. 5). Institute of British Geographers, London.

Blakeslee, H.W. and Grabowski, T.M. (1985) *A Practical Guide to Plant Environmental Audits*. Van Nostrand Reinhold, New York.

Blench, R. (1998) Biodiversity conservation and its opponents. *ODI Natural Resource Perspectives* No. 32, 4 pp.

Bliss, L.C., Heal, O.W. and Moore, J.J. (eds) (1981) *Tundra Ecosystems: a comparative analysis*. Cambridge University Press, Cambridge.

Bloemhofruwaard, J.M., Vanbeek, P., Hordijk, L. and Van Wassenhove, L.N. (1995) Interactions between operational research and environmental management. *European Journal of Operational Research* 85 (2), 229–243.

Blowers, A. (ed.) (1993) *Planning for a Sustainable Environment*. Earthscan, London.

Boardman, R. (1986) *Pesticides in World Agriculture: the politics of international regulation*. Macmillan, London.

Bocking, S. (1994) Visions of nature and society: a history of the ecosystem concept. *Alternatives* 20 (3), 12–18.

Bodansky, D. (1991) Scientific uncertainty and the precautionary principle. *Environment* 33 (7), 4.

Boehmer-Christiansen, S. (1994) Politics and environmental management. *Journal of Environmental Planning and Management* 37 (1), 69–86.

Bohoris, G.A. and O'Mahoney, E. (1994) BS–7750, BS–5750 and the EC's Eco-Management and Audit Scheme. *Industrial Management & Data Systems* 94 (2), 3–6.

Bookchin, M. (1972) *Post-Scarcity Anarchism*. Black Rose Books, Montreal.

Bookchin, M. (1980) *Towards a Social Ecology*. Black Rose Books, Montreal.

Bookchin, M. (1982) *The Ecology of Freedom: the emergence and dissolution of hierarchy*. Cheshire Books, Palo Alto.

Bookchin, M. (1986) *The Modern Crisis*. New Society Publishers, Philadelphia.

Bookchin, M. (1990) *Remaking Society*. Black Rose Books, Montreal.

Booth, D. (1997) *The Environmental Consequences of Growth*. Routledge, London.

Bormann, B.T., Brookes, M.H., Ford, E.D., Kiesler, A.R., Oliver, C.D. and Weigand, J.F. (1993) *A Broad Strategic Framework for Sustainable-Ecosystem Management* (Eastside Forest Ecosystem Health Assessment vol. V). USDA Forest Service, Washington, 62 pp.

Born, S.M. and Sonzogni, W.C. (1995) Integrated environmental management: strengthening the conceptualization. *Environmental Management* 19 (2), 167–181.

Borri, F. and Boccaletti, G. (1995) From total quality management to total quality environmental management. *The TQM Magazine* 7 (5), 38–42.

Boserüp, E. (1965) *The Conditions of Agricultural Growth: the economics of agrarian change under population pressure*. Allen and Unwin, London.

Boserüp, E. (1981) *Population and Technology*. Blackwell, Oxford.

Boserüp, E. (1990) *Economic and Demographic Relationships in Development* (essays selected and introduced by T.P. Schultz). Johns Hopkins University Press, Baltimore.

Bouchet, J.-J. (1983) *Management of Upland Watersheds: participation of the mountain communities*. FAO, Rome.

Boulding, K.E. (1971) The economics of the coming Spaceship Earth. *Development Digest* (1), 12–15. (Reprinted from 1966 in H. Jarrett (ed.) *Environmental Quality in a Growing Economy*. Johns Hopkins University Press, Baltimore.)

Bouverie, J. (1991) Recycling in Cairo: a tale of rags to riches. *New Scientist* 130 (1775), 52–55.

Bowander, B. (1987) Integrating perspectives in environmental management. *Environmental Management* 11 (3), 305–315.

Bown, W. (1990) Trade deals a blow to the environment. *New Scientist* 128 (1742), 20–22.

Bowyer, J.L. (1994) Needed: a global environmental impact assessment. *Journal of Forestry* 92 (6), 6.

Boyce, M.S. (1997) *Ecosystem Management: applications for sustainable forest and wildlife management*. Yale University Press, New Haven.

Boyle, A.E. (1992) Protecting the marine-environment: some problems and developments in the Law of the Sea. *Marine Policy* 16 (2), 79–85.

Bradshaw, A.D., Southwood, R. and Warner, F. (eds) (1992) *The Treatment and Handling of Wastes*. Chapman and Hall, London.

Braidotti, R., Charkiewicz, E., Häusler, S. and Wieringa, S. (1994) *Women, the Environment and Sustainable Development: towards a theoretical synthesis*. Zed Press, London.

Bramwell, A. (1994) *The Fading of the Greens: the decline of environmental politics in the west*. Yale University Press, New Haven.

Brent, R.J. (1997) *Applied Cost–Benefit Analysis*. Edward Elgar, London.

Brenton, T. (1994) *The Greening of Machiavelli: the evolution of international environmental politics*. Earthscan, London.

Briassoulis, H. (1986) Integrated economic-environmental policy modelling at the regional and multiregional level: methodological characteristics and issues. *Growth & Change* 17 (1), 22–34.

Brick, P. (1995) Determined opposition: the Wise-Use Movement challenges environmentalism. *Environment* 37 (8), 16.

Briggs, D.J. and Courtney, F.M. (1985) *Agriculture and Environment: the physical geography of temperate agricultural systems*. Longman, London.

Brimblecombe, P. (1987) *The Big Smoke: a history of pollution in London since medieval times.* Methuen, London.

British Medical Association (1991) *Hazardous Waste and Human Health.* Oxford University Press, Oxford.

British Standards Institution (1992) *BS7750 British Standard for Environmental Management.* British Standards Institution, Manchester.

British Standards Institution (1994a) *Part I: auditing of environmental management systems* (guidelines for environmental auditing – audit procedures, ISO/CD 14011/1, Document 94/400414DC). British Standards Institution, Manchester.

British Standards Institution (1994b) *Environmental Management Systems* BS7750. British Standards Institution, Manchester.

British Standards Institution (1994c) *Draft BS ISO 14040: life cycle assessment: general principles and practices.* British Standards Institution, Manchester.

British Standards Institution (1996) *Environmental Management Systems: specifications with guidance for use.* British Standards Institution, Manchester.

Broecker, W.S. and Denton, G.H. (1990) What drives glacial cycles? *Scientific American* 262 (1), 42–50.

Brokensha, D.W. (1987) Development anthropology and natural resource management. *Uomo* II (2), 225–249.

Bromley, D.W. (1994) The enclosure movement revisited: the South African commons. *Journal of Economic Issues* 28 (2), 357–366.

Bromley, D.W. and Cernea, M.M. (1989) *The Management of Common Property Resources: some conceptual and operational fallacies* (World Bank Discussion Paper No. 57). World Bank, Washington.

Brower, D.J., Schwab, A.K. and Beatley, T. (1994) *An Introduction to Coastal Zone Management.* Island Press, Washington.

Brown, D.J.A. (1995) EU Eco-Management and Audit Scheme (EMAS). *Journal of the Institution of Environmental Sciences* 4 (3), 4–7.

Brown, J.R. and MacLeod, N.D. (1996) Integrating ecology into natural resource management policy. *Environmental Management* 20 (3), 289–296.

Brunner, R.D. and Clark, T.W. (1997) A practice-based approach to ecosystem management. *Conservation Biology* 11 (1), 48–58.

Brush, S.B. (1986) Farming systems research. *Human Organization* 45 (3), 220–238.

Bryant, R.L. and Bailey, S. (1997) *Third World Political Ecology.* Routledge, London.

Bryant, R.L. and Wilson, G.A. (1998) Rethinking environmental management. *Progress in Human Geography* 22 (3), 321–343.

Buarque, C. (1993) *The End of Economics? Ethics and the disorder of progress.* Zed Press, London.

Buckley, R.C. (1993) International trade, investment and environmental regulation: an environmental management perspective. *Journal of World Trade* 27 (4), 101–148.

Buckley, R.C. (1994) Strategic environmental assessment. *Environmental Planning and Law Journal* 11 (2), 166–168.

Buckley, R.C. (1995) Environmental auditing, pp. 283–301 in F. Vanclay and D.A. Bronstein (eds) *Environmental and Social Impact Assessment.* Wiley, Chichester.

Bunce, R.G.H., Ryszkowski, L. and Paoletti, M.G. (1993) *Landscape Ecology and Agroecosystems.* Lewis Publishers, Boca Raton.

Burch, W.R. Jnr, Cheek, N.H.,and Taylor, L. (eds) (1972) *Social Behavior, Natural Resources and the Environment* Harper and Row, New York.

Burde, M., Jackel, T., Dieckmann, R. and Hemker, H. (1994) Environmental impact assessment for regional planning with SAFRAN. *IFIP Transactions* (B-applications in technology) 16, 245–256.

Burdge, R.J. (1994) *A Conceptual Approach to Social Impact Assessment: collection of writings by Rabel J. Burdge and colleagues.* Social Ecology Press (PO Box 620863), Middleton.

Burdge, R.J. and Vanclay, F. (1996) Social impact assessment: a contribution to the state-of-the-art series. *Impact Assessment* 14 (1), 59–86.

Burk, T. and Hill, J. (1990) *Ethics, Environment and the Company.* The Institute of Business Ethics, London.

Burton, I., Kates, R. and White, G. (1977) *The Environment as Hazard.* Oxford University Press, Oxford.

Burton, M.L., Schoepfle, G.M. and Miller, M.L. (1986) Natural resource anthropology. *Human Organization* 45 (3), 261–269.

Butler, R.W. (1991) Tourism, environment, and sustainable development. *Environmental Conservation* 18 (3), 201–209.

Buttel, F.H. (1978) Environmental sociology: a new paradigm? *The American Sociologist* 13 (3), 252–256.

Cahill, L.B. (ed.) (1989) *Environmental Audits* (6th edn). Government Institutes Inc., Rockville.

Cairns, J. Jnr and Crawford, T.V. (eds) (1991) *Integrated Environmental Management.* Lewis Publishers, Chelsea.

Caldwell, L.K. (1989) A constitutional law for the environment: 20 years with NEPA indicates the need. *Environment* 31 (10), 6–11, 25–28.

Caldwell, L.K. (1990) *International Environmental Policy: emergence and dimensions* (2nd edn). Duke University, Durham (USA).

Cameron, J. and Fijalkowski, A. (eds) (1998) *Trade and the Environment: bridging the gap* (vols 1 and 2). Cameron May, London.

Cann, J. and Walker, C. (1993) Breaking new ground on the ocean floor. *New Scientist* 140 (1897), 24–29.

Canter, L.W. (1996) *Environmental Impact Assessment* (2nd edn – 1st edn 1977). McGraw-Hill, New York.

Capra, F. (1982) *The Turning Point: science, society and the rising culture.* Wildwood House, London.

Capra, F. (1997) *The Web of Life: a new synthesis of mind and matter.* Flamingo (Harper-Collins), London.

Carley, M. and Christie, I. (1992) *Managing Sustainable Development.* Earthscan, London.

Carley, M., Smith, M. and Varadarajan, S. (1991) A network approach to environmental management. *Project Appraisal* 6 (2), 66–75.

Carney, D. and Farrington, J. (1998) *Natural Resource Management and Institutional Change.* Routledge, London.

Carroll, J.E. (1988) *International Environmental Diplomacy: the management and resolution of transfrontier environmental problems.* Cambridge University Press, Cambridge.

Carson, R. (1962) *Silent Spring.* Houghton Mifflin, Boston.

Carter, R.W.G. (1988) *Coastal Environments.* Academic Press, London.

Cartwright, J. (1989) Conserving nature, decreasing debt. *Third World Quarterly* 11 (2), 114–127.

Cartwright, T.J. (1991) Planning and chaos theory. *Journal of the American Planning Association* 57 (1), 44–56.

Catton, W.R. (1994) Foundations of human ecology. *Sociological Perspectives* 37 (1), 75–95.

CEC (1992) *Towards Sustainability: the Fifth Environmental Action Programme for Europe.* Commission for the European Communities, Brussels.

Cernea, M.M. (1988) *Involuntary Resettlement in Development Projects: policy guidelines in World Bank-financed projects* (World Bank Technical Paper no. 180). World Bank, Washington.

Chadwick, M.J. and Goodman, G.T. (eds) (1975) *The Ecology of Resource Degradation and Renewal.* Blackwell Scientific, Oxford.

Chambers, R. (1983) *Rural Development: putting the last first.* Longman, Harlow.

Chambers, R. (1992) *Rural Appraisal: rapid, relaxed and participatory* (Discussion Paper No. 311). University of Sussex, Institute of Development Studies, Brighton.

Chambers, R. (1994a) The origins and practice of participatory rural appraisal. *World Development* 22 (7), 953–969.

Chambers, R. (1994b) Participatory rural appraisal (PRA): analysis of experience. *World Development* 22 (9), 1253–1268.

Chambers, R. (1994c) Participatory rural appraisal (PRA): challenges, potentials and paradigm. *World Development* 22 (10), 1437–1454.

Chandler, R. (1988) *Understanding the New Age.* Ward, London.

Chapman, C.R. and Morrison, D. (1994) Impacts on Earth by asteroids and comets: assessing the hazard. *Nature* 367 (6458), 33–39.

Chapman, M.D. (1989) The political ecology of fisheries depletion in Amazonia. *Environmental Conservation* 16 (4), 331–337.

Chappell, J.E. (1993) Social Darwinism, environmentalism, and ideology. *Annals of the Association of American Geographers* 83 (1), 160–163.

Charnovitz, S. (1993) Environmentalism confronts GATT rules: recent developments and new opportunities. *Journal of World Trade* 27 (2), 37–53.

Charter, M. (ed.) (1992) *Greener Marketing.* Greenleaf, Sheffield (UK).

Chatterjee, N. (1995) Social forestry in environmentally degraded regions of India: case-study of the Mayurakshi basin. *Environmental Conservation* 22 (1), 20–30.

Cheney, J. (1987) Eco-feminism and deep ecology. *Environmental Ethics* 9 (4), 115–145.

Cheney, J. (1989) Postmodern environmental ethics: ethics as bioregional narrative. *Environmental Ethics* 11 (2), 117–134.

Cheremisinoff, P.N. and Morresi, A.O. (1977) *Environmental Assessment and Impact Statement Handbook.* Wiley, Chichester.

Chiapponi, M. (1992) Environmental management and planning: the role of spatial and temporal scales. *Ekistics* 59 (356–357), 306–310.

Cigna, A.A. (1993) Environmental management of tourist caves: the example of Grotta di Castellana and Grotta Grande del Vento, Italy. *Environmental Geology* 21 (3), 173–180.

Ciracy-Wantrup, S.V. (1952) *Resource Conservation: economics and policies.* University of California Press, Berkeley.

Clark, B.D., Gilad, A., Bisset, R. and Tomlinson, P. (eds) (1984) *Perspectives on Environmental Impact Assessment.* D. Reidel, Dordrecht.

Clark, J.R. (1996) *Coastal Zone Management Handbook*. Lewis Publishers, Boca Raton.

Clark, M., Smith, D. and Blowers, A. (eds) (1992) *Waste Location: spatial aspects of waste management, hazards and disposal*. Routledge, London.

Clark, R.B. (1989) *Marine Pollution* (2nd edn). Oxford Science Publishers, Oxford.

Clark, R. (1999) *Countryside Management*. Routledge, London.

Clark, W.C. (1989) Managing planet Earth. *Scientific American* 261 (3), 19–26.

Clements, F.E. (1916) *Plant Succession. An analysis of the development of vegetation* (Publication No. 242). Carnegie Institute, Washington.

Cleveland, H. (1990) *The Global Commons: policy for the planet*. The Aspen Institute and University Press of America Inc., Lanham.

Clunies-Ross, T. (1993) Taxing nitrogen fertilizer. *The Ecologist* 23 (1), 13–17.

Coddington, W. (1993) *Environmental Marketing*. McGraw-Hill, New York.

Coenen, R. (1993) NEPA's impact on environmental impact assessment in European Community member countries, pp. 703–715 in S.G. Hildebrand and J.B. Cannon (eds) *Environmental Analysis: the NEPA experience*. Lewis Publishers, Boca Raton.

Colby, M.E. (1990) *Environmental Management in Development: the evolution of paradigms* (World Bank Discussion Paper No. 80). World Bank, Washington.

Colchester, M. (1993) Pirates, squatters and poachers – the political ecology of dispossession of the native peoples of Sarawak. *Global Ecology and Biogeography Letters* 3 (4–6), 158–179.

Collins, J.I. (1986) Smallholder settlement of tropical South America: the social causes of ecological destruction. *Human Organization* 45 (1), 1–10.

Commins, S.K., Lofchie, M.F. and Payne, R. (eds) (1986) *Africa's Agrarian Crisis: the roots of famine*. Lynne Rienner, Boulder.

Commission of the European Communities (1992) *Towards Sustainability: a European Community programme of policy and action in relation to the environment and sustainable development* COM (92) 23 (final – vol. II). CEC, Brussels.

Common, M.S. (1996) *Environmental and Resource Economics* (2nd edn). Addison Wesley Longman, Harlow.

Common, M.S. and Norton, T.W. (1994) Biodiversity, natural resource accounting and ecological monitoring. *Environmental & Resource Economics* 4 (1), 29–54.

Commoner, B. (1972) *The Closing Circle*. Knopf, New York.

Conroy, C. and Litvinoff, M. (1988) *The Greening of Aid: sustainable livelihoods in practice*. Earthscan, London.

Conway, G.R. (1985a) Agroecosystem analysis. *Agricultural Administration* 20 (1), 31–55.

Conway, G.R. (1985b) The properties of agroecosystems. *Agricultural Systems* 24 (2), 95–117.

Conway, G.R. and Barbier, E.B. (1990) *After the Green Revolution: sustainable agriculture for development*. Earthscan, London.

Conway, G.R. and McCracken, J.A. (1990) Rapid rural appraisal and agroecosystem analysis, pp. 221–236 in M.A. Altieri and S.B. Hecht (eds) *Agroecology and Small Farm Development*. Westview/CRC, Boulder.

Conway, G.R. and Pretty, J.N. (1991) *Unwelcome Harvest: agriculture and pollution*. Earthscan, London.

Cooper, C. (1981) *Economic Evaluation and the Environment: a methodological discussion with particular reference to developing countries*. Hodder and Stoughton, London.

Cooper, C. (1990) *Green Christianity: caring for the whole creation*. Spire (Hodder and Stoughton), London.

Cooper, D.E. and Palmer, J.A. (eds) (1992) *The Environment in Question: ethics and global issues*. Routledge, London.

Cooper, P.J. (1995) Toward a hybrid state: the case of environmental management in a deregulated re-engineered state. *International Journal of Administrative Sciences* 61 (2), 185–200.

Copithorne, M.D. (1991) *Circumpolar Environmental Management and Regulation: from coexistence to cooperation – international law and organizations in the post-Cold War era*. Martinus Nijhoff, Dordrecht.

Cornwall, A. (1997) *Environmental Taxes and Economic Welfare: reducing carbon dioxide emissions*. Edward Elgar, London.

Corwin, R., Heffernan, P.H. and Johnston, R.A. (1975) *Environmental Impact Assessment*. W.H. Freeman & Co., San Francisco.

Cosgrove, D. (1990) Environmental thought and action: pre-modern and post-modern. *Transactions of the Institute of British Geographers* (new series) 15 (3), 344–358.

Costanza, R. (ed.) (1991) *Ecological Economics: the science and management of sustainability*. Columbia University Press, Ithaca (New York).

Costanza, R. and Cornwell, L. (1992) The approach to dealing with scientific uncertainty. *Environment* 34 (9), 12–20, 42.

Cotgrove, S. (1982) *Catastrophe or Cornucopia?: the environment, politics and the future*. Wiley, Chichester.

Council of Economic Priorities of the United States (1989) *Shopping for a Better World: a quick and easy guide to socially responsible supermarket shopping*. Council of Economic Priorities of the United States, New York.

Covello, V.T., Mumpower, J.L., Stallen, P.J.M. and Uppuluri, V.R.R. (eds) (1985) *Environmental Impact Assessment, Technology Assessment, and Risk Analysis: contributions from the psychological and decision sciences*. Springer-Verlag, Berlin.

Cramer, J. and Zegveld, W.C.L. (1991) The future role of technology in environmental management. *Futures* 23 (5), 451–468.

Croner Publications Ltd (1997) *Croner's Environmental Policy and Procedures*. Croner Publications, Kingston upon Thames (also available as CD-ROM).

Cumberland, J.H. (1990) Public choice and the improvement of policy instruments for environmental management. *Ecological Economics* 2 (2), 149–162.

Dalal-Clayton, B. (1992) *Modified EIA and Indicators of Sustainability*: first steps towards sustainability analysis. Earthscan, London.

Dale, A.P. (1992) Aboriginal councils and natural resource use planning: participation by bargaining and negotiation. *Australian Geographical Studies* 30 (1), 9–26.

Dale, T. and Carter, V.G. (1954) *Topsoil and Civilisation*. University of Oklahoma Press, Norman.

Dalton, R.J. (1994) *The Green Rainbow: environmental groups in western Europe*. Yale University Press, New Haven.

Dankelman, I. and Davidson, J. (1988) *Women and Environment in the Third World*. Earthscan, London.

Darling. F.F. and Dasmann, R.F. (1969) The ecosystem view of human society. *Impact of Science on Society* 19 (2), 109–121.

Darwin, C. (1859) *The Origin of Species by Means of Natural Selection: or the preservation of favoured races in the struggle of life*. John Murray, London.

Dasmann, R.F., Milton, J.P. and Freeman, P.H. (1973) *Ecological Principles for Economic Development*. Wiley, London.

Davidson, J., Myers, D. and Chakraborty, M. (1992) *No Time to Wait: poverty and the environment*. Oxfam, Oxford.

Davis, J. (1991) *Greening Business: managing for sustainable development*. Basil Blackwell, Oxford.

Davos, C.A. (1986) Global environmental management. *The Science of the Total Environment* 56 (6), 309–316.

D'Ayala, P., Hein, P. and Beller, W. (1990) *Sustainable Development and Environmental Management of Small Islands* (MAB Series No. 5). Parthenan Publishing Group (for UNESCO), Paris.

De Bardeleben, J. (1986) *The Environment and Marxism-Leninism: the Soviet and East German experience*. Westview Press, Boulder.

De Groot, W.T. (1992) *Environmental Science Theory: concepts and methods in a one-world, problem-oriented paradigm*. Elsevier, Amsterdam.

De Miraman, J. and Stevens, C. (1992) The trade/environmental policy balance. *The OECD Observer* 176 (Jan./Jly, 1992), 25–27.

Department of Environment (1994) *UK Strategy on Sustainable Development*. HMSO, London.

DeRoy, O.C. (1997) The African challenge: Internet, networking and connectivity activities in a developing environment. *Third World Quarterly* 18 (5), 883–898.

Devall, B. (1991) Deep ecology and radical environmentalism. *Society & Natural Resources* 4 (3), 247–258.

Devall, B. and Sessions, G. (1985) *Deep Ecology: living as if nature mattered*. Peregrine Smith Books, Salt Lake City.

Devall, W. (1988) *Simple in Means, Rich in Ends: practicing deep ecology*. Peregrine Smith Books, Salt Lake City.

Diamond, I. and Drenstein, G.F. (eds) (1990) *Reweaving the World: the emergence of ecofeminism*. Sierra Club Books, San Francisco.

Diamond, J. (1997) *Guns, Germs and Steel: a short history of everybody for the last 13,000 years*. Jonathan Cape, London.

Diaz, H.F. and Markgraf, V. (1992) *El Niño: historical and palaeoclimatic aspects of the Southern Oscillation*. Cambridge University Press, Cambridge.

di Castri, F. and Hadley, M. (1985) Enhancing the credibility of ecology: can research be made more comparable and predictive? *GeoJournal* 11 (4), 321–338.

di Castri, F. and Robertson, J. (1982) The biosphere reserve concept: 10 years after. *Parks* 6 (4), 1–6.

Dickinson, G. and Murphy, K. (1998) *Ecosystems: a functional approach*. Routledge, London.

Dinham, B. (1991) FAO and pesticides: promotion 450 or proscription? *The Ecologist* 21 (2), 61–65.

Ditton, R.B. and Goodale, T.C. (eds) (1974) *Environmental Impact Analysis: philosophy and methods*. University of Wisconsin, Sea Grants Program, Madison.

Dixon, J.A., James, D.E. and Sherman, P.B. (eds) (1989) *The Economics of Dryland Management*. Earthscan, London.

Dobson, A. (1990) *Green Political Thought: an introduction*. Routledge, London.

Dobson, A. (1994) Ecologism and the relegitimation of socialism. *Radical Philosophy* 67 (1), 13–19.

Dobson, A. (1995) *Green Political Thought: an introduction* (2nd edn). Routledge, London.

Dodds, F. (ed.) (1997) *The Way Forward: beyond 'Agenda 21'*. Earthscan, London.

Dodds, S. (1997) Towards a 'science of sustainability': improving the way ecological economics understands human well-being. *Ecological Economics* 23 (2), 95–111.

Döös, B.R. (1994) Environmental degradation, global food production, and risk for large-scale migrations. *Ambio* XXIII (2), 124–130.

Döös, B.R. (1997) Can large-scale environmental migrations be predicted? *Global Environmental Change* 7 (1), 41–61.

Dorney, R.S. (1989) *The Professional Practice of Environmental Management* (posthumously edited by L.S. Dorney). Springer, New York.

Dorney, R.S. and McLellan, P.W. (1984) The urban ecosystem: its spatial structure, its scale relationships, and its subsystem attributes. *Environments* 16 (1), 9–20.

Douglas, M. and Wildavsky, A. (1990) *Risk and Culture*. Westview, Boulder.

Dovers, S.R. and Handmer, J.W. (1995) Ignorance, the precautionary principle, and sustainability. *Ambio* XXIV (2), 92–97.

Dower, N. (ed.) (1989) *Ethics and Environmental Responsibility*. Avebury (Gower Books), Aldershot.

Doxiadis, C. (1968) *Ekistics: an introduction to the science of human settlements*. Hutchinson, London.

Doxiadis, C. (1977) *Ecology and Ekistics*. Elek Books, London.

Duinker, P.N. (1989) Ecological monitoring in environmental impact assessment: what can it accomplish? *Environmental Management* 13 (6), 797–805.

Dunlap, R. and Mertig, A. (eds) (1992) *American Environmentalism: the US environmental movement 1970–1990*. Taylor and Francis, Philadelphia.

Earll, R.C. (1992) Common sense and the precautionary principle: an environmentalist perspective. *Marine Pollution Bulletin* 24 (2), 182–186.

Easter, K.A., Dixon, J.A. and Hufschmidt, M.M. (eds) (1986) *Watershed Resource Management: an integrated framework with studies from Asia and the Pacific*. Westview, Boulder.

Eckersley, R. (1988) The road to ecotopia? Socialism versus environmentalism. *The Ecologist* 18 (4–5), 142–148.

Eckholm, E.P. (1976) *Losing Ground: environmental stress and world food prospects*. Pergamon Press, Oxford.

Ecologist (1993) *Whose Common Future? Reclaiming the commons*. Earthscan, London.

Edington, J.M. and Edington, M.A. (1986) *Ecology, Recreation and Tourism*. Cambridge University Press, Cambridge.

Edwards, F.N. (ed.) (1992) *Environmental Auditing: the challenge of the 1990s*. University of Calgary Press, Calgary.

EEC (1993) *EMAS No.1836/93* (EEC Council Regulation). Council of the European Communities, Luxembourg.

Ehrlich, P.R. (1970) *The Population Bomb*. New Ballentine Books, New York.

Ehrlich, P.R., Ehrlich, A.H. and Holdren, J.P. (1970) *Ecoscience: population, resources, environment*. Freeman, San Francisco.

Ekins, P. (1992a) *Wealth Beyond Measure: an atlas of new economics*. Gaia Books, Bideford.

Ekins, P. (1992b) *A New World Order: grass roots movements for global change*. Routledge, London.

El-Hinnawi, E. (1985) *Environmental Refugees*. UNEP, Nairobi.

Elkington, J. and Burke, T. (1989) *The Green Capitalists*. Victor Gollancz, London.

Elkington, J. and Hailes, J. (1988) *The Green Consumer Guide: from shampoos to champagne*. Victor Gollancz, London.

Elkington, J. and Knight, P. (1991) *The Green Business Guide*. Victor Gollancz, London.

Elliott, H. (1997) A general statement of the tragedy of the commons. *Population and Environment* 18 (6), 515–531.

Elsworth, S. (1984) *Acid Rain*. Earthscan, London.

Elton, C.S. (1958) *The Ecology of Invasions by Animals and Plants*. Chapman and Hall, London.

Engstrom, K. (1992) The recycling of plastic bottles collected from public waste. *Endeavour* 16 (3), 117–121.

EPA (1988) *Annotated Bibliography on Environmental Auditing*. US Environmental Protection Agency, Office of Policy and Education, Washington.

Eriksson, E. (1989) Acid deposition and its effects. *Ambio* XVIII (3), 184–191.

Eröcal, D. (ed.) (1991) *Environmental Management in Developing Countries* (Development Centre Seminars). Development Centre, OECD, Paris.

Esty, D.C. (1994) *Greening the GATT: trade, environment, and the future*. International Institute for Economics, Washington.

Evans, B. (1995) Local environment policy: sustainability and 'Local Agenda 21'. *Area* 27 (2), 163–164.

Evernden, N. (1985) *The Natural Alien*. University of Toronto Press, Toronto.

Fairhead, J. and Leach, M. (1996) *Misreading the African Landscape: society and ecology in a forest–savanna mosaic*. Cambridge University Press, Cambridge.

Fairlie, S. (1992) Long distance, short life: why big business favours recycling. *The Ecologist* 22 (6), 276–283.

Fairweather, P.G. (1993) Links between ecology and ecophilosophy, ethics and the requirements of environmental management. *Australian Journal of Ecology* 18 (1), 3–19.

FAO (1978) *Report on the Agroecosystems Zones Project*, vol. 1: *Methodology and Results for Africa* (World Soil Research Paper No. 48). FAO, Rome.

FAO (1986) *Strategies, Approaches and Systems in Integrated Watershed Management*. FAO, Rome.

FAO (1988) *Guidelines for Economic Appraisal of Watershed Management Projects*. FAO, Rome.

Farber, S., Moreau, R. and Templet, P. (1995) A tax incentive tool for environmental management: an environmental scorecard. *Environmental Economics* 12 (3), 183–189.

Farmer, A. (1997) *Managing Environmental Pollution*. Routledge, London.

Farvar, M.T. and Milton, J.P. (eds) (1972) *The Careless Technology: ecology and international development*. Natural History Press/Doubleday, Garden City (New York).

Fava, J.A. (1994) Life-cycle assessment: a new way of thinking. *Environmental Toxicology and Chemistry* 13 (6), 853–854.

Febvre, L. (1924) *A Geographical Introduction to History*. Routledge and Kegan Paul, London.

Feeney, D., Berkes, F., McCay, B.J. and Acherson, J.M. (1990) The tragedy of the commons – 22 years later. *Human Ecology* 18 (1), 1–19.

Feitelson, E, (1992) An alternative role for economic instruments: sustainable finance for environmental management. *Environmental Management* 16 (3), 299–307.

Feshbach, M. and Friendly, A. (1992) *Ecocide in the USSR*. Arum, London.

Finsinger, J. and Marx, J.F. (1996) Eco–Management and Audit Scheme (EMAS): opportunities and risks for insurance companies. *International Journal of Environment and Pollution* 6 (4–6), 491–499.

Fitter, R. and Scott, P. (1978) *The Penitent Butchers*. The Fauna and Flora Preservation Society, London.

Fitzgerald, C. (1993) *Environmental Management Information Systems*. McGraw-Hill, New York.

Flamm, B.R. (1973) A philosophy of EIA: toward choice among alternatives. *Journal of Soil and Water Conservation* 28 (3), 201–203.

Foder, I. and Walker, G. (eds) (1994) *Environmental Policy and Practice*. Hungarian Academy of Sciences, Pecs.

Foley, G. (1988) Deep ecology and subjectivity. *The Ecologist* 18 (4–5), 120–123.

Fong, C.O. (1985) Integrated population–development programme performance: the Malaysian FELDA experience. *Journal of Developing Areas* 19 (2), 149–169.

Forman, R.T.T. and Godron, M. (1986) *Landscape Ecology*. Wiley, New York.

Forrest, R.A. (1991) Japanese aid and the environment. *The Ecologist* 21 (1), 24–32.

Forrest, W. and Morison, A. (1991) A government role in better environmental management. *Science of the Total Environment* 108 (1–2), 51–60.

Forsund, F.R. and Strom, S. (1988) *Environmental Economics and Management: pollution and natural resources*. Croom Helm, London.

Fortlage, C.A. (1990) *Environmental Assessment: a practical guide*. Gower, Aldershot.

Fowler, C. and Mooney, P. (1990) *The Threatened Gene: food, politics, and the loss of genetic diversity*. Lutterworth Press, Cambridge.

Fox, M. (1983) *Original Blessing*. Bear and Co., Santa Fe.

Fox, M. (1989) A call for a spiritual renaissance. *Green Letter* 5 (1), 4, 16–17.

Fox, W. (1984) Deep ecology: a new philosophy of our time? *The Ecologist* 14 (5–6), 194–200.

Fox, W. (1995) *Towards a Transpersonal Ecology: developing new foundations for environmentalism*. Green Books (Resurgence), Totnes.

Francis, J.M. (1996) Nature conservation and the precautionary principle. *Environmental Values* 5 (3), 257–264.

Frankel, B. (1987) *The Post-Industrial Utopias*. Polity Press, Cambridge.

Franklin, W.E. (1995) Life-cycle assessment – a remarkable tool in the era of sustainable resource and environmental management. *Resources Conservation and Recycling* 14 (3–4), R5–R7.

Fraser-Darling, F. (1963) The unity of ecology. *British Association for the Advancement of Science* 20, 297–306.

Freeman, C. and Jahoda, M. (eds) (1978) *World Futures: the great debate*. Martin Robertson, Oxford.

Freestone, D. (1994) The road from Rio: international environmental law after the Earth Summit. *Journal of Environmental Law* 6 (2), 193–218.

French, P. (1998) *Coastal and Estuarine Management*. Routledge, London.

Frenkel, S. (1994) Old theories in new places: environmental determinism and bioregionalism. *Professional Geographer* 46 (3), 289–295.

Freudenburg, W.R. (1986) Social impact assessment. *Annual Review of Sociology* 12, 451–478.

Freudenburg, W.R. (1989) Social scientists' contributions to environmental management. *Journal of Social Issues* 46 (1), 133–152.

Friedman, J. and Weaver, C. (1979) *Territory and Function: the evolution of regional planning.* Edward Arnold, London.

Frosch, R. and Gallopoulos, N. (1989) Strategies for manufacturing. *Scientific American* 261 (3), 94–98.

Fuller, R.B. (1969) *Operating Manual for Spaceship Earth.* Southern Illinois University Press, Carbondale.

Funkhauser, S. (1995) *Valuing Climate Change: the economics of the greenhouse.* Earthscan, London.

Funtowicz, S.O. and Ravetz, J.R. (1991) A new scientific methodology for global environmental issues, pp. 137–152 in R. Costanza (ed.) *The Ecological Economics.* Columbia University Press, Ithaca.

Funtowicz, S.O. and Ravetz, J.R. (1992) The good, the true and the post-modern. *Futures* 24 (11), 963–976.

Funtowicz, S.O. and Ravetz, J.R. (1993) Science for the post-normal age. *Futures* 25 (7), 739–755.

Funtowicz, S.O. and Ravetz, J.R. (1994) The worth of a songbird: ecological economics as a post-normal science. *Ecological Economics* 10 (3), 197–207.

Gardiner, J.E. (1989) Decision making for sustainable development: selected approaches to environmental assessment and management. *Environmental Impact Assessment Review* 9 (4), 337–366.

Gare, A.E. (1995) *Postmodernism and the Environmental Crisis.* Routledge, London.

Garlick, J.P. and Keay, R.W. (eds) (1970) *Human Ecology in the Tropics.* Pergamon Press, Oxford.

Garrod, B. and Chadwick, A. (1996) Environmental management and business strategy: towards a new strategic paradigm. *Futures* 28 (1), 37–50.

Geertz, C. (1971) *Agricultural Involution: the process of ecological change in Indonesia.* University of California Press, Berkeley.

George, S. (1988) *A Fate Worse than Debt.* Penguin, Harmondsworth.

George, S. (1992) *The Debt Boomerang: how third world debt can harm us all.* Plato, London.

Georgiou, S., Whittington, D., Pearce, D.W. and Moran, D. (1997) *Economic Values and the Environment in the Developing World.* Edward Elgar, London.

Geraghty, P.J. (1992) Environmental assessment and the application of an expert systems approach. *Town Planning Review* 63 (2), 123–142.

Geraghty, P.J. (1993) Environmental assessment and the application of expert systems – an overview. *Journal of Environmental Management* 39 (1), 27–38.

Gerasimov, I.P., Armand, D.L. and Yefron, K.M. (eds) (1971) *Natural Resources in the Soviet Union: their use and renewal* (translated from Russian, 1963 edn, by J.I. Romanowski). Freeman, San Francisco.

Ghai, D. and Vivian, J.M. (eds) (1992) *Grassroots Environmental Action: people's participation in sustainable development.* Routledge, London.

Ghatak, S. and Turner, R.K. (1978) Pesticide use in less developed countries: economic and environmental considerations. *Food Policy* 5 (2), 134–146.

Giddens, A. (1991) *Modernity and Self Identity in the Late Modern Age*. Cambridge University Press, Cambridge.

Gilmour, A.J. and Walkerden, G. (1994) A structured approach to conflict resolution in EIA: the use of adaptive environmental assessment and management (AEAM), pp. 199–210 in A.J. Gilmour and B. Page (eds) *Computer Support for Environmental Assessment* (vol. 16) (Proceedings of the IFIP Working Conference on Computer Support for Environmental Assessment 6–8 October, 1993, Como, Italy). TC5/WG5.11 Transactions: B-Applications in Technology. North-Holland, Amsterdam.

Gilpin, A. (1995) *Environmental Impact Assessment: cutting edge for the twenty-first century*. Cambridge University Press, Cambridge.

Gleckman, H. and Krut, R. (1996) Neither international nor standard: the limits of ISO 14001 as an instrument of global corporate environmental management. *Greener Management International* 1996 (No. 14), 111–124.

Gliessman, S.R. (1990) *Agroecology: researching the ecological basis for sustainable agriculture*. Springer, New York.

Gliessman, S.R. (1992) Agroecology in the tropics: achieving a balance between land use and preservation. *Environmental Management* 16 (6), 681–689.

Goeden, G.B. (1979) Biogeographic theory as a management tool. *Environmental Conservation* 6 (1), 27–32.

Goldsmith, E. (1990) Evolution, neo-Darwinism and the paradigm of science. *The Ecologist* 20 (2), 67–73.

Goldsmith, E., Allan, R., Allaby, M., Davol, J. and Lawrence, S. (1972) *Blueprint for Survival*. Penguin, Harmondsworth (also published in *The Ecologist* 2 (1), 1–43).

Goldsmith, E., Khor, M., Norberg-Hodge, H. and Shiva, V. (eds) (1992) *The Future of Progress: reflections on environment and development* (revised edn). Green Books (Resurgence), Totnes.

Golley, F.B. (1991) The ecosystem concept: a search for order. *Ecological Research* 6 (2), 129–138.

Golley, F.B. (1993) *A History of the Ecosystem Concept in Ecology: more than the sum of the parts*. Yale University Press, New Haven.

Gonzalez, O.J. (1996) Formulating an ecosystem approach to environmental protection. *Environmental Management* 20 (5), 597–605.

Goodall, B. (1995) Environmental auditing: a tool for assessing the performance of tourism firms. *The Geographical Journal* 161 (1), 29–37.

Gordon, T.J. and Helmer, O. (1964) *Report on a Long Range Forecasting Study* (RAND Corporation Paper no. P-2982), RAND Corporation, Santa Monica.

Gorman, M. (1979) *Island Ecology*. Chapman and Hall, London.

Gottleib, R.S. (1996) *This Sacred Earth: religion, nature, environment*. Routledge, London.

Gould, S.J. (1984) Toward the vindication of punctuational change, in W.A. Berggren and J.A. Van Couvering (eds) *Catastrophes and Earth History: the new uniformitarianism*. Princeton University Press, Princeton.

Gourlay, K.A. (1992) *World of Waste: dilemmas of industrial development*. Zed Press, London.

Gow, D.D. (1990) Rapid rural appraisal: social science as investigative journalism, pp. 142–163 in K. Finsterbusch, L.J. Ingersol and L.G. Llewellyn (eds) *Methods for Social Impact Analysis in Developing Countries*. Westview, Boulder.

Graham Smith, L.G. (1993) *Impact Assessment and Sustainable Resource Management*. Longman, Harlow.

Gramling, R. and Freudenburg, W.R. (1992) Opportunity-threat, development, and adaption: toward a comprehensive framework for social impact assessment. *Rural Sociology* 57 (2), 216–234.

Gray, A. and Stokoe, P. 1988: *Knowledge-Based or Expert Systems and Decision Support Tools for Environmental Assessment and Management: their potential and limitations* (Final Report for the Federal Environmental Assessment and Review Office). Dalhousie University, School for Resource and Environmental Studies, Halifax (Nova Scotia, Canada).

Gray, R.H. (1990) *The Greening of Accounting: the profession after Pearce*. Chartered Association of Certified Accountants, London.

Gray, W. (1993) *Coral Reefs and Islands: the natural history of a threatened paradise*. David and Charles, Newton Abbot.

Grayson, L. (ed.) (1992) *Environmental Auditing: a guide to best practice in the UK and Europe*. Technical Communications and British Library Science and Information Service, Letchworth.

Grayson, R.B., Doolan, J.M. and Blake, T. (1994) Applications of AEAM (adaptive environmental assessment and management) to water quality in the Latrobe River catchment. *Journal of Environmental Management* 41 (3), 245–258.

Greeno, J.L. and Robinson, S.N. (1992) Rethinking corporate environmental management. *Columbia Journal of World Business* 27 (3), 223–232.

Grey, W. (1986) A critique of deep ecology. *Journal of Applied Philosophy* 3 (4), 211–216.

Gribbin, J. and Gribbin, M. (1996) *Fire on Earth*. Simon and Schuster, London.

Grove, R.H. (1990) The origins of environmentalism. *Nature* 345 (6270), 11–14.

Grove, R.H. (1992) The origins of western environmentalism. *Scientific American* 267 (1), 42–47.

Grove, R.H. (1995) *Green Imperialism: colonial expansion, tropical island edens and the origins of environmentalism, 1600–1860*. Cambridge University Press, Cambridge.

Grubb, M., Koch, M., Munson, A., Sullivan, F. and Thomson, K. (1993) *The Earth Summit Agreements: an analysis of the Rio '92 UN Conference on Environment and Development*. Earthscan, London.

Grumbine, R.E. (1994) What is ecosystem management? *Conservation Biology* 8 (1), 27–38.

Grumbine, R.E. (1997) Reflections on 'what is ecosystem management?' *Conservation Biology* 11 (1), 41–47.

Guariso, G. and Page, B. (eds) (1994) *Computer Support for Environmental Impact Assessment* (vol. 16) (Proceedings of the IFIP Working Conference on Computer Support for Environmental Assessment 6–8 October, 1993, Como, Italy). TC5/WG5.11 Transactions: B-Applications in Technology. North-Holland, Amsterdam.

Gumbricht, T. (1996) Application of GIS in training for environmental management. *Journal of Environmental Management* 46 (1), 17–30.

Gunn, D.L. and Stevens, J.G.R. (1976) *Pesticides and Human Welfare*. Oxford University Press, Oxford.

Gutman, P.S. (1994) Involuntary resettlement in hydropower projects. *Annual Review of Energy and the Environment* 19 (2), 189–210.

Haefele, E. (1973) *Representative Government and Environmental Management*. Johns Hopkins University Press, Baltimore.

Haeuber, R. (1996) Setting the environmental policy agenda: the case of ecosystem management. *Natural Resources Journal* 36 (1), 1–28.

Haigh, N. and Irwin, F. (eds) (1987) *Integrated Pollution Control*. The Conservation Foundation, Washington.

Haines-Young, R., Green, D.R. and Cousins, S. (eds) (1993) *Landscape Ecology and Geographic Information Systems (GIS)*. Taylor and Francis, London.

Hall, A.L. (1978) *Drought and Irrigation in North East Brazil*. Cambridge University Press, Cambridge.

Hall, A.L. (1994) Grassroots action for resettlement planning: Brazil and beyond. *World Development* 22 (12), 1793–1810.

Hallman, D.G. (1994) *Ecotheology: voices from south and north.* (World Council of Churches Publications, Orbis Books, New York.

Hamilton, K., Pearce, D.W., Atkinson, G., Gomez-Lobo, A. and Young, C. (1994) *The Policy Implications of Natural Resource and Environmental Accounting*. CSERGE Working Paper GEC 94–18, University College London, London.

Hamlyn, M. (1992) El Niño fathers distant drought. *The Times*, 29 May 1992, p. 12.

Hanley, N. and Spash, C.L. (1994) *Cost–Benefit Analysis and the Environment*. Edward Elgar, London.

Hanson, J.A. (1977) Towards an ecologically-based economic philosophy. *Environmental Conservation* 4 (1), 3–10.

Harcourt, W. (ed.) (1994) *Feminist Perspectives on Sustainable Development*. Zed Press, London.

Hardin, G. (1968) The tragedy of the commons. *Science 162* (3859), 1243–1248.

Hardin, G. (1974a) *The Ethics of a Lifeboat*. American Association for the Advancement of Science, Washington.

Hardin, G. (1974b) Lifeboat ethics: the case against helping the poor. *Psychology Today* 8 (1), 38–43, 123–126.

Hardin, G. (1985) Human ecology: the subversive, conservative science. *American Zoologist* 25 (2), 469–476.

Hare, B. (1991) Environmental impact assessment: broadening the framework. *Science of the Total Environment* 108 (1–2), 17–32.

Harris, C.M. and Meadows, J. (1992) Environmental management in Antarctica: instruments and institutions. *Marine Pollution Bulletin* 25 (9–12), 239–249.

Harrison, L.L. (ed.) (1984) *The McGraw-Hill Environmental Auditing Handbook: a guide to corporate environmental risk management*. McGraw-Hill, New York.

Harrison, P. (1987) *The Greening of Africa: breaking through in the battle for land and food.* Paladin, London.

Harrison, P. (1990) Too much life on Earth? *New Scientist* 126 (1717), 28–29.

Harrison, P. (1992) *The Third Revolution: population and a sustainable world*. Penguin, Harmondsworth.

Harte, D. (1992) Environmental law, pp. 56–79 in M. Newson (ed.) *Managing the Human Impact on the Natural Environment*. Belhaven, London.

Hartshorn, G.S. (1991) Key environmental issues for developing countries. *Journal of International Affairs* 44 (2), 393–402.

Hartwick, J.M. (1990) Natural resources, national accounting and economic depreciation. *Journal of Public Economics* 43 (3), 291–304.

Harvey, B. and Hallett, J.D. (1977) *Environment and Society: an introductory analysis.* Macmillan, London.

Harvey, D. (1989) *The Condition of Postmodernity: an enquiry into the origins of cultural change.* Basil Blackwell, Oxford.

Harvey, T., Mahaffey, K.R., Velazquez, S. and Dourson, M. (1995) Holistic risk assessment: an emerging process for environmental decisions. *Regulatory Toxicology and Pharmacology* 22 (2), 110–117.

Hassan, L. and Anglestam, P. (1991) Landscape ecology as a theoretical basis for nature conservation. *Landscape Ecology* 5 (4), 191–201.

Hawken, P. (1993) *The Ecology of Commerce: how businessmen can save the planet.* Weidenfeld and Nicolson, London.

Hayter, T. (1989) *Exploited Earth: Britain's aid and the environment.* Earthscan, London.

Hecht, J. (1991) Asteroid 'airburst' may have devastated New Zealand. *New Scientist* 132 (1789), 19.

Hector, T. (1996) Biotechnology and environmental management. *Biochemical Educations* 24 (2), 112–113.

Heer, J.E. and Hagerty, D.J. (1977) *Environmental Assessments and Impact Statements.* Van Nostrand Reinhold, New York.

Heintzenberg, J. (1989) Arctic haze: air pollution in polar regions. *Ambio* XVIII (1), 50–55.

Hemmelskamp, J. and Brockmann, K.L. (1997) Environmental labels: the German 'Blue Angel'. *Futures* 29 (1), 67–76.

Henderson, H. (1981a) Thinking globally, acting locally: ethics for the dawning solar age, pp. 354–405 in H. Henderson (ed.) *The Politics of the Solar Age: alternatives to economics.* Anchor Books, New York.

Henderson, H. (1981b) *The Politics of the Solar Age: alternatives to economics.* Anchor-Doubleday, New York.

Henderson, H. (1994) Paths to sustainable development: the role of social indicators. *Futures* 26 (2), 125–137.

Henning, D.H. and Mangun, W.R. (1989) *Managing the Environmental Crisis: incorporating competing values in natural resource administration.* Duke University Press, Durham (USA).

Henry, R. (1996) Adapting United Nations agencies for Agenda 21: programme coordination and organisational reform. *Environmental Politics* 5 (1), 1–24.

Herberlein, T.A. (1989) Attitudes to environmental management. *Journal of Social Issues* 45 (1), 37–57.

Hershkovitz, L. (1993) Political ecology and environmental management in the Loess Plateau, China. *Human Ecology* 21 (4), 327–353.

Hester, G.L. (1992) Electric and magnetic fields: managing an uncertain risk. *Environment* 34 (1), 6–11, 25–32.

Hewett, J. (ed.) (1995) *European Environmental Almanac.* Earthscan, London.

Higgs, A.J. (1981) Island biogeographic theory and nature reserve design. *Journal of Biogeography* 8 (2), 117–124.

Hildebrand, S.G. and Cannon, J.B. (eds) (1993) *Environmental Analysis: the NEPA experience.* Lewis Publishers, Boca Raton.

Hildyard, N. (1991) An open letter to Edouard Saouma, Director General of FAO. *The Ecologist* 21 (2), 43–46.

Hildyard, N. (1992) Liberation ecology, pp. 154–160 in E. Goldsmith, M. Khor, H. Norberg-Hodge and V. Shiva (eds) *The Future of Progress: reflections on environment and development*. Green Books (Resurgence), Totnes.

Hill, A.R. (1987) Ecosystem stability: some recent perspectives. *Progress in Physical Geography* 11 (3), 313–333.

Hill, C. (1972) *The World Turned Upside Down: radical ideas during the English Revolution*. Temple Smith, London (Penguin edn 1975).

Hill, D., Smith, N. and Kenneth, Ip. (1994) *Small Companies, Partnership and Shared Experiences in Improving Environmental Performance* (Proceedings of the 1994 Business, Society and Environment Conference). University of Nottingham, Nottingham.

Hill, J.C. (1964) Puritanism, capitalism and the scientific revolution. *Past and Present* 29 (1), 88–97.

Hill, M.K. (1998) *Understanding Environmental Pollution*. Cambridge University Press, Cambridge.

Hillary, R. (ed.) (1995) *The Role of the Environmental Manager*. Stanly Thornes, Cheltenham.

Hindmarsh, R. (1990) The need for effective assessment: sustainable development and the social impacts of biotechnology in the Third World. *Environmental Impact Assessment Review* 10 (1–2), 195–208.

Hirsch, A. (1993) Improving conservation of biodiversity in NEPA assessments. *The Environmental Professional* 15 (1), 103–115.

HMSO (1956a) *Volta River Project, I: report of the Preparatory Commission* (Government of UK and Gold Coast). HMSO, London.

HMSO (1956b) *Volta River Project, II: appendices to reports of the Preparatory Commission* (Government of UK and Gold Coast). HMSO, London.

HMSO (1971) *Report of the Roskill Commission on the Third London Airport*. HMSO, London.

Hodge, I. (1995) *Environmental Economics: individual incentives and public choices*. Macmillan, Basingstoke.

Holden, C. (1991) World Bank Environment Fund. *Science* 251 (4996), 870.

Holdgate, M.W. (1990) Antarctica: ice under pressure. *Environment* 32 (6), 4–9, 30–33.

Holdridge, L.R. (1964) *Life Zone Ecology*. Tropical Science Center, San Jose.

Holdridge, L.R. (1971) *Forest Environments in Tropical Life Zones: a pilot study*. Pergamon Press, Oxford.

Holling, C.C. (1973) Resilience and stability of ecological systems. *Annual Review of Ecology and Systematics* 4 (1), 1–23.

Holling, C.S. (ed.) (1978) *Adaptive Environmental Assessment and Management*. Wiley, Chichester.

Holling, C.S. (1987) Simplifying the complex: the paradigm of ecological function and structure. *European Journal of Operational Research* 30 (2), 139–146.

Holmberg, J. (ed.) (1992) *Policies for a Small Planet*. Earthscan, London.

Holmberg, J., Thomson, K. and Timberlake, L. (1993) *Facing the Future: beyond the Earth Summit*. Earthscan, London.

Homer-Dixon, T.F. (1991) On the threshold: environmental changes as causes of acute conflict. *International Security* 16 (2), 76–116.

Hopgood, S. (1998) *American Foreign Policy and the Power of the State*. Oxford University Press, Oxford.

Hornsby, M. (1989) Farming's nitrate nightmare. *The Times*, 11 December 1989, p. 11.

Horowitz, M.M. (1991) Victims upstream and down. *Journal of Refugee Studies* 2 (2), 164–181.

Horton, S. and Memon, A, (1997) SEA: the uneven development of the environment. *Environmental Impact Assessment Review* 17 (3), 163–175.

Htun, N. (1990) EIA and sustainable development. *Impact Assessment Bulletin* 8 (1–2), 16–23.

Hudson, N. (1981) *Soil Conservation*. Batsford, London.

Hudson, N. (1992) *Land Husbandry*. Batsford Books, London.

Hufschmidt, M.M. (1986) A conceptual framework for watershed management, pp. 17–31 in K.A. Easter, J.A. Dixon and M.M. Hufschmidt (eds) *Watershed Resource Management: an integrated framework with studies from Asia and the Pacific*. Westview Press, Boulder.

Huggett, R. (1990) The bombarded Earth. *Geography* 75 (2), 114–127.

Hughes, B.B. (1980) *World Modeling: the Mesarovic–Pestel world model in the context of its contemporaries*. Lexington Books, Lexington.

Hughes, D. (1992) *Environmental Law* (2nd edn.). Butterworths, London.

Hülsberg, W. (1988) *The German Greens: a social and political profile* (English trans. by G. Fagan). Verso, London.

Hunt, D. and Johnson, C. (1995) *Environmental Management Systems: principles and practice*. McGraw-Hill, London.

Hunt, L. (1998) Send in the clouds. *New Scientist* 158 (2136), 28–33.

Hunter, S. and Leyden, K.M. (1995) Beyond NIMBY: explaining opposition to hazardous-waste facilities. *Policy Studies Journal* 23 (4), 601–619.

Huntington, E. (1915) *Civilisation and Climate*. Yale University Press, New Haven.

Hutchinson, A. and Hutchinson, F. (1997) *Environmental Business Management: sustainable development in the new millennium*. McGraw-Hill, New York.

Independent Commission on International Development Issues (1980) *North–South: a programme for survival*. Pan, London.

International Chamber of Commerce (1989) *Environmental Auditing* (ICC Publication No. 468). International Chamber of Commerce, Paris.

International Chamber of Commerce (1991) *ICC Guide to Effective Environmental Auditing* (ICC Publication no. 483). International Chamber of Commerce, Paris.

International Chamber of Commerce (1993) Business Charter for Sustainable Development: principles for environmental management. *Environmental Conservation* 20 (1), 82–83.

Irvine, S. (1989) Consuming fashions: the limits of green consumerism. *The Ecologist* 19 (3), 88–93.

Isard, W. (1972) *Ecologic–Economic Analysis for Regional Development*. Free Press, New York.

IUCN Inter-Commission Task Force on Indigenous Peoples (1997) *Indigenous Peoples and Sustainability: cases and Actions*. International Books, Utrecht.

IUCN, UNEP and WWF (1980) *World Conservation Strategy: living resource conservation for sustainable development*. International Union for Conservation of Nature and Natural Resources, Gland.

IUCN, UNEP and WWF (1991) *Caring for the Earth: a strategy for sustainable living*. Earthscan, London.

Ives, J.D. and Messerli, B. (1989) *The Himalayan Dilemma: reconciling development and conservation*. Routledge, London.

Ives, J.H. (1985) *The Export of Hazards*. Routledge and Kegan Paul, London.

Jackson, C. (1993) Environmentalism and gender interests in the Third World. *Development and Change* 24 (4), 649–678.

Jackson, R.W. and Jackson, J.M. (1996) *Environmental Science: the natural and human impact*. Longman, Harlow.

Jackson, S.L. (1997) *ISO14000 Implementation Guide: creating an integrated management system*. Wiley, Chichester.

Jacob, M. (1994) Sustainable development and deep ecology: an analysis of competing traditions. *Environmental Management* 18 (4), 477–488.

Jacobs, P. and Sadler, B. (eds) (1989) *Sustainable Development and Environmental Assessment: perspectives on planning for a common future*. Canadian Environmental Assessment Research Council, Hull (Quebec).

James, D.E. (1994) *The Application of Economic Techniques in Environmental Impact Assessment*. Kluwer Academic, London.

Janssen, R. (1995) *Multiobjective Decision Support for Environmental Management*. Kluwer Academic, Dordrecht.

Jansson, B.-O. (1972) *Ecosystem Approach to the Baltic Problem* (Ecological Research Committee Bulletin No. 16). Ekologicommitten, Statens naturvetenskapliga forskningsrad, Stockholm.

Jenkins, B.R. (1991) Changing Australian monitoring and policy practice to achieve sustainable development. *Science of the Total Environment* 108 (1), 33–50.

Jensen, M.E., Bourgeron, P., Everett, R. and Goodman, I. (1996) Ecosystem management: a landscape ecology perspective. *Water Resources Bulletin* 32 (2), 203–216.

Johnson, D.L. and Lewis, L.A. (1995) *Land Degradation: creation or destruction*. Blackwell, Oxford.

Johnson, J. (1990) Waste that no one wants. *New Scientist* 127 (1733), 50–55.

Johnson, S.P. (1993) *The Earth Summit – the United Nations Conference on Environment and Development (UNCED)*. Graham & Trotman, London.

Johnson, W.H. and Steere, W.C. (eds) (1974) *The Environmental Challenge*. Holt, Rinehart and Winston, New York.

Jolly, V. (1978) The concept of environmental management. *Development Forum* 8 (2), 13–26.

Jones, M.L. and Greig, L.A. (1985) Adaptive environmental assessment and management: a new approach to environmental impact assessment, pp. 21–42 in V.W. MacLaren and J.B. Whitney (eds) *New Directions in Environmental Impact Assessment in Canada*. Methuen, Toronto.

Jorgensen, S.E. and Goda, T. (1986) Scope and limit in the application of biological models to environmental management. *Ecological Modelling* 32 (1–3), 237–240.

Jorgensen, S.E., Halling-Sorensen, B. and Nielsen, S.N. (1996) *Handbook of Environmental and Ecological Modeling*. CRC Press, Boulder (Springer, New York).

Jorissen, J. and Coenen, R. (1992) The EEC Directive on EIA and its implementation in the EC member states, pp. 1–14 in A.G. Colombo (ed.) *Environmental Impact Assessment* (vol. 1). Kluwer, Dordrecht.

Jull, P. (ed.) (1994) *Surviving Columbus: indigenous peoples, political reform, and environmental management in North Australia*. North Australia Research Unit, Australian National University, Darwin.

Kahn, H., Brown, W. and Martel, L. (eds) (1976) *The Next 200 Years*. Abacus, London.

Karl, H. (1994) Better environmental future in Europe through environmental auditing. *Environmental Management* 18 (4), 617–621.

Kates, R.W. (1978) *Risk Assessment of Environmental Hazards*. Wiley, Chichester.

Kates, R.W. and Haarman, V. (1992) Where the poor live: are the assumptions correct? *Environment* 34 (4): 4–11, 25–28.

Kates, R.W. and Hohenemser, C. (eds) (1982) *Technological Hazard Assessment*. Oelgeschlager, Gunn and Hain, Cambridge, Mass.

Kearns, L (1996) Saving the creation: Christian environmentalism in the United States. *Sociology of Religion* 57 (1), 55–70.

Keating, M. (1993) *The Earth Summit's Agenda for Change: a plain language version of Agenda 21 and the other Rio Agreements*. Centre for Our Common Future, Geneva.

Kennedy, I. (1992) *Acid Soil and Acid Rain* (2nd edn). Wiley, Chichester.

Kennedy, P. (1993) *Preparing for the Twenty-First Century*. Harper Collins, London.

Keohane, R.O. and Levy, M.A. (1996) *Institutions for Environmental Aid: pitfalls and promise*. MIT Press, Cambridge, Mass.

Kerr, R.A. (1972) Huge impact led to mass extinction. *Science* 257 (5072), 878–880.

Kershaw, K.A. (1973) *Quantitative and Dynamic Plant Ecology* (2nd edn). Edward Arnold, London.

Kiely, R. and Marfleet, P. (eds) (1998) *Globalisation and the Third World*. Routledge, London.

Kimmins, J.P. (1993) Ecology, environmentalism and green religion. *Forestry Chronicle* 69 (3), 285–289.

Kirkman, R. (1997) Why ecology cannot be all things to all people: the 'adaptive radiation' of scientific concepts. *Environmental Ethics* 19 (4), 375–390.

Kirkpatrick, D. (1990) Environmentalism: the new crusade. *Fortune*, 12 February 1990, 24–30.

Kivell, P., Roberts, P. and Walker, G. (eds) (1988) *Environment, Planning and Land Use*. Ashgate, Aldershot.

Klassen, R.D. and McLaughlin, C.P. (1996) The impact of environmental management on firm performance. *Management Science* 42 (8), 1199–1214.

Klee, G.A. (ed.) (1980) *World Systems of Traditional Resource Management*. Edward Arnold, London.

Klijn, F., De Waal, R.W. and Oude Voshaar, J.H. (1995) Ecoregions and ecodistricts: ecological regionalizations for The Netherlands' environmental policy. *Environmental Management* 19 (6), 797–813.

Kneese, A.V. (1977) *Economics and the Environment*. Penguin, Harmondsworth.

Knight, P. (1997) Rally round the standard. *Green Futures* December 1997, 38–41.

Kok, E., O'Laoire, D. and Welford, R. (1993) Environmental management at the regional level. A case study: the Avoca–Avonmore Catchment Conversion Project. *Journal of Environmental Planning and Management* 36 (3), 377–394.

Komarov, B. (1981) *The Destruction of Nature in the Soviet Union*. Pluto Press, London.

Koninklijk Instituut voor de Tropen (1990) *Environmental Management in the Tropics: an annotated bibliography 1985–89*. Royal Tropical Institute, Amsterdam.

Kopitsky, J.J. and Betzenberger, E.T. (1987) Bankers debate . . . should banks lend to companies with environmental problems? *The Journal of Commercial Bank Lending* 68 (11), 3–13.

Kotlyakov, V.M. (1991) The Aral Sea basin: a critical environmental zone. *Environment* 33 (1), 4–9; 36–38.

Koutstaal, P. (1997) *Economic Policy and Climate Change: tradeable permits for reducing carbon emissions*. Edward Elgar, Cheltenham.

Kozlowski, J.M. (1986) *Threshold Approach in Urban, Regional and Environmental Planning*. University of Queensland Press, St Lucia (Queensland, Australia).

Kozlowski, J.M. (1990) Sustainable development in professional planning: a potential contribution of the EIA and UET concepts. *Landscape and Urban Planning* 9 (3), 307–332.

Krimsky, S. and Goulding, D. (eds) (1992) *Social Theories of Risk*. Praeger, Westport.

Kropotkin, P. (1974) *Fields, Factories and Workshops* (original 1899 in Russian – English edition 1899 publ. by Freedom Press, London). 1974 edition ed. C. Ward, publ. by Unwin, London – with addition of word 'tomorrow' to end of title.

Krutilla, J.V. and Fisher, A. (1975). *The Economics of Natural Environments*. Johns Hopkins University Press, Baltimore.

Kunstadter, P., Bird, E.C.F. and Sabhasri, S. (eds) (1989) *Man in the Mangroves: the socio-economic situation of human settlements in mangrove forests*. United Nations University Press, Tokyo.

Kurth, W. (1992) The mounting pile of waste paper. *The OECD Observer* no. 174, 27–30.

Kuzmiak, D.T. (1991) A history of the American environmental movement. *The Geographical Journal* 157 (3), 265–278.

Lajeunesse, D., Domon, G., Drapeau, P., Cogliastro, A. and Bouchard, A. (1995) Development and application of an ecosystem management approach for protected natural areas. *Environmental Management* 19 (4), 481–495.

Lane, P. and Peto, M. (1995) *Blackstone's Guide to the Environment Act 1995*. Blackstone Press, London.

Lang, R. (ed.) (1986) *Integrated Approaches to Resource Planning and Management*. University of Calgary Press, Calgary.

Lang, T. and Hines, C. (1993) *The New Protectionism: protecting the future against free trade*. Earthscan, London.

Lang, T. and Yu, D. (1992) Free trade versus the environment: a debate. *Our Planet* (UNEP) 4 (2), 12–13.

Lawrence, D.P. (1997) Integrating sustainability and environmental impact assessment. *Environmental Management* 21 (1), 23–42.

Leach, M., Joekes, S. and Green, C. (1995) Editorial: gender relations and environmental change. *IDS Bulletin* 26 (1), 1–8.

Leach, M. and Mearns, R. (eds) (1996) *The Lie of the Land: challenging received wisdom on the African environment*. James Currey, London.

Ledgerwood, G., Street, E. and Therivel, R. (1992) *Environmental Audit and Business Strategy*. Pitman, London.

Lee, N. (1978) Environmental impact assessment of projects in EEC countries. *Journal of Environmental Management* 6 (1), 57–71.

Lee, N. (1982) The future development of environmental impact assessment. *Journal of Environmental Management* 14 (1), 71–90.

Lee, N. and Walsh, F. (1992) Strategic environmental assessment: an overview. *Project Appraisal* 7 (3), 126–137.

Lee, R.G., Field, D.R. and Burch, W.R. Jnr (1990) *Community and Forestry: continuities in the sociology of natural resources*. Westview, Boulder.

Leistritz, L.F., Coon, R.C. and Hamm, R.R. (1995) A microcomputer model for assessing socioeconomic impacts of development projects. *Impact Assessment* 12 (4), 373–384.

Leitmann, J. (1993) Rapid urban environmental assessment: toward environmental management in cities of the developing world. *Impact Assessment Review* 11 (3), 225–260.

Leonard, H.J. (with Yudelman, M., Stayker, J.D., Browder, J.O., De Boer, A.J., Campbell, T. and Jolley, A.) (1989) *Environment and the Poor: development strategies for a common agenda*. US-Third World Policy Perspectives No. 11 (Overseas Development Corporation). Transaction Books, New Brunswick.

Leopold, A. (1949) *A Sand County Almanac*. Oxford University Press, London.

Leu, W.S., Williams, W.P. and Bark, A.W. (1995) An environmental evaluation of the implementation of environmental assessment by UK local authorities. *Project Appraisal* 10 (2), 91–102.

Levett, R. (1993) *A Guide to the Eco-Management and Audit Scheme for UK Local Government*. HMSO, London.

Levett, R. (1996) From eco-management and audit (EMAS) to sustainability management and audit (SMAS). *Local Environment* 1 (3), 329–334.

Levine, L. (1993) Gaia – goddess and idea. *Biosystems* 31 (2–3), 85–92.

Lewin, R. (1992) How to destroy the doomsday asteroid. *New Scientist* 134 (1824), 12–13.

Lewin, R. (1993) *Complexity: life at the edge of chaos*. Dent, London.

Lewis, M. (1992) *Green Delusions: an environmentalist critique of radical environmentalism*. Duke University Press, Durham.

Likens, G.E. (1992) *The Ecosystems Approach: its use and abuse*. Ecology Institute, Oldendorf (Germany).

Linear, M. (1982) Gift of poison: the unacceptable face of development aid. *Ambio* XI (1), 2–8.

Linear, M. (1985) *Zapping the Third World: the disaster of development aid*. Zed Press, London.

Lintott, J. (1996) Environmental accounting: useful to whom and for what? *Ecological Economics* 16 (3), 179–190.

Lise, W. (1995) Participatory development, a path to ecological preservation: an approach with case-studies and modelling. *International Journal of Environment and Pollution* 5 (2–3), 243–259.

Lister, C. (1996) *European Union Environmental Law: a guide for industry*. Wiley, Chichester.

Little, P.D. and Horowitz, M.M. (1987) *Lands at Risk in the Third World: local level perspectives*. Westview Press, Boulder.

Llewellyn, L.G. and Freudenburg, W.R. (1989) Legal requirements for social impact assessment – assessing the social-science fallout from Three Mile Island. *Society & Natural Resources* 2 (3), 193–208.

Local Government Management Board (1991) *Environmental Auditing in Local Government: a guide and discussion paper*. Local Government Management Board, Luton.

Local Government Management Board (1992) *Local Agenda 21 – Agenda 21: a guide for local authorities in the UK*. Local Government Management Board, Luton.

Local Government Management Board (1994) *Agenda 21, a Guide for Local Authorities in the UK*. Local Government Management Board, Luton .

Loehle, C. and Osteen, R. (1990) IMPACT – an expert system for environmental impact assessment. *AI Applications in Natural Resource Management* 4 (1), 35–43.

Lovelock, J.E. (1979) *Gaia: a new look at life on Earth*. Oxford University Press, Oxford.

Lovelock, J.E. (1988) *The Ages of Gaia: a biography of our living Earth*. Oxford University Press, Oxford.

Lovelock, J.E. (1992) *Gaia: the practical science of planetary medicine*. Gaia Books, London.

Lovelock, J.E. and Margulis, L. (1973) Atmospheric homoeostasis by and for the biosphere: the Gaia hypothesis. *Tellus* 26 (1), 2.

Low, N. and Gleeson, B. (1998) *Justice, Society and Nature: an explanation of political ecology*. Routledge, London.

Lowe, J. and Lewis, D. (1980) *The Economics of Environmental Management*. Phillip Alan, Oxford.

Ludwig, H.F., Ludwig, R.G., Anderson, D.R. and Garber, W.F. (1992) Appropriate environmental standards in developing nations. *Water Science and Technology* 25 (9), 17–30.

Lyell, C. (1830) *Principles of Geology, Being an Attempt to Explain the Former Changes of the Earth's Surface by Reference to Changes Now in Operation* (3 vols). Published between 1830 and 1834. John Murray, London.

Lyon, R.M. (1989) Transferable discharge permit systems and environmental management in developing countries. *World Development* 17 (8), 1299–1312.

McArthur, R.H. and Wilson, E.O. (1967) *The Theory of Island Biogeography*. Princeton University Press, Princeton.

McAuslan, P. (1991) The role of courts and other judicial bodies in environmental management. *Journal of Environmental Law* 3(2), 195–205.

McBurney, S. (1990) *Ecology into Economics Won't Go*. Green Books, Bideford.

MacCarthy, F. (1994) *William Morris: a life for our times*. Faber and Faber, London.

McCormick, J.F. (1988) *Acid Earth: the global threat of acid pollution*. Earthscan, London.

McCormick, J.F. (1989) *Reclaiming Paradise: the global movement*. Indiana University Press, Bloomington.

McCormick, J.F. (1992) *The Global Environmental Movement*. Belhaven, London.

McCormick, J.F. (1993) Implementation of NEPA and environmental impact assessment in developing nations, pp. 716–727 in S.G. Hildebrand and J.B. Cannon (eds) *Environmental Analysis: the NEPA experience*. Lewis Publishers, Boca Raton.

McDavid, L. (1995) Safety net: the Sacred Earth Network uses the Internet to protect the environment in the former Soviet Union. *Internet World* 6(8), 70.

McDonagh, P. and Prothero, A. (1997) *Green Management: a reader*. Dryden Press, London.

McDonald, G.T. and Brown, A.L. (1990) Planning and management processes and environmental assessment. *Impact Assessment Bulletin* 8 (1–2), 261–274.

McEldowney, J.F. (1996) *Environment and the Law*. Addison Wesley Longman, Harlow.

McEvoy, III, J. (1971) A comment: conservation an upper-middle class social movement. *Journal of Leisure Research* 3 (2), 127–128.

McGill, S. (1999) *Environmental Risk Management*. Routledge, London.

McGillivray, J.W. (1994) *Environmental Measures*. Environmental Challenge Group, London.

McGillivray, J.W. (1996) *Natural Resource and Environmental Economics*. Addison Wesley Longman, Harlow.

McGregor, J. (1993) Refugees and the environment, pp. 157–170 in R. Black and V. Robinson (eds) *Geography and Refugees: patterns and processes of change*. Belhaven, London.

McGregor, J. (1994) Climate-change and involuntary migration: implications for food security. *Food Policy* 19 (2), 120–132.

McHarg, I. (1969) *Design with Nature*. Doubleday (Natural History Press), Garden City (New York).

McKenna & Co. (1993) *Environmental Auditing – a Management Guide* (2 vols). Intelex Press, London.

MacKenzie, D. (1998) Waste not. *New Scientist* 159 (2149), 26–30.

McLain, R.J. and Lee, R.G. (1996) Adaptive management: promises and pitfalls. *Environmental Management* 20 (4), 437–448.

McNeely, J.A. (1989) How to pay for conserving biological diversity. *Ambio* XVIII (6), 303–318.

McNeely, J.A., Miller, K.R., Reid, W.V., Mittermeier, R.A. and Werner, T.B. (1990) Strategies for conserving biodiversity. *Environment* 32 (3), 16–20, 36–40.

Maddox, J. (1972) *The Doomsday Syndrome*. Maddox Educational, London.

Mahony, R. (1992) Debt-for-nature swaps: who really benefits? *The Ecologist* 21 (3), 97–103.

Mainguet, M. (1994) *Desertification: natural background and human mismanagement* (2nd edn). Springer-Verlag, Berlin.

Maltby, E. (1986) *Waterlogged Wealth: why waste the world's wet places?* Earthscan, London.

Malthus, T.R. (1798) *An Essay on the Principle of Population as it Affects the Future Improvement of Mankind*. J. Johnson, London.

Manheim, B.S. Jnr (1994) NEPA's overseas application. *Environment* 36 (3), 43–45.

Mannion, A. (1996) The new environmental determinism. *Environmental Conservation* 21 (1), 7–8.

Marcandya, A. and Richardson, J. (eds) (1992) *The Earthscan Reader in Environmental Economics*. Earthscan, London.

Margaris, N.S. (1987) Desertification in the Aegean Islands. *Ekistics* 54 (323/324), 132–137.

Margerum, R.D. and Born, S.M. (1995) Integrated environmental planning and management: moving from theory to practice. *Journal of Environmental Planning and Management* 38 (3), 371–391.

Marion, M. (1996) *Environmental Issues and Sustainable Futures: a critical guide to recent books, reports, and periodicals* (World Futures Society, Bethesda, Md.). Norton, New York.

Marsh, G.P. (1864) *Man and Nature: or physical geography as modified by human action*. Charles Scribner, New York.

Marsh, J.S. (1994) GATT and the environment. *Global Environmental Change* 4 (2), 91–95.

Marsh, W.M. (1991) *Landscape Planning: environmental applications* (2nd edn.). Wiley, New York.

Martin, P.S. (1967) Prehistoric overkill, pp. 75–12 in P.S. Martin and H.E. Wright (eds) *Pleistocene Extinctions*. Yale University Press, Newhaven.

Martin, P.S. and Klein, R.G. (eds) (1984) *Quaternary Extinctions*. University of Arizona Press, Tucson.

Mason, P. (1993) Spare tyres drop into uncharted waters. *The Times*, 5 Feburary 1993.

Matthews, W.H., Perkowski, J.C., Curtis, F.A. and Martin, W.F. (1976) *Resource Management for Environmental Management and Education*. MIT Press, Cambridge, Mass.

Max-Neef, M.A. (1986) *Economía descalza: señales desde el mundo invisible*. Nordan, Stockholm.

Max-Neef, M.A. (1992a) *From the Outside Looking In: experiences in 'barefoot economics'* (originally publ. in 1982 by Dag Hammarskjold Foundation). Zed Press, London.

Max-Neef, M.A. (ed.) (1992b) *Real-Life Economics: understanding wealth creation*. Routledge, London.

Maxwell, S. (1986) Farming systems research: hitting a moving target. *World Development* 14 (1), 65–77.

Mayda, J. (1993) Historical roots of EIA? *Impact Assessment Bulletin* 11 (4), 411–415.

Meadows, D.H., Meadows, D.L., Randers, J. and Behrens, W.W. III (1972) *The Limits to Growth* (a report to the Club of Rome's project on the predicament of mankind). Universal Books, New York.

Meadows, D.H., Meadows, D.L. and Randers, J. (1992) *Beyond the Limits: global collapse or sustainable future?* Earthscan, London.

Mellanby, K. (1970) *Pesticides and Pollution*. Fontana, London.

Mercer, K.G. (1995) An expert system utility for environmental impact assessment in engineering. *Journal of Environmental Management* 45 (1), 1–23.

Merchant, C. (1992) *Radical Ecology: the search for a livable world*. Routledge, London.

Merchant, C. (1996) *Earthcare: women and the environment*. Routledge, New York.

Mesarovic, M. and Pestel, E. (1975) *Mankind at the Turning Point* (the Second Report to the Club of Rome). Hutchinson, London (published 1974 in USA).

Messerschmidt, D.A. (1986) 'Go to the people': local planning for natural resource development in Nepal. *Practising Anthropology* 7 (4), 1–15.

Middleton, N. (1995) *The Global Casino: an introduction to environmental issues*. Arnold, London.

Mies, M. (1986) *Patriarchy and Accumulation on a World Scale*. Zed Press, London.

Mies, M. and Shiva, V. (1993) *Ecofeminism*. Zed Press, London.

Mikesell, R.F. (1995) *Economic Development and the Environment*. Cassell, London.

Miller, G.T. Jnr (1991) *Environmental Science: sustaining the Earth* (3rd edn.). Wadsworth Publishing Co., Belmont.

Miller, R.I. (1978) Applying island biogeographic theory to an East African reserve. *Environmental Conservation* 5 (3), 191–195.

Milne, R. (1988) Conservation clouds choke Britain's forests. *New Scientist* 117(1604), 27.

Milton, K. (ed.) (1993) *Environmentalism: the view from anthropology*. Routledge, London.

Milton, K. (1996) *Environmentalism and Cultural Theory: exploring the role of anthropology in environmental discourse*. Routledge, London.

Ministerie VROM (1989) *National Environmental Policy Plan: to choose or lose?* SDU, The Hague.

Mintel (1990) *The Green Consumer*. Mintel, London.

Mitchell, B. (1997) *Resource and Environmental Management*. Addison Wesley Longman, Harlow.

Mitsch, W.J. and Gosselink, J.G. (1993) *Wetlands* (2nd edn). Van Nostrand Reinhold, New York.

Mnaksakanian, R.A. (1992) *Environmental Legacy of the Former Soviet Union*. Centre for Human Ecology, Edinburgh.

Moffatt, I. (1990) The potentialities and problems associated with applying information technology to environmental management. *Journal of Environmental Management* 30 (3), 209–220.

Moghissi, A.A. (1995) Eco-environmentalism vs human environmentalism. *Environment International* 21 (3), 253–254.

Momsen, J.H. (1991) *Women and Development in the Third World*. Routledge, London.

Montgomery, D.R. (1995) Input- and output-oriented approaches to implementing ecosystem management. *Environmental Management* 19 (2), 183–188.

Montgomery, J.D. (1990a) Environmental management as a Third World problem. *Policy Sciences* 23 (2), 163–176.

Montgomery, J.D. (1990b) Environmental management as behavioral policy. *Canadian Public Administration – Administration Publique du Canada* 33 (1), 1–16.

Moran, E.F. (1981) *Developing the Amazon*. Indiana University Press, Bloomington.

Moran, E.F. (ed.) (1990) *The Ecosystem Approach in Anthropology: from concept to practice*. University of Michigan Press, Ann Arbor.

Morris, D. (1990) Free trade the great destroyer. *The Ecologist* 20 (5), 190–5.

Morris, W. (1891) *News from Nowhere*. Reeves and Turner, London (more recent edn. published by Routledge and Kegan Paul, London).

Morrison, D.E. (1986) How and why environmental consciousness has trickled down, pp. 187–220 in A. Schnaiberg, N. Watts and K. Zimmerman (eds) *Distributional Conflicts in Environmental Resource Policy*. Gower, Aldershot.

Moser, W. and Peterson, J. (1981) Limits to Obergurgl's growth. *Ambio* X (2–3), 68–72.

Moss, T.H. and Stills, D.L. (eds) (1981) *Three Mile Island Nuclear Accident: lessons and implications* (Annals of the New York Academy of Sciences vol. 365). New York Academy of Sciences, New York.

Mott, J.J. and Tothill, J.C. (1985) *Ecology and Management of the World's Savannas*. Commonwealth Agricultural Bureaux, Slough.

Müeller, F.G. and Ahmad, Y.J. (eds) (1982) *Integrated Physical, Socio-economic and Environmental Planning*. Tycooly International, Dublin.

Mueller-Dombois, D. (1975) Some aspects of island ecosystem analysis, pp. 353–366 in F.B. Golley and E. Medina (eds) *Tropical Ecological Systems: trends in terrestrial and aquatic research*. Springer-Verlag, Berlin.

Mueller-Dombois, D., Bridges, K.W. and Carson, H.L. (eds) (1981) *Island Ecosystems. Ecological organization in selected Hawaiian communities*. Hutchinson Ross, Stroudsburg.

Mumme, S.P. (1992) New directions in United States–Mexican transboundary environmental management – a critique of current proposals. *Natural Resources Journal* 32 (2), 539–562.

Munda, G., Nijkamp, P. and Rietveld, P. (1994) Qualitative multicriteria evaluation for environmental management. *Environmental Economics* 10 (2), 97–112.

Musgrave, R.K. (1993) The GATT tuna–dolphin dispute: an update. *Natural Resources Journal* 33 (4), 957–976.

Myers, N. (1986) Economics and ecology in the international arena; the phenomenon of 'linked linkages'. *Ambio* XV (5), 296–300.

Myers, N. (1992) Population/environment linkages: discontinuities ahead. *Ambio* XXI (1), 116–118.

Myers, N. (1993) Environmental refugees in a globally warmed world. *BioScience* 43 (11), 752–761.

Myers, W.L. and Shelton, R.L. (1980) *Survey Methods for Ecosystem Management*. Wiley, New York.

Naess, A. (1973) The shallow and the deep, long range ecology movement, a summary. *Inquiry* 16 (1), 95–100.

Naess, A. (1988) Deep ecology and ultimate premises. *The Ecologist* 18 (4–5), 128–132.

Naess, A. (1989) *Ecology, Community and Lifestyles: outline of an ecosophy*. Cambridge University Press, Cambridge.

Naiman, R.J. (1992) *Watershed Management: balancing sustainability and environmental change*. Springer-Verlag, London.

Napier, C. (ed.) (1998) *Environmental Conflict Resolution*. Cameron May, London.

Narveson, J. (1995) The case for free-market environmentalism. *Journal of Agricultural & Environmental Ethics* 8 (2), 145–156 (pp. 126–144 present a case against).

Nash, J. and Ehrenfeld, J. (1997) Codes of environmental management practice: assessing their potential as tools for change. *Annual Review of Energy and the Environment* 22 (5), 487–535.

Nellor, D.C.L. (1987) Sovereignty and natural resource taxation in developing countries. *Economic Development and Cultural Change* 35 (2), 367–392.

Newby, H. (1990) Environmental change and the social sciences. Paper to 1990 Annual Meeting of the British Assoc. for the Advanacement of Science (mimeo), 22pp.

Newson, M. (ed.) (1992) *Managing the Human Impact on the Natural Environment: problems and processes*. Belhaven, London.

Ngwa, N.E. (1995) The role of women in environmental management: an overview of the rural Cameroonian situation. *GeoJournal* 35 (4), 515–520.

Nicholson, E.M. (1970) *The Environmental Revolution*. Hodder and Stoughton, London.

Nijkamp, P. (1980) *Environmental Policy Analysis*. Wiley, New York.

Nijkamp, P. (1986) Multiple criteria analysis and integrated impact analysis. *Impact Assessment Bulletin* 4 (3–4), 226–261.

Nijkamp, P. and Soeteman, F. (1988) Ecologically sustainable economic development: key issues for strategic environmental management. *International Journal of Social Economics* 15 (3–4), 88–102.

Nisbet, R. (1982) *Prejudices: a philosophical dictionary*. Harvard University Press, Cambridge, Mass.

Nixon, A. and Harrop, O. (1998) *Environmental Impact Assessment*. Routledge, London.

Nolch, G. (1994) Australia could become target for environmental refugees. *Search* 25 (9), 269.

Norris, S. (1990) The return of impact assessment: assessing the impact of regional shopping centre proposals in the UK. *Papers in Regional Science* No. 69, 101–119.

North, K. (1992) *Environmental Business Management: an introduction*. International Labour Office, Geneva.

North, R.D. (1995) *Life on a Modern Planet: a manifesto for progress*. Manchester University Press, Manchester.

Norton, B.G. (1991) *Towards Unity among Environmentalists*. Oxford University Press, Oxford.

O'Callaghan, P.W. (1996) *Integrated Environmental Management Handbook*. Wiley, Chichester.

O'Connor, M. (1997) The internalization of environmental costs: implementing the polluter pays principle in the European Union. *International Journal of Environment and Pollution* 7 (4), 450–482.

ODA (1984) Checklist for screening environmental aspects in aid activities (mimeo, amended 1984) Overseas Development Administration, London.

ODA (1989a) *The Environment and the British Aid Programme*. Overseas Development Administration, London.

ODA (1989b) *Manual of Environmental Appraisal* (revised 1992). Overseas Development Administration, London.

Odum, E.P. (1975) *Ecology: the link between the natural and the social sciences* (2nd edn.). Holt, Rinehart and Winston, London.

Odum, E.P. (1983) *Systems Ecology: an introduction*. Wiley, New York.

OECD (1975) *The Polluter Pays Principle: definition, analysis and implementation*. Organization for Economic Cooperation and Development, Paris.

OECD (1991) *Environmental Indicators*. Organization for Economic Cooperation and Development, Paris.

OECD (1993) *Coastal Zone Management: integrated policies*. Organization for Economic Cooperation and Development, Paris.

Oliver, S. (1994) The political ecology of deforestation – the case of the Basilicata region of Italy. *Environmental Conservation* 21 (1), 72–75.

Omernik, J.M. (1987) Ecoregions of the coterminous United States. *Annals of the Association of American Geographers* 77 (1), 118–125.

Ooi, Jin Bee (1983) *Natural Resources in Tropical Countries*. Singapore University Press, Singapore.

O'Riordan, T. (1976) *Environmentalism*. Pion, London.

O'Riordan, T. (1979) The scope of environmental risk management. *Ambio* VIII (6), 260–264.

O'Riordan, T. (1991) The new environmentalism and sustainable development. *Science of the Total Environment* 108 (1–2), 5–15.

O'Riordan, T. (ed.) (1995) *Environmental Science for Environmental Management*. Longman, Harlow.

O'Riordan, T. and Cameron, J. (eds) (1995) *Interpreting the Precautionary Principle*. Cameron & May, London.

O'Riordan, T. and Rayner, S. (1991) Risk management for global environmental change. *Global Environmental Change* 1 (2), 91–108.

O'Riordan, T. and Turner, R.K. (eds) (1983) *An Annotated Reader in Environmental Planning and Management*. Pergamon Press, Oxford.

Ortolano, L. and Shepherd, A. (1995) Environmental impact assessment, pp. 3–30 in F. Vanclay and D.A. Bronstein (eds) *Environmental and Social Impact Assessment*. Wiley, Chichester.

Osborn, F. (1948) *Our Plundered Planet*. Little, Brown and Co., Boston.

Osborn, F. (1953) *Limits of the Earth*. Little, Brown and Co., Boston.

Osborn, F. and Bigg, T. (1998) *Earth Summit II: outcomes and analysis*. Earthscan, London.

Owen, L. and Unwin, T. (eds) (1997) *Environmental Management: readings and case studies*. Blackwell, Oxford.

Parasuraman, S. (1994) Economic and social marginalization of irrigation project displaced people. *Journal of Rural Development* 13 (2), 227–242.

Park, A. (1997) Trees, people, food and soil: a case study of participatory development in Malawi. *Forestry Chronicle* 73 (2), 221–227.

Park, C. (1980) *Ecology and Environmental Management*. Dawson and Sons, Folkstone.

Park, C. (1987) *Acid Rain: rhetoric and reality*. Methuen, London.

Park, C. (1997) *The Environment: principles and applications*. Routledge, London.

Parkin, S. (1989) *Green Parties: an international guide*. Heretic Books, London.

Parson, E.A. (1995) Integrated assessment and environmental policy making. In pursuit of usefulness. *Energy Policy* 23 (4–5), 463–476.

Partidário, M. do R. (1996) Strategic environmental assessment: key issues emerging from recent practice. *Environmental Impact Assessment Review* 16 (1), 31–55.

Paruccini, M. (ed.) (1995) *Applying Multiple Criteria Aid for Decision to Environmental Management* (Euro Course Series: environmental management vol. 3). Kluwer Academic, Dordrecht.

Pasqualetti, M.J. (ed.) (1990) *Nuclear Decommissioning and Society: public links to a new technology*. Routledge, London.

Paterson, D. (1993) Did Tibet cool the world? *New Scientist* 139 (1880), 29–33.

Patlis, J.M. (1992) The Multilateral Fund of the Montreal Protocol: a prototype for financial mechanisms in protecting the global environment. *Cornell International Law Journal* 25 (1), 181–183.

Patricos, N.N. (1986) *International Handbook on Land Use Planning*. Greenwood Press, Westport.

Patterson, A. (1990) Debt-for-nature swaps and the need for alternatives. *Environment* 32 (10), 4–13, 31–34.

Patterson, A. and Theobald, K.S. (1995) Sustainable development, Agenda 21 and the new local governance in Britain. *Regional Studies* 29 (8), 773–778.

Pearce, D.W. (1992) Sustainable development and environmental impact appraisal, pp. 13–22 in CISP (ed.) *Forum Valulazione: semestrale a cura del Comitato Internazionale per lo Sveluppo dei Popoli* (CISP) (IT) No. 4.

Pearce, D.W. (1994) Commentary. *Environment & Planning-A* 26 (9), 1329–1338.

Pearce, D.W. (1995) *Blueprint 4: capturing global environmental value*. Earthscan, London.

Pearce, D.W. and Brisson, I. (1993) BATNEEC: the economics of technology-based environmental standards, with a UK case illustration. *Oxford Review of Economic Policy* 9 (4), 24–40.

Pearce, D.W. and Turner, R.K. (1990) *Economics of Natural Resources and the Environment*. Harvester Wheatsheaf, Hemel Hempstead.

Pearce, D.W., Markandya, A. and Barbier, E.B. (1989) *Blueprint for a Green Economy*. Earthscan, London.

Pearce, D.W., Barbier, D. and Markandya, A. (1990) *Sustainable Development: economics and environment in the Third World*. Edward Elgar, London.

Pearce, D.W., Barbier, E., Markandya, A. and Barrett, S., Turner, R.K. and Swanson, T. (1991) *Blueprint 2: greening the world economy*. Earthscan, London.

Pearce, F. (1989) Kill or cure? Remedies for the rainforest. *New Scientist* 123 (1682), 40–43.

Pearce, F. (1998) Burn me. *New Scientist* 156 (2109), 31–34.

Peat, D. (1988) *Superstrings and the Search for the Theory of Everything*. Cardinal-Sphere Books, London.

Peattie, K. (1995) *Environmental Marketing Management: meeting the green challenge*. Pitman, London.

Pepper, D. (1984) *The Roots of Modern Environmentalism*. Croom Helm, London.

Pepper, D. (1993) *Eco-Socialism: from deep ecology to social justice*. Routledge, London.

Pepper, D. (1996) *Modern Environmentalism: an introduction*. Routledge, London.

Pereira, H.C. (1989) *Policy and Practice in the Management of Tropical Watersheds*. Westview Press, Boulder.

Perez-Trejo, F., Clark, N. and Allen, P. (1993) An explanation of dynamic systems modelling as a decision tool for environmental policy. *Journal of Environmental Management* 39 (4), 305–319.

Perkins, P.E. (1995) An overview of international institutional mechanisms for environmental management with reference to Arctic pollution. *Science of the Total Environment* 161 (9), 849–857.

Perman, R., Yue Ma and McGilvray, J. (1996) *Natural Resource and Environmental Economics*. Longman, Harlow.

Pernetta, J. (1993) *Monitoring Coral Reefs for Global Change*. IUCN, Cambridge.

Pichon, F.J. (1992) Agricultural settlement and ecological crisis in the Ecuadorian Amazon frontier: a discussion of the policy environment. *Policy Studies Journal* 20 (4), 662–678.

Pichon, L. (1993) *Environmental Management for Hotels: the industry guide to best practice*. Butterworth-Heinemann, Oxford.

Pidgeon, S. and Brown, D. (1994) The role of lifecycle analysis in environmental management: general panacea or one of several useful paradigms? *Greener Management International* (No. 7, July), 36–44.

Pigou, A.C. (1920) *The Economics of Welfare* (1st edn.). Macmillan, London.

Pimbert, M.P. (1991) *Designing Integrated Pest Management for Sustainable and Productive Futures* (IIED Gatekeeper Series No. 29). IIED, London.

Pimm, S.L. (1984) The complexity and stability of ecosystems. *Nature* 307 (5949), 321–326.

Pinchot, G. (1910) *The Fight for Conservation*. University of Washington Press, Seattle.

Pinstrup-Andersen, Per (1982) *Agricultural Research and Technology in Economic Development*. Longman, London.

Pirages, D. (1994) Sustainability as an evolving process. *Futures* 26 (1), 197–205.

Pollard, S.J., Harrop, D.O., Crowcroft, P., Mallett, S.H., Jeffries, S.R. and Young, P.J. (1995) Risk assessment for environmental management: approaches and applications. *Journal of the Chartered Institution of Water and Environmental Management* 9 (6), 621–628.

Porritt, J. (1984) *Seeing Green: the politics of ecology explained*. Basil Blackwell, Oxford.

Prasad, K. (1993) Environmental impact assessment: an analysis of the Canadian experience. *International Studies* 30 (3), 299–318.

Prestcott, R. (1996) *Coastal Zone Management: towards best practice* (Department of the Environment). HMSO, London.

Princen, T. and Finger, M. (1994) *Environmental NGOs in World Politics: linking the local and the global*. Routledge, London.

Pritchard, D. (1993) Towards sustainability: first steps towards sustainability analysis. *Ecos* 14 (3–4), 10–15.

Pritchard, P. (1993) *Managing Environmental Risks and Liability*. Technical Communications, Letchworth.

Proost, S. and Braden, J.B. (eds) (1998) *Climate Change, Transport and Environmental Policy: empirical applications in a federal system*. Edward Elgar, London.

Prothero, R.M. (1994) Forced movements of populations and health hazards in tropical Africa. *International Journal of Epidemiology* 23 (4), 657–664.

Pryde, P.R. (1991) *Environmental Management in the Soviet Union*. Cambridge University Press, Cambridge.

Quammen, D. (1997) *The Song of the Dodo: island biogeography in an age of extinctions*. Pimlico (Random House), London.

Rabe, B.G. (1996) An empirical examination of innovations in integrated environmental management – the case of the Great Lakes Basin. *Public Administration Review* 56 (4), 372–381.

Rabinovitch, J. (1996) Innovative land-use and public transport policy: the case of Curitiba, Brazil. *Land Use Policy* 13 (1), 51–67.

Raghavan, C. (1990) *Recolonization: GATT, the Uruguay Round and a new global economy*. Zed Press, London.

Ramlogan, R. (1996) Environmental refugees: a review. *Environmental Conservation* 23 (1), 81–88.

Rao, B. (1991) Dominant constructions of women and nature in social science literature. *Capitalism, Nature, Socialism* CES/CNS Pamphlet No. 2. CES/CNES, PO Box 8467, Santa Cruz.

Rapoport, R.N. (1993) Environmental values and the search for a global ethic. *Journal of Environmental Psychology* 13 (2), 173–182.

Rau, B. (1991) *From Feast to Famine: official cures and grass roots remedies to Africa's food crisis*. Zed Press, London.

Raup, D.M. (1988) Diversity crisis in the geological past, pp. 51–57 in E.O. Wilson (ed.) *Biodiversity*. National Academy Press, Washington.

Raup, D.M. (1993) *Extinction: bad genes or bad luck?* (first published in 1992 by Norton, London). Oxford University Paperbacks, Oxford.

Ravenhill, J. (1986) *Africa in Economic Crisis*. Macmillan, London.

Redclift, M.E. (1984) *Development and the Environmental Crisis: red or green alternatives?* Methuen, London.

Redclift, M.E. (1985) *The Struggle for Resources: limits of environmental 'managerialism'* (IIUG ks 85–5). Internationale Institut für Umwelt und Gesellschaft, Berlin.

Redclift, M.E. (1987) *Sustainable Development: exploring the contradictions*. Methuen, London.

Redclift, M.E. (1992) A framework for improving environmental management: beyond the market mechanism. *World Development* 20 (2), 255–259.

Redclift, M.E. (1995) The environment and structural adjustment: lessons for policy interventions in the 1990s. *Journal of Environmental Management* 44 (1), 55–68.

Redclift, M.E. and Benton, T. (eds) (1994) *Social Theory and the Global Environment*. Routledge, London.

Reed, D. (ed.) (1992a) *Structural Readjustment and the Environment*. Earthscan, London.

Reed, D. (1992b) *Structural Adjustment and the Environment*. Westview Press, Boulder.

Reed, D. (ed.) (1996) *Structural Adjustment, the Environment, and Sustainable Development*. Earthscan, London.

Rees, J. (1985) *Natural Resources: allocation, economics and policy*. Methuen, London.

Reich, C. (1970) *The Greening of America*. Random House, New York.

Reisenweber, R.L. (1995) Making environmental standards more reasonable. *Environment* 37 (2), 15–32.

Rensvik, H. (1994) Who sets the environmental standards for tomorrow's industry: industry, consumers, government regulations, the green lobby? *Marine Pollution Bulletin* 29 (6–12), 277–278.

Renwick, W.H. (1988) The eclipse of NEPA as environmental policy. *Environmental Management* 12 (3), 267–272.

Repetto, R., Dower, R.C., Jenkins, R. and Geohagen, J. (1992) *Green Fees: how a tax shift can work for the environment and the economy*. World Resources Institute, Washington.

Ricci, R.F. (ed.) (1981) *Technological Risk Assessment*. Martinus Nijhof, Boston.

Rich, B. (1986) Environmental management and multilateral development banks. *Cultural Survival* 10 (1), 4–13.

Richards, L. and Biddick, I. (1994) Sustainable economic development and environmental auditing: a local authority perspective. *Journal of Environmental Planning and Management* 37 (4), 487–494.

Richerson, P.J. and McEvoy III, J. (1976) *Human Ecology: an environmental approach*. Duxbury Press, North Scituate.

Richey, J.S., Horner, R.R. and Mar, B.W. (1985) The Delphi technique in environmental assessment 2: consensus of critical issues in environmental monitoring program design. *Journal of Environmental Management* 21 (2), 147–160.

Riddell, R. (1981) *Ecodevelopment: economics, ecology and development*. Gower, Farnborough.

Risser, P.G. (1985) Toward a holistic management perspective. *BioScience* 35 (7), 414–418.

Ritchie, M. (1990) GATT, agriculture and environment: the US double zero plan. *The Ecologist* 20 (6), 214–220.

Ritchie, M. (1992) Free trade versus sustainable agriculture: the implications of NAFTA. *The Ecologist* 21 (5), 221–227.

Robinson, K.S. (1992) *Green Mars*. Harper Collins, London (there are a further two related science fiction books by the same author).

Robinson, N. (1992) International trends in environmental impact assessment. *Boston College Environmental Affairs Law Review* 19 (3), 591–621.

Rodda, A. (1991) *Women and Environment*. Zed Press, London.

Rodhe, H., Callaway, J. and Dianwu, Z. (1992) Acidification in Southeast Asia – prospects for coming decades. *Ambio* XXI (2), 148–150.

Rodhe, H. and Herrera, R. (eds) (1988) *Acidification in Tropical Countries* (SCOPE No. 36). Wiley, Chichester.

Roe, E. (1996) Why ecosystem management can't work without social science: an example from the California Northern Spotted Owl controversy. *Environmental Management* 20 (5), 667–674.

Rogers, M.F., Sinden, J.A. and De Lacey, T. (1997) The precautionary principle for environmental management: a defensive-expenditure application. *Journal of Environmental Management* 51 (4), 343–360.

Roggeri, H. (1995) *Tropical Freshwater Wetlands: a guide to current knowledge and sustainable development*. Kluwer Academic, Dordrecht.

Roszak, T. (1972) *Where the Wasteland Ends: politics and transcendence in post-industrial society*. Faber, London.

Roszak, T. (1979) *Person/Planet: the creative disintegration of industrial society*. Victor Gollancz, London.

Rothery, B. (1993) *BS7750: implementing the environment management standard and the EC eco-management scheme*. Gower, Aldershot.

Royston, M.G. (1978a) Introduction to environmental management (Seminar Kebangsaan Pergurusan Alam Sekitar dan Penilaian Kesan Kesan Alam Sekitar, Petaling Jaya, Kuala Lumpur 16–20 October 1978). Universiti Kebongsaan, Kuala Lumpur (mimeo), 24 pp.

Royston, M.G. (1978b) The modern manager in the human environment. Paper presented to Symposium on the Malaysian Environment, RECSAM Complex, Penang, 16–20 September, 1978 (mimeo).

Rudderian, W.F. and Kutzback, J.E. (1991) Plateau uplift and climatic change. *Scientific American* 264 (3), 42–50.

Ruddle, K. and Manshard, W. (1981) *Renewable Natural Resources and the Environment: pressing problems in the developing world*. Tycooly International, Dublin.

Rugman, A.M. and Kirton, J.J. (1998) *Trade and the Environment: economic legal and policy perspectives*. Edward Elgar, London.

Ruivenkamp, G. (1987) Social impacts of biotechnology in agriculture and food processing. *Development* 4 (1), 58–59.

Ryecroft, R.W., Regens, J.L. and Dietz, T. (1988) Incorporating risk assessment and benefit cost analysis in environmental management. *Risk Analysis* 8 (3), 415–420.

Ryle, M. (1988) *Ecology and Socialism*. Radius, London.

Sachs, C.E. (ed.) (1997) *Women Working in the Environment*. Taylor and Francis, Washington.

Sandgrove, K. (1992) *The Green Manager's Handbook*. Gower, London.

Sadler, B. (1994) Environmental assessment and sustainability at the project and programme level, pp. 3–19. In R.G. Goodland and V. Edmundson (eds) *Environmental Assessment and Development*. World Bank, Washington.

Sagan, C. (1997) *The Demon-Haunted World: science as a candle in the dark*. Hodder and Stoughton, London.

Samson, F.B. and Knopf, F.L. (eds) (1996) *Ecosystem Management: selected readings*. Springer, New York.

Sandbach, F. (1980) *Environment, Ideology and Policy*. Basil Blackwell, Oxford.

Sands, P. (ed.) (1993) *Greening International Law*. Earthscan, London.

Sargeant, F. II (ed.) (1974) *Human Ecology*. North-Holland Publishers, Amsterdam.

Sarkar, A.U. and Ebbs, K.L. (1992) A possible solution to tropical troubles? Debt-for-nature swaps. *Futures* 24 (6), 653–668.

Saull, M. (1990) Nitrates in soil and water (Inside Science Supplement No. 37). *New Scientist* 127 (1734), 4 pp.

Savory, A. (1988) *Holistic Resource Management*. Westview (Island Press), Boulder.

Scher, C.A. (1991) Proactive environmental management. *Environmental Progress* 10 (1), F2–F3.

Schibuola, S. and Byer, P.H. (1991) Use of knowledge-based systems for the review of environmental impact assessments. *Environmental Impact Assessment Review* 11 (1), 11–27.

Schmidheiny, S. (1992) *Changing Courses: a global business perspective on development and the environment*. MIT Press, Cambridge, Mass.

Schneider, S.H. (1990) Debating Gaia. *Environment* 32 (4), 5–9.

Scholz, U. (1992) Transmigrasi – ein desaster? Probleme und chancen des indonesischen umsiedlungsprogramms. *Geographische Rundsschau* 44 (1), 33.

Schramm, G. and Warford, J.J. (eds) (1990) *Environmental Management and Economic Development*. Johns Hopkins University Press, Baltimore.

Schultz, J. (1995) *The Ecozones of the World: the ecological divisions of the geosphere*. Springer-Verlag, Berlin.

Schumacher, E.F. (1973) *Small Is Beautiful: a study of economics as if people mattered*. Harper and Row, New York.

Schuman, R.W. (1996) *Eco-Data: using your PC to obtain free environmental information* (2nd edn.). Government Institutes Inc., Rockville (Maryland 20850).

Scitovsky, T. (1976) *The Joyless Economy*. Oxford University Press, Oxford.

Scolimowski, H. (1988) Eco-philosophy and deep ecology. *The Ecologist* 18 (4–5), 124–127.

Seager, J. (1993) *Earth Follies: feminism, politics and environment*. Earthscan, London.

Seda, M. (ed.) (1993) *Environmental Management in ASEAN: perspectives on critical regional issues*. Institute of Southeast Asian Studies, Singapore.

Seldner, B.J. and Cothrel, J.P. (1994) *Environmental Decision Making for Engineering and Business Managers*. McGraw-Hill, New York.

Selin, S. and Chavez, D. (1995) Developing a collaborative model for environmental planning and management. *Environmental Management* 19 (2), 189–195.

Semple, E.C. (1911) *Influences of Geographic Environment*. Henry Holt, New York.

Sessions, G. (ed.) (1994) *Deep Ecology for the 21st Century: readings on the philosophy and practice of the new environmentalism*. Shambhala Press, Boston.

Sewell, G.H. (1975) *Environmental Quality Management*. Prentice-Hall, Englewood Cliffs.

Seymour, S., Cox, G. and Lowe, P. (1992) Nitrates in water: the politics of the polluter pays principle. *Sociologia Ruralis* 32 (1), 82–103.

Shaner, W.W., Philipp, P.F. and Schmehl, W.R. (1982) *Farming Systems Research and Development: guidelines for developing countries*. Westview Press, Boulder.

Shankar, U. (1986) Psychological dimensions of environmental management. *Current Science* 55 (6), p. 297.

Sharratt, P. (ed.) (1995) *Environmental Management Systems*. Institution of Chemical Engineers, Rugby.

Shaw, R.P. (1993) Warfare, national sovereignty, and the environment. *Environmental Conservation* 20 (2), 113–121.

Sheldon, C. (ed.) (1997) *ISO14001 and Beyond: environmental management systems in the real world*. Greenleaf Publishing, Sheffield.

Shepherd, A. (1995) Participatory environmental management: contradictions of process, project and bureaucracy in the Himalayan foothills. *Public Administration and Development* 15 (5), 465–479.

Shillito, D. (ed.) (1994) *Implementing Environmental Impact Management*. Institution of Chemical Engineers, Rugby.

Shiva, V. (1988) *Staying Alive: women, ecology and environment in India*. Zed Press, London.

Shiva, V. (1993) *Monocultures of the Mind: perspectives on biodiversity and biotechnology*. Zed Press, London.

Shiva, V., Anderson, P., Schücking, H., Gray, A., Lohmann, L. and Cooper, D. (1991) *Biodiversity: social and ecological perspectives*. Zed Press, London.

Shrader-Frechette, K.S. and McCoy, E.D. (1994) What ecology can do for environmental management. *Journal of Environmental Management* 41 (4), 293–307.

Shrybman, S. (1990) Free trade vs. the environment: the implications of GATT. *The Ecologist* 20(1), 30–34.

Shutkin, W.A. (1991) International human rights law and the Earth: the protection of indigenous peoples and the environment. *Virginia Journal of International Law* 31 (3), 479–511.

Simmons, I.G. (1989) *Changing the Face of the Earth: culture, environment, history*. Basil Blackwell, Oxford.

Simon, J.L. (1981) *The Ultimate Resource*. Princeton University Press, Princeton.

Simonis, U.E. (1990) *Beyond Growth: elements of sustainable development*. Edition Sigma (WZB), Berlin.

Simons, P. (1988) Costa Rica's forests are reborn. *New Scientist* 120 (1635), 43–47.

Sinclair, J. (1990) Rising sea-levels could affect 300 million. *New Scientist* 125 (1700),

Singh, G.S. (1997) Sacred groves in western Himalaya: an eco-cultural imperative. *Man in India* 77 (2–3), 247–257.

Sinner, J. (1994) Trade and the environment – efficiency, equity and sovereignty considerations. *Australian Journal of Agricultural Economics* 38 (2), 171–187.

Slocombe, D.S. (1993) Environmental planning, ecosystem science, and ecosystem approaches for integrating environment and development. *Environmental Management* 17 (3), 289–303.

Smil, V. (1983) *The Bad Earth: environmental degradation in China*. Zed Press, London.

Smit, B. and Spaling, H. (1995) Methods for cumulative effects assessment. *Environmental Impact Assessment Review* 15 (1), 81–106.

Smith, C.P., Feyerabend, G.B. and Sandbrook, R. (1994) *The Wealth of Communities: stories of success in local environmental management*. Earthscan, London.

Smith, D. (ed.) (1992) *Business and the Environment: implications for the new environmentalism*. Paul Chapman, London.

Smith, D. and Dawson, A. (1990) Tsunami waves in the North Sea. *New Scientist* 127 (1728), 46–49.

Smith, F. (1996) Biological diversity, ecosystem stability and economic development. *Ecological Economics* 16 (3), 191–204.

Smith, J.F. (1998) Does decentralization matter in environmental management? *Environmental Management* 22 (2), 263–276.

Smith, S. and Reeves, E. (eds) (1989) *Human Systems Ecology*. Westview Press, Boulder.

Smuts, J.C. (1926) *Holism and Evolution* (2nd edn; 3rd edn 1936). Macmillan, London.

Snipp, C.M. (1986) American Indians and natural resource development: indigenous peoples' land, now sought after, has promoted new Indian–White problems. *American Journal of Economics and Sociology* 45 (4), 457–474.

Soderstrom, E.J. (1981) *Social Impact Assessment: experimental methods and approaches*. Praeger, New York.

Solomon, B.D. (1985) Regional econometric models for environmental impact assessment, *Progress in Human Geography* 9 (3), 378–399.

Sontheimer, S. (ed.) (1991) *Women and the Environment: a reader*. Earthscan, London.

Soroos, M.S. (1993) The odyssey of Arctic haze: toward a global atmospheric regime. *Environment* 34 (10), 6–11, 25–27.

311

Sorsa, P. (1992) GATT and the environment. *World Economy* 15 (1), 115–134.

Soule, M.E. (ed.) (1987) *Viable Populations for Conservation*. Cambridge University Press, Cambridge.

Sowman, M., Fuggle, R. and Preston, G. (1995) A review of the evolution of environmental evaluation procedures in South Africa. *Environmental Impact Assessment Review* 15 (1), 45–68.

Spaling, H. (1994) Cumulative effects assessment: concepts and principles. *Impact Assessment* 12 (3), 231–251.

Spaling, H. and Smit, B. (1993) Cumulative environmental change: conceptual frameworks, evaluation approaches, and institutional perspectives. *Environmental Management* 17 (5), 587–600.

Spash, C.L. (1996) Reconciling different approaches to environmental management. *International Journal of Environment and Pollution* 7 (4), 497–511.

Spedding, L.S., Jones, D.M. and Dering, C.J. (eds) (1993) *Eco-management and Eco-auditing: environmental issues in business*. Chancery Law Publishers, London (Wiley, Chichester).

Spellerberg, I.F. (1991) *Monitoring Ecological Change*. Cambridge University Press, Cambridge.

Spencer-Cooke, A. (1996) *From EMAS to SMAS*. SustainAbility Ltd, London.

Spretnak, C. (1990) *Reweaving the World: the emergence of ecofeminism*. Science Book Club, San Francisco.

Spretnak, C. and Capra, F. (1985) *Green Politics: the global promise*. Paladin, London (US edn 1984).

Steel, D. (1995) *Rogue Asteroids and Doomsday Comets*. Wiley, Chichester.

Steinbeck, J. 1939 *The Grapes of Wrath*. Heinemann, New York.

Steiner, D. and Nauser, M. (eds) (1993) *Human Ecology: fragments of anti-fragmentary views of the world*. Routledge, London.

Stigliani, W.M., Doelman, P., Salomons, W., Schulin, R., Schmidt, G.R.B. and Van der Zee, S.E.A.T.M. (1991) Chemical time bombs: predicting the unpredictable. *Environment* 33 (4), 4–9, 26–33.

Stiles, D. (ed.) (1995) *Social Aspects of Sustainable Dryland Management*. Wiley, Chichester.

Stoett, P.J. (1994) Global environmental security, energy resources and planning. *Futures* 26 (7), 741–758.

Stoett, P.J. (1995) *Atoms, Whales and Rivers: global environmental security and international organization*. Nova Science Publishers, New York.

Stone, L., Gabric, A. and Berman, T. (1996) Ecosystem resilience, stability, and productivity: seeking a relationship. *American Naturalist* 148 (5), 892–903.

Stonehouse, D.P., Giraldez, C. and VanVuuren, W. (1997) Holistic policy approaches to natural resource management and environmental care. *Journal of Soil and Water Conservation* 52 (1), 22–25.

Stonich, S.C. and Browder, J.O. (1996) I am destroying the land – the political ecology of poverty and environmental destruction in Honduras. *Latin American Research Review* 30 (3), 123–137.

Stout, B.B. (1992) Environmental determinism. *Journal of Forestry* 90 (7), 4–5.

Stouth, R., Sowman, M. and Grindley, S. (1993) The panel evaluation method: an approach to evaluating controversial resource allocation proposals. *Environmental Impact Assessment Review* 13 (1), 13–35.

Sunderland, T.J. (1996) Environmental management standards and certification: do they add value? *Greener Management International* April 1996 (No. 14), 28–36.

Susskind, L.E. (1992) New corporate role global environmental treaty-making. *Columbia Journal of World Business* 27 (3), 62–73.

Suter, G.W. II (ed.) (1993) *Ecological Risk Assessment*. Lewis, Boca Raton.

Sutton, K. (1989) Malaysia: a land settlement model in time and space. *Geoforum* 20 (3), 339–354.

Sylvan, R. and Bennett, D. (1988) Taoism and deep ecology. *The Ecologist* 18 (4–5), 148–158.

Syms, P. (1997) *Contaminated Land: the practice and economics of redevelopment*. Blackwell Science, Oxford.

Székely, A. (1990a) The International Law of Natural Resources and the Environment: a selected bibliography. *Natural Resources Journal* 30 (4), 765–917.

Székely, A. (1990b) The International Law of Natural Resources and the Environment: a selected bibliography. Part II. *Natural Resources Journal* 31 (2), 265–412.

Tansley, A.F. (1935) The use and abuse of vegetational concepts and terms. *Ecology* 16 (2), 284–307.

Taylor, B. (1991) The religion and politics of Earth First! *The Ecologist* 21 (6), 258–266.

Taylor, S.R. (1992) Green management: the next competitive weapon. *Futures* 24 (7), 669–680.

Teilhard de Chardin, P. (1959) *The Phenomenon of Man*. Harper and Row, New York.

Teilhard de Chardin, P. (1964) *The Future of Man*. Collins, London.

Therivel, R. (1993) Systems of strategic environmental assessment. *Environmental Impact Assessment Review* 13 (3), 145–168.

Therivel, R. and Partidário, M.R. (1996) *Practice of Strategic Environmental Assessment*. Earthscan, London.

Therivel, R., Wilson, E., Thompson, S., Heaney, D. and Pritchard, D. (1992) *Strategic Environmental Assessment*. Earthscan, London.

Theutenberg, B.J. (1984) *The Evolution of the Law of the Sea: a study of resources and strategy with special regard to the polar regions*. Tycooly International, Dublin.

Thomas, C. (ed.) (1994) *Rio: unravelling the consequences*. Frank Cass, London.

Thomas, D.S.G. and Middleton, N.J. (1994) *Desertification: exploding the myth*. Wiley, Chichester.

Thomas, W.L. (ed.) (1956) *Man's Role in Changing the Face of the Earth*. University of Chicago Press, Chicago.

Thomson, D.R. (1993) *The Growth of Environmental Auditing*. Institute of Environmental Assessment, East Kirkby.

Thomson, D.R. and Wilson, M.J. (1994) Environmental auditing: theory and applications. *Environmental Management* 18 (4), 605–615.

Thompson, M., Hatley, T. and Warburton, M. (1986) *Uncertainty on a Himalayan Scale*. Ethnographica, London.

Thompson, S. and Therivel, R. (eds) (1991) *Environmental Auditing* (Oxford Polytechnic, School of Planning, Working Paper No. 130). Oxford Polytechnic, Oxford.

Thoreau, H.D. (ed.) (1854) *Walden, or Life in the Woods* (1854 edn, Boston, Houghton Mifflin). 1960 edn. – New American Library, New York.

Thukral, E.G. (1992) *Big Dams, Displaced People: rivers of sorrow, rivers of change*. Sage, New Delhi.

Tietenberg, T. (ed.) (1997) *The Economics of Global Warming*. Edward Elgar, London.

Tietenberg, T. and Folmer, H. (1998) *The International Yearbook of Environmental and Resource Economics 1998/1999: a survey of current issues*. Edward Elgar, London.

Tiffen, M. (1993) Productivity and environmental conservation under a rapid population growth: a case-study of Machakos District, Kenya. *Journal of International Development* 5 (2), 207–224.

Tiffen, M. (1995) Population density, economic growth and societies in transition: Boserüp reconsidered in a Kenyan case-study. *Development & Change* 26 (1), 31–65.

Tiffen, M., Mortimore, M. and Gichuki, F. (1994) *More People, Less Erosion: environmental recovery in Kenya*. Wiley, Chichester.

Tilman, D. (1996) Biodiversity: population versus ecosystem stability. *Ecology* 77 (2), 350–363.

Tisdell, C. (1993) *Environmental Economics: policies for environmental management and sustainable development*. Edward Elgar, London.

Tiwari, K.M. (1983) *Social Forestry for Rural Development* International Book Distributors (India), Dehra Dun.

Tobey, J.A. and Smets, H. (1996) The polluter pays principle in the context of agriculture and the environment. *World Economy* 19 (1), 63–87.

Todaro, M.P. (1994) *Economic Development* (5th edn). Longmans, Harlow.

Tokar, B. (1988) Social ecology, deep ecology and the future of green political thought. *The Ecologist* 18 (4–5), 132–142.

Tolba, M.K. (1982) *Development without Destruction: evolving environmental perceptions*. Tycooly International, Dublin.

Tornell, A. and Velasco, A. (1992) The tragedy of the commons and economic growth: why does capital flow from poor to rich countries? *Journal of Political Economy* 100 (6), 1208–1231.

Treshow, M. (1976) *The Human Environment*. McGraw-Hill, New York.

Treweek, J. (1995a) Ecological impact assessment. *Impact Assessment* 13 (3), 289–316.

Treweek, J. (1995b) Ecological impact assessment, pp. 171–191 in F. Vanklay and D.A. Bronstein (eds) *Environmental and Social Impact Assessment*. Wiley, Chichester.

Triggs, G.D. (ed.) (1988) *The Antarctic Treaty Regime: law environment and resources*. Cambridge University Press, Cambridge.

Tromans, S. (1992) International law and UNCED: effects on international business. *Journal of Environmental Law* 4 (2), 189–202.

Troumbis, A.Y. (1987) Disturbance in Mediterranean islands: a demographic approach to changes in insular ecosystems. *Ekistics* 54 (323–324), 127–131.

Troumbis, A.Y. (1992) Environmental management: theoretical inputs of ecology – the guest editor's introductory statement. *Ekistics* 59 (356–357), 250–259.

Trudgill, S. (1990) *Barriers to a Better Environment: what stops us solving environmental problems?* Belhaven, London.

Tucker, K.C. and Richardson, D.M. (1995) An expert system for screeening potentially invasive alien plants in the South African fynbos. *Journal of Environmental Management* 44 (4), 309–338.

Tudge, C. (1995) *The Day before Yesterday: five million years of human history*. Pimlico (Random House), London.

Turner, B.L. and Ali, A.M.S. (1996) Induced intensification: agricultural change in Bangladesh with implications for Malthus and Boserüp. *Proceedings of the National Academy of Sciences of the USA* 93 (25), 14984–14991.

Turner, K. and Jones, T. (eds) (1991) *Wetlands: market and intervention failures*. Earthscan, London.

Turner, M.G. and Gardiner, R.H. (eds) (1991) *Quantitative Methods in Landscape Ecology: the analysis and interpretation of landscape hererogeneity*. Springer, New York.

Turner, R.K., Pearce, D.W. and Bateman, I. (1994) *Environmental Economics: an elementary introduction*. Harvester Wheatsheaf, New York.

Turnham, D. (1991) Multilateral development banks and environmental management. *Public Administration and Development* 11 (4), 363–380.

Turton, C. and Farrington, J. (1998) Enhancing rural livelihoods through participatory watershed development in India. *ODI Natural Resource Perspectives* No. 34, 4 pp.

Tussie, D. (1987) *The Less Developed Countries and the World Trading System: a challenge to the GATT*. Frances Pinter, London.

Tylecote, A. and Van der Straaten, J. (eds) (1997) *Environment, Technology and Economic Growth: the challenge to sustainable development*. Edward Elgar, London.

UN (1992) *Agenda 21: programme of action for sustainable development*. United Nations, New York.

UN (1993) *Systems of National Accounts*. United Nations, New York.

Underwood, A.J. (1995) Ecological research and (research into) environmental management. *Ecological Applications* 5 (1), 232–247.

UNDP (1991) *Human Development Report* (for UN Development Programme). Oxford University Press, Oxford.

UNDP (1992) *Handbook and Guidelines for Environmental Management and Sustainable Development*. UN Development Program (UNDP), New York.

UNHCR (1992) *Refugees and the Environment: special report* (special issue of *Refugee* No. 89). UN High Commission for Refugees, Geneva.

Usher, M.B. and Thompson, D.B. (eds) (1988) *Ecological Change in the Uplands* (British Ecological Society Special Publication No. 7). Blackwell Scientific, Oxford.

Vanclay, F. and Bronstein, D.A. (eds) (1995) *Environmental and Social Impact Assessment*. Wiley, Chichester.

Vandermeer, J. (1996) Tragedy of the commons – the meaning of the metaphor. *Science & Society* 60 (3), 290–306.

Van Dyne, G.M. (ed.) (1969) *The Ecosystem Concept in Natural Resource Management*. Academic Press, New York.

Van Pelt, M.J.F. (1993) *Ecological Sustainability and Project Appraisal*. Avebury, Aldershot.

Vastag, G., Kerekes, S. and Rondinelli, D.A. (1996) Evaluation of corporate environmental management approaches: a framework and application. *International Journal of Production Economics* 43 (2–3), 193–211.

Vaughn, D. (ed.) (1991) *Current EC Developments: EC environmental and planning law*. Butterworths, Oxford.

Vaughn, D. and Michle, C. (1993) *Environmental Principles for European Business*. Earthscan, London.

Velikovsky, I. (1950) *Worlds in Collision*. Victor Gollancz, London.

Velikovsky, I. (1952) *Ages in Chaos*. Victor Gollancz, London.

Velikovsky, I. (1955) *Earth in Upheaval*. Victor Gollancz, London.

Viles, H.A. and Spencer, T. (1995) *Coastal Problems*. Edward Arnold, London.

Vink, A.P.B. (1983) *Landscape Ecology and Land Use* (English transl. from German ed. by D.A. Davidson). Longman, London.

Virtanen, Y. and Nilsson, S. (1993) *Environmental Impacts of Waste Paper Recycling*. Earthscan, London.

Vivian, J. (1994) NGOs and sustainable development in Zimbabwe: no magic bullets. *Development & Change* 25 (1), 167–193.

Vlachos, E. (1985) Assessing long range cumulative impacts, pp. 49–80 in V.T. Covello, J.L. Mumpower, P.J.M. Stallen and V.R.R. Uppuluri (eds) *Environmental Impact Assessment, Technology Assessment, and Risk Analysis: contributions from the psychological and decision sciences* (NATO ASI series G, Ecological Science, vol. 4). Springer-Verlag, Berlin.

Vogler, J. and Imber, M. (eds) (1995) *The Environment and International Relations: theories and processes*. Routledge, London.

Vogt, K.A., Gordon, J.C., Wargo, J.P., Vogt, D.J., Asbornsen, H., Palmiotto, P.A., Clark, H.J., O'Hara, J.L., Keeton, W.S., Patel-Wayland, T. and Witten, E. (1997) *Ecosystems: balancing science with management*. Springer, New York.

Vogt, W. (1948) *Road to Survival*. William Sloane, New York.

Voisey, H., Beuermann, C., Sverdrup, L.A. and O'Riordan, T. (1996) The political significance of Local Agenda 21: the early stages of some European experience. *Local Environment* 1 (1), 33–50.

Von Moltke, K. (1992) The United Nations development system and environmental management. *World Development* 20 (4), 619–626.

Von Weizsäcker, E.U. and Jesinghaus, J. (1992) *Ecological Tax Reform: a policy proposal for sustainable development*. Zed Press, London.

Vos, C.C. and Opdam, P. (eds) (1993) *Landscape Ecology of a Stressed Environment*. Chapman and Hall, London.

Walker, K.J. (1989) The state in environmental management: the ecological dimension. *Political Studies* 37 (1), 25–38.

Wallington, T.J., Schneider, W.F., Worsnop, D.R., Neilsen, O.J., Sehested, J., Debruyn, W.J. and Shorter, J.A. (1994) The environmental impact of CFC replacements – HFCs and HCFCs. *Environmental Science and Technology* 28 (7), 320A–326A.

Walters, C. (1986) *Adaptive Management of Renewable Resources*. Macmillan, New York.

Ward, B. and Dubos, R.E. (1972) *Only One Earth: the care and maintenance of a small planet*. Penguin, Harmondsworth.

Warford, J. and Partow, Z. (1989) Evolution of the World Bank's environmental policy. *Finance & Development* December 1989, 5–9.

Warren, K.J. (ed.) (1997) *Ecofeminism: women, culture, nature*. Indiana University Press, Bloomington.

Warwick, C.J., Mumford, J.D. and Norton, G.A. (1993) Environmental management expert systems. *Journal of Environmental Management* 39 (4), 251–270.

Wathern, P. (ed.) (1988) *Environmental Impact Assessment: theory and practice*. Unwin Hyman, London.

Watson, A. (1991) Inside science No. 48: 'Gaia'. *New Scientist* 131 (1776), 4 pp.

Watt, K.E.F. (ed.) (1966) *Systems Analysis in Ecology*. Academic Press, New York.

Watt, K.E.F. (1969) *Ecology and Resource Management: quantitative resource*. McGraw-Hill, New York.

Watts, D. (1971) *Principles of Biogeography*. McGraw-Hill, New York.

Watts, M.J. (1989) The agrarian crisis in Africa: debating the crisis. *Progress in Human Geography* 13 (1), 1–41.

Weale, A. (1993) *The New Politics of Pollution*. Manchester University Press, Manchester.

Weber, M. (1958) *The Protestant Ethic and the Spirit of Capitalism* (English translation by T. Parsons – originally published in 1904 and 1905 in 2 vols). Charles Scribner, New York.

Weeks, W.W. (1997) *Beyond the Ark: tools for an ecosystem approach to conservation*. Island Press, Washington.

Wehrmeyer, W. (ed.) (1996) *Greening People: human resources and environmental management*. Greenleaf, Sheffield.

Weir, D. and Shapiro, M. (1981) *Circle of Poison: pesticides and people in a hungry world*. Institute for Food and Development Policy, San Francisco.

Welford, R. (1992) *Environmental Auditing: the EC Eco-Audit Scheme and the British Standard on Environmental Management Systems*. University of Bradford, Bradford.

Welford, R. (1993) Local economic development and environmental management – an integrated approach. *Local Economy* 8 (2), 130–142.

Welford, R. (1996) *Corporate Environmental Management: systems and strategies*. Earthscan, London.

Welford, R. (1997) *Hijacking Environmentalism: corporate responses to sustainable development*. Earthscan, London.

Wellburn, A. (1988) *Air Pollution and Acid Rain: the global threat of acid pollution*. Earthscan, London.

Wellburn, A. (1994) *Air Pollution and Climate Change* (2nd edn.). Longman, Harlow.

Wells, S. (1992) *The Greenpeace Book of Coral Reefs*. Blandford, London.

Wells-Howe, B. and Warren, K.J. (1994) *Ecological Feminism*. Routledge, London.

Werner, P. (1991) *Savanna Ecology and Management: Australian perspectives and intercontinental comparisons*. Blackwell Scientific Publications, Oxford.

Wesche, R. (1996) Developed country environmentalism and indigenous community controlled ecotourism in the Ecuadorian Amazon. *Geographische Zeitschrift* 84 (3–4), 157–168.

West, K. (1995) Ecolabels: the industrialization of environmental standards. *The Ecologist* 25 (1), 16–20.

Westing, A.H. (1992) Environmental refugees: growing category of displaced persons. *Environmental Conservation* 19 (3), 201–207.

Westlund, S. (1994) Is free trade compatible with sustainable development? *Stockholm Environmental Institute* (December 1994 No. 4/94). SEI, Stockholm.

Westman, W.E. (1985) *Ecology, Impact Assessment and Environmental Planning*. Wiley, Chichester.

Weston, J. (ed.) (1986) *Red and Green: the new politics of the environments*. Pluto Press, London.

White, G.F. (1968) Organising scientific investigations to deal with environmental impacts. Paper delivered to the Careless Technology Conference, Washington. (Later published pp. 914–926 in M.T. Farvar and J.P. Milton (eds) (1972) *The Careless Technology: ecology and international development*. Natural History Press – Doubleday, New York).

White, L. Jnr (1967) The historical roots of our environmental crisis. *Science* 15 (3767), 1203–1207.

White, R.R. (1993) *North, South, and the Environmental Crisis*. University of Toronto Press, Toronto.

White, R.R. (1994) *Urban Environmental Management: environmental change and urban design*. Wiley, New York.

Wilkinson, C.R. and Buddemeier, R.W. (1994) *Global Climate Change and Coral Reefs: implications for people and reefs* (Report of UNEP-IOC-ASPEI-IUCN Global Task Team on the Implications of Climate Change on Coral Reefs). IUCN, Gland, Geneva.

Wilkinson, P. (1979) Public participation in environmental management: a case study. *Natural Resources Journal* 16 (1), 117–135.

Williams, P.J. (1979) *Pipelines and Permafrost: physical geography and development in the circumpolar north*. Longman, London.

Williams, P.W. and Todd, S.E. (1997) Towards and environmental management system for ski areas. *Mountain Research & Development* 17 (1), 75–90.

Willig, J.T. (ed.) (1994) *Environmental TQM* (2nd edn – 1st edn 1992). McGraw-Hill, New York.

Wilson, E.O. (1992) *The Diversity of Life*. Penguin, Harmondsworth.

Wilson, G.A. and Bryant, R.L. (1997) *Environmental Management: new directions for the twenty-first century*. University College London Press, London.

Wilson, J. (1994) Environmentalism and political theory: toward an ecocentric approach. *Political Science* 46 (1), 129–311.

Winter, G. (1988) *Business and Environment: a handbook of industrial ecology with 22 checklists for procedural use*. McGraw-Hill, New York.

Winter, G. (1994) *Blueprint for Green Management: creating your company's own environmental action plan*. McGraw-Hill, London.

Winter, G. (1996) *European Environmental Law: a comparative perspective*. Dartmouth Publishing, Aldershot.

Wirth, D.A. (1986) Law: the World Bank and the environment. *Environment* 28 (10), 33–44.

Wisemann, G. (1994) Europe braces for eco-audit – standardizing the acronyms. *Chemical Week* 154 (13), 54–56.

Wisner, B. (1990) Harvest of sustainability: recent books on environmental management (review article). *Journal of Development Studies* 26 (2), 335–341.

Woehlcke, M. (1992) Environmental refugees. *Aussenpolitik* 43 (3), 287–296.

Wolf, E.C. (1986) *Beyond the Green Revolution: new approaches to Third World agriculture* (Worldwatch Paper No. 73). Worldwatch Institute, Washington DC.

Wolters, G.J.R. (1994) Integrated environmental management: the Dutch Governmental view. *Marine Pollution Bulletin* 29 (6–12), 272–274.

Wood, C.M. (1988) EIA in plan making, pp. 98–114 in P. Wathern (ed.) *Environmental Impact Assessment: theory and practice*. Unwin Hyman, London.

Wood, C.M. (1992) Strategic environmental assessment in Australia and New Zealand. *Project Appraisal* 7 (3), 137–143.

Wood, C.M. (1995) *Environmental Impact Assessment: a comparative review*. Longman, Harlow.

Woodcock, C.E., Sham, C.H. and Shaw, B. (1990) Comments on selecting a geographic information system for environmental management. *Environmental Management* 14 (3), 307–315.

Woolston, H. (ed.) (1993) *Environmental Auditing: an introduction and practical guide*. British Library, Science Reference and Information Service, London.

World Bank (1994) *Economy-Wide Policies and the Environment: emerging lessons from experience*. World Bank, Washington.

World Commission on Environment and Development (1987) Our Common Future (Brundtland Report). Oxford University Press, Oxford.

WRI, IIED and UNEP (1988) *World Resources 1988–9*. Basic Books, New York.

Wright, J.R., Wiggins, L.L., Jain, R.K. and Kim, T.J. (eds) (1993) *Expert Systems in Environmental Planning*. Springer-Verlag, Berlin.

Yaffee, S.L. (1996) Ecosystem management in practice: the importance of human institutions. *Ecological Applications* 6 (3), 727–730.

Yar, N.T. (1990) Round the peg or square the hole? Populists, technocrats and environmental assessment in Third World countries. *Impact Assessment Bulletin* 8 (1–2), 69–84.

Yasui, H. and Kobayashi, E. (1991) Environmental management of the Seto Inland Sea. *Marine Pollution Bulletin* 23 (5), 485–488.

Yearley, S. (1991) *The Green Case: a sociology of environmental issues, arguments and politics*. Harper Collins, London.

Yost, N.C. (1990) NEPA's promise – partially fulfilled. *Environmental Law* 20 (3), 681–702.

Young, A.L. (1994) An overview of ISO–9000 application to drug, medical device, and environmental management issues. *Food and Drug Law Journal* 49 (3), 469–483.

Young, J. (1990) *Post Environmentalism*. Belhaven, London.

Young, J.E. (1990) *Discarding the Throwaway Society* (Worldwatch Paper No. 101). Worldwatch Institute, Washington.

Young, L. (1985) A general assessment of the environmental impact of refugees in Somalia with attention to the Refugee Agricultural Programme. *Disasters* 9 (2), 122–133.

Young, M.D. and Solbrig, O.T. (1992) *Savanna Management for Ecological Sustainability, Economic Profit and Social Equity*. UNESCO, Paris.

Young, O. and Osherenko, G. (eds) (1993) *Polar Politics: creating international environmental regimes*. University of Columbia Press, New York.

Young, S. (1994) An Agenda 21 strategy for the UK? *Political Science* 3 (2), 325–342.

Zarsky, L. (1994) *Borders and the Biosphere: environment, development and world trade rules*. Earthscan, London.

Zeba, S. (1996) *The Role of NGOs in Reforming Natural Resource Management: policies in Burkina Faso* (Issues Paper, Drylands Programme, IIED No. 68). International Institute for Environment and Development, London.

Ze'ev, N. (1994) *Landscape Ecology: theory and application* (2nd edn.). Springer-Verlag, London.

Zhu, X., Healey, R.G. and Aspinall, R.J. (1998) A knowledge-based systems approach to design of spatial decision support systems for environmental management. *Environmental Management* 22 (1), 35–48.

Zimmermann, E.W. (1993) *World Resources and Industries* (revised edn). Harper and Brothers, New York.

Zimmerman, M. (1987) Feminism, deep ecology, and environmental ethics. *Environmental Ethics* 9 (1), 21–44.

Zwarteveen, M. (1996) A plot of one's own: gender relations and irrigated land allocation policies in Burkina Faso. *IIMI Abstract* (Research Report No. 10). International Irrigation Management Institute, Colombo, 2 pp.

Index

1491